The Establishment Man

A PORTRAIT OF POWER

Peter C. Newman

SEAL BOOKS

McClelland and Stewart-Bantam Limited

Toronto

THE ESTABLISHMENT MAN

*A Seal Book / published by arrangement with
McClelland and Stewart Limited*

PRINTING HISTORY

McClelland and Stewart edition published October 1982
A Selection of Literary Guild Book Club 1982
Seal edition / September 1983

ISBN 0-7704-1839-2

*Seal Books are published by McClelland and Stewart-Bantam Limited. Its trade-
mark, consisting of the words "Seal Books" and the portrayal of a seal, is the
property of McClelland and Stewart-Bantam Limited, 60 St. Clair Avenue East,
Suite 601, Toronto, M4T 1N5. This trademark has been duly registered in the
Trademarks Office of Canada. The trademark, consisting of the words "Bantam"
and the portrayal of a rooster, is the property of and is used with the consent
of Bantam Books, Inc. 666 Fifth Avenue, New York, New York 10103. This trademark
has been duly registered in the Trademarks Office of Canada and elsewhere.*

PRINTED IN CANADA

COVER PRINTED IN U.S.A.

U   0 9 8 7 6 5 4 3 2 1

With affection and gratitude
for my friend and mentor
Jack McClelland

The measure
of a man
is what he does
with power.

—Pittacus of Mytilene
(650–570 B.C.)

Contents

Contents

Prologue

The smug stalwarts who man the ramparts of the Canadian Establishment deeply resent his assault on their primacy, dismissing him as a pretender to their throne. But whether they like it or not, Conrad Black is the Establishment's heir rampant whose time has come.

Ever since I began my probes of the Canadian Establishment, of which this is the fourth instalment, I have by choice and by necessity dealt with groupings. In my first volume the aim was to define and detail the inner workings of the country's economic elite, its interconnections, rivalries, and peccadilloes. The very idea of such a stratification – the existence of a class structure in this country – came as a profound shock to many Canadians. It negated the populist belief in wide-open opportunities and the notion of unlimited upward mobility. Because the Establishment in Canada is neither reinforced by an aristocracy (as it is in Britain) nor based on several generations of wealth (as it is in the United States), most Canadians had tended to regard class designations as referring mainly to lifestyles and levels of sophistication.

That initial study documented the Establishment's existence as a circle of approximately a thousand men who deal with one another on a wide spectrum of intimacy, depending on the commonality of their objectives at any given moment. A loose confederation of like-minded men and a few women, they take one another into account, accept, understand, and protect each other. My first volume, published in 1975, undertook to delineate Canada's great business dynasties. At the same time it certified the fact that the wealth and authority once organized around families were being displaced by the national and multinational grip of large corporations.

An intriguing exception was the Bronfman family, a mysterious clan of complex Montreal and New York Jews who had come to rank among the world's richest citizens. Originally conceived as a wider study of Canada's Jewish Establishment, my research revealed so many lines of authority leading into various branches of the Bronfman dynasty that I realized this remarkable tribe of hot-headed dreamers with wounded eyes and hyper egos demanded to be chronicled as a separate volume. It was published in 1978.

11

The equations of power kept changing. By the start of the 1980s, it was clear that the Establishment's centre of gravity was shifting to the west. As well as flowing from oil and real estate, new wealth was emerging from such unexpected sources as cheeseburgers, vampire films, and microchips. The future was being claimed by the new breed of hucksters who populated my second Establishment volume: *The Acquisitors*—strangers, by birth and behaviour, to the Canadian Establishment who combined in their heyday a now-tempered *macho* approach to business with extravagant lifestyles.

The firestorm of monetary success ignited by these flashy newcomers largely burned itself out in the severe recession that set in shortly after that book was published in November 1981. But another group, the Establishment's natural heirs, was surviving very well indeed. Unlike most elites, which drive themselves into oblivion through the congenital profligacy or genuine idiocy of their offspring, Canada's Establishment managed to spawn an impressive clutch of Inheritors. Members of an enduring power network, they possess a dominant ethic easily distinguishable from that of their more acquisitive cousins: feeling themselves secure within the Establishment's hermetic confines, the Inheritors recognize that however elusive and abstract the precise quality of their adherence might be, their style is more easily envied than copied. Their self-confidence remains rooted in the notion that their way of doing things is the enemy of pretence; that unlike fashion, grace can never be purchased. Character and elegance, so their prevailing wisdom goes, ultimately depend on inner conviction—which is why, unlike the Acquisitors, the Establishment's very own Inheritors can command attention without appearing to crave it.

Even in the dismal business climate of 1982, the pursuit of personal power goes on and the ordination of the Canadian Establishment's princes continues unimpeded. Its members are, as always, a hegemony of regents dedicated to keeping alive the notion that they alone are the natural beneficiaries of the economic authority that counts.

The most interesting variation on the dual theme characteristic of the current Canadian Establishment is Conrad Black, the heavy-set Toronto millionaire who has turned himself into a Roman candle among the wet firecrackers littering Canada's business landscape. An Inheritor by upbringing, an Acquisitor by temperament, Black has come to symbolize Canadian capitalism on the hoof. His astonishing 1978 takeover of the Argus Corporation, one of the country's great pools of capital and influence, was the most daring—and most rewarding—*coup d'état* in Canadian corporate history. Using an inherited $7 million as the trigger, Black and his personal search-and-destroy squad grabbed control of companies with assets worth about $4 billion in four months of frantic manoeuvring. In the process, his personal fortune soared.

"I have," Black admits, "always had the twin ambitions to have at least $100 million and to get away from Canadian winters." Having realized both goals, and seeking ever-expanding corporate fields of battle, he has become the most controversial and most fascinating member of Canada's ruling economic elite. But Black's prominence within the Canadian business scene is hardly due to his remarkable personal wealth, which places him only in the middle ranks of Canada's richest citizens. Nor does his significance flow from the directorships he holds, despite his place on the boards of seventeen companies with total assets of $100 billion.* Instead, it is his indisputable ability to mesmerize his peers and critics alike that sets Conrad Black apart.

At the tender age of thirty-eight, he has become Canada's quintessential Establishment Man.

His career has blossomed with unusual speed and taken unexpected directions. The smug stalwarts who man the ramparts of the Canadian Establishment deeply resent his assault on their primacy, dismissing him as a pretender to their throne. But whether they like it or not, Conrad Black is the Establishment's heir rampant whose time has come.

Within the narrowing circle of Canada's business Establishment, Black has become something of a metaphor. His name has passed into the language as a generic term signifying either wealth and influence youthfully gained, or corporate manoeuvres too clever by half. "He's no Conrad Black," Bay Streeters murmur, using the name with equal frequency as an accolade or as a gibe. The *Globe and Mail* has cited him

---

*In a restructured Argus organization, Conrad Black—with his brother, George Montegu Black III, and partners David Radler and Peter White—exercises control over major corporations such as Dominion Stores, Hollinger Argus, Standard Broadcasting, Labrador Mining and Exploration, and Norcen Energy Resources. Black's non-Argus directorships include the Canadian Imperial Bank of Commerce, Confederation Life, Carling O'Keefe, and Eaton's. He shares with his brother and two partners private ownership of a newspaper chain (Sterling Newspapers), Canada's second-largest malting company (Dominion Malting), a majority holding in a B.C. motel company (Slumber Lodge), a 20-per-cent share of Bytec Management Corp. (in which the majority holder is Michael Cowpland, president of high-flying Mitel Corp. of Ottawa), and considerable California real estate holdings. With their Riley cousins, the Blacks control United Canadian Shares; with Radler and White they have a majority position in Sterling Energy Corp. Three West Coast entrepreneurs—Peter Brown (Canarim Investment Corp. Ltd.), Harbanse S. (Herb) Doman (Doman Industries Ltd.), and Joseph Segal, who made a fortune in retailing (Zeller's Ltd. and Fields Stores Ltd.)—also have holdings in Sterling Energy. See chart, page 225.

as personifying "the rebirth of the political right – with brains." In the autumn of 1980, Théâtre Passe Muraille presented a play entitled *Torontonians*, centred on a characterization of Conrad. "Black fascinates me," John Jarvis, the actor who portrayed him, mused. "He's a kind of Napoleonic hero – the prince of business who is despised and admired at the same time."

His grab for Argus was a power play in the classic manner. Black knew that to make the fantasies that have haunted him since youth become real, he first had to capture a power base, then corner enough money to make it unassailable. After that he would be his own man, free to follow the crusades of mind and spirit that lie closer to his real purposes in life. The true leader gains power by challenging existing social and economic structures. Black has done that in spades. But to date, few investors outside his own tight circle of partners have benefited very much from his financial sleight-of-hand, the main effect of which has been to move control of the Argus empire from crones to cronies.

The darker side of Black's nature is governed by a brash certainty, all too common in the offspring of the rich, that he is somehow exempt from evil intent. There exists a mile-wide streak of righteousness in the man, a glut of self-confidence that transcends run-of-the-mill arrogance. Knowing he has so much, Conrad presumes he should have it all. This divine right of things shows itself in the ferocity with which he condemns his competitors, assuming that any corporate or private behaviour that runs counter to his convenience constitutes wilful denial of his due. Within his imperious bearing there thrives a decided inclination toward avarice. "Greed," he confesses with a defiant twinkle, "has been severely underestimated and denigrated – unfairly so, in my opinion. I mean, there is nothing wrong with avarice as a motive, as long as it doesn't lead to dishonest or anti-social conduct. I don't think greed, as such, is anything to be proud of, but a spirit of moderate acquisitiveness is not un-akin to a sense of self-preservation. It is a motive that has not failed to move me from time to time."

THE PREVALENCE OF SELF-IMAGES that add up to his unique personality is dominated by Black's obsessive desire to be recognized as the personification of the traditions of Toronto's mighty Argus Corporation. As Argus chairman he is heir to two men who previously occupied that august office and were acknowledged deans of the Canadian Establishment: E.P. Taylor and John A. "Bud" McDougald.

Like his predecessors, Black regards capitalism primarily as a useful ordering of human affairs designed to shift maximum benefit to those who are its most adroit practitioners. But unlike the possessors of most other great Canadian fortunes – particularly the Bronfmans and Ken Thomson – Black employs no surrogates to ride herd on his investments. To the consternation of his more sedate partners, he loves being in the thick of the action, taking the kinds of gambles that make safety seem banal. "The escalation of factionalism following Bud McDougald's death was a tremendous risk," he admits. "There was a question of conquest and the stakes were very high. The excitement became a tangible thing."

"He *is* a young Bud," says Doug Ward, the honorary chairman of Dominion Securities, who was McDougald's best friend, "except that he is far better educated and more of a builder. I'd hate ever to be on the wrong side of him."

AT A TIME WHEN CANADA'S ECONOMIC CLIMATE is reminiscent of the bubonic plague, it is rare enough to isolate a corporate paladin who retains his faith in the ultimate triumph of free enterprise, rarer still to discover an individual whose private compulsions and public statements illuminate the systems he is defending.

Even more significant has been the capture of the Canadian imagination by Black's antics. His outrageous behaviour and equally outrageous pronouncements have provided ammunition both to the critics of capitalism, who view it as a system that rewards avarice and greed, and to its defenders, who see him as the living symbol of its flexibility and endurance. No one can deny that he has brought to the corporate wars a highly developed sense of the dramatic, a barely suppressed instinct for mischief, and a love of the power game – the excitement that comes from being the trainer in the tent with the tiger.

It was precisely because of these qualities that I recognized in Conrad Black the opportunity, for the first time, of focusing an entire book not on a class, a group, or a family, but on one individual. Somewhere between Inheritor and Acquisitor, Black has a foot in each camp and possesses a sharpness of intellect and edge of determination rare in either category. (Anyone who managed to get himself kicked out of Upper Canada College and Trinity College School and flunked out of Osgoode Hall can't be totally uninspiring.)

Ever since the spring of 1974, when he returned to Toronto from his self-imposed exile in Montreal, I have met with Black every few months to compare impressions of his corporate adventures. It would be too much to impute any Boswellian impulse to these early encounters. Initially, they were merely informal debriefing sessions conducted by a journalist curious about this new breed of black tomcat stalking the Canadian Establishment. As Black's activities accelerated, so did the frequency of our meetings. But it was not until the autumn of 1981 that I decided to write a book based on our conversations, plus the nearly one hundred other interviews I had accumulated about him in the interval.

This volume, then, is a study of personal power: how it was gained, has been exercised, and is being perpetuated by a Renaissance entrepreneur in a pinstriped suit named Conrad Moffat Black.

The Establishment Man

A Portrait of Power

CHAPTER ONE

Growing Up Rich

Jack Campbell, a family friend, recalls blinking in disbelief as he watched, through the summer haze, an eight-year-old Conrad on the patio outside the Blacks' living room carefully washing dollar bills and hanging them out on a line to dry.

For most of Conrad's compadres, growing up was a magic interval during which they matured into their fathers' sons—with all the baggage of tradition and continuity these rites of passage imply. Youth was a time of being wafted through sunny apprenticeships of promises kept and wishes fulfilled, of being enrolled in Daddy's private school at birth and spending languid vacations at large summer homes on the manicured shores of cool green lakes.

The rich don't have children; they have heirs.

Their progeny learn at their father's knee how to exude that air of besieged innocence that marks Canada's typical Establishment scions—an attitude nurtured in the hushed drawing rooms of homes protected by moats of privilege and discriminatory bylaws. Parents extend themselves only far enough to protect their offspring from life's more unpleasant realities by swaddling them in a cotton-batting world of material goodies. They transmit affection, like family heirlooms, via fiduciary agents, usually exquisitely trained, semi-disinterested nannies.

George Montegu Black, Jr., firmly rejected this preppy approach to his second son's upbringing.

Young Conrad, never very close to his mother, grew up instead as his father's intellectual and spiritual protégé. The elder Black spent the last eighteen years of his life in self-imposed exile, the Canadian Establishment's hermit-in-residence. Rarely stirring from his gloomy mansion, easing his loneliness with a hefty diet of neat vodka and Old Fashioneds, George Black channelled his declining energies into one life-sustaining purpose: the nocturnal teach-ins of his younger son, which would become the most important formative influence in Conrad's life. "It was much more a man-to-man than a father-to-son relationship," recalls Gordon Osler, one of Conrad's uncles.

The psychology of the two Blacks is so intimately intertwined that the one way to understand the forces at play in Conrad's mind and to appreciate the ultimate reach of his ambitions is to trace the oddly unfulfilled life of his father.

Seldom has a son's career been dedicated with such single-mindedness to a fairytale resolution of the unique circumstances in which he simmered up. Nostalgia has retroactively ennobled their time together, but to a surprising degree Conrad's life thus far has been the saga of an heir discovering unexpected resources within himself, so that through him the world might acknowledge the worth of his father.

While stoutly dismissing the relationship's transparent psychological dimensions, Conrad readily admits to "a certain sense of vindication." He mutters darkly about the way his father was "*used*" by some of the other Argus partners and fondly remembers those nightly sessions with Father, spent learning his family history, being taught the rudiments of high finance, debating the mysteries of the deep.

THE BLACK FAMILY moved in 1882 from Halifax to Winnipeg, where the first George Montegu Black became a partner in an insurance and investment agency. He eventually gained control of the Drewrys beer plant, which later became Western Breweries Ltd., but his investment income dried up during the Depression. His son studied French and English literature at the University of Manitoba, doing so well that he was in the running for the 1931 Rhodes Scholarship. But young George fell in love with Jean Elizabeth Riley, a daughter of Conrad Stephenson Riley, and deliberately removed himself from academic pursuits. He decided to go into business in order to rustle up enough money to get married. As it was, his engagement to Betty Riley lasted six years, from 1931 to 1937.*

The Riley family into which Conrad's father married then stood at the summit of Winnipeg society, tracing its roots to Robert Thomas Riley, who was born at Beverley, Yorkshire, on July 1, 1851. His father had founded the *Maritime Gazette* in London and was a member of the syndicate that owned the *Daily Telegraph*. The young Riley entered the Adjutant-General's department of the War Office as a clerk but suffered a physical breakdown as the result of an eighty-two-mile walking race. He finished alone when at the seventy-third mile the only other remaining contestant dropped out. He came to Canada in 1873 on a two-year

---

*Conrad Black has three double first cousins because his mother's brother, Ronald T. Riley, married his father's sister, Margaret Montegu Black.

leave of absence, planning to work outdoors in the hope of recovering his health. Headed for Dane County in Wisconsin, he stopped off in Hamilton, Ontario, where he married Harriet Murgatroyd. His well-being restored, he returned to Great Britain in 1875, informed the Adjutant General's office that he had no intention of living in England, and returned to Canada after only twenty-eight days. For the next six years he worked his farm near Hamilton and became associated with W.E. Sanford, a local businessman who had large landholdings in Manitoba. (Sanford was appointed to the Senate as a Conservative in 1887 and drowned at Windermere, in Muskoka, in 1889.) Sanford dispatched Riley to Winnipeg in 1881 to look after his western interests. With J.H. Brock, Riley was one of the organizers of the Great-West Life Assurance Company in 1891 and became a director and the holder of policy No. 1 – $5,000 for a ten-year term – when the company began operations in August 1892. He remained on the board until 1943 and was vice-president from 1910 onward. He became managing director (1895) and later president of the Canadian Fire Insurance Company and president of the Northern Trusts Company (1904) and the Canadian Indemnity Company (1912). He was also a director of the Manitoba and North-West Loan Company, Compagnie Hypothèque of Antwerp, Canadian National Railways, and the Union Bank of Canada. Worried about the bank's management, he quit the board and then rejoined it and was instrumental in getting the Royal Bank to take over the Union, after which he became a Royal director. Equally ardent as a Conservative, a Methodist, and a Mason, he was an exponent of provincial rights and a determined municipal philanthropist. From his early days as a champion pedestrian, when he walked thirty to fifty miles some days, he became in later life a horseman, raising hunters and jumpers.

When he died in 1944 at the age of ninety-three, R.T. was survived by three sons and a daughter – and a brood of twenty-two grandchildren and twenty-four great-grandchildren. As the family chart on pages 24-25 indicates, the Rileys have been and remain one of the Canadian Establishment's most impressive clans.

R.T.'s second son, Conrad Stephenson, was born at sea during a transatlantic crossing aboard the Dominion Line's *Ontario* (whose ship's bell later graced his Winnipeg home) but listed his birthplace as Hamilton because of problems he encountered crossing the border. After an early tangle with U.S. Immigration (when he told the examining officer that he had been born at sea), he took to describing his birthplace as Ontario, neglecting to note that this particular Ontario was a ship. (Later, when the *Ontario* was broken up, a brother acquired the bell and presented it to him. It remains in Riley hands in Winnipeg.) He succeeded his father as president of Canadian Indemnity, Canadian Fire Insurance, and Northern Trusts, and became chairman of the Canadian committee of the Hudson's Bay Company and a member of its London board. He served overseas in the First World War as a major in the Canadian Field Artillery, was a director of the Beaver Lumber Company and, like his father, of the Royal Bank and Great-West Life. A noted oarsman, he was made a member of Canada's Sports Hall of Fame.

YOUNG GEORGE BLACK FITTED IN WELL with staunch Riley traditions, choosing as he did to become an accountant. By the outbreak of the Second World War, he was employed as comptroller of the Black family brewery. Tall and ungainly (having grown twelve inches in one year during a childhood illness), he played no sports except golf.* Poor eyesight prevented him from enlisting in the army ("They said there was very little point in having a tall blind man stand in a trench, looking like an idiot and popping off a rifle at something he can't see") so he joined the accounting branch of the Royal Canadian Air Force. When Winnipeg auditor Walter Macdonald was soon afterwards called to Ottawa to put the Air Force headquarters pay records in order, he requested that Black be seconded to help him. George Black shed his Air Force uniform for civvies and started in on the required paperwork – but didn't bother to inform his service superiors. When he didn't show up for his basic training, he was listed as a deserter, and the RCMP was instructed to track him down. The mystery was cleared up when Harold (Gus) Edwards, then head of the RCAF's personnel branch, happened to mention the cross-country manhunt for George Black to one of Ottawa's dollar-a-year men. He was curtly informed that it was no wonder the Mounties couldn't find Black because he was working in an office next door – and had been for the previous six months.

In the spring of 1941, the Canadian government was asked to supply the Allied forces with airplane propellers. A factory was built in Quebec, and George Black moved to Montreal as president of Canadian Propellors Ltd.† His was one of the very few wartime Crown corporations to show a profit. After turning out 12,500 propellers, the company had a

---

*George Black played at the St. Charles Golf and Country Club. One afternoon he managed to break the course record. He decided then and there that he'd never play golf any better; he quit and didn't go near a golf course again.

†It was during his Montreal sojourn – on August 25, 1944, the day Paris was liberated – that George Black's second son, Conrad, was born.

$5,000 surplus, which Black donated to McGill University's department of mechanical engineering with the comment, "If anybody says I was a war profiteer, he's a goddamn liar." His performance attracted the attention of E.P. Taylor, the Canadian Breweries chairman then on special duty funnelling Canadian-made war supplies to the United States and Britain. The two men were invited to dinner at Ottawa's Rideau Club in July 1944 by Terence Sheard, a Toronto lawyer who was a friend of Black's and spent the war as an assistant to Massey-Harris president James S. Duncan, then serving as deputy minister for air. Taylor, who by that time was in the process of demobilizing himself, immediately took to the young Winnipeg accountant and offered him a job as $15,000-a-year executive assistant to D. Clive Betts, the Canadian Breweries president. Black accepted fifteen months later and by February 1950 had replaced Betts in the top operating job.

During Black's successful stewardship, Canadian Breweries increased its production by annual leaps of 25 per cent, invaded the U.S. market (moving its Carling brand from sixty-second to third in sales volume), and eventually became the world's largest and most profitable brewing complex. While E.P. Taylor received all the public acclaim, the company probably owed an equally large measure of its success to George Black's decentralized management approach, put into effect in November 1951. "It created a hell of a convulsion," Black remembered. "I called a meeting of all the important people in the Canadian operation; I guess there would have been about fifty of them. There was no discussion. I simply distributed copies of my memorandum and read it aloud. That was that. I subsequently learned that there were all kinds of meetings of people who thought of resigning, but they relented and it turned out to be a great success."

The relationship between Taylor and Black fluctuated from mutual admiration to mutual irritation. Taylor managed money; Black managed people. Taylor felt that Black was much too informal and unstructured in his approach, more interested in the immediate bottom line than in building up the great international beer empire its chairman dreamed of creating. Black believed that Taylor's social ambition (to become the world's greatest brewer and collect a British peerage in the process) had overcome his basic business sense and that he was making far too many deals with highly eccentric characters. "Eddie would deal with the devil, though he'd sup with a long spoon," Black once commented. "He'd negotiate with anybody. With Hitler. Not that I mean it in a pejorative sense. He'd just feel his way through each situation until some agreement or disagreement was arrived at. He didn't give a damn what a fellow's character, appearance, or manners were like." In private, Black invaria-

The Black Family Ties

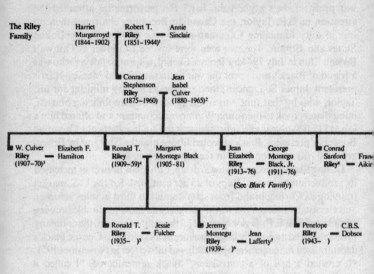

The Riley Family

Harriet Murgatroyd (1844–1902) — Robert T. Riley (1851–1944)[1] — Annie Sinclair

Conrad Stephenson Riley (1875–1960) — Jean Isabel Culver (1880–1965)[2]

W. Culver Riley (1907–70)[3] — Elizabeth F. Hamilton

Ronald T. Riley (1909–59)[4] — Margaret Montegu Black (1905–81)

Jean Elizabeth Riley (1913–76) — George Montegu Black, Jr. (1911–76)

(See *Black Family*)

Conrad Sanford Riley[8] — Fran Aikir

Ronald T. Riley (1935–)[5] — Jessie Fulcher

Jeremy Montegu Riley (1939–)[6] — Jean Lafferty[7]

Penelope Riley (1943–) — C.B.S. Dobso

---

[1] He had two daughters and seven sons. Conrad Stephenson was the second child. There were no children of the second marriage.

[2] Daughter of William H. Culver, partner of Sir James Aikins in the Winnipeg law firm of Aikins, Culver. His two sons, George W. and Albert F., both had careers with Izaak Walton Killam's Royal Securities. G.W.'s sons, both in Vancouver, are Gerald, a retired Hudson's Bay Co. manager, and Dennis, a chartered accountant. Albert's sons, in Montreal, are Bronson, a lawyer, and David, president of Alcan Aluminium.

[3] Chairman, Canadian Indemnity and United Canadian Shares; director, Royal Bank, Dominion Bridge, Southam Press. Head of Pan-American Games organization, Winnipeg, 1967; president, Winnipeg Blue Bombers; member, Canadian Olympic rowing team, 1928.

[4] President, Canadian Pratt & Whitney.

[5] Vice-president, CPR.

[6] Former headmaster, Stanstead College.

[7] Granddaughter of Louis S. St. Laurent.

[8] President, United Canadian Shares; director of Canadian Imperial Bank of Commerce.

[9] Granddaughter of Sir James Aikins and daughter of G.H. Aikins, Winnipeg lawyer, whose daughter Margaret Anne married George Henry Sellers of Winnipeg, president of Riverwood Investments and Sellers, Dickson Securities; another daughter, Jean Somerset Aikins, married R.D. (Peter) Mulholland, later president of Bank of Montreal and chairman of Brinco.

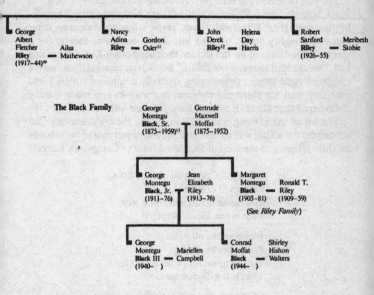

| George Albert Fletcher Riley (1917–44)[10] | — Ailsa Mathewson | | Nancy Adina Riley | — Gordon Osler[11] | | John Derek Riley[12] | — Helena Day Harris | | Robert Sanford Riley (1926–55) | — Meribeth Stobie |

The Black Family

George Montegu Black, Sr. (1875–1959)[13] — Gertrude Maxwell Moffat (1875–1952)

George Montegu Black, Jr. (1911–76) — Jean Elizabeth Riley (1913–76)

Margaret Montegu Black (1905–81) — Ronald T. Riley (1909–59)

(See *Riley Family*)

George Montegu Black III (1940–) — Mariellen Campbell

Conrad Moffat Black (1944–) — Shirley Hishon Walters

[10]Killed in action in Italy, 1944. Married daughter of J. Arthur Mathewson, Provincial Treasurer of Quebec in 1939–44 Liberal Government of J. Adélard Godbout and later chairman of Ogilvie Flour Mills.

[11]Toronto corporate director, former head of Winnipeg investment firm of Osler, Hammond & Nanton. His brothers include John Harty Osler, a judge of the Ontario Supreme Court, and E.B. Osler, Winnipeg author and former insurance executive. E.B. Osler married Jean Cameron Stobie, whose sister Meribeth was the widow of Robert Sanford Riley and later married James E. Coyne, former governor of the Bank of Canada. Susan Harty Osler, a daughter of the Gordon Oslers, is the wife of Toronto lawyer Robert Beverley (Biff) Matthews, son of Brig.-Gen. Beverley Matthews. The Osler brothers are sons of Hugh Osler of Winnipeg and grandsons of Toronto financier Sir Edmund Osler.

[12]Winnipeg corporate director.

[13]President of Black & Armstrong, Western Breweries, the Drewrys Ltd., Moose Jaw Brewing, Premier Brewing, Saskatchewan Brewing, and Barry Hotel Co.

bly referred to Taylor, with only slightly veiled sarcasm, as "the great man."

For some unaccountable reason, Taylor was both pleased and frustrated by George Black's prodigious dexterity in mental calculation. He could, for example, multiply two six-digit figures in his head and come out almost instantly with the correct sum down to two decimal points. At Canadian Breweries' board meetings, Taylor would often ask him: "What percentage is that, George?" And when the answer ("12.36 per cent") snapped right back, he'd get annoyed and call in an accountant to check the calculations, which always turned out to be correct.

The two men enjoyed little social contact, but on January 29, 1951, Black helped stage E.P. Taylor's gala fiftieth birthday party. The celebration was held at Windfields Farm, Taylor's Toronto residence. After dinner the eighty guests trooped into E.P.'s basement theatre for a special "show" emceed by Jim Baxter, then head of McKim Advertising Ltd. "We decided to really fox Eddie," Black later recalled, "and used a troupe of eight chorus girls singing specially composed songs. I had probably seen ten thousand chorines but seldom any more facially ill-favoured than those. However, they did their little jigs."

The hit of the evening was a skit involving the eight scantily clad women cake-walking with canes that had little papier mâché horseheads on them, singing to the tune of Stephen Foster's "Camptown Races":

> Of Argus Corp. you are the boss,
> Doo-dah! doo-dah!
> You make it run without a loss,
> That is the Taylor way.

> Eddie works all night,
> Eddie works all day,
> That's the secret of his success,
> That is the Taylor way.

> Of soya beans you are the king,
> Doo-dah! doo-dah!
> You control most everything,
> That is the Taylor way!

That same winter Black introduced Taylor to Bahamian society. During a 1949 southern holiday, the Blacks had been invited to the Hog Island "beach house" of Izaak Walton Killam, the Montreal financier, who had purchased the property from U.S. aluminum tycoon Arthur

Vining Davis and had spent $4 million having it refurbished.* The Killams eventually put the Blacks up for membership in the Porcupine Club, then the Bahamas' most exclusive private resort. "It had all the big hitters, including the Mellons and the du Ponts," Black recalled. "When Eddie Taylor and Lord Hardinge were visiting Nassau in the winter of '51, I asked them over and introduced them to Killam. From that time on, Eddie took a great business interest in the Bahamas."†

Taylor picked Black to negotiate the sale in 1954 of the Toronto soybean plant operations of Victory Mills Ltd. that he had purchased in 1945 for $2 million. Black persuaded Procter & Gamble to pay nearly four times as much for the waterfront plant, now Victory Soya Mills.

In 1955, when brewery workers threatened the Taylor company with a long strike, Black demonstrated his toughness by tricking strikers into picketing an empty building. On the day before pickets were to go on duty around Canadian Breweries' head office on Victoria Street in downtown Toronto, Black moved some furniture out and established himself and his senior staff in rented quarters on Adelaide Street. "It's the most brilliant labour-relations manoeuvre I've ever seen!" trilled Wally McCutcheon, one of the Argus partners.

*The Killam house had a main living room the size of two squash courts with high vaulted ceilings, and a trio of sleeping wings with three double suites each. A moving force in Calgary Power, Newfoundland Light & Power, and several other utilities, Killam owned Toronto's *Mail and Empire* and Royal Securities Corp. in Montreal, where his ace salesman was Ward Pitfield, father of Michael, who later became secretary to the Trudeau Cabinet. Killam died at his fishing camp near Cascapedia, Que., in 1955, leaving an estate of well over $100 million. The death duties, together with those on a similar fortune left by Sir James Dunn, were used to provide the original financing for the Canada Council. Killam's widow, Dorothy, once instructed a senior vice-president of Royal Securities to engage a suite on a train to bring her dog down to New York, carefully specifying that the animal was to sleep only on a lower berth.

†Three years after this encounter, Taylor formed the Lyford Cay Development Company to start converting 2,800 previously uninhabitable acres into one of the world's most luxurious communities. He eventually sank $35 million into the project, moved there himself in 1961, and six years later became a Bahamian citizen. Originally, Taylor invited George Black, J.A. McDougald, W. Eric Phillips, and M. Wallace McCutcheon (his Argus partners) to put a million dollars each into the Lyford project, but they turned him down. Eric Phillips told Taylor at the time: "Eddie, I'll give those islands twenty years. After that the cruise ships will come and the natives will get hostile, and they won't be worth a damn." When Taylor began to discuss the notion of transferring his citizenship, Black exploded: "You're out of your skull, Eddie. For God's sake, your people have lived here for a long time. Why are you so bloody jumpy about taxes? Don't you think that the country where you made your money is where you should keep it?" To which, Black remembered Taylor replying with a sigh, "I can't *afford* to die in Canada."

27

By the mid-1950s, Black had so decentralized the company's operations and delegated so much of his own authority that there wasn't much left for him to do. He spent an average of ten hours a week in his office, usually from two to four o'clock in the afternoon, and considered that morning appointments were part of what he called "the dawn patrol," a squad he wasn't about to join. During every World Series, Black refused to appear in the office at all. Under his hands-off management technique, Canadian Breweries continued to prosper in North America, though the overall results were being dragged down by Taylor's territorial ambition to take his company into the hotly competitive British market by negotiating for control of Hope & Anchor Breweries Ltd. and Hammonds United Breweries Ltd.

It was another strike at about this time that helped bring the shaky working partnership between Taylor and Black to an end. The unions struck the Canadian plants, but largely because of George Black's efforts the brewing industry faced them with a solid bargaining front. With his closed-down company losing $100,000 a day in beer sales, Taylor favoured settling separately, but Black refused. "If you can't turn around and snarl at these guys," he told Eddie in one transatlantic telephone exchange, "they'll cut you to pieces."

When the Canadian Breweries chairman returned to Toronto, he expressed dissatisfaction with Black's handling of the strike, adding that he thought the time had come to *re*centralize the company's chain of command. Then Taylor dropped his bombshell: "Perhaps it's time, George, we had a new president of Canadian Breweries."

Black calmly replied, "Well, that's fine with me. But as to recentralization, I think you're out of your skull, Eddie—and I won't have any part of it."

At the time, Black was getting a salary of $75,000; his pension amounted to only $15,000 a year. Taylor eventually reconsidered his harsh verdict and offered to rehire Black with an iron-clad five-year contract at an annual $150,000 if he would take charge of the recentralization program. But Black wouldn't even discuss it. He cleaned out his desk and never went near the Canadian Breweries head office again. When Maurice Hecht, a University of Toronto professor of business administration, was interviewing Black in 1973 for the research that eventually led to Richard Rohmer's official biography of Edward Plunket Taylor, his bitterness had not yet subsided. "When I was at Canadian Breweries—and Eddie, I hope you're listening—the morale was high," Black told Hecht's tape recorder. "I may not have been your ideal of a president but, by God, the employees thought I was!"

FINDING HIMSELF WITHOUT A JOB at forty-seven and feeling no desire to re-enlist in the corporate wars, George Black turned full time to the profitable private passion he had nurtured since leaving the University of Manitoba—searching out undervalued stocks and bonds. This preoccupation had been sparked in the mid-1930s when he decided that even though the Alberta government was on the verge of bankruptcy, it was not likely to default on its bonds. He bought the securities as fast as panicky investors discarded them, and when they were redeemed at par in 1940, he realized his first fortune.

His next big windfall came out of a tip from Alfred Duffield, then with Wood Gundy's Montreal office, who put him into Abitibi Power and Paper second-preferreds. The papermaker was in receivership at the time, and its shares were begging for buyers. As the company recovered, they climbed from $6 to $180. Black eventually used this formidable nest egg to buy into the original Argus public offerings, becoming the holding company's largest investor. In 1951 he was named to the Argus board.

After his retirement from the brewery post, he gave most of his time to his lucrative hobby. He rode IBM common shares both down and up in the 1967 market panic that saw the stock drop a hundred points and rise two hundred almost as quickly and became the second-largest shareholder in Industrial Acceptance Corp., which ultimately became the Continental Bank of Canada. The one stock he never sold was Argus. "In 1945 I was one of Argus's original shareholders. I decided right then that never before in the history of Canadian business had four such brilliant partners got together. It certainly hasn't happened since, and I doubt if it will ever happen again. No other combination of business acumen could equal them. They had a community of interest that held them together: making money. So did I. Argus was really a quadrumvirate—and I was the fifth wheel. Eddie Taylor was the promoter; the real brain of the whole complex was Colonel Phillips; the principal executive who carried out our agreed instructions was Wally McCutcheon; and the craftiest one of all was Bud McDougald."

Black became a member of the Argus executive committee in 1955 and actually served longer on it than McDougald. Through Western Dominion Investment Company Ltd., his private holding company, Black eventually acquired 561,000 Argus Class C shares as well as 231,297 (13 per cent) of Argus's common stock.

The dozen other stocks George Black followed brought him profitable results almost unerringly. Since he received few visitors and hardly ever went out, most of Black's stock decisions were based not on brokers' tips or market intelligence but on his close study of the Dow Theory.* Black had his own tickertape installed at home so that he could play the market without having to leave his living room. He enjoyed testing his wits against professional traders, using an approach similar to that of U.S. financier Bernard Baruch, who claimed: "I just sat and thought until I realized the obvious."

Black was equally adept in his real estate dealings. During the early 1950s, Major James Emanuel Hahn, the head of John Inglis Co. Ltd. (who had introduced the Bren gun to Canada), controlled a Toronto company called Property Holdings Ltd. It owned most of the land on Park Lane Circle and the Bridle Path in what was then Toronto's most fashionable outskirt and later the site of some of the most valuable housing in North America.† Hahn wanted to break the area into seventy small lots, but Black purchased from him the entire expanse (150 acres), having already bought seven acres on which stood an Eric Arthur designed house. He placed a minimum two-acre restriction on the size of lots and gradually sold them off at a considerable capital gain.

Apart from telephoning his brokers (Lord Hardinge or Charlie Burns or Brian Heward), he relaxed at home, sequestered from the world. During the eighteen years between his departure from Canadian Breweries and his death, George Black spent most of the time reading, smoking (sometimes two cigarettes simultaneously), and ringing for Fernando Aranda, his Spanish butler, to refill his drinking jug. Reading became progressively more difficult as the cataracts in both his eyes got worse; he had to use a magnifying glass to follow words from the end of one line to the beginning of the next, so that his head moved as if he were watching a tennis match.

Black was a very precise person. Norman Elder, the author-explorer who lived next door to the Blacks for most of two decades, recalls being

---

*Named after Charles Dow, the first editor of the *Wall Street Journal,* it postulated that there were three basic movements in the stock market: "The first is the narrow movement from day to day; the second is the short swing running from two weeks to a month or more; the third move develops out of economic forces, and is beyond control by any group of speculators." Dow developed complicated sets of indicators to follow these fluctuations.

†Hahn fought with distinction in the First World War (he was awarded the DSO, mentioned in dispatches twice, and wounded three times) and spent the Second World War as director-general of the Canadian Army's Technical Development Board, also helping to run Victory Aircraft Ltd., the country's largest bomber-producing plant. An avid fisherman, hunter, and yachtsman, he helped finance Sir Thomas Octave Murdoch Sopwith's attempt to wrest the America's Cup from Harold S. Vanderbilt. When he built his Park Lane Circle house, it was far enough from "downtown" Toronto to have a separate postal address. It is now occupied by Tom and Sonja Bata.

told by him that the lines of the marble on the floor of his garden room ran exactly due north. "I'd call George," Elder remembers, "and say, 'I'll be over in about ten minutes.' I'd arrive in fifteen and be told, 'You are now five minutes and thirty seconds late.'"

On the few occasions when George attempted the odd round of croquet (followed at two paces by Fernando and his magic martini cart), it was not a great success. "He was physically one of the laziest persons you could find anywhere in the world," recalls John Garfield (Jack) Campbell, Black's eventual successor in the Canadian Breweries presidency. "We lived near the Blacks and I phoned him a couple of times to ask him over so he could see the indoor swimming pool we'd bought for our daughter* as a Christmas present. When he finally arrived, he looked at the pool and said, 'Well, Garf, I think that's about all of the house I'll see today.' He just wouldn't make the effort to look around upstairs and, of course, he never came back."

Among the few visitors George Black did receive during his long years as a voluntary outcast were his wartime colleague Terence Sheard† and Michael de Pencier, now publisher of *Toronto Life*, who had married Honor Bonnycastle of Winnipeg. But his chief joy was to sit long into the evening with Conrad, playing chess. Father and son pitted their talents against history's great chess masters, replaying gambits devised by José Raúl Capablanca (the Cuban child prodigy who started to play the game at the age of four and became world champion in 1921) and Aleksandr Aleksandrovich Alekhine, the Russian master who took the world championship from Capablanca in 1927 and held it for more than sixteen years. Evans's Gambit became Conrad's favourite opening.

It was also during those times that the elder Black spun the tales of corporate derring-do that ignited the youngster's imagination and would eventually dominate his life.

---

*George Black's son Montegu III married Campbell's daughter Mariellen in 1964.

†Sheard, who also handled George Black's legal work, was a Cambridge graduate with an independent bent. He was the only member ever to question Bud McDougald at an annual meeting of the Toronto Club. In 1969, when the Argus president tried to push through the usual token resolutions, Sheard challenged him by complaining about, of all things, the sad state of the club's salt and pepper shakers. McDougald muttered something about being richer than Sheard, therefore a lot smarter and as a result not obliged to pay any attention. Sheard got up and gave a speech that never made it into the club minutes. "I'm not interested in coming to these annual meetings if I'm going to be insulted by Bud McDougald," he said. "Why, I remember when he was just a bond runner and spent his time emptying inkwells. He thinks that just because he has more money, he can insult me." To which McDougald answered, "Yes I can—and that's not the only reason."

UNLIKE THE WEALTHY PATRIARCHS who rush to endow their favourite offspring with the material rewards of their own hard-won success, George Black began to bestow in his lifetime a legacy that was different and very much more useful. He taught young Conrad the fundamentals of the market economy, steeped him in the lore of Argus, and explained how stock-value fluctuations can be forecast and exploited. He instilled in his teen-aged boy an appreciation for the relevance of historical perspective and, most important of all, tutored him in the art of seeing through grownups' deceptions. He demonstrated why gambling on any scale was wrong by installing a slot machine in his living room to teach the children that such devices were fixed and never paid off. When Mrs. C.O. Dalton, the wife of a Canadian Breweries executive vice-president, happened to hit the jackpot three times in a row, she was politely requested to return the money. Black always ceremoniously introduced Conrad to the isolated household's occasional visitors, a polite custom George had picked up from his own father. "He took me to shake hands with all the dignitaries who came to Winnipeg, always putting me in the picture, even at an early age. When you grow up you can sometimes astound people by saying, 'I shook hands with His Royal Highness the Prince of Wales.' I did, too, in 1919 though I was only eight at the time."

Conrad learned his priorities early.

He had been determined to become chairman of Argus since he was seven years old. Laurier LaPierre, the historian –TV commentator who first taught Black at Upper Canada College, remembers accosting him one day after school. "I said, 'It seems to me, Conrad, that you're waiting – what is it you're waiting for?'"

Black told him about his resolution and added, "It will come, one day."

"Even then," LaPierre recalls, "he was like a champion runner. I sometimes watch those contestants at the Olympics and find myself fascinated by the tension as they wait to spring into the pool or onto the running tracks. Conrad was like that – except that he seemed to know precisely when the starting gun would go off. His entire sense of life revolves around the idea that through a combination of circumstance, accidents, and evolution, God is granting him this extraordinary power that he must guard well and pass on. He has always felt himself to be a genuine instrument of history, with the capacity to create events."

Conrad was only eight when, of his own accord, he saved sixty dollars in pocket money to purchase a share in General Motors. "When I bought that share," he would later recall, "it was for motives that were then widely held by my elders. The Korean War was on at the time; Stalin was still in power; it was the height of the Cold War. To buy stock in General Motors was a wise means of participating in the growth of capitalism, supporting a great institution and casting one's vote with the side of justice and freedom in the worldwide struggle with the Red menace which was then generally assumed to be lurking behind every bush and under every bed. It was the act equivalent to the purchase of a victory bond during the Second World War. These were the early days of television; John Cameron Swayze and David Brinkley announced the kills in the aerial dogfights over Korea every night. I rushed home early from school to watch the McCarthy hearings on TV; 'Victory at Sea' was the most popular television program of the time.

"Notwithstanding my extreme zeal as a stockholder and as a Cold Warrior, I was appalled when the president of General Motors, Frederic Donner, announced that the U.S. automobile industry's policy was one of planned obsolescence. He claimed that because of the beneficial effect of this policy on the American economy, it should be described not as planned obsolescence but as *dynamic* obsolescence. I was young and reasonably credulous, but I instinctively knew that this was non-sense. Still, I always felt I was better off investing in General Motors, despite my reservations about management, than in record albums and the like."

His worship of money was precocious, to put it mildly. Jack Campbell, a family friend, recalls blinking in disbelief as he watched, through the summer haze, an eight-year-old Conrad on the patio outside the Blacks' living room carefully washing dollar bills and hanging them out on a line to dry.

When Ronald T. Riley, Conrad's uncle, came calling, George complained with considerable exasperation; "How in hell do you teach the Pythagorean theorem to a ten-year-old kid who hasn't had geometry in school yet?" Ian Dowie, another Canadian Breweries executive, recalls returning to George a borrowed biography of Napoleon and asking for a more detailed rundown of the relationship between Bonaparte and his marshals. The elder Black gestured toward his son: "Ask Conrad; he's the authority." The youngster, just shy of his tenth birthday, told Dowie far more than he wanted to know about Napoleon's Byzantine intrigues in keeping his ambitious adjutants at bay. "I tended, even from my very early years, to look at the world from a slightly different vantage point," Conrad recalls. "Although I might have had trouble articulating it at the age of ten, I wasn't unduly convinced of the durability of the Anglo-Saxon world as we had come to know it in the postwar period, a world of latter-day materialism advancing around the globe on the wings of the English language and the American dollar. I had a sneaking suspicion that we were living in a bit of a fool's paradise and began to be

33

much more interested in French culture, particularly Napoleon and de Gaulle."

Conrad emerged from his father's intense tutorials too undisciplined and too mentally overheated to handle more conventional learning. He gravely disappointed his father by managing to get himself expelled from two private schools, failing his law courses, and enduring rather than absorbing formal education.

Conrad's schooling was hardly a promising incubation period. The young Black felt that the private school milieu into which he had been involuntarily thrust was artificial, academically inferior, and too devoted to the concept of good sportsmanship, on and off the playing field. Conrad's mother once reported to her sister, Nancy Osler, with a considerable degree of puzzled outrage, that her young son regarded the official school prospectus issued by Upper Canada College, where he was enrolled, as "nothing but a tissue of lies."

Part of the problem was that UCC at the time was basically designed to appeal to the Toronto elite who wanted their sons to learn how to be unobtrusively rich. The school taught them about authority and how to cope with it, instilling in its graduates a smooth insouciance about perpetuating true Establishment values, not as an avowed creed but as a series of throw-away gestures. This was not a skill or attitude that Conrad required any lessons to absorb.

John Fraser, the *Globe and Mail* columnist and author of a brilliantly crafted book on China, was one of the few good friends Conrad made at UCC's prep school. "My earliest memory of him would be in about Grade Six and how terribly, terribly conscious he was of wealth and power," Fraser recalls. "We were walking around the school grounds one day and Conrad was raving on about the stupid masters. At one point he swept his hand to indicate the whole of the college and said, 'E.P. Taylor could buy this silly place fifty times over. He'd subdivide and make some money off it.' He was constantly sketching scenarios for taking over the college. Childhood was a prison for him. I remember Conrad as someone whose head was practically splitting because he was so impatient to get out into the real world and away from this nonsense of a boys' school."

Conrad recalls saying to Fraser, "Do you realize this is exactly the format of those death camps in the Third Reich? Here we are at compulsory games, compulsory changes of clothes, being herded like animals to the showers – and I hope to God it's water and not Cyclon-B that comes out."

Another pal from this period was George Hayhurst (whose father's advertising agency had handled the Canadian Breweries account), who spent five years with the youthful Black at UCC. "Conrad," he recalls, "was driven to school by Tommy Dair, the family chauffeur, in one of the Blacks' five cars, usually the Cadillac, and that's when he did his homework."

Hayhurst spent many memorable weekends at the Black residence. "Sunday lunch would be in the big dining hall, and, God, it was an enormous room. Mark, the cook, would serve the stuff, and it would be a pretty nice lunch, but Mr. Black would be about thirty-five feet away from me at the end of the table, sitting up there, talking about the Napoleonic wars, the internal combustion engine, American politics, or something else which I didn't really know an awful lot about. Conrad certainly knew a lot more than I did. After lunch we might play a game of pool Conrad had devised in which the coloured balls were battleships and we tried to sink them. He would always win. The slot machine was then in *his* room, and we used to play with it all the time. I fed quite a few nickels into that thing, and every once in a while I'd say, 'Look, I haven't won anything … let's break it open.' He had the key and we'd unlock it and start again. It was a real neat thing in those days to have your own slot machine. The house was kind of big and it was lots of fun. We also used to play in the family cars. Pushbutton windows were a great novelty, and we'd mess around with them for a while. I remember, at the beginning of the model year, we'd phone up the car dealerships and find out what the horsepower of their biggest models was, and the next day would compare notes to see which car had the most horsepower."

Norman Elder remembers that as a teenager Conrad had his own pleasantly decorated apartment within the household "where we would sit and chat for hours, pull out a *Canadian Who's Who* and go through a bunch of different people, the dates they did what, to see how we were doing. I used to give some pretty neat parties at Park Lane and he'd come, claiming that I was a great 'social engineer,' whatever that meant. We'd trick people. We would go up to one of the big houses around there whenever somebody new moved in and say, 'Why don't we bring a few of the neighbours around to meet you?' They'd agree, and we'd round up a couple of dozen local people as well as twenty-five others from the wrong side of the tracks. So everybody would arrive and the hosts were never sure who were the proper guests and who were from Scarborough. Conrad always loved those occasions."

One acquaintance vividly remembers driving Conrad and a babble of teenagers home from a birthday party in a station wagon and overhearing the young Black questioning every kid in the car about how many servants they had at home, wanting to make sure he was on top. He had few girlfriends. Jack Campbell recalls Conrad dropping in to see his daughter Mariellen late one afternoon and asking her to teach him how to waltz because he was attending his first dance that very evening.

When George Black was invited to give an informal talk to the boys at Upper Canada College, young Conrad was beside himself with pride, telling everybody exactly how important his father really was and precisely how wealthy his family would be. His only other passably pleasant memory of UCC was that it taught him to admire individuals who did their best at things for which they had no aptitude, especially sports. "I was always grateful," Conrad remembers, "for the few people around who were physically even less well co-ordinated than myself, one of whom was John Bosley.* He was an overweight kid with thick glasses always covered with fingerprints, a figure of almost universal derision. I became quite fond of him, thinking that as long as everybody disliked him, he must be pretty good."

The climax of Conrad's dubious career at Upper Canada College occurred in 1959. There is no mention of the event in school records. Officially, it never happened. Yet it was Conrad's first business venture, and in the context of the 1950s, when student pranks at UCC were something of a novelty, the great exam robbery caper set the Toronto Establishment's tongues wagging and eventually influenced Conrad's decision to exile himself to Montreal.

The college was at the time undergoing major repairs, its main building having been condemned as unsafe, and most teaching was being done in portable classrooms set about the grounds. In the confusion, security had been relaxed, and Conrad managed to get a key to the office of Rev. C.W. Sowby, the school principal. Along with two accomplices he decided it would be a great prank to go into Sowby's office and peek at people's confidential files. While rummaging around, the trio discovered copies of questions for that year's final examinations, which were to be written the following week. Struck by the profit potential of the find, Conrad secretly reproduced the documents on an Argus copying machine and sold them to worried students. Ever the democrat, young Black devised a variable price system that reduced the amount for kids who couldn't afford to pay and doubled the cost to those dunderheads who would almost certainly fail. "It was all organized with James Bond élan and was the first example of Conrad's adminis-

---

*Bosley, later a Toronto real estate broker, went into both municipal and federal politics, becoming one of the most intelligent members of the Joe Clark caucus. "In those days," he recalls of his UCC period, "what mattered was either if you were a jock, and that eliminated 80 per cent of the students, or if you convinced yourself you were a whiz kid. That meant you became part of a little group of about ten. Conrad fit neither category."

trative brilliance," says Ralph Heintzman, an Ottawa historian who was a UCC student at the time. "Conrad watched the movement of masters around the principal's office for weeks, had the keys copied in the Spadina Village hardware store, and then sold the exam-paper copies on a sliding scale."

Conrad and his pals netted close to five thousand dollars but unfortunately for them a student nicknamed "Pogo" Diakiw was caught with his prepared answers by J.L. Coulton, one of the masters, who quickly got the unnerved youth to confess exactly what had happened. Principal Sowby immediately called a meeting in the UCC assembly hall and told the whole school they would have to write a new set of exams. Some overexcited UCC non-graduates even marched to the Black household and shouted abuse at their classmate.

Conrad was summarily expelled.* George Black dispatched his lawyer, Terence Sheard, to intercede on his son's behalf. Although he himself was an Old Boy (1910-15), Sheard didn't have much of a brief. His argument for the defence – that cheating has always been common in high schools but "nobody had thought to put it on a commercial basis until Conrad came along" – was not particularly persuasive.

"One of the people to whom we sold an examination was discovered, and he sang like a canary flying backward at three o'clock in the morning," Conrad recalls. "I left Upper Canada on June 9, 1959, and as I was walking out the gates a number of students who literally twenty-four hours before had been begging for assistance – one of them on his knees – were now shaking their fists and shouting words of moralistic execration after me. I've never forgotten how cowardly and greedy people can be."

Schoolless, fifteen-year-old Conrad was enrolled by his exasperated parents at Trinity College School in Port Hope, Ontario, with scarcely better results. "If Upper Canada was an uninspiring and somewhat unconvivial environment," he says, "it was paradise itself compared to TCS. My experience there temporarily convinced me that the so-called Establishment in this country was a complete farce. As far as I could see,

---

*It is a striking coincidence that Conrad's chief mentor, John A. McDougald, enjoyed a similarly abbreviated stay at the college. When he was only twelve, young Bud insisted on driving himself to school in a Briggs & Stratton Buckboard to avoid the ignominy of streetcars. This was clearly against school regulations and he was regularly caned for the offence by J.L. Somerville, the prep school's headmaster. McDougald finally left the college in 1921 when he tied the rear axle of Principal W.L. "Choppy" Grant's Model T to a tree branch, so that when the unmechanically minded schoolmaster gunned his motor, the wheels just spun – until Bud cut him down. McDougald switched to St. Andrew's College but skipped most classes to place his schoolmates' bets on nags at the nearby Thorncliffe racetrack.

people were elevated exclusively on the basis of athletics." One of Black's less pleasant duties was acting as "fag" to Ronald Atkey, later to be Minister of Employment and Immigration in the Clark Government.* This was all part of the new-boy hazing system, which involved having to make beds and run errands. "I did not," says Black, "shine Atkey's shoes. I drew the line at certain indignities, and that was one of them. I thought most of the TCS students were chuckleheads and knew in my heart that just because by the standards of that place someone was a good football player (though he probably wouldn't have made the lowest intramural team at any American high school), it didn't mean he was going to be any hell-beater when he got going in a career." Atkey remembers Conrad as "a delightful eccentric who we all thought would become something very exotic like an engineer leading a major consortium into the Middle East."

His stay at TCS, like the UCC sojourn, ended with the school's strongly suggesting that Conrad might be happier elsewhere. ("There was nothing dramatic about it – they just kicked me out. I was invited to withdraw and become an extramural student, a status that had never existed before but allowed me to write the examinations without attending school.")

As a final resort, George Black enrolled his rebellious son in a private Toronto institution that specializes in rehabilitating the Establishment's less malleable offspring. Lodged in a modest three-storey converted private house at 241 Poplar Plains Road, and modelled on a Swiss finishing school, Thornton Hall maintains its enrolment at less than fifty, with a ratio of one teacher per seven students. It charges $4,000 in annual tuition fees. Founded in 1947 by Stuart Mackey, Thornton Hall gives such heady courses as "A Study of Liberal Democracy and Its Enemies" and "The Art of the Mediaeval World and Byzantium." The school's educational philosophy is summed up by Vice-Principal Angela Greig: "I take the position strongly that there is no such thing as a worthwhile human being who does not respond to Shakespeare, Milton, Keats, Michelangelo, and Goya. These greats judge us, we do not judge them. For a person to take the position, 'I do not like Milton,' or 'I find Shakespeare boring,' or even, 'I am not interested in Goya,' gives us no information about these artists, but it certainly tells us a great deal

---

*The Establishment wheel keeps turning. The same private school was attended by Michael Meighen, grandson of the former Canadian prime minister, whose uncle Max was to be Conrad's chief opponent in the grab for Argus. Young Michael Meighen's "fag" at TCS was none other than George Montegu Black III, Conrad's older brother.

about the person. He is revealing a spirit so shallow, an intellect so ego-centric, that he cannot be called a human being. In my twenty-five years of teaching I have come across about four such persons.... Often, just before a class begins, I look at these young people sitting before me with their pens, notebooks, scissors, glue, and serious expectant looks. It is a very special thing that they are sitting there in front of me and I feel keenly that I owe them something—something important, exciting, un-forgettable, something that will change their lives. I give them Dante, Isaiah, and Rembrandt."

Graduates have included three Eatons, a Bassett, a Gardiner, three Phelans, a Sifton, several Oslers, a Weston, and Robertson Davies's daughter Rosamond. There is no sports program but students have to paint self-portraits and help stage a play the first Saturday of every June in the school's miniature backyard Greek amphitheatre. Angela Greig has a memory of Conrad as "a thin hairpin of a boy with red hair, quite shy, very alert, though sometimes he annoyed me deeply because I felt there was more ability there than he was really using."

Another Thornton teacher was Eric Johnson, who remembers young Black as "a fascinating combination of tremendous sensitivity and tremendous force, enthralled by literature and history. He must have been pretty good because he did very little work and yet got top marks." After his sojourn at Thornton Hall Conrad finally managed to graduate from high school, writing the exams on his own. That was the first time he remembers his father congratulating him for anything.

LOOKING BACK over this patchwork educational process, Conrad vivid-ly remembers a puzzling exchange in 1956 with Laurier LaPierre while he was teaching at UCC. LaPierre had arrived in class that morning nearly in tears over Duplessis's victory at the polls. Young Black put up his hand to ask, "If Duplessis's so bad, why does he always win?" Bitter laughter was all that LaPierre could muster in exchange, though it seemed a fair question. "I felt for Duplessis, even then," says Conrad, "the way I felt toward the New York Yankees and the Montreal Cana-diens. It was the pride of champions."

The champion whose antics particularly intrigued Black was Cana-diens' star right-winger, Maurice "Rocket" Richard. "The Rocket and Ted Lindsay of the Detroit Red Wings had a terrible rivalry for years," he says. "In those days the teams would play in a Canadian city on Saturday nights and an American rink Sunday nights. After Richard and Lindsay had had this awful fracas, they got on the overnight train to Detroit, but the Rocket was so annoyed he couldn't sleep. Finally, he got up and went through each coach, pulling the berth-curtains apart to find out where Lindsay was, so that he could smash his face in. I've never had much tendency to physical violence, but I was always impressed by how highly motivated he was."

Black's other, much more intense, preoccupation was keeping track of the intrigues at Argus. "Conrad was wrapped up in the thing from the age of seven," claims H.N.R. (Hal) Jackman, later an Argus director. Peter White, who became one of Conrad's three main partners, disagrees with the Jackman assessment, claiming that the bug really bit a year earlier. "I think it was in part Bud McDougald's instinct, too," White contends. "Conrad certainly has been aware at least since the age of six that sooner or later he might have a shot at Argus. He was a precocious young man. But it didn't take any great genius to see that McDougald had no children, that Max Meighen had no children, that the Phillips, McCutcheon, and Taylor children were out of it – so the only available inheritors were the Black children."

Both McDougald and Taylor made a special point of being nice to the two Black boys. McDougald reminisced many years later about the first serious conversation he had with Conrad, who was about seven and had been boasting about his knowledge of maritime lore. To test him, McDougald said that he was planning a trip to Britain soon and asked Conrad which passenger liner might be the most suitable. "Well," McDougald recalled the youngster earnestly replying, "the greatest ship, the *Normandie*, isn't here any more, and the second-greatest, the old *Mauretania*, isn't either. So what you're left with is the *Queen Mary* for the best service, though the *Île de France* would have the most transatlantic atmosphere, which I suspect you're not really interested in. The *Queen Elizabeth* is a nice working ship, but it just doesn't have the aura. So I'd recommend you stick with the *Queen Mary*."

Properly impressed, McDougald could only mumble, "That confirms my judgement exactly," and went on to tell little Conrad how, on a previous crossing aboard the *Queen Mary*, he had happened to meet a fascinating Hollywood actor named Ronald Reagan.

In 1951, George Black bought his elder son, George Montegu III, an eighty-pound inflatable punt for his eleventh birthday. As soon as E.P. Taylor saw it, he insisted upon a proper launching in his pool and sent his gardener (an ex-RCMP constable) with a station wagon to pick it up. The boat slid down a mattress as both families watched and the proud father recorded the splash with a movie camera. *La-di-dah*.

George Black remembered Eddie Taylor once telling him about Conrad, "You know, judging by the size of his skull, that young man is going to have a tremendous brain." Taylor had dropped in to see the

Blacks after a horse auction in North Carolina and just for the hell of it asked Conrad, then twelve, "Where do you think North Carolina ranks in population among the states of the Union?"

Conrad shot back immediately: "Fourteenth!"

Taken aback, Taylor replied, "If you're correct on that, I'll give you a quarter."

The youngster scuttled upstairs and came back with a gazetteer, shouting, "You see, right there!" and was given his reward.

After George Black had been dismissed from Canadian Breweries, he tried to smooth out the growing tensions between Taylor and McDougald. "I begged them, beseeched them practically on bended knee, to bury the hatchet. When they solemnly assured me they had, I told them, 'All I can say, gentlemen, is that if you have, you buried it about one-sixteenth of an inch below the brain with the handle still sticking out."

As the possibility of reconciliation evaporated, Black sided more and more with McDougald, a trend that Bud helped promote by occasionally holding Argus executive committee meetings in George's living room. Then came the clincher: Conrad on his twenty-first birthday received a plain white envelope from McDougald. It contained a membership card for the Toronto Club.

Conrad had thus been slipped past the club's complicated admission procedure. When the story was told by a mutual friend to Paul Desmarais, the chairman of Power Corporation of Canada, he quipped: "Hell, Bud probably signed Conrad up the day he was born!"

IN 1962, CONRAD LEFT HOME to enrol in history and political science at Carleton. Few other universities would accept him, but he was just as happy to be in Ottawa because he was becoming interested in Canadian politics. When he neglected his studies, Naomi Griffiths, then a history professor and later Carleton's Dean of Arts, wrote him a curt note: "It appears you're failing this course. I would appreciate it if you would decide to withdraw or otherwise come to see me and decide to do some work." She recalls their subsequent meeting when Conrad sheepishly appeared at her office: "He was so astonished at somebody giving him the choice that he was grateful for it. I think one reason he majored in history was that the department really did care for its students."

Although he spent the decade of undergraduate revolt on various campuses, Conrad never became a child of the sixties, no roaring boy enlisting in the prevailing counterculture or lightfooting it into the hills. "He was very well read, well spoken, very interested in French politics,

Napoleon and de Gaulle, military strategy of any kind—and the only one of my contemporaries who followed the stock market," recalls Brian Stewart, who became his best campus friend. "He started to get involved with one or two girls at Carleton but I don't think he was very skilled at it. He had quite a lively interest in that area, but he was probably waiting for some kind of sophistication to come over him. His manner would tend to put off a lot of women. I mean, if you introduced him to a girl and he started off by talking about the exigencies of Napoleon's campaign in Flanders, she'd wonder how on earth to respond—and usually didn't."

He helped David Smith (later a federal Liberal M.P.) to throw out the NDP, then ruling Carleton's model parliament. Conrad was a Liberal at the time. But his chief non-academic exploit was a brief fling as a moving force in the university's theatre club. It sponsored a vaguely erotic film called *Bitter Ash*, ensuring brisk ticket sales by telephoning the morality squad of the Ottawa police department from the office of the university newspaper. The cops promptly threatened to raid the show, which they did at the end of the first reel. The next venture was called *A Thousand and One Freudian Delights*. "We correctly judged that all good freshmen from Arnprior and Smiths Falls would flock to this one, and they did," he recalls. "One of my fellow club members came out naked, painted in psychedelic hues from head to toe, and crawled around the stage to the Beatles' 'Yellow Submarine.' Then the record ended, the curtain came down, and he was zipped off the stage, leaving a frustrated and infuriated audience."

Conrad spent most summers travelling through Europe with Brian Stewart. "He was a tremendous travelling companion—funny, interested in films and plays, chasing women, all the normal things," his friend recalls. "Anywhere we went, he kind of knew the history of the place. It's the only time I remember him not wearing three-piece suits. He even managed to look rumpled occasionally and once ran out of money. I was in Spain and he was in France, and I got this urgent telegram asking that I meet him at the Madrid railway station. When I got there he was down to a few francs and remained broke for nearly two weeks before another cheque from home arrived. It was interesting to see him trying to scrape together enough money to eat."

After graduating with shaky grades from Carleton and not at all certain what he wanted to do, Conrad enrolled in Osgoode Hall, the Toronto law school. By the end of the first year he hadn't even made the 35 per cent grade in one key subject required for admittance to the supplemental examination courses. He wandered around England, worked briefly as a tour guide in Paris, toyed with the idea of taking a job in London's financial district, completed a course of studies toward becoming a psychoanalyst, did some writing and, in the autumn of 1966, fled Toronto for Quebec. He spoke little French at the time but found himself drawn to the province, especially to the militant nationalism sweeping its campuses, the pre-Centennial excitement of Montreal, and a growing fascination with an almost forgotten politician named Maurice Duplessis.

CHAPTER TWO

Bohemian Interlude

*Conrad slipped easily into the bistro milieu of
downtown Montreal and lower-town Quebec City,
arguing the night away with radical students and
becoming infatuated with a string of pretty girls.*

Between the hopeful summer of 1966 and the gloomy winter of
1974, Conrad Moffat Black, the failed WASP, evolved as a
successful entrepreneur and knowledgeable Québécois. He took
to French-Canadian society with the fanaticism of a convert. When
Black arrived in Montreal, he knew fewer than a hundred words of
French and had no credentials apart from his Anglophobe sentiments.
(He felt especially contemptuous of the way the British had given their
empire away, condemning Harold Wilson's 1966 decision to pull out of
the Persian Gulf and scrap the Royal Navy's aircraft carriers. He
regarded the subsequent resignation of Christopher Mayhew, Minister
of Defence for the Navy, as "the last resonance of good sense in that
country until Maggie Thatcher came in.") By the time he returned to
Toronto in the spring of 1974, Black had become thoroughly bilingual
(mastering even the colloquial twang of Quebec *joual*), had graduated
with honours in Civil Law from Laval University, and had obtained an
M.A. in history from McGill. He could count himself among the
confidants of two Quebec premiers and was the biographer of a third, as
well as having been a temporal adviser and fund-raiser to Paul-Émile
Cardinal Léger, Archbishop of Montreal and the province's outstanding
churchman. At the same time, he had discovered the world of women –
and was on his way to founding his impressive business empire.

Conrad had initially been attracted to the French character by Charles
de Gaulle's fascinating sequential incarnations as strategist, exile, saviour, recluse, saviour, savant, and saint. Although he never reached the
stage of sharing the General's ecstatic vision of France as "the Madonna
in the frescoes," he was immensely attracted by the idea that the
aesthetic of French civilization is predominantly based on the creative

faculty of choice. According to this notion, options are exercised not in response to the pull of advertising or the push of competitiveness but for their appropriateness to an individual's tastes and preferences—on the basis of what the French call *la mesure*, the proper proportion of things. "I was always impressed by even trivial illustrations of the extreme elasticity of the French mind," he says. "I remember reading a book about a famous criminal case in 1924 involving two chambermaids working for a well-to-do lady in a Paris suburb. She had asked them to press one of her dresses, but the iron broke and the maids worked themselves into quite a rage about one thing and another. When their employer came back they murdered her and chopped up her body. In due course they were discovered and charged. Their lawyer argued that the court must understand that the apparent crime was merely the inevitable outcome of frustration under the weight of which any human might buckle, giving an unbelievable and very eloquent pitch that was really absolute drivel. But he managed to get them off the murder charge, which may not have been admirable but certainly was illuminating."

His sojourn in Quebec was what passes for Conrad's Bohemian period. He slipped easily into the bistro milieu of downtown Montreal and lower-town Quebec City, arguing the night away with radical students and becoming infatuated with a string of pretty girls—Monique Benoit, Margaret Jones, and Odette Beaudoin among them.

At about this time, Black also came to know Dr. Clifford Scott, founder of the Canadian Institute of Psychoanalysis, who had treated Rudolf Hess and succeeded Dr. Ernest Jones (biographer of Sigmund Freud) as head of the Royal Psychoanalytic Society in London. A graduate of the University of Toronto medical school and a practising analyst since 1932, Scott returned to Canada in the mid-fifties. "Really a remarkable man," says Black, "but I would never ask him what kind of investments to make."

His most frequent companion was a wry and witty reformer named Nick Auf der Maur, one of the founding editors of the *Last Post* and later a member of the Montreal city council. "At the time, I was in the anti-Vietnam war movement while Conrad constituted almost the entire LBJ fan club in Canada," Auf der Maur remembers. "I used to go out for dinner and fight with him. It got to be quite a regular thing. We'd go back to his apartment at the Port-Royal, sit up until six or seven in the morning, drinking his Napoleon brandy, screaming and yelling at each other. We got along famously. He was, of course, madly pro-business and I was completely pro-labour. He was a terrible blabbermouth and so was I. We were both kind of double agents. Even at the height of my

46

crazy, radical days I was convinced of his sincerity, in the sense of wanting his ambitions to result in some good."

Conrad Black's most endearing quality is that he has the courage of his condescensions. His sense of indignation is often tested but seldom found wanting. Auf der Maur recalls running into Black on Sherbrooke Street and suggesting they have a drink. "As a lark, I decided to take Conrad into the Truxx Cruising Bar on Stanley Street, then Montreal's most notorious homosexual hangout. It was three flights up, an awful place, raided by the morality squad a couple of weeks later. I knocked on the door, but they wouldn't let us in: with his three-piece suit Conrad looked much too straight. He went through this hilarious transformation. For the first thirty seconds he was totally indignant because we were standing at what he later called 'the portals of depravity.' He then turned just as indignant because as a free citizen he was being refused entry. He got quite confused because he couldn't quite decide which to be more indignant about. We never did go in, but I'll always remember that moment of twin consternations."

At one point Auf der Maur, who hadn't played chess since high school, challenged Black to a tournament, which their friends quickly escalated into an ideological confrontation. The match was to be the best of seven games, played on subsequent days at the Rainbow Bar & Grill. "We fixed the date three weeks ahead of time and were both supposed to practise. Our pals went around betting madly on the winner. I didn't take it very seriously, and in our first game he narrowly beat me. Conrad has this terrible discipline—he won't drink during chess games. And I have this terrible non-discipline. I was drinking away, so I immediately challenged him to a second game. He beat me a little more easily. I ordered more liquor and decided we'd have the third game right away. He beat me fairly handily. More drinks, and I insisted on the fourth game. By this time I was drunk and Conrad was still sipping his bloody Perrier. He totally humiliated me in the fourth game and happily sat around collecting hundred-dollar bets from the out-of-work actors and other unemployed buddies who had bet on me."

Despite their many differences, the two young men found common ground in their contempt for the lack of leadership in Montreal's English business community and its inability to cope with events. Black became for a time a vocal supporter of Quebec's aspirations, steeping himself in the nuances of its nationalism. "He was far more sympathetic and understanding of Quebec than I would expect any Anglo businessman to be," recalls Auf der Maur. "He was also becoming deeply knowledgeable about Quebec history, far better informed than most French-Canadian intellectuals, who often don't know anything prior to

1950." Black grew particularly attracted to Montreal's French-speaking business leaders because they were nearly all self made, having worked their way up against tough odds. He constantly stressed his identification with these *arrivistes* rather than with Westmount's inheritors of wealth. He insisted on explaining to anyone who would listen that he wasn't daddy's boy, that he had made it on his own, that while he might have been born to privilege, he'd started his own business and its success had been based on his own merit, his own brain, his own ability to function.

This interpretation of Black's founding of the Sterling newspaper chain, which was the object of his boasting, magnified somewhat the series of events involved. Moreover, as Auf der Maur loved to point out, "Conrad had a slightly better line of credit than most of us."

GENESIS OF THE STERLING IDEA dated from Conrad's days at Carleton University and his friendship with Peter Gerald White. An intense young man, all shoulders and dedication, White had been born in São Paulo, Brazil, in 1938 and had studied French at a *lycée* in Lausanne, Switzerland. He graduated from Bishop's College School at Lennoxville in the Eastern Townships and went on to obtain a law degree at Laval. Attending a Progressive Conservative party convention in Ottawa while still a law student, he ran into an old chum from BCS, Jeremy Riley (later principal of Stanstead College), who introduced White to his cousin Conrad Black. The two students hit it off, and the following year, when White arrived in Ottawa to be an executive assistant to Forestry Minister Maurice Sauvé, Conrad invited him to move into his fancy digs at the Juliana, then Ottawa's most luxurious apartment building. In the penthouse just above Black and White lived John C. Doyle, the mining promoter, who used to play his Hammond organ until four or five in the morning. The building had also been the site of most of the assignations of Gerda Munsinger, the Montreal prostitute with underworld connections who was linked to Pierre Sévigny, Associate Minister of National Defence in the Diefenbaker Cabinet.

"Conrad was the apple of his father's eye," White recalls. "When we were sharing that apartment, George was in Toronto at Park Lane Circle and he'd be doing whatever he did all night long. At around four o'clock nearly every morning, he'd decide to telephone Conrad. I'd be asleep, but Conrad, after having been through this probably every day of his life in Ottawa, would know damn well that this phone call was coming, so he would have the dilemma of either going to bed and being wakened up at four o'clock or staying up and waiting for it. He generally opted for the latter because he was very much a nocturnal animal in those days. And so—the phone would ring around four or whatever, George would come on, and they would talk for an hour at the very least, sometimes two or three. I visualized George sitting back in his chair at Park Lane Circle, just sort of passing the time of night with his son, because the father found him a stimulating intellectual conversationalist, someone to talk to. Conrad enjoyed the exchanges but did view them as something of an imposition on his time. He was supposed to be studying for university. George obviously either assumed that his son could handle both things easily—or it never even occurred to him. I'd never met anybody who spent up to three hours every day talking on the long-distance telephone. It was astonishing."

A political and commercial entrepreneur with fast wits and a nose for profit, White had purchased for one dollar a decrepit Quebec weekly called the *Knowlton Advertiser*, which claimed a summer circulation of three hundred. He persuaded Black, at loose ends following his disastrous year at Osgoode, to run it. They changed the paper's name to the *Eastern Townships Advertiser*, decided to publish the year round, bought a companion French-language weekly in nearby Cowansville, and within six months were turning a monthly profit of $350. Black moved into a boathouse belonging to Peter White's mother on the shores of Brome Lake, near Knowlton. The tiny cottage was usually occupied by a priest named Jonathan Robinson, the son of Maurice Duplessis's Minister of Mines, who was then secretary to Cardinal Léger. He had placed a sign over the top of the cottage door, spelling out in Hebrew "The House of Jonathan, The Secretary."

What had started as a lark gradually turned into a real business. With a staff of only two (including brother Monte, who acted as financial editor), Conrad wrote most of the copy, sold much of the advertising, and looked after the subscriptions, which climbed to 2,100.

Through the brooding solitude of a Quebec winter, Black lived in the cramped hut, spending the long nights by himself. A snifter of Napoleon brandy at hand, he would muse romantically about his future, gazing across the frozen lake toward Tyrone, the baronial summer house of the late John Bassett, a *real* publisher, who had commanded the Montreal *Gazette* and owned the *Sherbrooke Record*. "I may have been tempted to shake my fist at it many nights," he later recalled, "but I don't think I ever actually did."

White had by this time become a special assistant to Daniel Johnson and introduced Conrad to the Quebec Premier at a rally in Granby. Black continued to run the two weeklies but decided to get a little closer to the centre of things by enrolling in the law faculty of Laval University and moving into the modish Sillery Plaza in Quebec City. No more nocturnal flights of envy peering across Brome Lake at the material expression of Bassett's achievements. Conrad spent his Quebec City evenings gazing down instead at the St. Lawrence River, enviously watching the navigation lights of Paul Desmarais's Canada Steamship Lines and Jack Leitch's Upper Lakes Shipping freighters steaming by.

Partly because White was a Johnson aide, but probably just as much because Black was such an oddity around Quebec in those days – this upper-crust WASP in a dark three-piece suit who spoke good French – he grew quite close to the Premier and his successor, Jean-Jacques Bertrand. Black's favourite recollection is of sitting around Johnson's office with several cabinet ministers, sipping beer late on a Friday, when an assistant burst in with an important position paper on the environment. Johnson vaguely promised to read it, but the aide insisted that the problem required immediate action. He finally subsided when the Premier ruled, "No. I've worked hard to get to this position, where I can sit around on a Friday afternoon and drink beer with the guys. That's what I'm going to do."

Black gradually insinuated himself into Daniel Johnson's entourage, writing half a dozen speeches for the Premier, even though only one was ever delivered. And he met Franklin David Radler.

It was White who pointed Black toward his first business venture and helped guide him through it. But it was Radler, a streetfighter with the fastidiously tuned intellect of a classical scholar, who became and has remained Conrad's chief alter ego. Unimpressed with the whole Establishment scene, Radler has an unswervable dedication to the bottom line on balance sheets, yet he is instinctively aware of the appearance of things, suspicious that the social contract lurks everywhere.

Radler's father, who later became an executive at Miami's Fontainebleau Hotel, had owned a Montreal restaurant called Au Lutin Qui Bouffe (The Elf Who Eats Too Much), which attracted customers by allowing them to play and pose with piglets that wandered among the tables (at ten weeks the piglets became too big and were replaced). A onetime waiter at the nightclub was Mario Beaulieu, who eventually rose to occupy the finance portfolio in the Quebec government of Jean-Jacques Bertrand. It was in March 1969, during a party held to celebrate Beaulieu's by-election victory at the Renaissance Club, a Union Nationale hangout in Montreal, that Radler first met White, who introduced him to Black.

After graduating in arts from McGill, Radler had taken an MBA degree at Queen's and while still at university was asked to create a handicrafts marketing program for the Curve Lake Indian Reserve north of Peterborough, Ontario. Under his guidance, Clifford Whetung, the band's most imaginative craftsman, became Canada's first native Indian millionaire through his own efforts. Radler later developed similar schemes at thirty Indian communities ("There's always one guy on every reserve who wants to get rich – that's all you need") and set himself up as a successful management consultant.

In June 1969, Black, White, and Radler decided to go into partnership and bid for the Sherbrooke newspaper. Purchased by John Bassett in 1936, the *Record* was the only English-language daily in the Eastern Townships. It had been taken over by the owner's son, Major John W. Bassett, as a kind of postwar demobilization project. The managing editor, Doug Amaron, earned eighty dollars a week. "Every Christmas," Amaron later recalled, "we were given a turkey. The size of the bird depended on the rank you held. I had no children and I used to get a twenty-two pounder. A fellow who worked in the composing room had seven children, but he'd get one weighing eight pounds. For years, I used to switch with him." Ivan Saunders, the paper's general manager, purchased a $144,000 Goss press, hoping to expand into the printing business. But the *Record* started losing money and after the younger Bassett moved to Toronto, his family lost interest in the property. It was sold in 1968 to Saunders, by then president of the *Record*, for the equivalent of its breakup value. The paper's losses continued to escalate. Black, White, and Radler were able to buy it (without the new press, which had already been sold) for $20,000. This was to be the only actual cash the three partners ever invested in Sterling. White obtained his downpayment through a loan from the Bank of Montreal in Knowlton and Black financed his share out of the profits of the *Eastern Townships Advertiser*, although by then he and Monte had inherited $200,000 from their paternal grandfather – an amount that the elder brother eventually ran up to a million dollars through market investments.

The new owners looked around for the cheapest press facility and chose Newport, Vermont – giving the *Record* the dubious distinction of being the only Canadian daily newspaper ever to be printed in a foreign country. They moved to Sherbrooke, with Black and Radler installing themselves in L'Ermitage Motel on King Street at $8.50 a night; Peter White opted for a four-dollar room at the Royal Hotel, casting loud and frequent aspersions at his partners' extravagance. They cut the paper's payroll in half, instituted a tight cost-accounting system, and started an aggressive advertising sales drive. The first month, July, ended with a loss of $8,000 – which became a $1,132 profit in August. "As a publisher," remarked George MacLaren, a Sherbrooke lawyer who observed Black's cost-cutting techniques, "Conrad could have given a few lessons to Lord Thomson, right down to counting rolls of toilet paper and the number of pencils used by reporters." Lewis Harris, one of the *Record*'s managing editors during that time, recalls being chauffeured in Black's obese Cadillac to a business luncheon conference – at a locally renowned hamburger drive-in beside the river.

The paper's editorial independence was tested when Peter White decided to run in the 1970 provincial election, and Black ordered that his partner's campaign receive blanket coverage. "There seemed only two choices: quit or knuckle under," recalls John Fraser, who started as a *Record* reporter in 1963. "Instead, the staff responded brilliantly by overfulfilling their mandate. White turned up nearly every second day on the front of the paper in embarrassingly eulogistic circumstances, whereas his Liberal opponent appeared only twice – once in a comparison with Adolf Hitler and the second time by mistake. The result, of course, was that White became a laughingstock, which no doubt contributed to his subsequent defeat."

"After we saw the profits coming in, we said to ourselves, 'God, where's this business been all our lives?'" Black recalls. His brother, Monte, who was then with Draper Dobie and Company Ltd., had been visiting the Toronto investment firm's Vancouver office, where he got hold of a list of fifteen British Columbia weeklies up for sale. At about the same time, Senator Keith Davey's Committee on Mass Media issued its report, and Conrad used one of its appendices to provide himself with a handy tabulation of likely papers to buy. Another source of information was the media source book *Canadian Advertising Rates & Data.* "One afternoon," Radler later recalled, "Conrad, Peter, and I started to wade through its listings. The first section is on B.C. and the Yukon. We phoned dozens of the proprietors, then and there, and asked them if they were interested in selling. There were just two people interested in even talking with us. Most of them hung up. But we did talk with Dan Murray in Fort St. John and with the Milner papers in Prince Rupert. So Conrad and I flew to B.C. and did the deals."

In March 1972, Radler moved to Prince Rupert to take full-time command, and during the next decade there was hardly a B.C. newspaper that wasn't sold to Sterling.* Using bank loans of $6.7 million and

*

Paper	Circulation	Cost to Sterling
Alaska Highway News (Fort St. John)	5,000 weekdays	$240,000
Mackenzie Times (Mackenzie)	1,350 Wednesdays	$10,000

gradually accumulated profits (but no family money), Black and his partners eventually ended up owning a group of twenty-one publishing properties. They were frequently able to outmanoeuvre the Thomson

Northern Horizons (Dawson Creek)	26,000 every second Monday	
Peace River Block News (Dawson Creek)	5,000 weekdays	$480,000
Chetwynd Echo (Chetwynd)	1,500 Wednesdays	
Trail Daily Times (Trail)	6,500 weekdays	
Nelson Daily News (Nelson)	9,600 weekdays	$1.3 million
Alberni Valley Times (Port Alberni)	8,000 weekdays	$690,000
Lloydminster Daily Times (Lloydminster, Sask.)	8,000 weekdays	$350,000
Weekly Times (Lloydminster, Sask.)	17,400 Wednesdays	
Summerside Journal- Pioneer (Summerside, P.E.I.)	11,500 weekdays	$500,000
North Shore Citizen (North and West Vancouver)	49,200 Wednesdays (Ceased publication in 1980)	$725,000
The Enterprise (Port Coquitlam area)	36,300	$50,000
Surrey-Delta Messenger (Suburban Vancouver)	37,000	$52,000
White Rock & Surrey Sun (White Rock and Surrey)	18,000	$125,000
Richmond Review (Ladner and Tsawwassen)	23,000	$459,000
Daily Townsman (Cranbrook)	4,200 weekdays	
Courier Merchandiser (East Kootenays)	23,000 Mondays	$480,000
Kimberley Bulletin (Kimberley)	2,000 weekdays	
Terrace Daily Herald (Terrace)	3,100 weekdays	
Prince Rupert Daily News (Prince Rupert)	4,500 weekdays	$160,000

chain because they avoided the creation of any bureaucracy. "We were easier to deal with than Thomson," says Radler. "We could just look at each other, wink, and agree to a deal in minutes."

When he was once asked what marketing criterion the group applied in its choice of newspapers to buy (was it a question of projecting circulation area demographics; counting storefronts owned by potential advertisers; or, perhaps, a detailed analysis of big-city-daily overflow?), David Radler replied: "We'd visit the offices of each prospective property at night and count the desks. That would tell us how many people worked there. From our experience at Sherbrooke we realized that if a place had, say, forty-two desks, we'd only need thirty. We knew a dozen people would be leaving the payroll, even though we hadn't seen their faces yet." Most of Sterling's dailies operate with an editorial complement of only three or four full-time editorial employees, a curmudgeonly attitude that at least once had absurd consequences. On February 11, 1978, when a Pacific Western Airlines jet crashed at Cranbrook, B.C., killing forty-three of those aboard, the Sterling-owned *Daily Townsman* in Cranbrook covered the tragedy mostly by running dispatches from the Toronto-based Canadian Press news agency.

Sterling's only Maritime purchase was the *Journal-Pioneer* in Prince Edward Island, which cost a discounted $500,000.* "Conrad phoned me from the Holiday Inn at Summerside when he was negotiating the deal," Monte recalls. "He said he didn't want to be overheard and was sitting under a blanket because the walls were so thin."

In June 1973, Harlequin Enterprises Ltd. offered $5 million (and was turned down) for the chain founded only four years before for $20,000. By 1981, Sterling's revenues had exceeded $20 million, with a $5-million profit; its ownership was shared by Black (42 per cent), Radler (33 per cent), and White (25 per cent). The *Sherbrooke Record* was sold in 1977 to George MacLaren, the Townships lawyer, for $840,000. This represented an impressive margin on the original investment put in eight years before, particularly considering that the three Sterling partners had taken about $1 million in profits out of the paper to help finance the chain's growth. (The partners' non-Argus assets now include ownership of Dominion Malting, majority positions in the Slumber Lodge chain of more than a dozen B.C. motels and in a junior oil and gas company called Sterling Energy, and rapidly growing investments in California real estate.)

In 1978, Maclean Hunter Ltd. of Toronto offered to buy Sterling for $14 million, but the deal fell apart on differing interpretations of its tax

*The Black brothers, backed by their father, Bud McDougald, and the Canadian Imperial Bank of Commerce, also made a $15-million bid for the *Toronto Telegram* just before it folded, but nothing came of it.

implications and disagreement over the newspaper chain's audited results. When the sale seemed to be going ahead, Radler called in Phil Adler, then the Vancouver bureau chief for Canadian Press, to grant a rare interview. "I'm now buying my first lunch in ten years," he declared, half seriously. "I don't own the petty cash any more." Lunch at the newspaper-littered desk – only a constantly used calculator was clearly in view – consisted of two hot dogs with lemonade and two cardboard sandwiches for his visitor, a meal in keeping with the frugal image of Radler painted by some of his employees.

Radler's publishing philosophy was probably best summed up in his broadside swipe at the Royal Commission on Newspapers in the *Financial Post* on October 17, 1981. Dismissing the commission's report as "an elitist manifesto for government control which tells Canadians they are not intelligent enough to know what they want to read in their newspapers," Radler viewed it as a threat not merely to the freedom of the press but to the capitalist system itself. "What a convenient way for any government to deal with its detractors and curb unwanted editorial criticism – legislate your detractors out of existence. The spectre of a government willing, if not eager, to fill this void is the most dangerous threat to freedom of the press ever proposed in this country. A commission which believes it knows best could be replaced by a government that knows it knows best. It is this that must be recognized by all Canadians and fought with every resource at our disposal."

Radler's personal approach to journalism is simplicity itself: "You have a pile of newsprint on one side, a stack of papers filled with ads on the other – and the printing press in the middle."

BEFORE STERLING RAN AWAY WITH ITSELF and Black was still living in Quebec City, completing his studies at Laval, he became involved in one of his few altruistic ventures. He had met Paul-Émile Cardinal Léger through his friend Father Jonathan Robinson and immediately fell under the eminent churchman's spell. "I used to talk with Léger a fair amount," Conrad recalls, "not on religious matters, but because of his political insights. He was, without a shadow of doubt, the most brilliant man in French Canada, and not only about Quebec. His knowledge of the general drift of world affairs was most extraordinary. He was pretty friendly with de Gaulle for some time."

Black eventually became one of Léger's fund-raisers and wrote the thirty-one-page document nominating the Cardinal for the 1973 Nobel Peace Prize. It describes Léger's decision to leave Montreal and minister to the untreated lepers of Central Africa in terms better suited to a beatification. "In this man," Black exulted, "and in his Sisyphean but voluntarily-assumed burden is the union of the material need and the spiritual good, the marriage of the advancements of the West to the enduring strength of more venerable cultures. Here is an epochal reaffirmation of the power of an individual's passive example and active benefactions to prove the limitlessness of hope and the untarnishable value of human life, no matter how lowly its condition. Paul-Émile Léger has crowned a career brilliant in word and deed, great in charity and abstract leadership, with an example both symbolically and substantively forceful, historic and durable, in an area critical to the world's future and central to its conscience."

Conrad's rhetoric notwithstanding, the Nobel Peace Prize for 1973 was awarded to Henry Kissinger and Le Duc Tho. During his dealings with Léger, Black became an expert in Catholic politics and loved to repeat the comment that Maurice Duplessis had once made to Malcolm Muggeridge, the British critic and professional iconoclast: "There is no great difficulty in governing Quebec. All one must do is keep the Jesuits and Dominicans fighting."

His relationship with Léger, at least in its early stages, was a case of unremitting hero-worship. "Late one evening, a few of us were in Conrad's apartment," recalls Brian McKenna, a Montreal TV journalist, "when he jumped up and said, 'Listen to this!' He put on a recording of a long sermon by Léger, his mouth moving to the Cardinal's words. Then he shut it off and gave the whole text back, using its exact intonation – it was no coincidence that Black became such a close confidant of Léger's. Basically, I think of Conrad as the reincarnation of an eighteenth-century cardinal. The red hat would have suited him perfectly."

A less charitable interpretation of the Black-Léger link comes from Nick Auf der Maur. "I always felt that Conrad intended to be his campaign manager for the papacy – he would have liked nothing better than to have access to the Pope. He was endlessly fascinated by how a guy such as Léger could reach the bearing and natural grace of aristocracy without having been born to it," Auf der Maur says. "But when the Cardinal gave up his post to become an ordinary parish priest and then went to look after lepers in Africa, Conrad felt he'd blown his chance for the Holy See and got quite exasperated. He saw his whole entrée to the Vatican going down the drain. He kept complaining that Léger wasn't being consistent, that nobody was going to take him seriously any more. As the whole thing disintegrated, Conrad got increasingly short-tempered, and whereas he'd once spoken in total awe of Léger, he would mutter about the Cardinal having become a bit eccentric and how he'd better clean up his act."

"Perhaps," Black now admits, "Léger suffered from what they call in French a taste for the sensational. He was like one of those matadors who, as the cadence of the *olés* gets more and more rapid, are always trying to find something more daring to do. He grew hasty in his desire to produce new spectacles and maybe did a few ill-considered things. But on the whole I remain impressed with him."

In an age when the meltdown of moral absolutes is a common occurrence, Black maintains a private spiritual dimension which has taken him to the brink of ditching his Anglican upbringing to join the Roman Catholic Church. "That's between Conrad and his God," says G. Emmett Cardinal Carter, Archbishop of Toronto, when the question is posed. He eschews such speculation but has succeeded Cardinal Léger as Black's spiritual adviser. "Certainly, it wouldn't surprise me. He is a very deep person and really feels himself a part of the Catholic Church. Whether he can continue to find his spiritual home in the Anglican branch of the Catholic Church—that has to be his decision."

Black became the Cardinal's close confidant after moving back to Toronto. The two men spend many a long evening debating the finer points of Vatican intrigue, Quebec history, and theological verities. "Conrad really is extraordinary," says the Cardinal. "He puzzles me. I don't know how he does it. I can hardly bring up a subject he's not up on. I lived much of my life in Quebec, and he knows more about French Canada than I do. He is very history conscious, in some ways more of a traditionalist than I am. He loves to talk about what goes on among the cardinals and is always fleshing out some historical church figure I didn't remember anything about or had only heard as a name. He certainly knows more about how the Vatican worked in the eighteenth century than I do. He is quite incredible."

DURING THE EIGHT YEARS he spent in Quebec, Black stayed in touch with Toronto, treating it more and more as the imperial city from which he was exiled but to which he would return in triumph, like some latter-day Clive of India. The main object of his affections was Bud McDougald at Argus, who found himself the recipient of every Sterling financial report, accompanied by suitable comments describing the youthful trio's latest financial exploits.

In 1968, Black persuaded the Montreal *Gazette* to send him on a tour of South America. The series of articles he produced was fairly prescient, including this file from Buenos Aires, foreseeing Juan Perón's later return to power: "Juan Perón rose to prominence in the ranks of the military in the late 1930s but with great agility and foresight took leave of his martial associations to become the champion of the industrial workers and rural *descamisados*, the shirtless ones. Much more than an average swaggering Latin American despot, Perón was, and remains, an original populist leader with demagogic skills often imitated but seldom surpassed. The last few years of his regime were marked by an erratic, terror-stained leftism that was climaxed in 1954, when he burned down the aristocratic Jockey Club and seven churches on the same night. His excesses forgotten by all but the victims of them, Perón's reputation has acquired lustre with years and, like the Napoleonic legend, has achieved an almost dreamlike quality in the minds of many of his countrymen."

That series of dispatches must have triggered something in McDougald's mind because on September 11, 1968, he presented Conrad with a magnificent portrait of Napoleon by Lefebvre that had belonged to Eric Phillips, an original Argus partner. The accompanying letter, in which Bud joked that it was far better "for Bonaparte to be in Conrad's living room than on the island of St. Helena," didn't fool Black for a minute. "My father was getting ready to set up the Ravelston holding company at the time," he says, "and Bud was assiduously applying himself to the fiscal act of pulling the rug out from underneath Eddie Taylor. As usual, his apparently spontaneous act of generosity was inspired by perhaps slightly less than admirable sentiments." But he did frame McDougald's two-line note and hung it beside the painting.

Apart from his contacts with McDougald, Conrad began to cultivate the circle of young Toronto Inheritors thrusting their way into contention.* Chief among them was Fred Eaton, the department store heir, who worked up quite an interest in Sterling's activities. ("Conrad—thanks for the operating results, which are most interesting. I am by nature a doubting Thomas. You seem to have things on the right track and I wish you every success in keeping them there.")

On July 15, 1970, the twenty-five-year-old Conrad sat down with his friend Peter White for a heart-to-heart session about his—and the country's—future. White kept notes of Black's musings, which included the forecast that Canadian "federal and provincial governments will succeed one another with dazzling inconsequentiality." On a more personal basis, Black decided that he would write a book "to estab-

---

*In 1970, Black agreed to finance the Montreal version of *Hair*, being produced in Canada by Johnny F. Bassett. By unfortunate coincidence, the opening of the exuberant rock musical took place on the night Pierre Laporte's body was found in the trunk of a car during the FLQ crisis.

lish academic, political, journalistic and pundit credentials" so that he could issue "future policy statements and calls to arms" that might be taken seriously.

At first he toyed with the notion of trying a sympathetic biography of Lyndon Johnson and went to discuss it with Herman Kahn at the Hudson Institute. But in the end, Black decided that he was ideally equipped to document one of the most controversial figures in Canadian political history. The late Joseph Maurice Le Noblet Duplessis had been Premier of Quebec for an unprecedented four terms between 1936 and 1959 during what French-Canadians themselves described as *la grande noirceur*, the dark ages.

"While he was still studying at Carleton," his friend Brian Stewart recalls, "Conrad exhibited more interest in the former Quebec politician than Duplessis's own mother would probably have shown. He was fascinated even then by powerful men who he felt had been misjudged by their contemporaries. He used to visit Quebec City all the time. He would go to Montreal just to study how the place had been put together, stop off at small towns to see where the authority was—how the whole political system operated. That was how his early interest in Duplessis grew, as a man who had brilliantly mastered that power network and yet had received a bum rap from history."

At first, Black had shared "the conventional sixties view of Duplessis as virtually a domestic Hitler, at best an ogre-primitive, corrupt and altogether a bad premier." But as he probed further into the Duplessis period, Conrad began to grow excited about the possibility of placing on the record a dissenting view. "When I was born in Quebec, in 1944, most of the province's French-language school commissions, many of its municipalities, and even the University of Montreal were on the verge of bankruptcy or beyond it. The government didn't even have the means to pay for snow-clearance on the province's highways, except for a couple of major arteries. French Quebec was, in almost every sense, underdeveloped. The conventional wisdom has been that the ensuing fifteen years, part of the Duplessis period, was a time of unrelieved backwardness and corruption. In fact, that period was the only one in history in which Quebec was, by any social or economic yardstick, gaining on Ontario. While this was happening, the provincial debt declined by 40 per cent and taxation levels were significantly reduced....
As with most modernizers, Duplessis had recourse to rather crude methods, but he was the first politician to establish the authority of the state in Quebec as being absolutely pre-eminent over that of the church

59

and the first to reverse the process of accumulating centralized constitutional powers in Ottawa."

It was after completing his final law exams at Laval that Black began to think concretely about doing some writing, since his duties at Sterling were hardly a full-time occupation. On May 1, 1971, he attended a colloquium on Duplessis at Trois-Rivières. Following the standard condemnations of the former Union Nationale leader and all his works by the gathering of academics, a quavering-voiced elderly gentleman seated directly in front of Black got up, waving sheafs of documents, and harangued the panel about the inaccuracies they had inflicted upon the memory of Duplessis. He turned out to be Robert Rumilly, then seventy-six, who had written the forty-one-volume *Histoire de la Province de Québec* and was the late premier's chief literary executor. The two men quickly became friends. Rumilly introduced Black to Auréa Cloutier, who had been Duplessis's secretary for thirty-six years and now roosted among his papers in the Premier's former residence at Trois-Rivières. During Conrad's subsequent fifty-five visits, she gradually permitted him to see increasingly private correspondence; on his twentieth call, she emerged from the basement bathroom with a bulging accordion file, commenting, "Everything in here is something that was handed to me by M. Duplessis himself with the words, 'Set that aside for when we write our memoirs.'"

Conrad found historically significant letters from Rodrigue Cardinal Villeneuve side by side with hand-written, ungrammatical requests for jobs with the Quebec Liquor Board, unpaid bills, the returns of his ministers who were cheating on their taxes, a number of scribbled notes for Assembly speeches, tidbits of political espionage, compromising photographs, a ledger listing the political contributions of every tavern-keeper in the province—all sorts of bric-à-brac from a long, event-filled life.

Mlle Cloutier eventually entrusted all the documents to Conrad, and his friends vividly remember his regaling them with Duplessis anecdotes while driving his automobile—then pulling over to the curb, jumping out, and getting the original document from the trunk to pass it around for their edification. Once, on the road from Mansonville to Knowlton, Conrad got so excited that he went off the road. "The car flew through the air like a rather unaerodynamic aircraft, and I got bounced around a bit. I've still got a scar from it. In retrospect, I have this rather humorous picture in my mind of cows wandering down and poking around the Oldsmobile, which was all bashed in at the front and back."

To give his project some form, Black enrolled as a part-time M.A.

student at McGill, and under Prof. Laurier LaPierre's tutelage during the next two years produced his thesis: "Career of Maurice L. Duplessis As Viewed through His Correspondence, 1927–1939." LaPierre considered it worthy of a degree, but Black's external examiner, Prof. Ramsay Cook of York University, condemned the work on the basis of "slip-shod research and uncritical use of evidence." Cook scathingly damned and dismissed Black's 700-page paper as "of marginal acceptability in almost every respect," accusing Black of being "a totally, or almost, undisciplined writer." Worse yet, Cook described Black as having "verbal diarrhoea" and being addicted "to words that have no place in the vocabulary of academic writing—'cop-out,' 'dipsy-doodling,' 'wanting to have at it,' 'snafu' and many more."

In reply to Cook's fairly chilly assessment, Conrad reworked his thesis but enclosed a four-page note that ended with this Gaullist stinger: "Having read all the other works on the same subject, including M. Rumilly's recently published effort; having spent innumerable days and evenings in the dusty and poorly-illuminated archival chaos of Maurice Duplessis' basement, and having conscientiously revised the original version of this thesis in conformity with many objections, some of which were uninformed and unjust, I am unpretentiously conscious of presenting herewith the definitive work in its field, in any language."

Black was granted his degree in the autumn of 1973, but he never did forgive Cook. Their initial exchange was to be the opening salvo in one of Canada's minor but obdurate literary feuds. Four years later, after Black had turned his thesis into a 743-page book,* the two men confronted each other again.

The volume is crammed with intimate details, such as that Duplessis had suffered from hypospadias, a condition in which the urethral aperture is at some remove from the end of the penis—in his case, about an inch. Black traces the path followed by the late Quebec premier in transforming the absurd Quebec Conservative party of 1932 into the most powerful political machine in Quebec history, not exactly whitewashing the tactics employed but certainly condemning Duplessis's critics for their "depraved calumny." If Black presents his central character as innocent of some accusations of blatant corruption, his portrait

---

*It was published as *Duplessis* by McClelland and Stewart in 1977. To reduce the selling price of the huge volume to a manageable $16.95, the publisher printed 10,000 copies, of which only half were bound at McClelland's expense. Conrad paid for the other 5,000 and sold the unbound pages back to the publishing house as sales warranted. To date, the book has sold 8,000 copies in English and 15,000 in the two-volume French edition.

of the period's supporting characters is merciless. It includes documentation that a Chief Justice of Canada (Thibaudeau Rinfret) had sought and was granted Duplessis's intervention in the transfer of a hotel liquor licence; that journalists of the period were on the government payroll (Tracy S. Ludington, news editor of the Montreal *Gazette*, simultaneously served as a member of the Premier's staff responsible for English-language public relations); that in the 1952 and 1956 provincial elections *Montreal Star* publisher J.W. McConnell sent donations of $50,000 to $100,000 in fresh banknotes delivered in cartons "for ... [Duplessis's] own attention." Black reported that Duplessis garnered an incredible $100 million in graft during his stormy stewardship.

The portrait that emerges is of a master politician who manipulated the folk memory of the Conquest to maintain his voters in a constant state-of-siege mentality at a time when the double bed and not the television set was still the focal point of family life. "Duplessis' political party was one of his greatest achievements," Black writes. "All-conquering while he lived, the Union Nationale crumbled gradually into dust after he died. His adversaries and the uninitiated of posterity could claim dumb tenebrous primitivism as an explanation for his success. The real explanation was a masterful combination of sincere patriotism, social conservatism, economic modernization, a taste for grandeur, and a talent at the common touch—brilliant advocacy and ward-heeling poll-captaincy."

Without glossing over the Premier's cruder moments (such as the winter afternoon in 1938 when Duplessis was driving past the Liberals' Reform Club in Quebec City and told his chauffeur to stop, rushed in past the astonished members, urinated in the fireplace, and walked briskly out again, never having said a word), Black did allow his admiration to shine through: "Maurice Duplessis had too great a sense of the farcical to be arrogant. Much of what his critics decried as dictatorship and corruption was really a puckish love of farce."

A reader of the thick volume can easily spot the clues to Black's personal identification with his subject, almost as if he were using the act of placing someone else's life on paper to exorcise his self-doubts. Conrad praises Duplessis for abstaining from all physical activities except croquet, endorses his conservative ideology, lauds the Premier's photographic memory, defends his use of police as strikebreakers, and supports his condemnation of the press. ("*Le Devoir*'s leaders were lionized in English Canada, even though their opinions were overtly racist, stridently nationalistic, libellous, and in gross contravention of professional standards of research, impartiality, or common decency.")

A powerful work, the book bristles with evocative passages, such as this description of Trois-Rivières in 1890, the year and place of Duplessis's birth: "Its massive stone buildings symbolized the stern, watchful, immutable supremacy of the Church. Neat frame homes revealed the modest ambitions of the town's bourgeoisie.... On the docks, in the paper mills, and in the rushing water of the rivers that gave the town its name and its origins, there was a muscular quality that lent the citizens of La Mauricie a discreet swagger. The surrounding agricultural community had not changed its beliefs or techniques for centuries. The farms were small, families large; life was hard, virtuous, and uncomplicated.... Where once seigneurs had ruled their elongated domains that marched inland from the banks of the vast St. Lawrence toward the frieze of the resigned old Laurentian Mountains, the ecclesiastical authority oversaw, encouraged, and gave purpose to the *habitant* valorously fighting his indifferent circumstances."

Just before the book was to be published, Black began hearing ominous rumours. Prof. John English, a friend of his who had been doing some research at the Public Archives in Ottawa, reported that Ramsay Cook had made vague noises about critically dismembering Black's book in the *Globe and Mail*. Conrad immediately contacted his friend Brig. R.S. Malone, then the paper's publisher, who confirmed that the volume had indeed been assigned to Cook for review. "I can take it away from him, but he would only go some place else," Malone told Conrad. "Then his review would be twice as bad, because he could claim you had muscled him out of the assignment."

When the review appeared on December 18, 1976 (prior to publication of the book), it was fully as devastating as Black had expected. "As history," wrote Cook, "it is often little more than regurgitated source material spiced with an intensely partisan hostility to any individual or institution which refused to recognize Duplessis as the saviour of Christian civilization, Quebec branch." Cook could discover not a single redeeming virtue in Black's labours. "Indeed, anyone who can endure this ramshackle volume to the end," he wrote, "will likely conclude that though ... Duplessis triumphed rather easily over most of his enemies, he has finally come a cropper in the hands of an admiring biographer."

Within hours of the review's publication, Black was on the doorstep of Malone's Forest Hill house. The Brigadier was not surprised to see the aggrieved author advancing toward him, tirade at the ready. Black's accusations were eventually fitted into a letter to the editor and edited for libel. He challenged Cook's motives, describing him as "a slanted,

63

supercilious little twit." Cook replied a few days later, trying to wash his hands of the whole affair, denying that he was engaged in any kind of personal vendetta.

This served merely to redouble Conrad's fury. "Remember those old games with the Montreal Canadiens in the Montreal Forum when, two minutes into the game, the Rocket would knock down a Maple Leaf and you'd have a bench-clearing brawl?" he badgered his friend Brian McKenna. "Well, I'm going to have a bench-clearing brawl with Ramsay Cook."

The professor's main reaction was to try to get out of Black's life as soon as possible. But Conrad wouldn't let up. He asked his friend Doug Bassett to write a supportive letter to the *Globe* and had John Robarts, Jack McClelland, and John Bassett in reserve with follow-up missives. Sputtered Black: "To put Ramsay in focus: he's an ex-CCF Methodist Manitoban and doesn't really see the humour in some of the things Duplessis did. It's a very moralizing and to me rather tiresome conception of the world, but he's entitled to it."

There were in fact a number of favourable reviews. Prof. Robert Bothwell of Trinity College at the University of Toronto wrote that the book "while exhausting to read…is honest and authoritative and deserves no stigma because it is somewhat favourable to its subject. No other volume stands up to it in terms of Quebec history during the 1940s and 1950s."

Some critics took their lead from Cook. Prof. Walter Young, head of the political science department at the University of Victoria, wrote the volume off in the *Vancouver Sun* as "absurdly long, disconnected, superficial," only to receive a counterblast from Conrad, who claimed that twenty-six of twenty-eight sentences in Young's review had been wholly or partly false. Black's letter ended with the petulant dismissal, "I had never heard of Young before, and I do not expect to hear from him again."

In contrast, the Quebec press took the work very seriously, giving it generally glowing reviews. In 1979, when *Le Devoir* paid tribute to Duplessis on the twentieth anniversary of his death, it was Black's book that was used as the main reference source.* Conrad's proudest moment

---

*Black still fires off letters to *Le Devoir* whenever any of his interpretations of Duplessis are questioned. "Every now and then some old priest will write in complaining about Duplessis's row with the Church in 1952 or something," says Nick Auf der Maur, "and Conrad will take great delight in ripping off a letter in flowing French, taking total umbrage, denouncing the guy as a crumbbum. I'm sure his only sorrow is that he can't do it in Latin."

following publication of the book probably occurred when he walked into the Toronto Club on the day his letter attacking Ramsay Cook was published in the *Globe*. "It's a slight exaggeration to say that I was applauded," he recalls, "but I got several encouraging slaps on the back, and one guy sort of clapped his hands a couple of times."

ALTHOUGH HE HAD MASTERED ITS LANGUAGE and become a serious student of its politics, Black was by the early seventies finding Quebec an ever-less-hospitable arena for his talents. The province's intellectuals were not in a hurry to forgive his offhand comment during a TV interview that imposition by Pierre Trudeau of the War Measures Act amounted to little more than an uncomfortable week or so in jail for five hundred people.

It was in 1974 that Susan Farkas, a CBC producer in Montreal, took advantage of his controversial opinions and cast Black along with Laurier LaPierre in a weekly dialogue on CBM Montreal. "Conrad played the uptight WASP and did it very well," she says. "It's a role that comes to him naturally." LaPierre, who was a vice-president of the NDP at the time, recalls some lively exchanges. "Conrad was not very keen on social welfare and felt there were plenty of jobs. But people who accused him of being anti-French misunderstood his concepts."

Having no philosophical structure within which to fit the tides sweeping the province into an era of unprecedented social change, Black interpreted each intrusion by the state into the private sector as the hot breath of revolution. This was particularly true of Bill 22, the language legislation that Premier Robert Bourassa introduced that spring. "I was having near-apoplexy every morning when I got up to read the newspaper," Conrad recalls. "I felt double-crossed by the French but could work up no strong identification with the English. I was not mentally prepared to cast my psychological lot with Quebec. There was this interminable process of misrepresenting the cultural framework of the province. The English had no rights; they had privileges.... The politicians alternated ever more illiberal measures with self-congratulation on their treatment of the so-called minorities, as if the 800,000 to a million non-French in Quebec were Romanians rather than the local representatives of the 98 per cent majority language group of this continent."

On July 26, 1974, Black rebelled. In a radio broadcast that is still remembered with considerable awe by Montreal's nationalistic journalists, he delivered this ferocious broadside: "The present government of

Quebec is the most financially and intellectually corrupt in the history of the province. There are the shady deals, brazenly concluded, and the broken promises, most conspicuously that of last October to retain Bill 63. But above all we remember the agitation of the political and intellectual leadership of French Quebec in the fifties and sixties for greater bilingualism, particularly among the English. Now that this is occurring, we learn almost every day in *Le Jour, Le Devoir*, and even from the government that bilingualism is the means *par excellence* of assimilation. Moderation, then, is no longer possible, under the leadership of the province's technocratic elite, personified by Robert Bourassa—scheming, emotionless, dull, and amoral.

"The government dragged out the ancient and totally fictitious spectre of assimilation to justify Bill 22 and its rejection of the right of free choice in education, its reduction of English education to the low echelon of ministerial whim, its assault upon freedom of expression through regulation of the internal and external language of businesses and other organizations, and its creation of a fatuous new linguistic bureaucracy that will conduct a system of organized denunciation, harassment, and patronage. At second reading, the Minister of Education withdrew the assimilation argument and revealed what everyone already knew: that the French language in Quebec is stronger in every way than it has ever been.

"There is a paralytic social sickness in Quebec. In all this debate, not a single French Quebecker has objected to Bill 22 on the grounds that it was undemocratic or a reduction of liberties exercised in the province. The Quebec Civil Liberties Union, founded by Pierre Trudeau, from which one might have expected such sentiments, has instead demanded the abolition of English education, and this through the spokesmanship of Jean-Louis Roy, who derives his income from McGill University.

"As for the political leadership of the English community, where Jonathan Robinson and George Marler and even Eric Kierans once sat we now have the painfully naive Dr. [Victor] Goldbloom, and…[William] Tetley and [Kevin] Drummond.

"It is clear that Mr. Bourassa, having persuaded Mr. Trudeau and Jean Lesage to help him cheat Claude Wagner and Pierre Laporte out of the Liberal leadership, having eliminated the non-separatist opposition by turning two consecutive elections into referenda on separation, is now going to try to eliminate the Parti Québécois by a policy of gradual scapegoatism directed against the non-French elements in the province.

"It is clear that the only significant difference between Mr. Bourassa and René Lévesque is that Mr. Bourassa knows how to count. He is content, for the time being, to bilk the other provinces in order to dispense patronage in Quebec. This is his idea of 'profitable federalism.'

"Instead of *bonne entente* there will be cat and mouse. The English community here, still deluding itself with the illusion of Montreal as an incomparably fine place to live, is leaderless and irrelevant, except as the hostage of a dishonest government.

"Last month one of the most moderate ministers, Guy St-Pierre, told an English businessmen's group, 'If you don't like Quebec, you can leave it.' With sadness but with certitude, I accept that choice."

That evening, Conrad Black cleared out of his Port-Royal apartment and permanently transferred himself back to Toronto.

CHAPTER THREE

Pre-emptive Manoeuvres

*In its time, Argus has been the most successful
nest-feathering operation in the country.*

lack's return from his self-imposed exile in Montreal was a
joyful homecoming. Feeling as vulnerable as Gulliver after his
last voyage, Conrad need not have worried. Toronto's Establishment adopted him with that welcoming spirit it reserves for its bright
offspring who show the slightest sign of believing in and wanting to
carry on its traditions.

During the next half-decade, Black methodically prepared himself
for the Argus chairmanship, behaving like a hermit crab, which inhabits
other people's shells, consumes what it needs to grow, and moves on. It
was during this interval that Black served his corporate apprenticeship,
learning along the way, latching on to contacts who would serve him
well when he made his putsch on Argus. He collected corporate mentors
as if he were an over-aged flower child accumulating bedmates. "I was
formed by them," he admits. "I always get on well with the old guys. I
am a historian, after all. You have to feel a basic respect for what they've
done, and I don't mean just because they're old. It is a prodigious
achievement to be rising eighty-four, like P.C. Finlay of Hollinger, and
still know precisely what you're doing. Besides, I don't think of myself as
being young. David Radler, my partner, claims I have a psychological
age of eighty."

For succession duty purposes, Conrad and his brother, Monte, had,
by the end of 1974, transferred to themselves all but 125 shares of their
father's Argus ownership position by assuming control of family companies, mainly Western Dominion Investment, that held the stock. This
allowed Conrad for the first time to institutionalize his contact with the
holding company that had preoccupied him since childhood.

ARGUS, NAMED AFTER THE EVER-WATCHFUL HUNDRED-EYED GIANT
of Greek mythology, had been formed by E.P. Taylor in 1945 as a

closed-end investment trust with initial capitalization of $8.5 million.*
The new company's operating philosophy was deceptively simple: it
would conserve its capital by acquiring investments in companies in
which dominant but not majority holdings were sufficient for control.
After the satellite companies had paid their shareholders (including the
Argus partners) dividends of up to 65 per cent of annual income, the
balance would be reinvested to extend the arc of Argus's influence. The
original portfolio included Taylor's Canadian Breweries complex (sold
off to Rothmans in 1968 for a $17.7-million profit); control holdings of
Dominion Stores (acquired from French interests on VE Day); Standard Chemical (folded into Dominion Tar and Chemical Company
Ltd. in 1951; Argus sold its Domtar position in 1978); Massey-Harris
(later Massey-Ferguson, jettisoned in 1980); Canadian Food Products
(sold in 1961); Orange Crush (disposed of in 1959); and Dominion
Malting (eventually purchased by the Black family as a private holding).
During 1946 Argus put together B.C. Forest Products (selling off
control to its U.S. partner in 1973 for a $9-million profit) and acquired
control of Standard Broadcasting (then Standard Radio and mainly
CFRB in Toronto but later supplemented by CJAD in Montreal and radio
and TV outlets in Ottawa and the United Kingdom).

Argus rapidly multiplied its influence through the 1950s and 1960s.
On a typical trading day, such as June 5, 1964, fully 10 per cent of all the
shares traded on the Toronto Stock Exchange were in Argus-controlled
enterprises. Earnings attributable to its investment holdings had escalated from the $1.5 million of the founding year to $34 million in 1974.
While the company's portfolio briefly held such exotic curiosities as
Peruvian International Airways (which operated a short-lived Mont-

*The company's first board of directors consisted of Eric Phillips (chairman); E.P.
Taylor (president); Wallace McCutcheon (vice-president and managing director);
David G. Baird of New York (who along with Roger Gilbert represented Atlas Corp.,
Floyd Odlum's U.S. holding company, on which the Argus concept had been
based); W.L. Bayer, a Montreal industrialist who was a fellow director of Taylor's at
Canadian Breweries and chairman of Canadian Bronze Co. Ltd.; E.W. Bickle, a
Toronto investment dealer, then president of Maple Leaf Gardens; H.J. Carmichael,
one of Taylor's fellow dollar-a-year men who had just been appointed a director at
the Bank of Toronto; James S. Duncan, president of Massey-Harris; W. Kaspar
Fraser, one of Taylor's chief legal advisers; J. William Horsey, president of Dominion
Stores Ltd.; K.S. Maclachlan, president of Standard Chemical Co. Ltd.; H.R.
MacMillan, another former Ottawa associate of Taylor's and the tallest tree in the
B.C. forest industry; Allan Miller of London, chairman of Broadcast Relay Services;
Felix E. Notebaert, an influential Montrealer who was also a director of Asbestos
Corp. and Dosco; and J.S.D. Tory, one of Canada's most important corporate legal
counsel. Argus's first portfolio consisted mostly of Taylor's personal holdings,
which were folded into the new holding company. In return, his bank loans were
paid off and he received half the issued stock.

real-to-Lima service in the late 1940s), its most notable acquisition was the purchase, between 1961 and 1968, of effective control of Hollinger Mines Ltd.

Hollinger is one of Canada's great mining ventures, dating from a syndicate formed in 1903 by the brothers Noah and Henry Timmins, storekeepers at Mattawa in the upper Ottawa Valley, David Dunlap, a young lawyer from the same village, and the McMartin brothers, John and Duncan, the contractors hired to punch a pioneer railway through the Precambrian Shield of Northern Ontario. The syndicate's first investment was a silver mine in the rich ore outcrop at Cobalt that revealed itself when Fred LaRose, a blacksmith with the railway gang, carelessly tossed his hammer aside at lunch break. Their next major project was to purchase in 1909 the claims of Benny Hollinger, which became the Porcupine district's richest mine, yielding gold worth $600 million before it closed in 1968. They went on to chart and exploit dozens of other mines, and in 1925 the company acquired its initial stake in Noranda, which eventually totalled 10.7 per cent.

In 1960, when Bud McDougald was in charge of Argus's acquisitions, Percy Finlay, then and forevermore Hollinger's senior counsel, called to say that the Noah Timmins branch of the family was about to dispose of a block of Hollinger stock to Gilbert W. Humphrey, president of the M.A. Hanna Company of Cleveland, and that any Canadian counter-offers would have to be mobilized immediately. McDougald was aware of Hollinger's understated values because he'd been a Hollinger director since 1950 and was a cousin of the McMartin heirs, who sat on the Crown Trust board with him. He made a winning bid on behalf of Taymac Investments, a trust privately owned by the Argus partners. By purchasing the Hollinger stock through an intermediary company which then resold the shares to Argus, the partners were able to extract for themselves a net capital gain of $1.25 million in an afternoon.

This toll-gating approach to business was solidly in the Argus tradition. Ten years before the Hollinger stock transaction, the same group had set up a paper tiger called Arbor Corporation Ltd. to gather in the shares of St. Lawrence Corporation, a Quebec-based pulp processor, at an average price of thirty dollars. The stock was sold to Argus in 1955 at seventy-five dollars—for a private capital gain of up to $9 million.

The Argus partners were successful ($1,000 invested in Argus at its founding in 1945 was worth $8,400 by 1975), and they knew how to work the system, building up their own legends, becoming pivotal figures in the new Upper Canadian elite as economic power shifted from Montreal to Toronto. In its time, Argus has been the most successful nest-feathering operation in the country. It is something of a tribute to the lack of sophistication of Canada's financial Establishment that the Argus partners could have become its spiritual leaders. Any society evolves an elite that reflects its sense of values. The Argus executives gave the postwar Establishment its public face, shaping its character far out of proportion to their actual contribution. It was their inordinate sense of style that provided that Establishment with whatever panache it possessed.

Of the four key partners, Col. Eric Phillips was perhaps the most interesting. A graduate of Upper Canada College and the University of Toronto (in analytical chemistry), he joined the British Army as a private at the outbreak of hostilities in 1914. Taken prisoner, he escaped and fought with such distinction that he won field promotion to lieutenant-colonel—the youngest in the British Army—and was awarded the Distinguished Service Order and the Military Cross. During the interval between the world wars he built his parents' modest framing business into the major glass supplier for General Motors of Canada—a move helped by the fact that his first wife was a daughter of Sam McLaughlin, founder of GM's predecessor company. During the Second World War, Phillips headed Research Enterprises Ltd., a Crown corporation. It was during this stint that he became E.P. Taylor's partner.

Once installed at the Argus table, Phillips quickly became the holding company's intellectual heavyweight, a distinction for which there was not much competition. Phillips was an inveterate reader, skimming through four or five books a night and remembering nearly everything in them. A friend of the artists Pietro Annigoni, Augustus John, and Picasso, he was also the owner of a major collection of Gainsboroughs. His other great pleasure was motor-boating, particularly aboard his great yacht *Sea Breeze*, a converted Fairmile he kept on Georgian Bay, and her sister ship in the Bahamas. A tough disciplinarian who could make a success of any enterprise that caught his fancy, Phillips put in several terms as chairman of the University of Toronto's Board of Governors. His sense of humour could take some strange turns. "Eric was a rather naughty boy at times," recalls Maj.-Gen. Bruce Matthews, the former Argus executive, who was one of his best friends. "Both he and his wife Doris had been married before. One night they were entertaining this chap she had gone around with for two years before she met Eric. He was being subtle and correct, paying attention entirely to Eric. At one point, trying to emphasize the existence of Doris's children by her previous marriage, the visitor slyly commented: 'I'm astounded how you have settled in with these young children. The noise and so on...'

"'Not at all, old fellow,' Phillips grandly replied. 'Why, I wouldn't know they were in the house.' At this point there was a loud crash, making the whole building shake.

"Doris raced up to the bedroom floor, two stairs at a time, and found that her youngsters had overturned a huge chest in the upstairs hall, obviously at a prearranged signal. 'I don't want another sound out of you,' the upset Doris threatened the mischievously grinning children, 'or I'll whip each one of you within an inch of your life.'

"To which the youngest replied: 'Daddy said we'd get another five dollars if you did!'"

The most capable manager among the partners, Phillips took over at Massey after the Argus-inspired firing of its chairman, James Duncan. Once Taylor's closest ally, Phillips grew increasingly impatient with E.P.'s grandstanding, and by the time he died at Palm Beach on the day after Christmas, 1964, he was hardly speaking to Argus's senior presence.

In mid-century Canada, Edward Plunket Taylor stood out in the classic struggle between the haves and the have-nots as the ultimate symbol of wealth and power. Taylor's grey-top-hatted visage on the country's sports pages, binoculars perched on portly stomach as he accepted yet another racing trophy, did little to dispel the ordinary citizens' concern that no matter how their paltry pay cheques were spent, they would inevitably enrich the ubiquitous Eddie. He was condemned by left-wingers as "E(xcess) P(rofits) Taylor – the mad miser of millions," and by churchmen as the beer baron personally responsible for the plight of every Canadian alcoholic. Taylor was a natural enthusiast, with all the confidence that comes to self-made men who make it big. (His family had more breeding than money, and his father, Lt.-Col. Plunket Bourchier Taylor, left Eddie exactly $12,225.)

Taylor at his best probably equalled the grasp and imagination of any entrepreneur spawned since Adam Smith first gave voice to the capitalist ethic.* But as his Argus stable of companies matured, Taylor grew increasingly restless, devoting more of his time and capital to thoroughbred racing and the golden township he had developed at Lyford Cay in the Bahamas. He was very proud that when a summit meeting with Prime Minister Harold Macmillan was held at Lyford in 1962, President John Kennedy chose to stay at the Taylor residence.

Taylor became one of the world's most successful horse breeders, with bloodstock and land-holdings at his farms in Oshawa and Maryland valued at more than $100 million. Probably his best-known horse is Northern Dancer, which won the Kentucky Derby and the Preakness in 1964 and has since collected the highest aggregate stud fees in the history

*For a description of E.P. Taylor's life and career, see Chapter 11 in *Flame of Power*, Toronto, Longmans Canada Ltd., 1959.

of the sport. A French syndicate offered to buy the prolific sire for $40 million, and British soccer pool tycoon Robert Sangster paid $3.5 million for one of the foals, while Greek shipowner Stavros Niarchos spent $1.7 million for a grandson of the great champion. Stud fees are a quarter of a million dollars a shot. When Taylor retired to the Bahamas, his stables were taken over by his last child and only son, Charles, who instead of attempting to become an Argus successor chose to be a journalist and writer.*

Very different from Taylor and the other Argus founders was Wallace McCutcheon, whose service inside Eddie's court dated back to some of the bloodiest mergers and takeovers that went into forming Canadian Breweries. Named a director of the young brewing empire to represent the Dominion Bank, McCutcheon soon established himself with Taylor for his organizational ability and nerve. His counsel was so widely recognized that when he abruptly decided to leave business for a place in John Diefenbaker's 1962 Cabinet, McCutcheon had to resign from seventeen boards. A florid personage with a retired-British-brigadier's face, McCutcheon during his brief political fling became the authentic if lonely voice of Canadian conservatism. There was something valiant about this old Bay Street lion standing up before dwindling audiences across the country, defending an approach that no longer found expression or even echoes in any Canadian political party—least of all his own. The last angry Tory in a lapping sea of liberalism, McCutcheon in making a stout defence of a world safe for Canadian millionaires may have placed himself outside the mainstream of political thought. But he fought hard for his principles, and when he died in 1969, his passing was genuinely mourned.

McCutcheon's death set off a major power struggle inside the Argus hierarchy, but the trouble had started earlier. One of the points of contention had been Taylor's venture into real estate through Canadian Equity and Development Company Ltd., formed in 1953 to buy a 2,100-acre tract outside Toronto that became the residential suburb of Don Mills. Bud McDougald, the partner then reaching for the Argus crown, was particularly critical of the methods used by Taylor and his fellow real-estate developers.† ("They had this arrangement," Conrad

---

*The author of three particularly sensitive books, Taylor left an enviable legacy as a journalist at the *Globe and Mail*. Its editor, Dic Doyle, has commented: "Of all the assets of E.P. Taylor, the one which has been most productive and of which he can be most proud is his son Charles."

†For a description of McDougald's role in Argus, see Chapter 1, *The Canadian Establishment*, Vol. 1, Toronto, McClelland and Stewart, 1975.

Black later commented, "where they took all the profit and threw it up in the air. What stayed up, they gave to the other shareholders; what came down, they took for themselves.")

"I remember one meeting the four partners had up at E.P. Taylor's office on Bayview Avenue," recalls Harry Edmison, the Argus economist, "and after a while the air really got blue. They were fighting about whether they should stay in real estate or not. Taylor wanted them to invest in Lyford Cay, but Colonel Phillips and Bud would have none of it. When it was all over, I walked out with McCutcheon, who turned to me and asked, 'Now, Harry, you didn't hear anything, did you?'

"And I said, 'No, Wally, not a word.'"

In these and other battles, E.P. Taylor found himself increasingly isolated. George Black, fired by Taylor as president of Canadian Breweries (and not even accorded the customary corporate accolades in the following year's annual report for his contributions), had turned against his former employer to join the McDougald faction. After the Diefenbaker Government fell, the partners refused to readmit McCutcheon. When Phillips died, his widow, Doris, granted McDougald, her brother-in-law, power of attorney over her shares. Maxwell Meighen, a Toronto investor who had joined the Argus board in 1961 and had accumulated considerable stockholdings, had been offended when he heard that Taylor privately made slighting references to him. McDougald did little to hide his contempt for Taylor, accusing him within the whispering galleries at the Toronto Club of having become an expatriate egomaniac who was making a fool of himself by chasing a British knighthood in the Bahamas. Taylor, on the other hand, felt that McDougald would not be a good Argus successor because he was too conservative in his outlook and could not provide a renewal of the entrepreneurial spark that Argus required. They were both right. The partnership had run its course.

Paranoia and cunning ruled the roost. Anxious to benefit from the succession, the remaining partners expended most of their energies nominating one another as candidates so that Taylor would get the message that he wasn't running the place any more. At these meetings, Meighen, who had served in the Canadian Army as a colonel, would draw himself up to rigid attention and proclaim, "*I* will bell the cat!" But nothing much happened until the anti-Taylor conspirators met in George Black's house in the spring of 1969, to activate a holding company called Ravelston, specifically incorporated to drive Eddie out of Argus.

The approximately 50 per cent of Argus stock represented by McDougald, Black, Meighen, Matthews, the Phillips estate, and some extra shares Bud had stashed away in Dominion Stores and Crown

Trust were rolled into Ravelston. The agreement provided that the new partners could exercise a first-refusal "put" on one another's shares.* McDougald later negotiated a seven-year voting arrangement with Taylor, who retained his 10.34 per cent of Argus common and a block of more than 18 per cent of the preferred shares outside Ravelston. Shortly afterward, Taylor was replaced by McDougald in the Argus presidency, and two years later he vanished from the company's list of executive officers.

Once Argus was safely in his grasp, McDougald allowed the company to lapse into a sleepy personal fiefdom. "We don't make anything. We don't sell anything," remarked Bruce Matthews, Argus's executive vice-president. "We merely look after our own affairs." When Matthews, whose position on the board of Dome Mines allowed him an advance look at what its sister company, Dome Petroleum, was planning in western Canada, suggested that McDougald go out to Calgary, Bud saw no point in such a journey. The Argus directors met only four times a year, seldom exceeding their seven-member quorum; the satellite companies were effectively controlled through the executive committees of their boards.

What stirred McDougald into a frenzy of defensive action was the unexpected $150-million takeover attempt, in the spring of 1975, by Paul Desmarais, chairman of Power Corp. The Montreal holding company had accumulated 10.37 per cent of Argus's voting stock on the market and arranged to buy out E.P. Taylor's stock. Under the Power offer, Desmarais raised his holdings to an eventual 26 per cent of Argus common and 59.8 per cent of its Class C preferreds—giving him control over more than half the company's equity position. But the Ravelston agreement held firm, and he had to be satisfied with the dispiriting, costly role of a passive shareholder. All through this scuffle, McDougald found an articulate ally in Conrad. The youthful Black publicly condemned "this kamikaze raid that just came out of the *blue* from Montreal" and was particularly adamant about Desmarais's hardly surprising claim that Argus wasn't being fair to its minority stockholders, namely himself.

*Ravelston, incorporated October 10, 1968, was originally divided into the following holdings: McDougald and the Phillips estate, 23.6 per cent each; Black, 22.4 per cent; Meighen interests, 26.5 per cent; Matthews, 3.9 per cent. The agreement, reproduced in Appendix A, also included a provision that if 51 per cent of Ravelston's shareholders ever wanted to buy out any partner, they could serve a compulsory transfer notice to force the sale. A Ravelston predecessor, Meadowbrook Holdings Ltd., which contained the Taylor, McDougald, Phillips, and McCutcheon blocks, had distributed its shares on March 5, 1969. (Wallace McCutcheon had died on January 23.)

Even though he already exercised absolute control over Argus, Mc-Dougald concentrated its ownership even more tightly by signing a voting agreement with Hal Jackman (who held 9 per cent of Argus through Empire Life Insurance) and purchasing for thirty dollars a share (eight dollars over market price) the approximately 11 per cent owned by McCutcheon's five heirs. This $25-million transaction was negotiated in a small private dining room on the second floor of the Toronto Club during the 1975 Hollinger Dinner. The secret meeting, attended by McDougald, Frederic and James McCutcheon, Max Meighen, Alex Barron, Bruce Matthews, and Conrad Black, was held in near-total darkness because, despite his vaunted influence at the Toronto Club, Bud never did get the lights turned on.

During the next three years, Conrad continued expanding his contacts, first from an office in the old Commerce building and later from Draper Dobie, a medium-sized investment house he and his brother bought to give themselves a recognizable Toronto base. Here they held weekly roast-beef lunches, entertaining Fred Eaton, John Robarts, Galen Weston, and Doug Bassett, among many others. Publication of his Duplessis book gave Black the right to pontificate on Quebec's political scene, particularly after the election of René Lévesque's separatist party in 1976. His prognosis was inevitably gloomy. ("Lévesque is no Dave Barrett. The B.C. Premier is merely a fat, silly social worker. Lévesque is the most dangerous man ever to appear in Canadian politics. His election set in motion an apparently irresistible juggernaut. The game is probably over for Canada.")

Black's own political activities were limited to acting as strategist and bagman for Claude Wagner's run at the Conservative party leadership. He gave a dinner for his candidate at the Toronto Club attended by most of the local Establishment, boosting the range of his acquaintances.

Although he is his own man now, while Black was still reaching for power he would try to match some of the Argus partners' mannerisms. "Conrad had a certain admiration for these guys who can drink a quart of scotch, pull themselves up, and walk out of the room erect," recalls David Smith, the Liberal M.P., who knows him well. "He would come over to our house in the early seventies and be there till three in the morning putting away an awful lot of scotch. When it was time for him to go, he would rise out of his chair and walk out with his head high. I knew that in his mind he was saying, 'I've got to carry this off, just like Wally McCutcheon.' I just *know* that's what he was thinking."

As he became better known inside Toronto's social set, Black moved into the Lonsdale, an apartment building across the road from Upper Canada College that houses many of the rich and powerful, and began to squire around town some strikingly attractive ladies. None of his dates was more exotic than Anna Maria Marston, born in Brazil of wealthy Italian parents and more recently divorced from John Marston of Toronto. Anna Maria is a charter member of what the *Toronto Star*'s Lynda Hurst dubbed Canada's "Concorde Crowd – who sunbathe in Cuernavaca, ski in Klosters, visit friends in Rio, and wouldn't dream of not popping in to see Roloff [Beny] in Rome." The former curator of the Henry Birks collection of Canadian antique silver, Mrs. Marston enjoys a highly visible aristocratic lifestyle, maintaining that "Toronto isn't Rio – it doesn't have the same tradition of servants."

IN THE LATE SPRING OF 1976, Alex Barron, Argus director and operating head of Meighen's financial empire, received an urgent invitation to drop in on the elder Black, who by then knew that his wife was terminally ill and was himself feeling increasingly feeble. Black told Barron he wanted to resign all his directorships and asked for his help in making sure that he would be replaced in them by his sons. Barron persuaded Black to delay his departure and McDougald pledged that the boys would indeed succeed the father as directors of Argus companies.

Conrad's parents died a month later, only ten days apart. George Black's last evening was spent with his younger son. At one point he delivered a savagely bitter valedictory, telling Conrad always to remember that "life is hell, most people are bastards, and everything is bullshit." Just before dinner, the elder Black walked painfully up the stairs; then, as he reached the landing, his knees gave way. He crashed through the railing and fell to the main floor, to die at Scarborough General Hospital four hours later.

George Black had wanted to be buried without fanfare at St. John's Cemetery in Winnipeg but the sons decided to revive the time of their father's greatness and programmed a ceremonial funeral on July 2, 1976, at Grace Church on-the-Hill near Upper Canada College. The list of pallbearers, who turned out thirty-two strong, was made up of some of the great Establishment names. The flag on both the Argus building and the Commerce headquarters flew at half-mast that day. When the young Blacks heard that E.P. Taylor was flying in from Europe, they scheduled a hymn called "My Own Dear Land" sung to the tune of "Danny Boy," which, at least by inference, condemned those who leave their home countries. Some of the congregation pointedly stared at Taylor as the choir's bass soloist sang the last lines:

No dearer land to me in all the earth;
By all sweet ties of home and love and beauty,
To thee I cleave, dear land that gave me birth.

Only eight days after the funeral, McDougald asked the Black brothers to Green Meadows, his Toronto estate, and anointed them with offers of directorships: Conrad would join the Ravelston and Argus boards; Monte would become a director of Dominion Stores and Standard Broadcasting. At about the same time, Conrad was invited to sit on the boards of Eaton's and Confederation Life. The boys folded Draper Dobie into Dominion Securities, assuming ownership positions and personal offices in the larger investment house. "To meet Conrad in those halcyon days was to be kept waiting for only forty-five minutes," wrote CBC producer Ron Graham in *Saturday Night*. "He glided down the corridor of Dominion Securities in Toronto, tendered an apology, extended his hand low enough that an involuntary bow was required to grasp it, and said hello with an ennui that contradicted his quizzical gaze. The petitioner was ushered graciously into an unkempt cubicle where, surrounded by unpacked boxes, a photograph of Joe Clark, a sheaf of pink phone messages, and a stack of his biography of Maurice Duplessis, Black entertained for several hours with droll verbiage, slanderous insights, and a hilarious piece of French vitriol he had just dispatched to the editor of *Le Devoir*. One laughed at his jokes, admired his intelligence, deferred to his position, and came away with the promise of an interview."

To credit Black with enough prescience to guess precisely how the course of events culminating in his grab for Argus would unfold may make him sound too Machiavellian. Yet it is a fact that in the interval between his return to Toronto and the death of Bud McDougald he met and courted every one of the men who would turn out to be key players in that transfer of power. He had come to know Alex Barron, Dixon Chant (the associate of Eric Phillips who represented the late colonel's estate), and Louis Guolla (McDougald's lawyer) during the negotiations that led up to the formation of Ravelston. McDougald introduced him to Ainslie Shuve, saying that he wanted the Crown Trust executive to know Conrad because "he could become a very important part in the whole scheme of things." At a party hosted by Roy and Lee MacLaren, Toronto Society's Renaissance Couple, Black met Derek Hayes, secretary of Massey-Ferguson, who in turn arranged for him to meet Victor Rice, the company's comptroller. From then on, Rice kept him informed about what was really happening at the troubled agricultural implement giant. Black also visited Dixon Chant in hospital several times after he suffered a severe heart attack.

But Black's most significant encounter was with Percy Finlay and his son, John. As a true Argusologist, Conrad recognized that it was here, in the custody of this father-and-son combination of lawyers, that the holding company's future direction, and perhaps his own, would eventually be decided. At that point, the senior Finlay had been associated with Hollinger as counsel for more than fifty years, though McDougald had bypassed him for the company's top job. The two Finlays still exercised great influence over Hollinger's affairs because they acted as legal advisers and guardian angels to many of the heirs from the original mining partnership. "Conrad and I met at the Hollinger dinners held after the company's annual meetings," John Finlay recalls. "There was always a table at the back where the pilots, office staff, and young people were seated. I recognized him as being particularly bright, and it was my guess that somewhere along the line he would become the power behind Argus. I was very unhappy with the lack of activity at Hollinger and so was he."

All this contact-making didn't pass unnoticed, particularly after McDougald confided to Hartland MacDougall, executive vice-president of the Bank of Montreal, that Conrad was the son he wished he'd had. "Unlike most of his contemporaries," the great Bud opined, "this boy has the ability to think in modern terms while still maintaining tradition."

That was enough to start the buzz. "I find the suggestion slightly irksome that I am standing next to Mr. McDougald like one of those bemedalled Soviet marshals who stood next to Stalin," Black declared during a television interview when he was asked about the rumours of his succession. "That people would speculate about my role in Argus is not surprising or unreasonable, since my brother and I own lots of shares and the company owns major assets plus $200 million in cash."

In public, Black adroitly sidestepped even the hint of ambition. "I would do myself an injustice," he said, with a straight face, "and indeed not serve the truth, in the representation that I am sitting about rubbing my hands and waiting for the grim reaper to carry off my older colleagues to the boardroom in the sky. Nothing could be further from the truth."

But inside the Argus orbit, Conrad was pushing hard for greater recognition. He knew that within the serried ranks of Canada's Establishment, the move that signifies ultimate acceptance is appointment to a major bank board.

John Hull, a friend of Black's who was then head of Public Relations

80

Services Ltd., suggested to W.O. Twaits, retired chairman of Imperial Oil and a Royal Bank vice-president, that Conrad might be available. Earle McLaughlin, the Royal's chairman, was anxious to heal the wound left behind by his support of Desmarais during the Argus takeover battle; he sounded Conrad out, but nothing was decided. Hull had meanwhile advised Page Wadsworth, the Commerce chairman, that the bank had better grab Conrad before it was too late, because the Royal was about to get him.

Black tentatively discussed the idea with McDougald, who disliked McLaughlin and told the young man, "I don't mean to be a mother hen, but you can't have that. I'll get you an invitation from the Commerce." Black pointed out that McLaughlin had already told him he could not be a Commerce director because, under the Bank Act, no more than a quarter of any board's members may be directors of the same bank, and four of Argus's sixteen were already on the Commerce's roster. "I don't want any lesson in the Bank Act from that *teller!*" Bud exclaimed, and promptly decided to enlarge the Argus board by five new directors to accommodate the legislation.

McDougald decided that two long-time back-office Argus executives— James R. Wright and Harry Edmison—should now become directors of the company. Then McDougald suggested that he and Conrad agree on another and each nominate one more. Fred Eaton, the department store heir, was their unanimous first choice. McDougald's nomination was Trumbull Warren, the chairman of Rheem Canada Ltd. and an able industrialist who was already on the Massey board. While Black was pondering his choice, Bud brought forward the name of Col. Charles "Bud" Baker, chairman of the Ontario Jockey Club.

Baker is a well-known businessman, but McDougald chose to put his case forward with an unusual recommendation: "They were bringing some horses back for the Olympic team in a plane from England a while ago, and one of the animals started to panic. They would have had to shoot him to prevent him from kicking a hole in the side of the plane— but Bud Baker held his tail all the way across the ocean!" Black pointed out in as kindly a manner as he could that holding a horse's tail was not the ideal qualification for becoming an Argus director.

When an angry McDougald asked him who *his* candidate was, Black replied, "Nelson Davis. He is going off the Commerce board for age reasons, he's a good friend of ours, a great businessman, and it's time we had some more proprietors around here."

"Goddamn it, you're right. Never thought of him. Nelson it is."

And that was how Nelson Davis, who would turn out to be the pivotal player in Conrad's grab for power, came to join the Argus board.

CHAPTER FOUR

Demise of a Titan

*Like a latter-day King Lear raging against his own
mortality as the outer reaches of his empire crumbled
away, McDougald kept dragging himself to his
shower-room phone booth, calling out to the world,
searching for some sleight-of-hand that might rescue
Massey — but finding he had no magic left to perform.*

B y the early winter of 1977–78, John Angus "Bud" McDougald,
the Argus chairman and self-appointed dean of the Canadian
Establishment, was not feeling quite himself.

He had spent his customary six weeks in England, but instead of
taking the usual joy in mingling with London's fiscal aristocracy, he
moved along his accustomed circuit of visits like an aging lion patrolling
his turf, still proud but no longer threatening. As always, he stayed in his
permanent suite (Room 358 at Claridge's) and was driven around
London in his Phantom V Rolls. He still visited his friends the Duke of
Wellington, the Marquess of Abergavenny, and Lord Crathorne, then
moved on to inspect his four-in-hand hackneys at their stalls in the
Cotswolds. He spent an inordinate amount of time at Kingsclere, the
historic Hampshire stables whose eighty-five boxes the McDougald
thoroughbreds shared with mounts belonging to the Queen, Paul Mellon, and Col. Julian Berry, one of the United Kingdom's best-known
racers. Few members of Britain's large and enthusiastic equestrian class
were aware that their most famous training stable had been quietly
acquired in 1976 by a little-known Canadian millionaire. Eight Derby
winners had trained at Kingsclere. Its magnificent Park House overlooks
a dozen cottages, a recently built covered ride, and two hundred acres of
downland gallops on which the McDougald horses (identified by their
French grey and cerise racing colours) could be worked any distance up
to two miles.

When Peter Towers-Clark, editor of the authoritative *Stud & Stable*,
asked the Canadian industrialist why he was investing in the ailing
British racing industry, McDougald replied: "Britain is a great sporting

country and racing is and always has been part of its way of life. It is certainly not going to die, and to quote that famous conversation between Bismarck and Disraeli, 'as long as you keep up your racing, you will never have a revolution in England.'"

McDougald loved the sport, but his horses (with the possible exception of Idiot's Delight, which placed in its first race at Ascot) won few trophies. He enjoyed most of all the fuss that accompanies horsy events. One season in Toronto when G. Allan Burton, Master of the Toronto and North York Hunt, asked permission to ride across McDougald's estate, he not only granted it but even invited the whole hunt of three hundred for a breakfast of Melton Mowbray pork pie on his front lawn. At the time, he had just planted rows of fifteen-foot trees along Green Meadows' driveways, but by the day before the hunt, many of them had died and turned brown. McDougald promptly hired an extra crew of gardeners and had the offending leaves sprayed green.

Feeling testy and preoccupied, McDougald paid little attention to the affairs of the British subsidiaries of Massey-Ferguson, Standard Broadcasting, or Dominion Stores. He spent much of his time organizing cosy little lunches at the Turf, his favourite London club, whose membership, he would boast, included sixteen dukes. When one of his British dining companions dared question the long-term usefulness of the Queen, he countered with an eccentric defence. "The monarchy," he puffed, "as far as I'm concerned, is a damn good piece of business. If I were an Englishman, I'd be full of the monarchy all the time – because you've something to sell. Now there are an awful lot of people in England … all for getting rid of the monarchy – the stupid bastards! I mean, it's all they've got to sell…. Just think of the number of films and cameras they must sell as a result of the monarchy. Whether you like the Queen, or whether you don't, doesn't enter into it with me. It's a good piece of merchandise. All you have to do is walk by Buckingham Palace any time you like and there's always a big crowd outside taking snapshots and standing waiting in the rain. Nobody can tell me the public don't like a parade. They do."

ON THE PLANE TRIP BACK ACROSS THE ATLANTIC, McDougald was seated directly beneath a faulty air vent and caught a touch of pneumonia. His return was marred by a cautious customs official who demanded to know what he had been doing in England for so many weeks. "I was over for Dominion Stores," he answered. "I'm sort of in retail sales. This was rather an important meeting and I'm not free to discuss it." The customs man replied: "Well, if you're in sales, I'd like to have a look at your sample case." McDougald, whose younger self might have been prompted to deliver a scathing lecture on the merits of freely conducted commerce and unrestricted travel, blandly mumbled, "I haven't got a sample case with me."

He couldn't shake the fever and his circle of intimates at the Toronto Club was shocked at how old and tired Bud looked. His jaw was slack; the topography of his face betrayed the full measure of his years. He worried about his age, particularly because Bank of Commerce directors face enforced retirement at seventy, then only months away. He launched a brief campaign to prove he was really two years younger than the records showed, ransacking the archives of the 48th Highlanders, airily maintaining that he had faked his birth date to rush his enlistment as a youngster. But no supporting documents were ever found. He retreated even further into the Jamesian world he'd created for himself, growling at the galloping imperfections of the liberal society he despised, but only occasionally reasserting the prejudices and obstinacy that had sustained his former vigour. When a policeman stopped his limousine one morning and noted that the occupants were not wearing seatbelts, McDougald fixed his accuser with an imperious gaze. "I believe that federal law takes precedence over this silly regulation you're trying to enforce, officer," he harrumphed. "In the Criminal Code there is some sort of prohibition against suicide. So, you see, by putting federal ahead of provincial law, I'm just being a good federalist." Then he ordered the chauffeur to drive on, leaving behind one thoroughly puzzled traffic cop.

He spent nearly every lunch hour at his beloved Toronto Club, but it just wasn't the same any more. On one occasion, McDougald looked around at a group of guests in the club's downstairs lobby and complained to his dining companion: "My God, it looks like a convention of plumbers in here. People are actually coming into the Toronto Club wearing wooden shoes!" McDougald, who controlled the club's membership even though he held no official title, would never allow anyone to join who wore diamond-patterned socks. His wife, Maude, known to everyone as Jim, recalled an occasion when a man's socks had ruined a career: "They were looking for quite a top executive for one of the Argus companies and they had tried everybody. Finally, this chap seemed as if he were going to be simply perfect. Some of the other executives had met and interviewed him and the poor fellow came into our living room, hitched up his trouser legs, and sat down. He had white socks on. My husband turned to the others and just said: 'Out... Useless.'"

It was during one of his visits to the Toronto Club that Bud ran into Jack Campbell, retired president of Canadian Breweries. A shrewd marketer who enjoyed practical jokes, Campbell had walked up to McDougald a few days after his daughter Mariellen had married Montegu Black III in 1964 and said: "Bud, I've worked out a plan. I know you've got no children and no successors. You've probably always wanted a boy like me.* Now I've got one of the Black boys all sewn up, so why don't you adopt me? We'll get Don McIntosh† to draw up the papers." McDougald laughingly agreed, and "the adoption" had been a running gag between the two men ever since. Catching sight of his sick friend at the club in early 1978, Campbell walked over to the McDougald table and said, "Bud, I hope you're not getting ill; we've got to get this adoption thing settled." McDougald's laughter was hearty, but his eyes remained vacant.

As his health continued to deteriorate, McDougald took the Argus jet down to Florida and settled into the Basque-style mansion on Ocean Boulevard that he'd purchased a couple of decades earlier from Mrs. Felix du Pont.

Over the years the du Ponts, who were in paints among other things, had covered most of the mansion's exposed surfaces, including a stone fireplace, with twenty coats of khaki semi-gloss. McDougald refurbished the *pied-à-terre* and used it to consolidate his American contacts, becoming a major figure in Palm Beach society. A governor of both the Everglades and the Bath and Tennis clubs and a shareholding board member of the First National Bank, he liked nothing better than to spend the long, languid afternoons with his cronies, the upper crust of the eastern seaboard's financial aristocrats.

One such companion was Benjamin Oehlert, Jr., a onetime Philadelphia lawyer who became president of the Minute Maid Corporation and served as U.S. ambassador to Pakistan in the late 1960s. McDougald relished the story of how Oehlert joined the ranks of the welfare state. "Ben has a lot of money," McDougald told a Toronto visitor, "and the other day there were two or three of us having lunch at the Everglades. We were talking about what a hell of a mess everything was in, with all this welfare and so on, when Ben said, 'Christ, when you come to think of it, I'm unemployed – I don't have a job. I think I'll go over to the West Palm Beach welfare office and see what I can do.' So, by God, he gets into his Rolls after lunch and lines up with all those other people.

"Finally his turn comes. The clerk says, 'Well, what can I do for you?'

"'I'm out of a job.'

*Campbell was forty-eight at the time, weighing in at 250 pounds.

†Donald A. McIntosh was the principal Argus lawyer and a director of the company.

"'What's your line of work?'

"'I'm an ambassador. I was let out, and I'd like another ambassador's job.'

"So they went all through their files to see if anybody was looking for an ambassador. Then they checked upstairs where they had a more sophisticated filing system and finally told him they'd be in touch if they could find any openings for ambassadors.

"So Ben comes back to the club and says, 'They're the stupidest bunch of buggers I've ever talked to.'... Well, Jeez, three days later, damned if he doesn't get this unemployment cheque!"

Bud regaled his friends with stories about his neighbour, one of Palm Beach's most colourful citizens, the redoubtable Marjorie Merriweather Post Close Hutton Davies May. The daughter of a Midwestern breakfast cereal manufacturer (whose Postum and Grape-Nuts company became General Foods), Marjorie had married four times. She lived on a scale that has yet to be equalled, even on Florida's Gold Coast.

Afloat, she relaxed aboard the 316-foot four-masted barque *Sea Cloud*, which required a crew of seventy-two to provide services for ten guests. She collected rooms full of Fabergé Easter eggs and other Czarist treasures, priceless diamonds, a fifty-one-carat sapphire, and a porcelain dinner service created for Catherine the Great. At Mar-a-Lago, her lavish fifty-room Palm Beach residence, staffed by sixty servants (including her private candy maker), she gave Thursday-night parties that were *de rigueur* for everyone who counted. Whether or not they felt like it, her hundred or so guests had to spend at least a couple of hours square-dancing to her house band, the women having first been supplied with slippers to prevent their sharp heels from marking the ballroom's mirror-finish floor. Anyone complaining about these compulsory hoedowns would hardly have penetrated Mrs. Post's immunity from life's little annoyances: she had become almost totally deaf. She died in 1973 and in the spring of 1982 Mar-a-Lago was listed with a Palm Beach real estate broker for $20 million.

In her heyday, she had occasionally sought advice from Bud McDougald, especially about the pressure for further diversification put on her by General Foods' management. "These boys were very anxious that she agree to go along and get into the hamburger business," McDougald reminisced. "McDonald's had been very successful and was a pretty good thing. The old girl didn't think much of that because, as she described it to me, 'My father always said we were in the cereal business and not in the meat business.'

"I said, 'I agree with you, Marjorie.'

"She said, 'What would you do? I have to go back to my meeting.'

"I said, 'I would bounce them out of the house and tell them you are sticking to Post Toasties.'

"That was that. She went back to lunch and these birds browbeat her, knocked her down, and I saw her a couple of weeks later and she said, 'We're in the hamburger business.'

"A year and a half ago General Foods wrote off $83 million from that hamburger investment."

In his final weeks, McDougald spent some happy hours at a ranch he had acquired in Florida, arranging to remove the alligators left behind by its former occupants. The farm had housed a private zoo, and McDougald's terms of purchase included removal of all its animals. When he asked the previous owner, the daughter of sportsman-industrialist Jim Norris, why the 'gators had not been carted off, it was explained that she had heard he liked to wear alligator shoes, and the animals would provide him with a lifetime supply. McDougald didn't have the heart to point out that he did indeed have a penchant for such footwear, but only for an English bench-made variety that he could buy at a small shop near Claridge's in London.

The McDougald house in Palm Beach has eighteen bathrooms, but none more important to its owner than Felix du Pont's former shower off the main bedroom that the Argus chairman had converted into an office. Fitted with a tiny desk, two telephones, wastebasket and pencil sharpener, it was the communications centre from which he called Toronto to monitor the pulse of his business empire.

IT WAS NOT A TRUTH he could or would ever accept, but Bud McDougald had in his later years become a museum-keeper. The six companies that had once been the pride of the Argus portfolio urgently required the energy and imagination of E.P. Taylor again or of a much younger McDougald. B.C. Forest Products had long before slipped from their grasp; Argus was still the largest shareholder of Noranda but exercised no influence on its policies; Dominion Stores, Domtar Inc., and Standard Broadcasting were all but comatose. Worst of all, reports about Massey-Ferguson, the multinational jewel within the Argus chain of holdings, spelled serious trouble. McDougald had become a lethargic spider squatting within a huge and complicated corporate web that seemed to have immobilized him.

He had lost the will to expand Argus's holdings. In the summer before McDougald died, Harry Edmison, the company's secretary, had walked into his office while he was on the phone and had stuck a note on his desk with the notation: "30,000 shares of Hollinger being offered at

$22." Even though this was a favourable price and Argus at the time had only a 23.1-per-cent interest in the profitable mining complex, McDougald scribbled "Not interested" on the paper and dismissed his friend. "I particularly remember how worried I was about Massey that summer," Edmison recalls, "and Mr. McDougald used to be annoyed about all those insider reports we had to file. He asked me if, as a new Argus director, I had to file them too. I reminded him that as a matter of policy I had decided not to hold anything that was in the Argus portfolio. In fact, I told him, there was nothing I would want to buy.

"'Are you kidding?' he wanted to know.

"And I replied that it was true that I certainly wouldn't want to buy Massey because it had far too much debt. Shortly after that, I found an article in the *Magazine of Wall Street* in which a professor hired by an American insurance company had formulated a complicated index by which to judge industrial debt positions. I ran Massey through it and they were right on the line. I left the calculations on Bud's desk, but all he said was, 'Who is this fellow?' When I told him the man was a professor, he lost all interest."

IN MID-JANUARY OF 1978, McDougald received an important visitor. Alex Ethelred Barron, president of Canadian General Investments Ltd. and a long-time Massey director, had a few months previously been invited to join the agricultural implement company's executive committee. This had allowed him for the first time access to details of its financial position. The examination had confirmed his worst fears about Massey's long-term viability. When in Miami, he phoned McDougald and asked if they could spend a few hours together. Barron was invited to Palm Beach on the same day Albert A. Thornbrough, president and chief executive officer of Massey, was also due for a visit. "I arrived a few minutes after Thornbrough," Barron later recalled, "so Bud and I didn't have a chance to chat in advance. To my surprise, he asked Al to step aside as the person who chaired the Massey meetings and declared that he was taking charge. Some days later I telephoned Bud and told him that I agreed Thornbrough should not continue but thought he wasn't physically capable of handling it himself. 'Alex,' he said, 'the company's in trouble and somebody's got to hold the banks in line and bear the brunt of the criticism. I have the responsibility, so I'll have to do it.'"

Blessed with the acute sensitivity of a closet paranoid, McDougald could smell the crisis at Massey half a continent away and tried desperately to stage an eleventh-hour rescue. He never let up, even though his energies continued to drain from him. Evelyn Young, his secretary in the Argus Toronto office, later remembered that during his daily calls her boss's voice kept growing weaker and she would gently interrupt his harangues to inquire, "Am I keeping you too long?"

By the beginning of March, McDougald was becoming so weak that he could hardly dress without help. He had somehow shrunk into himself: his shirts hung loosely on his frame and he had to keep hitching up his pants. The Florida sun made his eyes water. Like a latter-day King Lear raging against his own mortality as the outer reaches of his empire crumbled away, McDougald kept dragging himself to his shower-room phone booth, calling out to the world, searching for some sleight-of-hand that might rescue Massey—but finding he had no magic left to perform. Bruce Matthews, then executive vice-president of Argus, recalled that about this time, "the doctors really put the heat on Bud and told him to cool right out, to stay in his room. Word finally came through that he wasn't to get out of bed. But on one or two occasions when he heard Mrs. McDougald answer my calls, he grabbed the phone and got going on Massey."

On March 9, just five days before Bud's seventieth birthday, Jim McDougald gave a small dinner party for Bev Matthews (the Toronto lawyer and former Tory fund-raiser), his wife, Phyllis (the former Mrs. Neil McKinnon), Signy Eaton (John David's widow), and John Parkin, the Canadian Establishment's court architect. "We'd first had drinks at Doris Phillips's house," Parkin remembers, "then walked across the street to a beautiful dinner—the precision of the serving was just wonderful. Bev Matthews was thoroughly impressed, and I was overwhelmed. Jim McDougald wanted to show me the house, which of course had been built by Addison Mizner, and when she opened one closet door there was a suit left behind by the Duke of Wellington. I hadn't the wit to remind her that the Duke's father had been an architect and that, in fact, the present Duke had for years practised as an architect in London under the name Arthur Wellesley & Partners. I would have loved to tease Mrs. McDougald."

A few days before the party for Bev Matthews, Doug Ward, chairman of Dominion Securities and McDougald's best friend, telephoned Palm Beach. The two men had gossiped over coffee together each morning for thirty years, also lunching at least twice a week at the Toronto Club. Ward was McDougald's chief stockmarket adviser. They tended to converse in percentages. When Ward inquired how his friend was feeling, "25 per cent" was Bud's feeble reply.

On March 14, his seventieth birthday, Bud suffered a massive heart attack and was rushed to Good Samaritan Hospital. "I sort of had in mind taking him to the Mayo Clinic," Mrs. McDougald said, "but the doctors told me there wasn't any hope. The next morning he was really going and I was by his bedside."

"I've got to speak to Thornbrough," wheezed the dying Bud.

"Yes, I know, darling, as soon as you get up."

"No. I want Al to come here. I've got to talk to him – I've figured out a way to fix Massey..."

"Never mind. You leave that. Massey will get fixed. It always does fix itself eventually."

"No, not this time. It's in bad shape. I've got to speak to Al. Get him down here. Tell him only I can fix Massey..."

They were to be his final words. At 10:45 a.m. on March 15, 1978, John Angus McDougald reluctantly withdrew from the world of power and privilege he so loved.

FIFTEEN MINUTES LATER, Doris Phillips, the dead Argus chairman's sister-in-law, telephoned Evelyn Young in Toronto to tell her the news and asked her to notify Bruce Matthews. Called out of a directors' meeting at Canada Permanent, the retired major-general took over in typical military style: he wrote out an operations order, complete with appropriate countdown procedures, and set out to organize the plushest funeral since George Black's two years before.

Conrad Black and John Bassett were giving a luncheon that day at the York Club for Billy Graham, the American evangelist who uses the Bassetts' television facilities to videotape his crusades around the world. "I introduced Billy, and John Bassett thanked him, and we had some rather pleasant witticisms at each other's expense," Conrad later recalled. "When I got back to my office at Dominion Securities, I heard what had happened, and a good many people telephoned that afternoon to say what an unfortunate event it was... I appear to have been the only person who took note of the fact that Mr. McDougald had died on the Ides of March. He always had a Caesarian bearing, and his succession was not much better organized."

THE DEATH OF McDOUGALD was not just the end of a unique career or the final exit of a dominant personality in Canadian business for most of three decades. His demise had the ceremonial resonance of the passing of royalty – as much the symbolic end of an era as an actual event. In the dawning of the computer age, he imparted to everything he touched a sense of grandeur and air of chivalry that may have been old-fashioned, but at least he was an individual well aware of his worth and not afraid to show it.

In Palm Beach, Page Hufty, a McDougald confidant whose father-in-law had been a large shareholder in John D. Rockefeller's Standard Oil, telephoned the governor of Florida, persuading him to allow the family to bypass the tedious formalities so that the body could be flown north within twenty-four hours. The firm of Rosar-Morrison, in business since 1861 and the Toronto Establishment's leading Catholic buriers, was hired to run the funeral. Here the first difficulty arose. A family member noted that the firm's youthful sextet of professional attendants wore their hair almost to their shoulders. In keeping with Bud's aversion to lengthy coiffures, they were requested to get haircuts in time for the ceremony.*

IT WAS A COLD DAY FOR A FUNERAL, the sibilant March rain falling hard on the steps of St. Michael's Cathedral. The scene, with its muster of top-hatted mourners, their breath visible in the chill air, was reminiscent of a Czarist cortège in late nineteenth-century Russia. The genuine grief of the close family was openly expressed, but almost everyone else seemed less absorbed with the ceremony than with surreptitiously eyeing one another, ranking the pews they had been allocated, trying to guess which of them might be the dead Argus emperor's successor. The McDougald family had requested that Archbishop Philip Pocock officiate at the funeral, but he declined because of the highly inflammatory language the late Argus chairman had used when the churchman, supporting the California-based boycott on non-union-grown grapes, had asked Dominion Stores to co-operate. Bud had raked not merely the church and its earthly representative over the coals for that one but had even questioned the wisdom of Much Higher Authority in allowing such an outrage. It was only through the intercession of Senator Joseph Sullivan that Pocock finally agreed to attend the funeral; he sat stonily

*McDougald once had two shareholders ejected from a Crown Trust annual meeting purely on the grounds that he thought their hair was too long. Hartland MacDougall, executive vice-president and general manager of the Bank of Montreal, who is a kind of walking and breathing personification of the Canadian Establishment (being a Molson, having been educated at LeRosey in Switzerland, and belonging to ten of Canada's most eminent private clubs), ran into McDougald one day on his way out of the Toronto Club. MacDougall at that time was wearing his elegant hair slightly longer than usual – partly to fit his country-squire image (he had recently moved to an estate near Belfountain, Ontario). "Hartland!" McDougald beckoned. "Yes, sir," MacDougall replied. Came the barb: "Hold on a minute. What is the *matter* with your hair? Are you trying to be a middle-aged hippie?"

beside the altar through the ceremony and refused to officiate over the departed Bud.

"Until the day we die, our most singular prayer to God should be one of praise and thanks for the gift of life," intoned Monsignor Pearse Lacey, rector of St. Michael's. "To live even but a few years would be more than any of us have a right. But to have lived seventy years as the deceased, Bud McDougald, had done, endowed with precious God-given gifts and a will to work, surely calls forth from us profound and humble thanks to God for the wonder of Bud's works, for the wonder of his accomplishments.... And yet with all our high estate, created as we are in God's image, we walk with feet of clay in our humanity, often frail, often imperfect, often sinful. The whole thrust of this eucharistic celebration this morning in this funeral service is really to beseech a loving and compassionate God to be merciful and forgiving of the sins of our beloved deceased. Whatever purification and healing the Lord demands of Bud, may we his brothers and sisters call in confidence on Jesus the Lord to unbind him and let him go freely into the Kingdom of Heaven.... Amen."

The police outriders were out in full force that day, shepherding the procession of tug-sized Cadillacs and boxy Rollses to Mount Hope Cemetery. After the brief burial service and tearful family farewells, Conrad Black noticed the silhouette of a man in a camel-hair coat lingering close by, near the remaining mourners. Black recognized him as John Prusac, a mysterious Yugoslav-born Toronto developer who had been befriended by McDougald in his last years.

Prusac stayed by the burial mound for a full hour, sobbing in the rain.

BUD McDOUGALD HAD NO MORE ACKNOWLEDGED the idea of his own mortality than he would have accepted an invitation from people he hardly knew. McDougald used to astonish his acquaintances, whenever any of them was presumptuous enough to bring up the subject of succession, by prefacing his remarks with the comment, "*If* as and when I croak..." He was so stubborn about ignoring his inevitable demise that he had even avoided clearing the deed for the plot in which he was to be buried. A title search had to be quickly organized, when the time came, by Argus secretary Harry Edmison. Bud would not permit a whisper of the possibility of his death in his presence; his preparations were limited to reluctantly signing a will. He had made no contingency plan to assure continuity at Argus.

It was a sign of how deeply torpor had rigidified Argus that news of

McDougald's death had bumped up by three points (to $33.50) the value of the company's thinly traded common stock. Bay Street couldn't fathom what its complicated lines of succession might be, but in the market's cool judgement any change promised improvement in its activity and earnings.

"Bud really didn't think he was ever going to die," recalled Doug Ward of Dominion Securities, "or he would have made more adequate preparations at Argus. He probably realized that George Black's sons would eventually take a very prominent part in the company, but he thought they would come in sponsored by Max Meighen and General Matthews, then be elevated at the appropriate time."

Despite all the brave chatter about his pride in being a Canadian free-enterpriser, McDougald had lost faith in both his country and its system. Except for his Argus position, nearly all of his investments had been converted into cash. In addition to the bulk of his holdings he left his wife all his "furniture, sterling silver service and flatware, plate, jewellery, linens, glass, china, books, pictures, prints, provisions, consumable stores, automobiles, motorcycles, motor and other vehicles, horses, mares, dogs, harness, saddlery, livestock, stable and garage furniture and equipment, swimming pool equipment, tools, implements, and other equipment and accessories."*

IMMEDIATELY AFTER McDOUGALD'S DEATH nothing much seemed to happen. The two widows, Jim McDougald and Doris Phillips, returned to Palm Beach. Their lawyer, Lou Guolla, came to see Bruce Matthews to inquire whether some formal agreement should be drawn up with the estates to keep the Argus structure operating. The General replied that there had never been anything in writing between Bud and himself, and he certainly didn't require any documentation now. "Just tell Jim that I'm acting for her," he told Guolla. "Anything the estates want, I will see it done."

Asked by Adrienne Clarkson on CBC-TV's "the fifth estate" what might now happen to Argus, Conrad reached for his most ingratiating countenance:

> Well, I think that the many high offices left vacant by Mr.

---

*Apart from a few small family legacies, he left various amounts to his personal retinue: $15,000 to his secretary, Evelyn Young; $5,000 to his secretary, Ruth Smith; $10,000 to his wife's maid, Kathleen Coffey; $10,000 to his cook, Esther Kalio; $15,000 to his chauffeur, John Mous; $10,000 to his gardener, William Van Veen; $5,000 to Godfrey Lockyer, his head groom; $5,000 to Edith Jones, his housekeeper; $5,000 to his personal maid, Rose Coffey; and $20,000 to his butler, Arthur Durham.

94

McDougald's death will be filled by his senior colleagues, who are men of equivalent stature with long and distinguished careers. I'm thinking in particular of General Matthews, Colonel Meighen, and Mr. Alex Barron. As to whether there might be changes in corporate policy in the Argus companies, I really have no authority to say. I wouldn't anticipate any great breach of continuity. Mr. McDougald had his own style, and his prestige cannot be deprecated. He was always very careful to canvass his associates and acted in a pretty unanimous interest. I would say, business as usual.

Clarkson: People have said that you're the Dauphin. That you will take over. Will you?

Black: No. I don't think there's any suggestion of that. All I've ever heard of it is in the press. Whenever people have asked me, in the event of Mr. McDougald disappearing from the scene, what would happen, I invariably cited General Matthews, Colonel Meighen, and Mr. Barron, and I still do that. What in fact happens is not up to me. I think you might have, comparatively speaking, a little more collective rule than has generally been the case in those companies. But there is no Dauphin.

On air, Black marvelled at McDougald's sense of style: "I remember asking him once what he felt the finest car he had ever seen was, and he described the 1924 Isotta Fraschini originally built of tulipwood for Alfonso XIII, King of Spain. When I said, 'I wonder where it is now?' he replied, 'In my garage.'"

For the cameras, Conrad lauded Bud's talents as a raconteur. "I remember Mr. McDougald once telling me about his days as treasurer for Mitch Hepburn when he was running for leadership of the Opposition in Ontario back in the thirties. It was his job to dole money out to Hepburn's hecklers, those people who were paid to stand up and try to shout Mitch down at public rallies. Their interventions would have been arranged in advance and rehearsed; Hepburn would have been told exactly how to reply to them. Just at the height of the campaign, they came to Bud and said, 'You know, we're not getting paid enough for this job of making fools of ourselves in every auditorium in Ontario…' Bud strung that one out for fifteen minutes and it was just hilarious. He was an inexhaustible storehouse of anecdotes going back to the 1920s."

But in the studio banter that was never actually broadcast, Conrad was much less circumspect. At one point, Adrienne Clarkson asked him:

	What kind of a figure was Bud McDougald in the long sense of history? Was he Napoleonic? Did he exercise power like a pope?
Black:	A bit of each. Ahh...let me see...I don't want to be banal here, but I'd hate to offend his wife or anything like that. If you asked me that question and I gave the answer I just did, it might be thought a bit uncalled for, you know. I just want to be careful here. I suppose I could give you that line the *Star* quoted me on, about how he divided the world into friends and enemies...
Clarkson:	Yeah? O.K. Let's do that...How did he wield power? What kind of a figure was he? How did he see the world?
Black:	He tended to divide the world into friends and adversaries. He was a man of unshakable loyalty to his friends, but was capable of quite a high degree of unsentimentality toward adversaries. He had a profound conviction of the worthwhileness or correctness of those standards that he was endeavouring to maintain, which in large measure he embodied as an individual. That was part of his strength. He was a person of style, almost ostentatiously unashamed of his own success and of his own championship of his view of society, his idea of how to direct events.

WHILE McDOUGALD HAD NEVER ANOINTED ANY CROWN PRINCES, he had quietly during the year before his death recruited two friends to help him run Argus's corporate stable. Sixty-eight-year-old Bruce Matthews, who sat on the boards of fourteen companies and was working out of four offices (at Argus, Canada Permanent, Excelsior Life, and Dome Mines), found that he had spread his energies too thinly to be able to give the Argus holdings the attention they required. In the autumn of 1977, therefore, McDougald had approached Alex Barron to become a vice-president of Argus, an appointment that was to have been ratified at the company's 1978 annual meeting. By January 1978, Barron had partly moved into 10 Toronto Street, spending his mornings in Wally McCutcheon's old office and beginning to take over some of Matthews's management functions.

At this point seven very different men, representing widely dissimilar and occasionally competing interests, were closely monitoring the Argus situation. Besides Conrad Black and his retinue, they were:

Col. Maxwell Charles Gordon Meighen. At seventy, Meighen believed that if he simply did nothing Argus was eventually bound to fall into his lap. This was because under the complicated Ravelston agreement signed by Argus's main shareholders in 1969, his Canadian General Investments Ltd. and a related company held the largest block of stock (26.5 per cent). As the other owners died or sold their shares, his pro-rated slice would eventually command a control position – or so the theory ran.

Scott Fennell. The son-in-law of the late Eric Phillips was the only McDougald relative who could foresee precisely what would happen to the Argus empire. Having divined the fact that the key to control of Argus lay in Crown Trust, he had approached Bud early in 1977, asking if some arrangements could be made for him to buy into the trust company. "The first thing he said was, 'No, Scottie, I'm in control,'" Fennell later recalled. "I told him that I wasn't talking about right then, just that someday I'd like to have the opportunity. But he wouldn't talk to me about it."

Albert Thornbrough and Albert Fairley. As chief executive officers of Massey-Ferguson and Hollinger Mines, these gold-dust twins were aware that their corporate performances were being criticized by their own outside directors and other Argus shareholders. With their mentor and protector gone from the scene, both men started to scurry about, searching for lifelines.

John Prusac. The man who had lingered over Bud McDougald's grave now began actively to advance his ambition of presiding over Argus. He was indiscreet enough to discuss his plans with a Toronto real-estate man and even approached two prominent Toronto Establishmentarians about joining his future Argus board. Prusac's overtures quickly became noontime gossip at Winston's.

Percy Finlay. Rejected in 1964 by both McDougald and Phillips as being too old to head the Hollinger operation, Finlay at eighty was still the lawyer in charge of the Dunlap and Duncan McMartin estates and part of the Timmins estates. This 15 per cent, added to 8 per cent held at Crown Trust (through the John McMartin estate) and the 23.1 per cent tucked into the Argus portfolio, represented a control position. But Finlay was one of the few players who realized that without the strength of Bud McDougald's presence to hold this loose coalition together, Hollinger was vulnerable to a takeover bid.

BLACK'S MAIN ADVANTAGE at this juncture was that unlike everyone else within the Argus orbit, he had never been hypnotized by McDougald's in-group charisma. "Bud's exactly like my cat Sidney," he once told a fellow Argus director. "He's elegant and smart, but he just doesn't care. He can be very pleasant one day and destructive the next. It just depends on what's up."*

Black had always been fond of the Argus chairman but unlike most of Bud's doting entourage he had taken his mentor's measure in a particularly cold-blooded way. "Certainly, Mr. McDougald possessed a sense of style," he reminisces, "a little overdone at times – but particularly in a country as dull as Canada was for so long, he gave Toronto such zip as it had. There was also the matter of the relationship my family had with him. He was very much an ally of ours and vice-versa, but his greatest talent was as a very elegant kind of con-man. I knew perhaps even more about his entire career than he would have wished. It always astonished those boys who went to school with him just how prominent he became, especially people who worked with him when he was just – in the words of a friend of my father's – a bond salesman with the ass hanging out of his pants, trying to peddle municipal bonds up in Malton for Dominion Securities.... It's hard to imagine the Bud McDougald we knew in later years described that way. As time went by, he managed to convince virtually everybody that he was the supreme leader of Canadian business, and in many ways he was. But to me, he always seemed like an Italian cardinal, especially in his style of building personal loyalties."

While everyone else was busily trying to divine what form of succession McDougald might have had in mind, Conrad set about consolidating his position so that he and his brother would become the natural inheritors. "Bud was a true Darwinist," Black confided to a friend at the time, "so in his view, when he died – to the winner should go the spoils. It was a free-for-all. A lot of people, Nelson Davis for one, used to ask me what Bud would have thought of the somewhat unseemly scramble that went on after he died. I suspect it would have flattered him. Had he wanted an orderly succession, he would have organized one. He certainly told Monte and me that he wanted us to take over – but he told a few other people the same thing. Bud was very skilful at presenting the carrot and making sure it wasn't within anyone's grasp.

"One of the reasons my brother and I succeeded while the others didn't is that they never really understood his technique. They never recognized the McDougald system as I did. It was all based on manoeu-

---

*Sidney has since died and been replaced by new cats named Suzy and Oliver.

vring personalities and controlling estates. You put one man's son into the Toronto Club and let another one ride in an antique car—just the way he gave me that painting of Napoleon."

Having studied the McDougald method, Black was prepared to emulate it. He set about, with a dash that Bud might have envied, to exploit the vulnerabilities—both financial and personal—among the improbable cast of characters vying for the Argus crown.

CHAPTER FIVE

The Great Argus Grab

"Maybe St. Francis of Assisi
was the last living man who
wouldn't have liked control of Argus."
—Conrad Black

The struggle for Argus combined all the elements of a brilliantly conceived military *coup d'état* with the convoluted plotting of a Harlequin romance. In a hundred and twenty-five days of savage corporate infighting during the spring of 1978, control over assets worth about $4 billion changed hands—for $18 million. Conrad Black, exhibiting what one impartial observer called "the balls of a canal horse," toppled from power some of the Canadian Establishment's most respected figures, who found themselves befuddled by the improbable circumstances in which they were trapped.

Two posses of power-hungry snipers, divided by age, degrees of ruthlessness, conflicting interests, and mutual mistrust, went to war. Their weapons were words—open threats and hidden promises—but feeling about money the way they did, there was nothing make-believe about the battle they fought. It was a duel to the death, with the rawest of power plays somehow muted by the opulence of their settings. But the transfer of authority was very real.

Black's motives were clear: he was determined to capture ownership of the holding company that had been haunting him since childhood. "Maybe St. Francis of Assisi was the last living man who wouldn't have liked control of Argus," he openly confessed. Like Salvador Dali, who planned every aspect of his life right down to copying his moustache from Velásquez's portraits of Philip IV, Black took care of all the details. He fully applied his gift of timing. "You've got to have the cadence just right," he told a friend just before hostilities began, "and you must treat events with a certain rhythm, maintaining a kind of symmetry as if you were conducting a symphony orchestra."

In his conduct, Black was more reminiscent of Napoleon than of Toscanini, applying as he did the Little Emperor's favourite battlefield dictum, "Never interfere with the enemy when he is in the process of destroying himself." He based his strategy against the formidable forces massed opposite him on Bonaparte's tactics during the campaign leading to the Battle of Rivoli in January 1797. "Without being pretentious about it," Black later mused, "there were certain strategic similarities. Napoleon never really gave battle. He bundled the Austrians right out of two Italian provinces by moving faster than they did, seizing the bridge at Arcola in what was really a sapper action, constantly outflanking his opponents by crossing rivers. And that's what we did."

Like his hero, Black was merciless with his enemies, plucking their plumes of influence, living up to the observation of John Fraser, his Upper Canada College chum: "Conrad was a revenge-seeker, even then. I'd never met anyone else quite so intent on getting revenge for any perceived slight—until I went to Newfoundland, where the whole island is basically built on revenge."

The great grab for Argus and its linked companies is a Gothic tale in which loose coalitions formed and then dissolved; ancient regimes were toppled as young upstarts all but twirled their moustaches. Before the reconstruction of what happened, a dramatis personae is required.

Apart from Black and Bud McDougald's very active ghost, the cast included a former Yugoslav freedom-fighter aspiring to become the Canadian Establishment's ethnic Horatio Alger figure; wealthy former Olympic figure-skating contenders who thought they were being cheated out of their rightful inheritances; a reclusive colonel bound for glory; scions of wealth in Liechtenstein, Spain, France, and the Netherlands; an eccentric multimillionaire with money to burn; a beautiful divorcée whose great-uncle wrote the English words to "O Canada"; executors of formidable estates faced by conflicting interests; and an heiress ensconced in a resort town in upstate New York who proclaimed she was the Empress of China. Such a listing makes no mention of the countless sharpshooters, legal beagles, spear-carriers and, oh yes, an albino man-servant who flitted briefly through the fray before exiting stage left.

This was the cast of main characters:

Major-General Albert Bruce Matthews,
CBE, DSO, ED, CD

HE IS ONE OF THOSE THOROUGHBRED MILITARY MEN who, no matter what happens after they've departed the battlefields, remain strangely cool in their manner. Certainly a man to go tiger-shooting with –as long as you don't plan to spend much time discussing abstractions around the campfire.

Bruce Matthews, who was one of Canada's most distinguished divisional commanders during the Second World War, possesses a look which, if not precisely fit for Mount Rushmore, has that forward slant of jaw that suggests participation in great deeds. Born in 1909 to a prosperous Toronto stockbroker who became Ontario's sixteenth lieutenant-governor, Matthews attended Upper Canada College (where, like all other dedicated wicketkeepers, he dislocated the top joint of his middle finger playing cricket). In 1928, after a brief stint at the University of Geneva, he entered the investment business and joined the Canadian militia. (He had tried to join the Royal Canadian Naval Volunteer Reserve but was turned down because he was colourblind.) Three years later he went into the family firm, Matthews & Company. He was called up in September 1939 and went overseas in 1940 at the head of the 15th Field Battery. A major-general at thirty-five, he took command of the 20,000-man 2nd Canadian Division in November 1944 during the Allied advance into Belgium and the Netherlands. Twice mentioned in dispatches and winner of the Distinguished Service Order and the Croix de Guerre with Palm, he fought a good war.

After returning to Canada, Matthews joined the Excelsior Life Insurance Company, succeeded his father as president in 1949, and used his family's funds to buy control. On its board he renewed his acquaintance with E.P. Taylor. "I actually first met Eddie at the Dorchester Hotel in London, just after he was torpedoed on his way across the Atlantic in 1940," Matthews recalls. "I was an artillery officer in those days and was told by Andy McNaughton, then our corps commander, to see Taylor and his group about ammunition supplies. I really had nothing to do with supply. I was a user. But I went to see him and C.D. Howe for tea at the Dorchester. It was very pleasant." Taylor's office was next door to the Excelsior Life headquarters on Toronto Street, and Matthews soon found himself invited to join several Argus boards. Although Matthews was Lester Pearson's first choice to succeed George Vanier as Governor General, his previous tenure as president of the National Liberal Federation ruled out the appointment.

Long a favourite of Bud McDougald's, Matthews was appointed executive vice-president of Argus in June 1969 following Taylor's departure from the presidency. He described the job as "back-stopping Bud" –which really amounted to being the holding company's chief operating officer, at least in so far as it actually operated anything.

When Ravelston was formed, Matthews was allowed to purchase about 4 per cent of the shares in the partnership—the sliver that was to be a crucial element in Conrad Black's grab for Argus.

In the course of the events that decided Argus's eventual ownership, the General became something of a tragic figure. The perfect gentleman, he stuck to the immutable sense of loyalty that had been the animating spirit of his life. The problem was that events moved too fast for him, and it was not always clear where his loyalties should be invested to perpetuate the rightful order of things. Despite his good intentions, the General became an agent of confusion, throwing his support in different directions in quick succession and finally being frozen out by all the factions involved.

He was gracefully put out of his discomfort on December 14, 1979, when the Black brothers reserved the Toronto Club to stage a farewell dinner for him and Lord McFadzean, both of whom were leaving the board of Standard Broadcasting. The tables were decorated with waxed McIntosh apples arranged within the glow of maroon candles and their determinedly cheery red velvet bows. His daughter Taddy and his son Bryn were there, as were most of the Argus partners who had ever thought of lifting a knife toward Matthews's ramrod back. It was a grand evening. The General was piped in by Archibald Dewar of the 48th Highlanders to the strains of "The Bruce Matthews March," composed in 1945 by Neil Sutherland, pipe-major of the Calgary Highlanders. During dinner, Peter Appleyard played the medley of Scottish airs especially arranged for the Queen Mother when she had visited Toronto in 1974.

Conrad Black stood in a corner, observing the revelry and murmuring that Bruce Matthews certainly had his moments, that he was a lot smarter than he seemed to be, but that it.was easy "to get the jimjams" imagining him actually leading a division into battle...

The General sat beaming at the assembly, drinking in the graceful protocol of the moment—half-flattered at all the fuss and wholly delighted to have survived the Argus ordeal with his honour intact.

Igor Kaplan

IF THE ARGUS PUNCH-AND-JUDY SHOW had a puppetmaster, it was an obscure Lithuanian-born lawyer named Igor Kaplan. Only a legal adviser with Kaplan's unorthodox background and working habits could have provided Black with the risky and aggressive advice that won the day. (Does any other lawyer consulted by the Canadian Establishment work in a round office and own a nightclub named the Cav-A-Bob?) If Kaplan had been a typical Toronto Club lawyer, he would almost certainly have counselled much more caution, and Black would have lost his main chance. It is a mark of the respect and gratitude the present Argus chairman feels for Kaplan that in his corporate dining room, brimming as it is with the russet daubs of the Group of Seven, the only photograph in evidence is that of his late friend Igor—and Kaplan is wearing a very fitting Cheshire-cat grin.

Kaplan died of cancer at the age of forty-nine, less than two years after the Argus takeover. Had he lived, the droll and elegant counsel would have become a major force in Canada's legal community.

Having fled Lithuania in the turmoil of 1940 and settled in Williamstown, near Cornwall in eastern Ontario, Kaplan got a law degree in 1955 and began hustling for clients. Walking on the wild side, he was part of the Vancouver Stock Exchange scene during its worst bucketshop days; he represented groups seeking Ontario's off-track betting permits and overextended himself through the purchase on credit of a rundown hotel in Montreal, drive-in restaurants, and fifth-rate nightclubs. Finding himself $400,000 in debt, he declared personal bankruptcy. He met Black in 1974 through David Smith, a mutual friend, when Conrad was looking around for a tough lawyer to get him off a traffic-violation charge. Kaplan took care of it. From that time, he was the Black brothers' legal counsel. "Most lawyers are as dry as parsley," says Black. "It offends their egos to think they are working for people they consider to be of inferior education to themselves, so they affect a certain impartiality about the fate of their clients. Igor wasn't like that. He fought like a madman for us and did a terrific job—but we did a lot for him, too. When I first met him he was conducting business out of a circular room in the Colonnade. It was the most unusual law office I've ever seen."

When Black insisted that Kaplan ally himself with a major law firm, Igor found a berth at the ultra-respectable Aird & Berlis organization, but only fractionally toned down his zest and irreverence. "Most people in corporate law take themselves very, very seriously," he told Jack Batten, author of *Lawyers*. "The theory is that the big-buck work has to go to them in their big firms because they're the only lawyers who have the brains to handle the business. I disagree. There's no magic in corporate work. The guy sitting down with two immigrant butchers to hammer out a partnership agreement is doing the same thing as the guy who makes out an agreement between Massey-Ferguson and Hollinger. I should know. I've done both."

Rifet John Prusac

EVEN AMONG THE UNLIKELY CAST OF CHARACTERS involved in the Argus takeover, John Prusac stands out as the most improbable participant of them all.

He came the closest of all the also-rans to capturing the prize, yet he remained a mystery throughout, appearing at strategic turning points with impressive legal documents, then vanishing again, leaving a trail of numbers for disconnected phones and unused addresses. "I have always thought of him as the Scarlet Pimpernel of Canadian finance," says Toronto lawyer Rudolph Bratty, who is one of Prusac's legal advisers. "He is terribly enigmatic. No one can find out anything about his personal life. He has several homes in Toronto and hangs his hat wherever he happens to be. Once you meet John, you never forget him."

Tall, silver-haired, and athletically overbearing, he resembles one of those gallant Confederate cavalry colonels who are the heroes of old-style Westerns invariably titled "Seven Bugles to Sunset." Prusac is hardly ever seen in public without a long camel-hair coat draped over his shoulders like a sorcerer's cloak, a black homburg, and a fresh rose in his lapel – white in daytime and red at night. A classic loner, he belongs to that traditional breed of European elegants who click their heels as they bow to kiss their hostess's hand goodnight, then – in Prusac's case – vanish into the night riding a spotless black Lincoln.

A wartime fighter with the Yugoslav Partisans, Prusac arrived in Canada during the early fifties with no money. The former officer worked on a farm in the Ottawa Valley and got a job as a lineman with Ontario Hydro, walking ten miles a day to and from his job to save bus fare. He purchased a lot for eighty dollars on Bogert Avenue in the Willowdale area of North York and started to build a small house in his spare time. Once he had installed the floor, he moved into a corner of the basement to save on rent. He sold the bungalow as soon as it was finished, purchased the adjoining lot, and started all over again.

By 1964 he had saved enough cash to buy the discounted assets of W.B. Sullivan Construction Ltd., then in receivership, which he expanded into a major house-builder. He had married Gloria Griffith, a granddaughter of Canadian publisher Sir William Gage (she now lives in Zurich). "He is a very intense and secretive man," says Charles Tisdall, a public relations consultant in Toronto who is Prusac's brother-in-law. "There must have been a hurt somewhere in his background; he lives for his work. I recall him once remarking, 'I'm going to Nassau tomorrow morning.' I said that that was great, that at least he would have a bit of a rest. 'No,' he replied, 'I'm flying back tomorrow afternoon.' It was business as usual."

Apart from eating at La Scala, drinking Crown Royal whisky, and owning four homes (including a Florida condominium in the same building as Ontario Premier Bill Davis), Prusac seems to expend most of his energy cultivating an air of mystery. He never allows anyone, including his banker (George Hitchman at the Nova Scotia), to see his financial statements, and he once lost a $5-million lawsuit rather than reveal his net worth. "John is so close-mouthed," says Rudolph Bratty, "that he invariably answers questions with questions. If you ask him, 'How many houses did you sell last week, John?' he'll reply, 'How many *houses* did I sell last week?' and leave it at that."

Prusac eventually became the largest private real estate entrepreneur in Canada. He took over the powerful Y & R Properties (with the aid of German capital brought in through Dr. Hans Abromeit of the Lehndorff group of companies), Deltan Corporation, Imperial General Properties, and the Shalimar Hotel in Freeport in the Bahamas. But his main boast is that he sipped tea most Sunday afternoons with the great Bud McDougald.

Prusac had made a deal with the Argus president in the autumn of 1969 when McDougald decided to sell off part of his estate on Leslie Street in the northern reaches of Metro Toronto. It was not an ordinary $10-million land transaction. Keeping seventeen acres for himself, the fussy Bud insisted that the purchaser leave a buffer zone between the two properties, that a ridge planted with scotch pines be constructed so McDougald wouldn't have to look at ordinary backyards—which, by his edict (even though he couldn't see them), could contain no swimming pools, and the houses built there would all have wood-shingle roofs. Prusac agreed to all the conditions, paid $2 million cash, and McDougald took back a $7.9 million mortgage. The two men became friends. "John just worshipped Bud," recalls his brother-in-law. "He used to say that Mr. McDougald had taught him everything he knew. Since he was worth at least $30 million before he met Bud, that wasn't *quite* true. But he would go up there on Sundays, when help was off, and the two of them would slip out for a sandwich and tea."

McDougald never went so far as to entertain Prusac at the Toronto

Club or allow anyone outside his family to see them together, but his widow recalls Bud's suggesting: "John, why won't you get yourself a proper house and staff, join some clubs, and let people know who you are, instead of being the mystery man around here?"

Prusac later developed properties formerly owned by E.P. Taylor and the Phillips estate, becoming mesmerized by the mystique of his Argus association, marginal though it was. At some point in his friendship with Bud, the Yugoslav developer began to have a vision of himself as the inheritor of the McDougald mantle. In the spring of 1978, when McDougald was dying in Palm Beach, Prusac began to liquidate his holdings so that he would have the necessary cash to buy out his mentor's company. He sold control in Y & R to Donald Love, the Edmonton entrepreneur, for $27 million in one marathon nine-hour bargaining session.* He sold one of his development firms, Imperial General Properties, to Abacus Cities Ltd. in Calgary for $18.7 million and flipped most of his condominiums for $18 million through another Toronto developer, Karsten von Wersebe, to Bob Lee of Vancouver. Within a very few weeks he was sitting with $93 million in cash, ready to outbid all comers for a run at Argus.

Shirley Gail Hishon

MARUJA TRINIDAD JACKMAN, wife of Argus partner Hal, once quipped that Conrad Black was remarkable for only two reasons: his *inocente* flare of freckles and the fact that he had the good sense to marry Shirley. The wedding, which took place at the climax of the Argus fuss, created such a great stir because, snazzy lady though she is, Shirley hardly fitted the dynastic destiny the mavens of Rosedale had pre-ordained for the youthful Black.

They had regarded him as the catch of the decade. They pushed their coltish daughters at him, racehorse good looks at the ready to serve his cause, their emotional lives as spotless and ordered as their orthodontia

---

*Prusac had been having a running argument with Ken Rotenberg, president of Y & R, particularly on the issue of trying to establish a pension plan for company executives. Rotenberg had bought a book on how to go about it. Prusac not only vetoed the plan but was greatly annoyed about the money spent on the book. He also objected to purchase of elastic bands for the office at fifty cents a box, insisting that in future Rotenberg order the thirty-seven-cent kind.

and their Birks silver. But Black would have none of it. He wanted a marriage, not a merger. "There was a certain parallel between my romantic career and Duplessis's," he once told a friend. "There were a good number of one-night stands and a few liaisons that had a certain quality of seriousness to them, but until Shirley, none with matrimonial intent." He had met Shirley Walters (then about to be divorced from her first husband) while she was treasurer and corporate secretary to the Blacks' private companies at Draper Dobie. A lively and clear-eyed woman with an aura of quiet pride, she has a smile that twinkles as welcomingly as harbour lights after a foggy passage. A grandniece of Robert Stanley Weir, the Montreal judge who wrote the standard English words to "O Canada," and the daughter of a Montreal bank accountant, she has never accepted the artificial values of Toronto society, gently dismissing its most prominent pretenders as "a bunch of humpty-hooeys."

The marriage took place at Toronto's Grace Church on-the-Hill in the late afternoon of July 14, with Monte Black and Leigh Beauchamp of Ottawa as witnesses. No one gave the bride away.

The reception, catered by Winston's (where the couple had spent many a dinner courting), was a joyous evening. Peter White and Monte toasted the bride with Dom Perignon; Conrad replied with a rare show of understatement.

It was something of a tribute to their love that the couple could formalize the romance during the most frantic days of the Argus *coup d'état*. The experience brought them closer together in what has continued as one of the Canadian Establishment's happiest marriages.

Dixon Samuel Chant

A DEFERENTIALLY FRIENDLY CHARTERED ACCOUNTANT, Dixon Chant is one of those unobtrusive dependables who move through life betraying signs of wear rather than age. He has a slightly hurt look about him, as though he were suffering from an undetermined war wound. The stiff impression he creates is more than anything else the result of the precise geometry of his speech patterns: he talks as if he were reciting a clandestine bill of particulars. A man with a sure instinct for keeping his psychological alibis polished, he has moved through Canada's business community with few contrails to mark his considerable influence.

Chant, a son of an executive of Toronto's Shaw Business Schools, got his early training at Clarkson Gordon, then joined Duplate Canada Ltd. as treasurer and personal financial consultant for Col. Eric Phillips, an Argus founding partner. "I got to know Bud McDougald," Chant says, "because he was the Colonel's brother-in-law, and we held quite a few Duplate meetings at Oriole, the Phillips farm up on Sheppard Avenue." Chant quickly became the Colonel's chief confidant, was named president of Grew Corporation, one of Canada's best small-boat manufacturers, and in 1965 succeeded Phillips as the head of Duplate.

Following Phillips's death in December 1964, McDougald and Chant, along with the Colonel's widow, Doris, became the estate's executors, sold off the boat company, and channelled the stock portfolio (including his Argus holdings) into what became W.E.P. Investments Ltd.* During the next fourteen years, Chant managed the Phillips fortune, running up its value from $7 million to $35 million. His zeal and dedication were such that the only outside activity he allowed himself was one term as president of the Granite Club, and his only private holding was ownership of the miniature train that takes visitors on tours of Upper Canada Village near Morrisburg, Ontario.

Chant was treated as something of a hired gun by both Phillips and McDougald. Elected to the Argus board in June 1974 as a representative of the Phillips estate, he was approached by McDougald in August 1977 to become one of the holding company's full-time vice-presidents. Just recovering from a heart attack, Chant delayed his reply for another six months, by which time the Argus chairman was dying in Florida, so that nothing was finally settled.

Yet, in the dramatic events that followed, Chant was a key if secret player, performing some of the crucial spadework in the takeover's most bizarre turning points. The widows later blamed him as much as the Black boys for their downfall. Chant, who was named Argus's

*As well as the Colonel's widow, the Phillips family consisted of his three children by a first marriage: Derek, who works for Duplate and whose talented wife, Nancy, has a full-scale merry-go-round in her Toronto garden; Diana, who married Phil Jackson, the head of a construction company; and Michael, who is a prospector. From Doris's first marriage there are Timothy Phillips, an artist who has studied under Augustus John and Salvador Dali, and Cecil, whose first husband was Walter Pady, who now runs the Grew boatworks and is chairman of the jumping section of the Canadian Equestrian Team. She later married T. Scott Fennell, the M.P. for Ontario riding and parliamentary assistant to the Secretary of State in the short-lived administration of Joe Clark. Fennell, who may well be the most capable (and most underrated) of the Argus drama's supporting cast, now runs the Phillips portfolio.

executive vice-president by Conrad, blossomed in the partnership. It accorded him the chance, for the first time in his life, to be taken as seriously as he deserves. "It has been a marvellous opportunity," he says, "but I didn't buy it. Anybody who suggests that the position I hold was the result of anything I did for the Blacks is a goddamned liar. If Conrad is not happy with my efforts tomorrow, I'll leave. That's our understanding."

Colonel Maxwell Charles Gordon Meighen, OBE

THE BIG LOSER IN THE ARGUS SWEEPSTAKES, Max Meighen has about him the vaguely ecclesiastical air of a superannuated Archbishop of Rupert's Land, frozen in his quest. Deep into his seventies, he seems perpetually in mourning for himself and his times.

"Eddie Taylor always had a PR guy," he contends with great seriousness as he declaims on his favourite subject, the perfidies of the press. "When anybody is in the news all the time, you know damn well he's paying for it. Because the press people are lazy. If they're provided with copy, they'll use it. You don't see Jacqueline Kennedy in the press any more, do you? Because the Kennedy family stopped paying her PR agent, that's why!"

He is an upright gentleman in touch with all the arcane virtues of the initiated. "From the tribal states on, young men were only too anxious to offer their lives for the sake of the tribe," he pronounces. "That has not died out, but young men now don't have that opportunity. They're frustrated, and that's why they're raising hell all the time."

He genuinely believes that government functions should be limited to defence, the court system, and tariffs, admits he has lost his faith in democracy, and expects all Western nations to become dictatorships. (His opposition to Ottawa is not limited to its jurisdictions. He refuses to sanction the national capital with his presence and, except for one brief trip in 1952 on a tax appeal, has never visited the place.) He is a supercautious investor, even staying away from bonds and insurance, and is precise about every aspect of his life, whether it's his weight ("I was 160 pounds at Royal Military College in the spring of 1926, and by the middle of the war I was down to 135") or his holiday schedule ("I go to my villa in Jamaica for three and a half weeks in winter and twelve days in summer"). He goes to bed at precisely the same time every evening in his meticulously maintained Rosedale mansion and very seldom entertains.

The source of Meighen's behaviour patterns is not hard to divine. A metallurgist by training and a soldier by inclination, he was conscripted by his father—Arthur Meighen, Canada's eleventh prime minister—to go into business. "My father used to tell everybody I was the Second Coming and treated me like a four-year-old moron. You get the picture? I walked out of his office four times, intending never to go back, but my wife said, 'You made your decision, stick to it.'" The elder Meighen had temporarily left politics in 1927 to establish a series of portfolios, including Canadian General Investments and the Third Canadian General Investment Trust, which have prospered under his son's direction. (Net assets at the end of 1981 were $225,198,000.)

Ironically, Meighen first got into Argus because he had been such a close friend of the Black family, having worked for Conrad's maternal grandfather and often visited the Rileys at their cottage on Lake of the Woods. It was during a holiday at Favouring Winds, the Meighen villa in Jamaica, that Conrad's mother began to feel the first cancer pains.

The Colonel had often discussed Conrad's future with his friend Bud McDougald, who'd warned him, "We have to bring him along exceedingly slowly. He's too precipitate. We have to educate him." That was precisely what Meighen set out to do when he installed himself as McDougald's successor.

In the tumble of events that followed, Meighen was humiliated by Black's nerve and tactics, leaving a residue of bitterness. "I wouldn't do business with Con Black ever again. Never. Wouldn't think of it. And a good many other people feel the same way. Argus can never come back to what it was. It's gone. It has lost its integrity—and dignity."

Meighen's companies ended up by selling their Argus investment for about $30.4 million.* What really set him on his ear was that for once in his life he was quite clearly bested. During his brief tenure as head of the company, Meighen had told a friend he would rather be Chairman of Argus than Prime Minister of Canada.

Writing about Arthur Meighen, the late Ralph Allen commented: "When he left Rideau Hall on July 10, 1920, Arthur Meighen had just been sworn in as the youngest Prime Minister since Confederation.... He had everything he needed to succeed—except a chance to succeed.

---

*The original Ravelston investment was sold for $11,760,000 in 1978. The holding of 850,000 Class C Argus shares was purchased by Black from Meighen in 1981 at $12 a share for $10,200,000. In addition to these favourable transactions was the 1979 sale of the Hollinger shares Meighen's companies had received as a Class C Argus dividend, bringing in a further $8,475,000.

His prospects as prime minister were already hopeless before he became prime minister."

Like his father, the good colonel never realized that much of politics (and business) is a process of elimination, and that he was in the process of being eliminated.

Alex Ethelred Barron

THE BARRON NAME IS ALWAYS LINKED with that of Colonel Meighen in the Argus chronicles, almost as if they were a single corporate entity. This is unfair, because Alex Barron is a very much more enlightened individual, aware of contemporary realities. A compact and attractive man with a slightly patronizing air, he tries hard to please —so hard that he's never really able to claim his own space. His voice struggles for passion, so that no matter how serious or thoughtful he may be, his words come out sounding as pat as a weather forecast or grace at a Rotary Club luncheon.

He is careful, allowing his ideas to marinate rather than expand, and tends to approach the powerful proprietors he's been appeasing most of his life with extreme circumspection, measuring the thinness of the ice before each cautious step. Unlike most of the actors in the Argus drama, Barron has never enjoyed the privilege of being an owner. "If you inherit $10 million or so at twenty-five, you've got a hell of a head start," he pointedly comments, mentioning Conrad Black's circumstances but not his name. "If you don't end up with $100 million at sixty-five, you've been stupid. It's as simple as that. The first million is the tough one."

Barron should know. The son of a dentist in Paris, Ontario, Alex headed for Toronto's financial district at seventeen to job-hunt in 1935, and it took more than twenty interviews before he landed an office boy's slot at Thomson & McKinnon, a firm of stockbrokers. Three years later he joined another Bay Street investment house, Fry & Company, gradually rising to its presidency, as well as the chairmanship of Canadian Tire, one of the companies Fry had helped finance. In 1954 he first attracted Meighen's attention, and the Colonel eventually turned over operating direction of his investment portfolio to him, which led to Barron's appointment to several key Argus boards. Barron was not on the best of terms with McDougald. "Bud was very suspicious," says Black, "because he correctly recognized in Alex a threat to his sleepy little hegemony. Barron was right in having doubts whether the king had enough clothes. He was trying to stir up Monty Prichard, Hal Jackman, myself, and whomever else he could find with a warm body that had a few twitches left in it to see if we couldn't move Bud off dead centre. Alex is very intelligent and very insightful, but in the last analysis, we were just not compatible."

This absence of compatibility was due mostly to the age difference of the two men. "In their meetings, Conrad would walk away with a thirty-four-year-old's version of what had been said, and Alex would leave with a sixty-year-old's interpretation," says Peter Harris, then chairman of A.E. Ames & Company, who was close to the action. "That doesn't mean either was right or wrong, but there was a real generational thing going on, particularly because Conrad appeared to be so young and impulsive in the older company where he found himself."

Barron doesn't disagree. "Conrad's age and my age are quite different," he says. "There's a great difference as to whether one should incur large personal obligations, for example. He was obviously thinking of a thirty-year period of being with Argus, so he could afford to take longer risks.... Given that time, he might do all kinds of wonderful things and restore Argus's mystique and power, but when you're associated with something for many years and have had a very happy and pleasant relationship, you don't like to have the curtain drawn in thirty seconds. That's basically what happened to Colonel Meighen and me. All of a sudden, we discovered we didn't have a happy partnership—and that was an embarrassing situation."

Nelson Morgan Davis

IT WAS ENTIRELY APPROPRIATE that when Nelson Davis drowned on March 13, 1979, he was in Phoenix, planning a new "shack" as his third winter abode in the Arizona sunbelt. He found great contentment among his American peers, especially with the many friends he had made at the Scottsdale Paradise Valley Country Club, where the centurions of the American Midwest meet to fondle ("straight up") tumblers of Cutty Sark, compare golf scores, rail against "those buck-happy bastards in Washington," and point out the bungalow near the summit of Camelback Mountain where President John F. Kennedy is supposed to have spent a weekend with Angie Dickinson.

In his later years, Davis revelled in driving visitors in one of his six air-conditioned Cadillacs through Arizona's iridescent landscape, the horizon alive with the roaring of executive jets landing at the Phoenix Sky Harbor airport, the desert air fresh with the scent of jasmine. He would guide his car with Episcopalian grace between double rows of palm trees—their spiked heads swaying to the same wind that danced the odd tumbleweed across the wide boulevards—and end up at the private garage of his friend Tom Barrett III. There he and his guests would clamber through half a dozen antique cars, including Rudolph Valentino's 1927 Isotta Fraschini and Joseph Goebbels's original Maybach-Zeppelin roadster. His own rambling, six-bedroom villa of pink stucco walls and tile roofing had originally been built by Tommy Manville, the asbestos heir, who had lived there briefly with his eleventh wife. It was sold to Davis by Clare Boothe Luce in 1968. "Nels," as he was called by close friends, also owned a property at Sedona, a hundred-odd miles north of Phoenix. Late in 1978, needing a respite from the Argus wars, he started to get restless. At the turn of the year, he had acquired another house just off the fourth hole of the Paradise Valley golf course and on the morning of his death had been arranging the transplanting of a dozen large palm trees to his new domain. His physician had examined Davis on January 29, 1979, pronouncing him extraordinarily fit, the reward for a long life spent shunning alcohol, tobacco, and excess in all its forms. But nothing could save him when his forehead hit the ledge of his pool while he was taking an afternoon dip on March 13. He lost consciousness and sank to the bottom, his lungs filled with water. The gardener's punctured eardrums prevented him from attempting a rescue, and by the time Davis's wife, Eloise, could get there, it was too late.

At the time of his death, Davis had been chairman of Argus for eight months, having been elevated to that position as the result of his unexpectedly vigorous support of Conrad Black as Bud McDougald's natural heir. This was an extraordinary turn of events, because his leadership within the Black coalition was a decisive factor in the struggle's eventual outcome. It was the first time in a long and fascinating career that Davis had opened his actions to the glare of front-page publicity. His passion for anonymity knew few bounds. He didn't even publish his mailing address in *Canadian Who's Who*, and his chief private residence had five unlisted phone numbers.

Davis had built a conglomerate of fifty middle-sized manufacturing, marketing, and financing companies with annual sales of $200 million.* As their sole owner, he found himself the happy recipient of at least $4 million a year in net, after-tax profits. His problem was trying to find

*For a biography of Nelson Davis, see Chapter IX, *The Canadian Establishment*, Vol. I, Toronto, McClelland and Stewart, 1975.

ways of spending the cash fast enough before another $4 million came flowing into his private coffers. This was no easy task, but he did his valiant best. He built a private eighteen-hole golf course, owned five houses, employed a full-time staff of eighteen, and fussed over a collection of twenty antique powerboats. Despite such riches and the considerable if not widely known power he exerted within the Canadian Establishment during the final two decades of his life, it was his role as chief *agent provocateur* during the Argus crisis that would be his epitaph.

Certainly Jim McDougald, who still feels that her good friend Nels (or the Brig, as she liked to call him) had turned treacherous in urging her to sign any agreement with the Blacks —certainly *she* knew how to exact the appropriate retribution. "I've always wanted a Lincoln Continental," she told a friend not long after the Argus transfer, "but the Brig had a General Motors dealership, so we had to keep buying Cadillacs. Whenever I mentioned my Continental, Bud would say, 'No, we can't do that to the Brig. It's the principle of the thing; you don't do that to your friends.' Little did he know... Now I've *got* my Lincoln, and I'll never buy a Cadillac again."

Reuben Cohen

A GENTLE SLUMP OF A MAN with that special quality of taking people at face value that distinguishes Maritimers from their more cynical Upper Canadian cousins, Reuben Cohen was the financial victim of some mighty smooth hokey-pokey. Not involved directly in the Argus adventure, he made an attempt to gain control of Crown Trust that became a pivotal sub-plot, adroitly exploited first by McDougald and then by Black for their own hardly altruistic purposes.

Crown had started its corporate life as the Trusts and Guarantee Company in 1897 with assets under administration of only $165,000. Though it absorbed three other small trust companies, one of them called Crown Trust Company (whose name it took in 1946), it never became a major financial force. But when John McMartin, one of the original Hollinger partners, died on April 12, 1918, it took over administration of his $4.7 million estate; at about the same time the McMartin estate acquired a quarter of Crown's shares. Bud McDougald's father, Duncan, had been an executor of McMartin, who had married Duncan's sister Mary, and it was this connection that moved Crown Trust within the Argus orbit. By 1975 (with the original McMartin grubstake run up to $14.3 million), Crown shared half a dozen of its directors with Argus-associated companies, though McDougald himself had to be satisfied with being chief of the firm's Toronto advisory board because federal legislation barred bank directors from sitting on trust boards. Crown was not a large operation, but its assets under administration of $1.337 billion included the estates of Eric Phillips and later Bud McDougald. It also controlled the holdings of the surviving heirs of John McMartin, who owned 8 per cent of the outstanding Hollinger shares.

In 1975, Cohen and his partner, Leonard Ellen, a Montreal investment dealer, purchased a 25-per-cent interest in Crown on the open market, hoping to use it as a base to expand their trust operations to central Canada. A lawyer from Moncton, N.B., Cohen graduated with honours from the Dalhousie Law School, bought out Central Trust in his home town and merged it with Nova Scotia Trust Company and later Eastern Canada Savings & Loan Company of Halifax to form the region's most influential group of financial companies. He made a series of pilgrimages to central Canada and eventually met McDougald.

Cohen, whose main conversational gambit is to put himself down ("I'm a very dull fellow – I don't ride horses, I don't curl. I'm awfully drab"), had never been so impressed. "Mr. McDougald," he maintains, "was an exceptional human being in every sense of the word. He would take me to the Toronto Club, introduce me to all his friends, and never at any time attempt to hide me under the bush. A thorough and complete gentleman. There aren't too many successors in office who can match him." Cohen's wife, an extraordinarily dynamic lady from Cape Breton named Louise, became so captivated by the Argus chairman that she fashioned a copy of a *Maclean's* cover picture of McDougald on enamelled copper and presented it to him.

What Cohen didn't realize was that McDougald had been deliberately forestalling his takeover of Crown by getting the Commerce to buy 74,900 of its shares over a period of time. The trust company was not controlled directly by McDougald (who owned less than 10 per cent) – but by voting the McMartin shares (24.8 per cent), having the co-operation of the bank in its holding of 9.9 per cent, and controlling Crown's board of directors, he ran it as a minor but significant adjunct to his empire.

Cohen believed that if McDougald had lived another twelve months, he would have altered the ground rules and allowed the Maritimer to capture Crown. But the Argus chairman died before any of this could happen. Suddenly the trust company, holding in its grasp the estates of

McDougald, Phillips, and the John McMartin heirs, became a prime target for all the contenders in the Argus sweepstakes.

The Smith Sisters

THE LIVES AND LOVES of Doris, Cecil, and Hedley Maude (known as Jim) Smith could fill hope-chests full of Gothic novels. In Toronto society circles, they were snidely nicknamed "Bud McDougald's three wives" —a trio of proud outriders in the Argus homestead, saluting the distance they had travelled since their girlhood beginnings.

In some ways, they were woefully unprepared for the responsibilities they incurred. "The tragedy of it is that they were never given any training—no business training, no background in anything to do with this," says Scott Fennell, Doris's son-in-law. "When the Colonel died, Bud took over and ran everything for Doris, and she never knew what was going on. She said one day, in jest, 'The only filing I ever do is on my nails.' When their lawyer, Bill Somerville, asked Doris where she kept her files, she quipped, 'Oh, tucked in among my hankies.'"

Their father, Eustace Smith, had attended Royal Military Academy, Woolwich, and on the weekend before he was due to be shipped out from England for service in India, went hunting in Scotland. "His best friend shot him in the face," Jim blithely recounts. "Thought he was a pheasant. A complete accident. In those days, Edinburgh was the big medical centre, so his mother got a doctor to come down and look at Daddy. They thought he was going blind. There were no passenger trains due so the doctor stood on the front of the engine for the thirty-five-mile trip, and took as much shot as he could out of Daddy's face and eyes. The way they cured it was to put him in a dark room for a year. Never saw a bit of light. Daddy was very musical. They put a piano in the room, got him a violin, and hired a tutor to come out from Edinburgh twice a week to give him lessons in the dark. He played well enough and later gave a concert in Albert Hall."

Allowed out at the end of his convalescence, Smith could see again, but his hope of an army career was shattered. He joined Coutts Marjoribanks, third son of Lord Tweedmouth and brother of the Countess of Aberdeen, in running a ranch that the Aberdeens had bought in the Okanagan. Marjoribanks's father, whose family were partners in the old banking house of Coutts & Company, was a major holder of Hudson's Bay Company stock and a landowner with big tracts in Inverness-shire and Berwickshire. Coutts had tried his hand at raising Aberdeen Angus cattle in North Dakota without much success, and his sister wanted him back within the confines of Empire. She struck upon the B.C. property, named it Guisachan after a Marjoribanks family place in the Highlands, and in 1890 the two bachelors, Coutts and Eustace, set about turning the dry land — now part of Kelowna — into a fruit farm.

The Guisachan didn't prosper, and the first planting of fruit trees was ripped out after a few years. In the meantime Lord Aberdeen had gone ahead with the purchase of a much larger Okanagan property, the 13,000-acre Coldstream Ranch, and established a jam factory in nearby Vernon. He had also become Governor General of Canada and moved into Rideau Hall in 1893. Coutts Marjoribanks had married in 1895, and had a fair crew of hands to handle the Guisachan and the Coldstream. Smith headed for the East and landed on a dairy farm near Aurora, north of Toronto. It was during a viceregal visit to the Grange, the Toronto home of the author and Canadian nationalist Goldwin Smith, at which he was present that he met Maude Delano Osborne. The Osbornes had emigrated from England to Sutton, near Lake Simcoe, where young Maude learned tennis well enough to win five Canadian national championships. "They saw each other only nine times, and then they got married," says Jim. "They celebrated their fifty-fifth wedding anniversary, and I don't remember hearing Daddy say one cross word to Mummy ever in his life."

The Smiths later moved to Toronto, where he became superintendent of dining and sleeping-car services for the Canadian Northern. The family had little money, "but we always had candles on the table, even when we didn't have that much food," Doris remembered. While they lived largely on a diet of macaroni — and to this day don't like eating meat — the sisters enjoyed active social lives, encouraged by a mother anxious that they marry well. Doris drove an ambulance in the First World War and rode in the inaugural Royal Agricultural Winter Fair; the other two sisters became figure-skating champions, competing as Canada's representatives at the 1928 Olympics and giving exhibitions in half a dozen European capitals. (Cecil was 1925-26 Canadian Women's Champion and skated against Sonja Henie at two Olympics.*)

Jim met the young John A. McDougald while skating at the Granite

---

*Sonja Henie, who died in 1969 at fifty-six, amassed a fortune after she turned professional and toured in ice shows. She was married three times. Her husbands were Dan Topping, heir to a U.S. tin-plate fortune and later owner of baseball's New York Yankees; Winthrop Gardiner, Jr., scion of an old American family; and Niels Onstad, an Oslo shipowner. She held the world skating championship from 1927 to 1936 and won the Olympic title in 1928, 1932, and 1936. Cecil Smith was sixth in the 1924 Olympics and fifth in 1928.

Club. "Bud used to come on Sunday mornings on his way from church. He looked simply frightful, with morning coat, striped trousers, a yellow polo-neck sweater and derby hat," she said. "He must have been twenty at the time and had never taken a girl out in his life. He spoke to me because he knew I had met his sister. I was walking out with Eddie Mulqueen at the time, so for about a year we went out as a threesome before Bud invited me on his own. We were married two years later."

Doris was married to Col. Adair Gibson (who killed himself by jumping off a train) and later to Col. Eric Phillips, the Argus partner. A great beauty (she was painted by both Salvador Dali and Pietro Annigoni), she was also a bit of a scatterbrain. "One time," Jim reminisces, "all these big shots came from Oxford—professors and their wives. Eric was, as Doris used to say, mixed up in the university in those days. [He was chairman of the board of governors at the University of Toronto.] He had to entertain all these people, and she was left with the wives. Eric asked her to show them the university buildings. Doris got them all in the car and went down University Avenue. They drove around and around and she couldn't *find* the campus. She came home, and when they were all at dinner, he said to the ladies, 'Did you see the university?'

"They said, 'We didn't see too much of it, no.'

"He turned to Doris. 'Didn't you show it to them, Doris?'

"'I couldn't find it,' Doris replied. 'Why don't you have some gates? There's no entrance to it.'

"Some months later, Doris had the mail at breakfast one morning, and she picked up this bill from her alumnae association. She threw it over to Eric and said, 'You pay this—it's your university.'

"'Why would you get that?' he asked.

"'I belong to the alumnae.'

"'How ridiculous. You didn't even go to the university.'

"'Of course I went to the University of Toronto. I went for two years, and then I gave it up.'

"'I don't believe it. I'll find out from the registrar.'

"So on his way down to the office that morning he went in to see the president, Sidney Smith, who called and confirmed that she had gone for two years.

"When Eric came home, he said, 'Why didn't you tell me?'

"'I didn't think you'd be interested.'

"'Of course I am. But I want you to promise you'll never tell anybody you went to the University of Toronto.'"

Cecil, the youngest sister, married Ted Gooderham, a member of the distilling family, who worked for his father's brokerage house. He became an alcoholic, and the marriage broke up. Cecil moved away to become head pro at the Buffalo Skating Club. There she met and later married its president, Eric Hedstrom, but he succumbed to the identical malady of her first husband. "He was drinking an awful lot when she married him," says Jim, "and they had a beautiful place in East Aurora, outside Buffalo, one of the prettiest houses I've ever seen in my life. The people who'd had it before brought every stone from England, even the roof.

"The final touch was when Eric started swearing at her, and her young son, Teddy, came out of his room—this was about ten o'clock at night—and said, 'You can't talk to my mother like that,' and hit his stepfather. Cecil said she nearly died because they were at the top of a circular stone staircase. Eric was quite an athlete, actually, playing polo and good golf. So he hit Teddy and knocked him out. Cecil grabbed Teddy and got out of the house. Eric emerged with a gun and scared the life out of them both. Teddy would have been only about fourteen. There's a little police station east of Aurora, and they went in and the man said, 'Sure we'll help you. Get him out into the road and we'll arrest him if he does anything. But we can't go into the house after him; that's his own private property, he can do what he wants.' So she telephoned us, and we told her to come home, that we could take care of it." Cecil eventually moved back with her son, Ted, and settled into Doris's gatehouse. She later became one of Toronto's most successful real estate sales agents, a field in which she met and grew to admire John Prusac.

Doris died in 1980, but Jim continues to run her horses. Her racing colours are seen at Saratoga, and she maintains Bud's magnificent Kingsclere training establishment in England, where she recently completed a tiled swimming pool for the horses. Her hackneys have twice been world champions. She has six servants who travel with her and all the luxury money can buy (her fortune has been estimated at $60 million), but she misses her Bud and still wonders what really happened after he died—and why young Conrad, who had come to her house for a glass of milk when he was a little boy, pushed her out of Argus.

"The problem," says Al Thornbrough, a long-time McDougald friend, "was that Bud didn't appreciate how quickly things can change when one's presence is not around. That lack of understanding put both Jim and Doris in a position that was impossible. They were not equipped to cope. Once you've got a power struggle going on, it becomes self-generating, like a hurricane, and feeds on itself. The debris that can be caused by a power struggle may linger for years. The fallout from the battle for Argus is still floating around."

THIS IS A CHRONOLOGY of the hundred and twenty-five days that shook the Argus world:

March 8: The word is out among Argus insiders—Bud McDougald is dying. At 10 Toronto Street, the directors meet in their chairman's absence and discuss changes in the command structure. Barron and Black chat briefly in a corridor after the meeting, and the two men agree to have dinner (with Monte) on March 16.

In the Crown Trust boardroom, four blocks away on Bay Street, a significant power shift is taking place. Ainslie St. Clair Shuve succeeds Harold Kerrigan in the presidency and Dixon Chant, a director and member of the executive committee, is named vice-president of the board of directors.

March 9: McDougald sneaks away from his sickbed in Palm Beach to phone Evelyn Young, his Argus secretary. After a somewhat disjointed exchange, she hesitantly inquires what she should do "in the event the worst happens." Bud's reply is strong and unequivocal: "Call Crown Trust." It is their last conversation.

March 15: McDougald dies.

March 16: Barron arrives at Conrad Black's house for dinner with the brothers. He finds Conrad reading the 1969 Ravelston Agreement, but his suspicions are not aroused.* They discuss Argus's post-McDougald prospects, sharing the fear that Maj.-Gen. Bruce Matthews will perpetuate the prevailing immobilities. Conrad Black becomes convinced that Barron has agreed to "help nudge Bruce along towards a more activist policy," and that Barron has pledged his support in getting Conrad an Argus vice-presidency and Monte a place on the board of directors. At this point, Barron believes that Matthews, who was McDougald's closest business associate during the last decade of his life, has been

*Ownership of Ravelston, holding company of Argus Corp. put in force in 1969, was split five ways: the McDougald and Phillips estates held 23.6 per cent each; the Meighen interests, 26.5 per cent; the Black brothers, 22.4 per cent; and General Matthews, 3.9 per cent. Under this charter, any Ravelston partner who obtained control of 51 per cent or more of the company's shares could force the sale to himself of the holdings of the others.

named an executor of the chairman's estate, thus guaranteeing that the Argus lines of influence would be virtually undisturbed, and putting Conrad on hold indefinitely.

With the Meighen companies holding the largest proportion of the Ravelston stock and being the only corporate entities—as opposed to mortal individuals—Argus would, through the erosion of time, have eventually fallen to Meighen's heirs.

March 17: Barron reports to Max Meighen on his conversation with the Blacks. "Bud's just died, for heaven's sake," Meighen replies. "Let's leave the whole thing as to who's on first base until the summer months, when we can all sit down together and talk about the future."

March 18: McDougald is buried. Argusologists note that Jim McDougald has chosen General Matthews as her escort at the funeral, strengthening the assumption that he is about to don her late husband's Argus mantle. John Prusac's graveside appearance evokes comment. During the post-funeral reception at the McDougald residence, Matthews and Meighen are conspicuous in their morning coats, displaying their grief in front of Bud's widow. E.P. Taylor has flown in from Nassau to tidy up longstanding residues of ill will—or, as Conrad Black put it, to make sure Bud was dead.

March 20: McDougald's table at the Toronto Club remains unoccupied, a tribute to the institution's departed patron saint. But today there is an unusual buzz among the customarily somnambulant lunchers. Those in the know have become aware that General Matthews, eating at a table in the northwest corner, is *not* an executor of the late Argus chairman's estate. Instead, McDougald has created a posthumous sensation by having named his widow, Jim, his sister-in-law Doris, and Crown Trust to run his affairs.

March 21: "You know," Conrad remarks to Monte in a phone call, referring to the late mayor of Chicago and his power plays, "P.C. Finlay is the Richard J. Daley of this ball game. He's the key to the whole group—the only guy left who knows how Bud's system really worked." Black obtains a list of Hollinger shareholders. It reveals that the mining company, which is Argus's main cash-producing asset, is dangerously exposed to an outside takeover. Apart from Argus's 23-per-cent stake, the largest blocks of shares are the 15 per cent held in the estates of Hollinger heirs managed by Finlay and his son, John, and 8 per cent tucked into Crown Trust. Black pays a visit to P.C. at his law office, and because he knows John better, approaches him to suggest a voting agreement between the Hollinger estates and Argus. "I would guess," John Finlay later comments, "that as a direct result of looking through the shareholders' list, Conrad decided to acquire Crown Trust so that he could get his hands on the Hollinger shares represented there."

March 22: The Argus executive committee meets promptly at 10 a.m. to choose its slate of post-McDougald officers. The order of business is swift and leaves no doubt that the incumbents believe power should reside in their own hands. Meighen assumes the Argus chairmanship, Matthews becomes president, and Barron is nominated executive vice-president. (Matthews will take over the Massey, Dominion Stores, and Standard Broadcasting chairmanships, while Barron will get the chairmanship of Domtar and Massey's executive committee.) Black is late, held up by a traffic jam on the Don Valley Parkway. He arrives at 10:04, tiptoes into the Argus boardroom, and finds a full house. Argus's three principal officers regard him with the impassive look of faces on a pack of cards, bearing the stern expressions of the King of Clubs. When he is informed that all the executive titles have been dealt out, Black protests that while he is happy with those appointments, he thinks there should be something for everybody—to leave the Blacks out would be a deliberate slight against them. He hopes for some title to signify his acceptance within the new grouping. He congratulates the other office-holders, offers tribute to their age and experience, but asks them once more to make some gesture so he needn't endure the embarrassment of comment that he has been left out. "It'll look bad in the press if I'm not named a vice-president," he pleads.

"*We* are naming Bud's successor, not the press," is Meighen's stern reply. The card-faces remain impassive. Again Colonel Meighen speaks. "You're rushing your fences," he says. "Just take a look around. You won't have long to wait."

It is a reasonable reply. With an average age of sixty-six, Meighen, Matthews, and Barron hardly represent a long-term incumbency. Black replies that in the interest of the company he will not rock the boat, but he is not satisfied. Inwardly he is seething.

Up and away from the Argus meeting, Black all but runs to phone Nelson Davis, the McDougald ally who also sits on the Crown Trust and Argus boards and has been taking a fatherly interest in Conrad's activities for years. Speaking in the clipped accents of his Middle-Western upbringing, Davis offers his young protégé this advice: "Bide your time, bite your lip, and these guys will dig their own graves."

March 23: The Argus partners settle into their power slots. Barron orders a fancy new filing cabinet. They all feel satisfied that they have silenced the impatient young Black, assuring one another that he will get his proper due "when the time comes." They don't realize that in Conrad's view, the time has come. "It was an utterly disgraceful performance," Black later insists. "I am not one to take high ground about chicanery in general —that's part of life, and it's even somewhat enjoyable at times. But it should be conducted with a certain elegance, and they didn't have that. Under their arrangement, I couldn't even have an office at Argus; I could only go there and pay court to this triumvirate. It was a declaration of war. I don't know how they could claim to be astounded by what happened after that. It's like the Japanese saying, 'We didn't expect the Americans to sink our carriers at Midway. All we did was bomb Pearl Harbor.'"

April 4: The full Argus board meets to ratify the executive appointments. The agenda is routinely approved, but afterwards in the corridor Bruce Matthews takes Dixon Chant aside to whisper, "You must have been surprised not to be elected a vice-president." Chant admits that this is so, particularly since he has previously been promised a vice-presidency by both McDougald and Matthews. "We couldn't do it," Matthews says. "If we had, we would have had to make Conrad a vice-president too." Chant replies that Black *should* have been made an officer. When Chant asks whether Matthews would consider pledging his Ravelston shares to the ladies, the General says, "No, I should prefer to remain flexible."

Chant's internal alarm goes off. Without knowing the details, he senses that Meighen, using Barron and Matthews as his surrogates, is intent on retaining Argus permanently within his investment group.

That afternoon, Chant phones Doris Phillips and Jim McDougald and explains that to follow their wishes of preserving Argus as a living memorial to Bud, he must approach the Blacks, because only with such a coalition can the group attain majority control. "I still remember them telling me, 'Yes, we're all for that,'" Chant later recalls.

After the phone call, Jim McDougald retires to the parlour of her

Palm Beach mansion and begins writing notes to friends who expressed sympathy at her bereavement. Before her husband died, she had given him a new pocket day-book and had asked his secretary, Evelyn Young, to transfer the addresses from its battered predecessor. Now she needs it and calls Toronto, but Miss Young won't give it up. "I couldn't possibly," she says. "There might be something important come up that I have to do." Mrs. McDougald points out that something important might come up for *her*, too. "Oh yes," is the unyielding reply, "but it couldn't be as important a reason as *I* would have." Miss Young will not relent. Distraught, Jim goes for a walk along Lake Worth. Inconsequential in itself, the conversation gnaws at her. The world without Bud is not a friendly place.

April 5: Black sets into motion what he and his partners grandly refer to as Plan A, which calls for the acquisition of the John McMartin estate's 24.8-per-cent block of Crown Trust—and the subsequent purchase of the heirs' Hollinger holdings. It is the most daring gamble of Black's *coup.* The McMartin heirs' shares of Crown will cost him $6.3 million; the benefits of the move are unpredictable. A big foothold in the trust company may, as he puts it, "give us some input and a certain degree of moral suasion with the ladies, as well as consolidating the partnership with Chant." Most important, he feels that capturing an outpost of the McDougald empire is his bid to be taken seriously. "It's a matter of getting the attention of our elders," he explains.

He makes certain that the two ladies (who by now are referred to by everyone as the widows) are informed that by acquiring Crown, Young Conrad is saving Bud's trust company from "those outsiders" in the Maritimes.

April 6: The Maritimer most concerned with this development is Reuben Cohen, who, along with his partner, Leonard Ellen, has been trying to win control of Crown since 1975. Cohen arrives in Toronto from his Moncton home base to confer with Page Wadsworth, a former chairman of the Commerce. Over lunch at the Ontario Club, which is housed in the Commerce Court buildings, Cohen asks Wadsworth how he could best go about raising his stake in Crown. The retired banker advises him to contact Nelson Davis, who is on the Crown board as a friend and business associate of the late Bud. Cohen phones Davis but is refused an appointment. When the Crown board (including Davis) meets, the directors, who are aware that the company is on the takeover block, cast about for a saviour within the Argus group. Meighen is not eligible because his companies are the largest shareholder in Canada Trust, and the process of merging trust companies is a cumbersome one; the same is true of General Matthews, who is chairman of Canada Permanent. The directors decide to support any move by Black, and Ainslie Shuve makes plans to jet to Europe so he can talk to some of the John McMartin heirs.

April 20: Alex Barron, a widower, plans to marry Beverley Mollet on May 5. He invites Conrad and his fiancée, Shirley Walters, to dinner – appropriately enough at an utterly luxurious Toronto eatery named Napoleon's. The meal is festive, but afterward, as Barron and *his* fiancée drive away, Conrad pauses in the parking lot, turns to Shirley, and remarks, "Do you realize Alex believes that I am absolutely placated by this evening? He has the effrontery to think I'll forget his total double-cross by going out to dinner with him."

April 20 – May 4: The search to find the McMartin heirs and buy their Crown shares enters its final phase. Black is offering them $34 a share – twice the book value and $13 above the then current market quotes. Only two of John McMartin's daughters are still alive, Jean Mulford in New York City and Rita Floyd-Jones of Saranac Lake, N.Y. Jean's daughter Olga is married to a titled Dutchman and lives in a castle in the Netherlands; the widower of another daughter – killed in a 1954 plane crash – lives in France. Shuve tracks them down to obtain their consent as residual beneficiaries of the estate.*

Rita Floyd-Jones, formerly Rita LeMay, who lives in a hotel at the Adirondacks resort, "sat on a throne next to this tumbledown hotel – had delusions about being the Empress of China," Black recalls. She has a son, a partner in a fishing-tackle store called the Blue Line Sports Shop, and a daughter. The McMartin heirs sell out for $6.3 million.

April 21: Jim McDougald sends a note to Conrad Black, thanking him for the sympathy he showed at her husband's death. She remembers that Bud had thought Conrad was the only young man "that will be of

---

*Shuve, at that point a twenty-one-year veteran at Crown, performs beyond the call of duty for Black. But when the company is sold to CanWest in 1979, though Shuve is still Crown's president, he is not even notified in advance, having to read about his new owners in the newspapers. He departs soon afterward.

any account in the Country or Business World" and quotes his words, "'Thank God he has George's integrity,' as so many of the Young have never heard the word."

May 6: Black and Shirley Walters attend the wedding of Robert Beverley "Biff" Matthews and Susan Harty Osler (Conrad's cousin) at Trinity College Chapel. They approach the officiating clergyman, Rev. John Erb (a schoolmate of Biff's), to ask whether he will marry them after Shirley's divorce is official. He agrees and begins the process of obtaining the Anglican bishop's approval for the union.

May 8: Reuben Cohen, who has heard rumours of Black's move on the trust company, sends the Crown board a telegram offering two dollars a share more for the McMartin holdings than any competing bid.

May 12: It is the night of the Hollinger Dinner at the Toronto Club, the Establishment's annual hoedown, held for the first time in several decades without McDougald's august presence. Black has been invited, even though the Argus powers-that-be are firmly within the Meighen circle. Conrad fidgets through the meal, then rushes home and, using his grandmother's antiquated typewriter, pounds out a memorandum to himself, for the first time putting into written form his ambitions at Argus. "C. Black," he notes about himself, "will become Executive Vice-President and Chairman of the Executive Committee of Argus Corporation, it apparently being the consensus of the meeting that Matthews occupies too many chairs and that taking the chairmanship of the Executive Committee is a more certain and less controversial way of assuring the sound functioning of that committee than by packing it. Mr. Davis will join the Executive Committee, and the next two vacancies on that committee will be filled by G.M. Black, who will become a director of Argus Corporation immediately, and Fredrik S. Eaton. If Mr. Davis secures Mrs. McDougald's approval, C. Black will occupy Mr. McDougald's office at 10 Toronto Street....

"Time is an urgent consideration, and upon the above being approved by Mrs. Phillips, Mrs. McDougald, and Messrs. Black, Black, Chant, Davis, Ritchie [William Ritchie, head of Crown Trust's estates department] and Shuve, implementation should commence at once, preferably in the week of May 15-19, 1978. Extensive efforts will be made to avoid any publicity or rumours of a rift. No one is to be humiliated or embarrassed, and the general theme of continuity and the spirit of partnership, whose absence has necessitated the contemplated action, will be strongly emphasized. It is envisioned that Messrs. Davis and G. Black will speak to Matthews, and Messrs. Chant and C. Black will speak to Meighen, both in the most conciliatory way possible in the circumstances. (The latter, especially, promises to be an entertaining exchange.)"

May 15: It is the sixty-first day after Bud McDougald's death. News about the Blacks' purchase of 24.8 per cent of Crown Trust has become public. Shuve phones Reuben Cohen to point out that his offer tendered by telegram was not considered because it contained no firm price.

Bay Street observers sense that events at Argus are in flux, but no one knows precisely what's happening. The scene of action is moving to Palm Beach.

Ever since the Meighen triumvirate has taken over Argus, none of the partners has made contact with the widows. "Jim and Doris would pick up the papers and read about the latest Argus appointments, with no reference having been made to them at all, when in fact they had more stock, combined, than any of the others," noted Doug Ward, who had been Bud's best friend. Jim feels no great hostility to Meighen—but not much friendship either. "Bud used to say," she confides to a friend at the time, "'Max is all right. He always puts his hand up when you want him to go along with you.'"

Meighen, Matthews, and Barron are not particularly active, spending most of their time administering the existing structures and elevating themselves to the chairmanships of various Argus company committees. But Black is well aware that unless he moves fast, his chance to capture Argus will evaporate.

Then an approach is made to him that hands him the opportunity for which he is waiting. The three official representatives of the McDougald and Phillips estates, Dixon Chant, Bill Ritchie, and Lou Guolla (a partner in Daly, Cooper, Guolla & O'Gorman who had looked after Bud's private legal work for thirty years), suggest that the only way to fulfil the widows' wishes of perpetuating the status quo at Argus is for Black to enter into a contract that would grant the ladies a voting majority for the ten-year term of the agreement. The widows' emotional commitment, born equally of their grief and of their ignorance of how business really works, is to keeping Ravelston—and through it, Argus—untouched, somehow manipulating its awkwardly fractured ownership positions in a way that will allow it to function as if Bud were still alive.

Black joyfully agrees. Guolla proposes that a clause (which Black drafts) be inserted in the agreement that will allow only Black to trigger the original Ravelston buyback arrangement, whereby a majority of shareholders can force the minority to sell out. It is worded in such a way that Black is in sole control of when the compulsory transfer notices involved will be issued.*

Another agreement is drawn up the same day, granting Dixon Chant full authority to vote the widows' shares.

Guolla and Ritchie fly down to Palm Beach to get the widows' signatures on the documents in what is meant to be a routine transaction. "We paid for our plane to take Lou down there," Black maintains, "and explain everything to them, absolutely everything – in the most laborious detail, in monosyllables."

The widows did precisely what almost anybody else would have done in the circumstances: they signed where the lawyer pointed.† Only later, when the deal began to fall apart, would Jim McDougald complain: "Like absolute idiots and birdbrains, we signed and signed and signed, without reading at all. The definite impression I had was that Lou was going to fix something to do with Argus that Bud had arranged to have done before he died.... I never thought about controlling Argus. I don't even know the price of a tin of peas – so why would I think of controlling a company?"

An unexpected visitor at Jim's seaside mansion during the signing ceremonies is Al Thornbrough, Massey's chief executive officer, who lives in Boca Raton, just down the coast from Palm Beach. He is fearful for his job because Barron, who has criticized his stewardship in the past, has been named chairman of the farm implement company's executive committee. Thornbrough is a favourite of the widows; he reassures them with his presence and explanations. He flies back with Guolla.

In Toronto, Black is triumphant. No one else is aware of it yet, but he has won. Argus is his. Only the details of the actual Ravelston transfer remain to be negotiated. He telephones Max Meighen's secretary to request an appointment for himself and Dixon Chant the next day.

He then has lunch with John Finlay in the old Draper Dobie dining room (which continues to function as the Black brothers' primary

---

*For the full text of the voting agreement, see Appendix B.

†As a result of this meeting, Jim took the McDougald family business away from Guolla and later hired Bill Somerville. To compensate him for the loss, Conrad retained Guolla to draft the Black family wills.

downtown roost) and briefs him on the widows' agreement. It is at this luncheon that Black and Finlay reach the concept of a "put" arrangement that gives Black first refusal on the stock held by the Hollinger heirs represented by Finlay and his father.

May 16: Crunch Day. Black and Chant walk into Meighen's office to serve the compulsory transfer notice that will strip the Colonel of his place and power at Argus. For once, Conrad is nervous. There is simian menace in his posture as he whips out the document, hands it over, and explains its contents. Meighen blanches but says nothing. The room grows chilly and silent. Even the street noises are unaccountably subdued, as if Bay Street were holding its breath. The muscles of Meighen's mouth tighten in querulous disdain for this young pup.

Black stands there.

He starts rattling on about how Argus needs to be run by resident proprietors, how he doesn't *really* expect Meighen to sell all his Ravelston shares, how he has not been treated as promised, how he hopes this episode can be amicably settled.

Nothing.

In desperation, Black notices a painting of Taddy Meighen, the Colonel's wife, holding a poodle. Black moves to the next painting, which shows Meighen's father (the prime minister), to another of Alex Barron, and one of Louise Morgan. He asks who the lady might be, and Meighen brings Mrs. Morgan, a director of his companies, into the office. They shake hands and keep talking about dogs.

As Black and Chant leave, Conrad quickens his step and says, "Let's get out of here before he realizes what we've said."

"No," Chant replies. "My impression of Max has gone way up—there's no question he knew what we said."

At about the same time, Monte Black and Nelson Davis are calling on Bruce Matthews to brief him on the fact that his boss is about to be bounced. When Conrad phones Monte to ask how the meeting went, his brother replies, "The General is panting like a carthorse."

May 17: Barron, who has been away on his honeymoon, arrives home and is briefed by Meighen on the enormity of the previous day's events. It is the greatest surprise of Barron's life. "I'm sort of used to the Marquis of Queensberry rules," he laments to a friend later that evening. To his diary he confides: "9 P.M., phone Con Black at his home. Long chat, low voices, no bitterness. I express my shock at the news, as I felt we were partners and friends with common objectives...." As a protective counter-measure, Barron resolves to try to interest either Paul Desmarais or Hal Jackman in an anti-Black coalition.

May 27: A tea party for the widows and their sister, Cecil, at Black's house. Nelson Davis is in attendance. They ponder Max Meighen's ouster and discuss the pros and cons of back-tracking a bit and keeping the good Colonel within the Argus stable by urging him to maintain some of his stock and titles. Ever afterwards the sisters described it as the Mad Tea Party.

The singsong that follows, tolled off in perfect cadence with appropriate pauses, is reminiscent of a row of citizen judges pronouncing their verdicts on Meighen's acceptability.

"He has egg stains on his ties," says Doris Phillips.

There is a pause.

"He wore yellow socks to our house in Florida," says Jim McDougald.

The indictment hangs heavy in the air.

"He has thin lapels," says Cecil Hedstrom.

The room is shocked.

"He drives a gold Mercedes," says Nelson Davis.

Can this be true?

"He becomes boisterous after a couple of drinks," chimes in Conrad Black.

Doris Phillips, looking unusually grim, passes sentence. "Well, then," she says, "we can dispense with *him.*"

The party breaks up. Everybody seems pleased. Next morning, Doris Phillips sends Conrad a wooden statue of Napoleon with a note that thanks him for "the helpful time we spent with you. It is a comfort to feel that the companies will carry on. I was afraid they might disappear.... Bud...told me how interested you were in Napoleon and...Eric was a keen student of Napoleonic history—and I know he would be very happy for you to have [this figure] in your collection." Jim McDougald also writes of her gratitude to Conrad and Nelson in helping "to bring Doris and me up to date as to what is going on with my darling Bud's Companies.... We were so happy to hear all the good news you had to tell us, what you and Monty had done to help us."

June 12: Maclean's publishes a cover story on Conrad Black by Rod McQueen in which he outlines the anatomy of his Argus takeover. John Prusac, the real estate developer who was such a fervent admirer of the late Bud and is a friend of Cecil Hedstrom, comes to visit Jim McDougald. He tells her that he has read the magazine, that "the whole thing is wrong," that by signing those papers, she and Doris allowed Conrad to take Argus away from them. "He asked me for permission to work on it," Mrs. McDougald recalls. "I said, 'Sure, if you really think it's wrong.' By then, I had started believing him instead of Con."

A strategy is evolved whereby the widows (who together hold 47.2 per cent of Ravelston) will attempt to negotiate a pact with Bruce Matthews and his 3.9-per-cent slice—giving them a decisive 51.1 per cent of Ravelston's control over Argus.

June 13: Bruce Matthews is in the United Kingdom on Standard Broadcasting business when he gets a frantic call from the widows. They are distressed beyond belief. They are unhappy with Conrad; they misunderstood what they had done and want to unravel the Ravelston contract they signed. Matthews is sympathetic. When they ask the General to pledge his shares to them, he agrees, but warns that the situation is a difficult one.

"John Prusac was acting as their intermediary," Matthews remembers. "They actually gave him their proxies and said they wanted to start all over again. They were very determined, very wrought up, very emotionally disturbed. I told them that in keeping with the arrangement I had with Bud, I would give them my shares to vote as they wished."

No one mentions it, but what really seems to be taking place is an attempt to reapportion the Argus ownership so that out of the whole mess John Prusac—not Conrad Black—might emerge as the new dominant influence. Black has heard reports on the ladies' activities. The rumour mill at Winston's is also claiming that the sisters are about to sell their shares to Prusac and that Meighen is carrying through a major Argus reorganization that includes the auctioning off of Massey.

The *Toronto Star* headlines a story about Black by Jack McArthur and Richard Conrad, which claims: "Metro Mogul May Rule Giant Argus Corp." When a noise interrupts his telephone interview to the reporters, Conrad quips, "The grumbling you heard in the background, by the way, is not a captive stockholder struggling with his shackles."

It is a slow day at the Montreal *Gazette.* Business writer Ian Anderson decides to phone Mrs. McDougald and ask her to comment on Black's reaching out for Argus control. Did she indeed empower Conrad to grab Meighen's Ravelston shares? Much to his surprise, Anderson receives an uncertain reply from her: "I don't think I did, but I suppose I must have. I have a bird brain about business and I don't know anything about it." Anderson then phones Doris Phillips, who gives him a considerably less equivocal reaction to the Black moves. He writes his story, for the first time revealing the widows' unhappiness with Black. He includes quotes from Black at his most ingratiating: "'Any suggestion that I would hoodwink two bereaved septuagenarian widows is patently ridiculous,'" he contends, maintaining that his actions are "'not an obscene grab for Caesarian authority.'"

June 14: Nelson Davis, who is overseas, jumps into the controversy. "I agree with everything the Black boys have done," he explains to Hugh Anderson of the *Globe and Mail*'s *Report on Business*, who has been tipped off that Davis is available for an interview at Dromoland Castle in Ireland. "According to the original Ravelston agreement, they can kick anybody out — and that's exactly what they've done with Meighen." Of the widows' involvement with John Prusac, Davis pointedly remarks in a later interview with Anderson: "You can't suddenly decide to do business with anybody who walks down the street. You have to pick your partners and stick with it…. When you give your word, you have to stick with it. That's the way I do business, anyway."

June 15: Rev. John Erb meets Conrad — over a boiled egg — to discuss the details of his wedding to Shirley Walters. Erb suggests the couple take a course of instruction in Christian marriage.

June 18: Nelson Davis and his wife, Eloise, return to Toronto from Europe. They have been the McDougalds' close friends for thirty-five years, travelling with them as a foursome on many vacations together, and are upset by the Ravelston rift. Their concern turns to anger when Jim McDougald phones Eloise. "Tell Nelson he's a double-crossing rat!" she shouts, and hangs up.

Davis is beside himself with fury. He calls John Robinette, wishing to retain Canada's leading counsel in what he vows will be the trial of the century: his lawsuit for slander against Bud McDougald's widow. He plans to ask for $100 million in damages.*

---

*The case goes no further, but the bitterness persists. Davis and Mrs. McDougald never speak again, nor does she deign to recognize Black. "I haven't spoken to Con since," she declares. "Saw him at a distance in the York Club one night, that's all. He bought a house in Palm Beach. Bud would ordinarily have been pleased about that, gone along with it, and helped to see that Con got into the clubs and everything. Now there's no hope in the world of him joining and it's pretty miserable to be down in Palm Beach without belonging to the Bath and Tennis."

June 20: The Bishop of the Anglican Diocese of Toronto, the Right Reverend Lewis S. Garnsworthy, grants Conrad and Shirley permission to marry.

June 24: Maj.-Gen. Bruce Matthews returns from England and agrees to attend a secret conclave at Doris Phillips's house to discuss the anti-Black strategy. Prusac insists the meeting be held at the witching hour of midnight because he feels that whatever they do can be finished that business day.

June 25: Doris Phillips phones Bill Ritchie of Crown Trust and requests his presence at the midnight conference, ordering him to bring the trust company seal along. He agrees to appear but without the seal.

That day, Dixon Chant and Bill Ritchie drive to Doris Phillips's grey stone house on Teddington Park Boulevard.* They walk into an Agatha Christie play. There is Doris Phillips sitting at a card table in her study, reciting over and over again, like a mantra: "Fifty-one percent. It's better to have control. We *must* have fifty-one per cent. It's better to have control..."

Prusac enters from stage right, sweeping back his cape and kissing her hand. "I've never met a fellow like Prusac before," Chant later reminisces. "It was almost as if he had a Svengali effect on the ladies. He told me that he had this agreement I had to sign on behalf of the Phillips estate and that Bill Ritchie had to sign it on behalf of Crown Trust. He wouldn't show it to us, but kept saying: 'We're buying Bruce Matthews's shares and that will give us control.' He was ordering me to do this and that until I finally told him, 'Look, I don't have to do anything you say, but from what you've told me, that document of yours is a violation of existing agreements and would leave us wide open to legal action.'" (Under the May 15 agreement, each partnership had to undergo a self-canvass procedure which, in the case of the Phillips estate, required a vote of two out of three from Dixon Chant, Crown Trust, and Doris Phillips. By signing the agreement, Mrs. Phillips had, in effect, lost control of her own family inheritance.)

Prusac confronts Chant and tells him he can't leave the room without signing the new agreement. Chant draws himself up, turns to the ladies, and declares: "If Eric and Bud were here, they would give short shrift to this fellow."

*Doris Phillips died in November 1980. The following year, her house was purchased by Steven Stavro, president of Knob Hill Farms Ltd., for $2 million. Sales agent for the transaction was Cecil Hedstrom.

As if on cue, the Major-General walks in. Chant marches over and begins to throw agitated questions at him, asking if he really knows what's going on. "No," confesses Matthews.

"It's just like Fairyland," Chant agrees.

Chant prepares to leave. But Prusac is presenting the document (which would take Argus out of Black's hands) around for signatures — first to Doris Phillips, then to Jim McDougald, then to the General, who uses a briefcase on his lap as a writing surface. In theory at least, this diverse crew now has majority control of Argus.

June 26: Conrad gets a flash confirmation that Matthews has removed his Ravelston shares from the safety deposit box he rents at the Toronto-Dominion Bank's main downtown office on King Street and that Prusac has the stock certificate. Black also hears about Prusac's involvement from David Rogers, a distant relative of Bud's who is staying at the McDougald house. Black airily dismisses Prusac as "a vague Middle-European with visions of himself as living out a sort of Slovenian Horatio Alger story based on *Arsenic and Old Lace*" — but he realizes that unless the General can be stopped, Argus will slip from his grasp.

Prusac appears at the Crown offices bearing the signed transfer document, and requests the trust company's consent. He attempts to get someone in authority to accept the piece of paper, but nobody will touch it. The scene degenerates into a Keystone Kops situation, with briefcases being hot-potatoed from hand to hand. Prusac leaves a Xeroxed copy behind and vows to come back. Black phones Igor Kaplan and arranges a strategy session with three legal colleagues for the following morning to plan emphatic countermeasures.

June 27: At the 7:30 a.m. meeting in Kaplan's office, Kaplan contends that the widows have subverted their agreement with Black and should be restrained from doing so. Conrad, who joins the meeting, isn't satisfied. He is adamant about launching an action challenging the mental competence of the two women, then seventy-five and seventy-eight years old. "My point," he explains later, "was that we could have dumped them as executors because I didn't think they could stand cross-examination. All we had to do was slap them into a witness box."

Black and Kaplan call on Crown Trust, where Ritchie and Shuve vainly attempt to tone down the proceedings, genteelly pointing out that any further legal process will upset the ladies.

"Upset?" screams Kaplan. "The women are *upset*? Their behaviour is disgraceful. They should be ashamed of themselves."

The assembled company turns to Black, hoping for milder words. Only the volume is lower. "I don't give a damn how upset they are," he growls. "They totally double-crossed us...."

Doug Ward, the man who so often shared a friendly cup of Richmello coffee with Bud McDougald for thirty years, offers to mediate and drives out to the Phillips house with Crown Trust chairman Harold Kerrigan. Ward attempts to dissuade the ladies from their partnership with Prusac, pointing out as gently as he can that it makes little sense for them to seize control of Argus. To make his case, he invokes the notion that Bud never believed there was a place in business for women, and had never allowed a woman to sit on any Argus board. He counsels them to abide by the agreement they had already signed with Conrad, which would protect them but take the burden of management off their shoulders. He has a verbal tussle with Prusac over the issue, but nothing is resolved. Ward leaves, but is called back. (A description of the scene is contained in Kaplan's hand-written notes, based on the observation of R.S. Paddon, his legal-associate-on-the-spot: "Paddon saw Mr. Ward leave and then one of the servants, a tall lanky albino, loped out of the house after him. Ward went back in, then out again. Paddon [who is attempting to serve the demand for the compulsory transfer notice for Matthews's Ravelston shares] told Mrs. Phillips that this was not a court document or anything like that. She said, 'I certainly hope not.'" She refuses to sign.)*

At his law firm, Kaplan is drafting a writ suing the ladies for trying to subvert the May 15 agreement. He phones their lawyer, Bill Somerville, threatening court action.

Another theatre of war this day is the boardroom at Massey-Ferguson. During a break in the proceedings, Black rises, walks over to Page Wadsworth, a fellow Massey director, and says, "Now, Page, I want you to observe the fact that I am going to give this document to Bruce."

He marches over to Matthews, then Massey's chairman of the board.

The General stands there like a man waiting to be awarded a medal. He is handed an envelope instead.

"This is a preventive measure," Black intones.

*The fact that Doris Phillips had a servant who happened to be an albino complicated matters, because she also had a butler called Albino Gago, who shortly after this episode left her employ to work for the Blacks, later switched to the Doug Bassett household, went over to the Jack Danielses', then back to Scott Fennell, Doris's son-in-law.

137

The Massey chairman excuses himself and for the next few minutes vacates the chair. He has been served with a compulsory transfer notice by Black. Unlike the similar document handed to Colonel Meighen a month earlier, this has not been signed by the widows. It does bear the signature of Dixon Chant, who, in keeping with the rococo aspects of the Argus melodrama, proclaims: "I am an honest man," as he affixes his name.

After the end of the Massey meeting, Black, along with Chant and Nelson Davis, starts canvassing the directors of Argus by phone, trying to line them up against its incumbent officers. Fred Eaton is in Minneapolis, visiting Dayton's department store. His response is swift and reassuring: "I don't really understand all this, but you've got my vote." Arrangements are made for the anti-Meighen/Barron/Matthews caucus to meet in the Eaton's boardroom at 10 a.m. the following Friday, prior to the full-scale Argus board meeting. Black and Davis, invoking a little-used Argus bylaw that allows a minimum of two directors to call a meeting on two days' notice, summon the board for June 30.

Not everyone is onside. Al Fairley, the president of Hollinger, is trying to rescue himself (he is demanding semi-retirement as deputy chairman at full salary with a funded pension) and claims he cannot attend because of urgent commitments in Alabama.*

June 28: The legal offensive continues. Kaplan chairs the conclave of lawyers that has prepared a writ against the ladies, Prusac, and Matthews, charging them with conspiring to breach both the Ravelston and the May 15 agreements. Lou Guolla emerges as the chief bargaining agent between the Black group and Prusac. Black's main objective is to have action taken upon Matthews's compulsory transfer notice, but many side issues come up, and the lawyers eventually retreat to the Cambridge Club in the Sheraton Centre Hotel for a quick lunch, where the only consensus they reach is that the pecan pie portions are too small.

Guolla comes into the Crown Trust offices late in the afternoon and dramatically declares that he has reached agreement with Prusac on all outstanding issues. The real estate developer alleges that the widows are most concerned that Black may force them to sell their Ravelston shares before the expiration of the May 15 agreement. Kaplan prepares a

---

*After the conclusion of the Argus rumpus, Fairley came to Black, requesting that he be allowed to stay on the board. "Al," was the reply, "you should have thought of that when you didn't attend that meeting at Eaton's. We'd gone to bat for you and when we needed you, you weren't there—so you are not being re-elected."

clarifying document, reassuring the ladies that no such takeout is possible. Various deadlines pass on both sides, but nothing is resolved. Sensing that the dénouement is at hand, the ladies have transferred themselves to the Hotel Toronto, close to the Crown Trust building. They stay up until 3 a.m. consulting their lawyers and Prusac, unwilling to sign any more documents of any kind, all but paralysed with worry, deep in what one of their friends describes as "a vertical coma."

That evening, Conrad is having dinner at Winston's with Shirley. He excuses himself, borrows restaurant owner John Arena's office, and phones Doug Ward at home. The long-time McDougald ally, now well into his seventies, has been desperately anxious to keep the lid on any Argus disagreements. He reports on his day of shuttle diplomacy. His peace mission to his neighbour on Teddington Park has been a failure. Like every other WASP conscript to the Argus wars, he stresses his objection to Prusac's habit of bowing and kissing the ladies' hands. Then he delivers his verdict. "You've got no alternative but to be tough with those women," he tells Conrad.

A block away, the lonely figure of John Prusac appears in the office of Peter Harris, the chairman of A.E. Ames & Co. and son-in-law of Bruce Matthews. For the next four hours he recounts the chronicle of his efforts to "save the widows," and expresses the hope he can still stymie Black. The operatic recitation moves Prusac to tears.

June 29: Black lunches at the Toronto Club with two Bay Street habitués, Bill Wilder and Bill Harris, to discuss the possibility of turning Crown Trust into a merchant bank. The Argus infighting intensifies. Unless it can be resolved during the next twenty-four hours, Kaplan (acting on Black's instructions) will publicly launch the conspiracy suit against Prusac, Matthews, and the widows. The sanction is a daunting one. Such a trial would split the Canadian Establishment wide open, breaking all the unwritten rules according to which Canada's elite must never wash its dirty laundry in public.

Conrad spends most of the day consolidating his alliances within the Argus board, trying to rally a majority of the directors in his putsch to remove Meighen, Barron, and Matthews. At day's end, Hal Jackman is still undecided.

That night, there is a sixty-fifth birthday party for Signy Eaton at the York Club and a sixtieth anniversary party for Doug Ward at the Toronto Club in honour of his service at Dominion Securities. Conrad Black is invited to both but goes to the Ward celebrations and keeps ducking out to phone Jackman and others about the crucial vote.

139

June 30: The day of the *coup*. Black is proposing to remove Max Meighen, Alex Barron, and Bruce Matthews as the presiding officers of Argus. For two days now he has been talking to various board members, explaining his reasons, urging them to attend his wildcat meeting at the Eaton's boardroom. Chant approaches Kaplan to voice his concern about any conflict that might arise among his triple functions as executor of the Phillips estate, chairman of the executive committee at Crown Trust, and director of Argus. He is advised to act in the best interests of the Argus shareholders.

To provide more heft for his daring initiative, Black invites Doug Ward to sit in on the meeting at Eaton's. Ward is not a director of Argus, but he used to put through the stock trades for Sir John Eaton and carries the kind of moral authority that counts on Bay Street. In what Black later describes as "a febrile atmosphere," twelve of Argus's twenty-one directors gather at 11 a.m. Lawyers for the various factions keep interrupting the proceedings. Nelson Davis leads the attack against Meighen and his fellow triumvirs. Trumbull Warren, an Argus director since 1976 with all the right Establishment connections (he attended Upper Canada College, Lakefield, *and* Ridley College), is late arriving, having rushed in from Muskoka. He has hardly sat down before he exclaims, "These people aren't wanted. They've got to go. Those women... They've got to go."

This interjection sets the mood of the conclave. Of the dozen directors, eleven vote to support the Black putsch. Only Hal Jackman abstains. He states that he will not be a party to a gang-up, but if the Meighen group is removed he will support the new slate. At this point Davis whispers to Black, "We'd better bring this fellow into Ravelston, so we can give him a compulsory transfer notice too."

With enough votes to carry the day, Black moves his council of war to 10 Toronto Street. The official Argus directors' meeting is convened and then almost immediately adjourned. Nelson Davis, Dixon Chant, and Don McIntosh (the lawyer from Fraser & Beatty who assisted Kaspar Fraser on the incorporation of Argus for E.P. Taylor) march Colonel Meighen upstairs to Bud McDougald's former office. Meighen, who is not aware of General Matthews's attempted sale of his shares to the widows, is asked to entertain thoughts of resigning from the Argus chairmanship. He refuses, accurately pointing out that he doesn't support transfer of the General's stock to the ladies, either. He ends the increasingly heated exchange with a flourish. "If you want me out, you'll have to *throw* me out."

Argus is now split into three distinct factions: the Meighen group (which still retains the loyalty of nine directors); the Black caucus; and Bruce Matthews. He has been isolated. Conrad Black leaves the boardroom and finds the General standing alone in a corridor. "Look," Black says, "we're organized to bounce all the officers, and we're going to do it, too. But it's not the ideal solution. If you will give an undertaking, which will be repeated to the directors, that you'll stop this attempt to sell your shares to the women, we'd be prepared to let things take their course a bit. We have no particular desire to proceed with our transfer notice on you either, so long as that stock doesn't go elsewhere."

The General is beaten. "Well, that's fine," he concedes. "Do that."

They return to the boardroom. Matthews asks Black to speak. Conrad summarizes the day's events, throws Meighen a bone by underlining that the Colonel would not wish to leave his office indecorously – and, indeed, nothing indecorous should be inflicted on him. Then he mentions General Matthews's "extremely destabilizing" attempt to sell his shares, pointedly referring to "certain elements within the controlling group of shareholders" who had taken the situation to the verge of litigation… Black drones on, gently now, but still reciting what amounts to an indictment, so that ever so subtly his opponents are painted as intruders in Argus's sacrosanct halls, while he emerges as the established authority. The scene is somehow reminiscent of a muted mutiny in an Algerian officers' school. Generals and colonels are being deposed with exquisitely civilized decorum – but the epaulettes are being torn off just the same.

Black finishes his short address by asking Don McIntosh to read out the new slate of Argus officers. Nelson Davis will be chairman, Conrad Black president and the head of the board's powerful executive committee; Dixon Chant is elevated to executive vice-president; Hal Jackman is nominated as vice-president. A hastily pencilled-in Bruce Matthews is added in the token slot of deputy chairman.

The meeting is adjourned to July 13, when the new regime will take power. The resignations of Max Meighen and Alex Barron are to be gratefully accepted at that time.

That evening, Conrad is celebrating with Shirley and Tom Birks at Winston's. Igor Kaplan remains unconvinced about Matthews's real intentions, since the General has switched sides before. He bursts into the restaurant and presents Conrad with what he calls his "Lithuanian Triangle" – an ingenious, if slightly impractical, twist that would require the General to sign a compulsory transfer notice on himself, pledging his stock to Black. It's a Baltic form of hara-kiri that turns out to be both unworkable and unnecessary, but Black resolves to visit Matthews the next day, just to tie down the General's consent.

July 1: It is a Saturday morning and the Black brothers are driving out to Matthews's house. "We've nailed only one of Bruce's feet to the floor," says Monte to Conrad. "He's still hopping around, so we've got to nail the other one down." They arrive, and the conversation on the General's verandah is quite pleasant. He is as good as his word. There is only one brief heated exchange, when Monte demands, "General, we'll have those shares."

"I won't be bullied."

"Oh yes you will."

July 3: The widows send out the first peace feeler through their lawyer, Bill Somerville. One of the Blacks' lawyers suggests that the brothers would be interested in buying up the McDougald and Phillips stock in Ravelston. A meeting is arranged for the following evening at Conrad Black's house.

July 4: The powwow convenes in Black's dining room at 10:30 p.m. (No one there is aware of it, but for Conrad the highlight of the day has been Shirley's meeting with Rev. John Erb to plan their wedding. They have decided on the floral decorations and the actual choreography of the ceremony, since there is to be no rehearsal.) As well as a tort of lawyers and the Black brothers, John Prusac is there as the plenipotentiary emissary of the widows. Bill Somerville begins by giving a historical résumé of the Argus struggle, which Black dismisses as being inaccurate and unimportant. Monte appears ready to pop out of his seat to respond, but Kaplan restrains him. The meeting drags on. Prusac and Somerville are drinking Scotch; the Black boys sip wine.

Somerville unexpectedly springs a price on the group: the widows would sell their Ravelston holdings for $10 million each. Kaplan demands to know whether Somerville and Prusac have adequate power of attorney to negotiate and conclude a deal. When the two men assure him that they have, Conrad offers $18 million for the lot. Somerville counters with $18.4 million.

Black can hardly contain himself. He had previously told Kaplan he would pay as high as $23 million for the widows' stock. The Blacks hastily agree to the Somerville offer, and Prusac leaves with a handwritten note to obtain the ladies' signatures. Behind the kitchen door, Kaplan congratulates Black, who replies, "It's a goddamn steal."

While Prusac is out obtaining the ladies' consent, Black phones Russ Harrison, chairman of the Canadian Imperial Bank of Commerce. It is just before 11 p.m.

"I hope I'm not disturbing you," says Black.

"No," is the reply, "I'm just watching the Miss Universe contest."

"Well, I've just concluded a deal with two star candidates for the title... By the way, we're going to need about $18 million tomorrow at five o'clock."

"Fine. Done. Just call the office in the morning and say where you want the cheques delivered and payable to whom... Does that mean this goddamn drama is about to end?"

"Yep."

"Well, that's too bad, because I've been enjoying it."

Prusac returns at midnight bearing the signed document.

Everyone relaxes. More drinks are served.

Prusac prepares to leave and says that he is happy to have met Black. Conrad replies that his reputation had preceded him.

They part like generals exchanging farewells over broken swords.

Kaplan is broke. Referring to himself in the third person, he describes the long night in his diary: "Kaplan said that although this was a huge closing, he had only 37 cents in his pocket but would stay if someone would lend him ten dollars to get home. Kaplan was out of cigarettes and smoked butts till 4:30 a.m. He left, having had many scotches and warm conversation with Conrad Black."

July 5: Up at an unusual 9 a.m. the following day, Conrad is on the phone to his friend Hal Jackman. When Black tells his confrère what has happened, Jackman responds with a Shakespearean reference: "One must go back to *Richard II*. In the second act young Bolingbroke arrives in England with thousands of men to repossess his father's estates, and in the last act he is crowned Henry IV of England... Well done. It has been high drama."

The formal closing ceremonies are scheduled for 5 p.m. in the Crown Trust boardroom. At 4:53 Monte Black, a director of the Toronto-Dominion Bank, decides there is really no reason why the Commerce should get the whole account. He telephones J. Allan Boyle, the new president of the T-D, and says: "I need $9.2 million right away secured by Ravelston shares. If you can get it here in seven minutes, you've got some business for the bank, but if you can't make it, don't worry because the Commerce is advancing the funds." Boyle calls John Fitzpatrick, manager of the T-D's City Hall branch, and tells him to get the money there fast.

The group stands in the old Crown Trust building, looking out the second-storey window. At precisely one minute to five, Fitzpatrick (who measures six-feet-five in stocking feet) comes charging down Bay Street, dodging pedestrians like a champion running quarterback.

The control of Argus changes hands.

July 10: In Montreal, Brian Mulroney, president of the Iron Ore Company of Canada, a firm associated with the Argus group, is asked by the *Gazette* to comment on the takeover. "I don't think anything like this had ever happened in the history of Canadian business," he says, tidily summing up the Canadian Establishment's reaction. "But if anyone was going to do it, it was going to be Conrad."

In Toronto, power never stops moving. Black has just finished lunch in the Toronto Club when he happens to bump into Peter Harris, the Ames chairman, who has been eating with his father-in-law, Bruce Matthews. Black and Harris stand near Wellington and York streets, watching the General climb into a large green Cadillac. "Whose car is Bruce getting into?" Black asks.

"Ah, Con," Harris replies, "it's either his own or it belongs to Dome Mines, where he is chairman. I can't tell one from the other. They're both green. But in any event, it isn't one of *yours*, so you can relax…"

CHAPTER SIX

Messing with Massey

*"I am amazed by the number of so-called
financial experts luxuriating in the view that I am some
sort of punch-drunk prizefighter on the ropes.
Well, screw them."*

—Conrad Black

His triumphant capture of Argus and the successful manoeuvres that followed left Conrad Black exposed to that most malignant and most indigenous of Canadian fevers: the rush to humble any individual who dares push ahead of the herd.

Black's flash accomplishments had transformed him from the business community's darling into its prime target. His peers and rivals mobilized their incipient jealousy into a kangaroo court assessing his intentions and his worth. Even if neither the case against him nor the rules of evidence were ever made clear, the jury was seldom out.

By late 1980, Conrad-bashing had become the chief sport at the Toronto Club members' table where such things are decided. Nearly everyone, it seemed, was anxious to join the chorus of condemnation. "In those days," remarked one of the more acid-tongued regulars, "taking turns attacking Black was like going into a Jewish bakery to buy bagels. You had to take a number."

The reason for all this scorn was Black's performance during the tumultuous twenty-five months he spent between the autumns of 1978 and 1980 as chairman and dominant stockholder of Massey-Ferguson, the huge multinational agricultural implement company. His conduct in that office and in particular his abrupt departure were judged to be his Waterloo. This was a silly comparison, except for one fact: like the Little Emperor's defeat, the humiliation the Argus chairman may have suffered (and he admitted to remarkably little) was rooted as much in historical circumstance as in his own actions.

THE FORCES THAT ANIMATED MASSEY'S DIFFICULTIES in the late 1970s stretched back to the early 1940s, when E.P. Taylor was serving out his term as wartime dollar-a-year man with C.D. Howe's Department of Munitions and Supply in Ottawa. He'd become a friend of James Duncan, president of Massey-Harris, then Deputy Minister for Air with National Defence. Duncan, a suave French-born industrialist who had served the company since 1911, filled Taylor's ears with tales of Massey's glorious past and prophecies of an even more glorious future.

Founded in 1847 by Daniel Massey, who had originally supplied the farmers of Durham County in central Ontario with sap-boiling kettles, the company had grown rapidly from its start in a small machine-shop at Newcastle. After the amalgamation with Alanson Harris's similar operation in 1891, the combination burgeoned into a major industry, eventually turning out bicycles, windmills, home freezers, milking machines, stoves, kerosene engines, and washers, plus a wide-ranging line of agricultural machinery. During the opening of the Canadian west, a Massey marching band would lead parades of newly delivered farm machines into the raw towns, with the company treating the purchasers to free concerts and dinners. Massey's reputation spread overseas when its technology became a hit of the 1867 Paris International Exposition, and operations were extended into the United States with purchase of the Johnston Harvester Company of Batavia, N.Y., in 1910. Introduction (in 1938) of the self-propelled combine, developed mainly in Argentina by Australian-born engineer Tom Carroll, revolutionized harvesting methods. The Second World War transformed Massey, already Canada's showcase multinational, into a major weapons supplier, adding significantly to its capacity for turning out sophisticated goods.

Anxious to attract imaginative risk-takers to his board, Duncan invited Eddie Taylor, who before his Ottawa sojourn had whipped together a straggle of beer-making plants into the mighty Canadian Breweries Ltd., to join the Massey board in March 1942. Nine months later, Taylor persuaded Duncan to recruit Eric Phillips to Massey, and the two men surreptitiously began buying up gobs of the company's stock. By the winter of 1945, the duo had acquired 55,195 Massey preferred shares, transferring them a year later into 8 per cent of the company's common stock one minute before the deadline specified by an obscure bylaw. Taylor and Phillips next cooked up a secret deal with Victor Emanuel, president of Avco Manufacturing Corporation in the United States, who bought a 6.4-per-cent share of Massey in the expectation that his small Ohio-based farm-equipment company (New Idea Inc.) would be merged with the Canadian giant. Duncan scotched that deal, but the Argus partners bought Emanuel out, making them the company's largest equity holders. At the 1947 annual meeting, they put enough of their own candidates on the Massey board to gain effective control.

From that time on, a showdown between Duncan and Taylor became inevitable. Duncan, who from 1949 onward had been chairman as well as president of Massey, was concerned with reinvesting the company's earnings in new production facilities; the Argus crowd kept voting themselves higher dividends to service the bank loans required for their stock purchases. In classic Argus tradition, they were trying to force Massey to finance its own takeover. Duncan fought a valiant rearguard action against great pressures. In 1950, for example, although Massey's $15-million earnings represented a twelve-month increase of only $1.7 million, the Argus directors forced a dividend payout of $7 million. Duncan found himself overruled time after time, but went on to negotiate the successful merger with Harry Ferguson's British tractor company and the expansion of Massey's overseas empire. By the summer of 1956, lax cost-control systems and a general economic downturn had allowed unsold inventories to reach $182 million. Argus board members moved in to demand Duncan's resignation.

The circumstances of Duncan's departure remain something of a mystery. The Argus partners maintained it was a straight business decision. Wallace McCutcheon privately commented that Duncan's record, though great, had been "sullied by vanity." Conrad Black puts forward a more intriguing interpretation. "What Jim Duncan did," he says, "was psychologically indistinguishable for me from General MacArthur's performance during the Korean War. He wanted to be fired, and acted in a way he must have known was going to get him fired. He completely ignored the efforts of Eric Phillips and Eddie Taylor to reason with him and left them absolutely no choice. So they fired him."

Following a five-year stint as chairman of Ontario Hydro, Duncan retired to his beloved Somerset House in Bermuda, and Massey moved into a period of hard-nosed management under Eric Phillips. He fixed up the bottom line (by October 1958, he reported an $18-million turnaround) and moved Massey into new markets. Sir Edmund Hillary used the company's tractors on his historic overland expedition to the South Pole, and Massey purchased the prestigious F. Perkins Ltd. of Peterborough, England, the world's largest manufacturer of diesel engines. The Argus partners began to recruit British aristocrats (with Lord Crathorne, the Duke of Wellington, and the Marquess of Abergavenny leading the way) to decorate the company's board.

Massey endowed the Argus partners with the international prestige and connections they craved. Its London office, overlooking as it did

147

Claridge's Hotel, where Massey maintained an ostentatious permanent suite for Bud McDougald, became a social climber's paradise. Another and only slightly less sumptuous *pied-à-terre* was leased for Massey president Albert Thornbrough in the Carlton Tower in Cadogan Place. The company also splurged on two Rolls-Royces and a Daimler for exclusive use by its Canadian visitors. (The Phantom VI was such a grand automobile that it was decorated in royal colours and, to McDougald's panting delight, was borrowed by the Queen for ceremonial occasions.)

After Phillips's death in 1964, operational duties fell to Thornbrough, originally a Ferguson employee who had become Phillips's chief lieutenant. Massey sales continued to multiply. The company, by then employing 65,000 people, was selling its products in 120 countries. By the end of 1975, Argus's unrealized gain on its Massey investment amounted to $23.2 million, but the Argus partnership had been crumbling for some years. The only item on which Taylor and McDougald could agree was that neither should become the new Massey chairman; as a result, the key position went unfilled for an astounding fourteen years. Taylor remained content to be chairman of the company's executive committee, being alternately indifferent to its affairs (he once left a Massey board meeting only half an hour after it started, with the comment: "Well, I've got to be out at Woodbine for the fourth") and issuing erratic commands (such as when he stormed into Thornbrough's office and instructed him to shut down all North American operations in "an all-out retreat to Europe").

The full slate of directors gathered only quarterly, and the meetings were fairly desultory affairs. "The board usually convened at 2:15 and the meeting would be over by 3:15 – an hour at the most," recalls Derek Hayes, a cousin of Bud McDougald's and at the time Massey's assistant secretary. "A half-hour would be taken up by McDougald telling anecdotes about the social circuit in Palm Beach and court gossip from the U.K. It was fun because he was a marvellous raconteur, but there was little business discussed. There was no regular reporting procedure about what was going on.

"The same attitude applied to plant tours. I remember board members being taken through a factory in Des Moines, Iowa; it was total farce. They put the directors into golf carts and whizzed them through at thirty miles an hour. The maintenance people spent $580,000 prettying up the place and were still painting the bloody floor when the visitors arrived. One director noticed the assembly-line workers' spotless garb, and vaguely commented to his guide: 'I didn't realize before this that people who work on assembly lines actually wear white coats.' It was farcical."*

Without a chairman or active major shareholder, Massey's direction passed into the hands of Al Thornbrough. A native of Kansas and a Harvard graduate in economics, he had worked with John Kenneth Galbraith in wartime Washington's Office of Price Administration, had risen to the rank of lieutenant-colonel in the Corps of Engineers, and had fought his way up the corporate ladder in Harry Ferguson's U.S. operation. After the Massey merger in 1953, he moved to Toronto and in 1956 became president under Phillips's tutelage. One of those likeable Midwesterners who lope instead of walk, Thornbrough speaks with an accent of American assurance, whatever the circumstances or subject. The man who made Massey work and thrive through the 1960s and early 1970s, Thornbrough in his later years had trouble entering into realistic dialogue with his managers. He became a captive of his dreams, reporting to his Argus principals just the optimistic side of the ledger. He discouraged movement toward succession by bringing in managers and discarding them before they could become serious rivals. Only one senior vice-president, John Staiger, made it through to retirement during Thornbrough's stewardship—and his son was married to Thornbrough's daughter.

One of Thornbrough's peculiarities was that he operated Massey as if it were an American rather than a Canadian company. He refused to take out Canadian citizenship, favoured Americans for senior jobs, established the crucial job-creating large-tractor production plant at Des Moines, and commuted to work in Toronto from his beach home in Boca Raton, Florida.

Addison Mizner's original "dream city," Boca Raton is a tranquillity base for the American rich, second in its luxurious appointments only to Palm Beach. (It boasts the Royal Palm Polo Club, a twenty-seven acre bird sanctuary, and twenty-one golf courses.) Thornbrough's house there is built around an atrium with almost no outward-facing windows. He ran Canada's best-known multinational corporation from one of his

*The story is reminiscent of a plant tour conducted by Harry Ferguson for Bud McDougald. Ferguson was fanatical about cleanliness on his tractor assembly line and was explaining his operating philosophy to the Canadian visitor, when McDougald interrupted. "I'm sorry, Harry," he said, "but I've got to have a leak." After turning down Ferguson's offer of the executive washroom, McDougald bolted into a factory toilet, went about his business, and was walking back when Ferguson noticed one of the assembly-line workers coming out after a similar mission. "Here, here, my good man," Ferguson exclaimed, "whenever you do that, always wash your hands before you go back to work!" Came the reassuring reply: "It's all right, Mr. Ferguson. I'm not going back to the line, I'm on my way to lunch."

two garages (converted to an office), taking time out for cruises aboard his forty-two-foot fishing cruiser, the *Yonder*. Every Monday night he would climb into one of Massey's three jets and fly to Toronto. He'd be met at the airport by a chauffeur-driven Massey Cadillac and taken to the six-bedroom Massey apartment at the Old Mill Towers. After three days at the office, he would reverse the procedure and arrive back in sunny Florida each Thursday evening. For this schedule he was collecting an annual salary (in 1977) of $471,000 (plus a pension allowance of $156,000), ranking him as the highest-paid corporate executive in Canada.*

Through the 1970s, Massey went on expanding. "We borrowed ourselves to the hilt to carry out an acquisition spree," says a Massey executive who later resigned in disgust. "When the market turned up, we rode along with it, though nothing was cured underneath. None of the productivity problems were dealt with, none of the manpower problems, none of the quality-control problems—in fact, they had all intensified, because with the increase in the market, we just poured people and money into new plants to turn out product, whether it was good, bad, or indifferent."

The only distant early warning that the company was out of control came from Alex Barron, president of Canadian General Investments, who had been invited to join the Massey board by McDougald in 1974. "During the second or third directors' meeting after I joined the board," he commented, "Mr. Thornbrough recommended that Massey buy Hanomag, a German construction machine manufacturer. This was a surprise to the outside directors, because we had been sent no information in advance. I was the only member of the board to question the advisability of the purchase. When I could get no answers, I committed the unforgivable: I asked Mr. Thornbrough whether the recommendation had the unanimous support of the three other corporate officers who sat on the board. Dead silence. Then I asked whether I could poll the inside directors. Dead silence. Finally, two of them said they favoured the proposal. Sir Montague Prichard, who was the head of the Perkins organization, then stood up, declared that he was opposed to the transactions, and gave his reasons. But Mr. Thornbrough insisted

*Thornbrough was matched in lifestyle only by John Mitchell, head of Massey's North American division, who also lived beside the Atlantic in Florida but maintained his headquarters in Des Moines. He persuaded Massey to purchase a Lockheed JetStar, mainly for his use, because it was the only executive aircraft that enabled him to commute from Des Moines without a refuelling stop. Mitchell once ordered all of Massey's senior U.S. executives to purchase Cadillacs so that the company would project an aura of prosperity.

on recommending the motion. Some director seconded it—so we were in the Hanomag business."

It turned out to be the worst deal Massey ever made—and that's taking in a lot of territory. Hanomag bled Massey's balance sheets for $250 million before it was sold off in 1979. "The ill-prepared and predictably disastrous construction machinery project," Prichard wrote of the deal in a confidential internal memorandum, "delivered the final blow to MF's ambitions by drawing off the profit of the other divisions and adding a crushing burden to the financial requirements.... Looking back on this unfortunate venture and the euphoria surrounding it, one can only sum it up with a single word: 'idiotic.'"

In October 1974, Barron decided to visit England to tour the Massey plants there. Prichard welcomed him and requested an opportunity to brief McDougald personally on his imaginative eleven-point proposal for regenerating his own division and much of the rest of Massey. "When I got back to Canada," Barron recalls, "I saw Bud and gave him my letter describing Sir Monty's ideas requesting the audience. He read it very carefully. Ten days later he phoned and told me, 'Thornbrough won't meet with Sir Monty. He thinks it's a waste of time.' About six months after that, Thornbrough abruptly retired Prichard, five years ahead of the normal date. When he announced it at the board meeting, he looked down the table meaningfully at me, as if to say: 'That'll teach you to interfere.' From that time on, Thornbrough and I were poles apart. I felt Massey was on the wrong course, but there was nothing I could do about it."

Massey's problems were both structural and managerial. Its growth and diversification had been born of opportunism rather than of long-range product and market development, which required steady inputs of capital and personnel. Massey moved into the United States and lost Canada without ever winning the American market; that would have required development of a big 100-horsepower tractor, which Massey bungled. With the notable exception of the self-propelled combine, Massey had never really been a product innovator, due to lack of capital for research and an inability to identify what its customers wanted and what the manufacturing facilities could actually produce.

An only slightly overstated case could be made that, in modern times, Massey *never* produced satisfactory returns on capital. Even in 1976, its most profitable year, $93 million of the $118-million net profit was accounted for by currency gains, traceable to the collapse of the British pound. During the fifty years between 1929 and 1979, the company had made more than 4 per cent on its sales only five times. One reason for this performance was that the company's dominant shareholders at

Argus would neither float any equity issues nor allow anyone else to invest more capital—because that might have diluted their control position. Although the Argus position floated between 8.2 and 16.4 per cent, no one else was able to exert the kind of pressure that might have lightened Massey's debt load. (All the while, Bud McDougald sat on the executive committee of the Commerce, which continued to extend Massey credit with such generosity that the bank eventually became the company's largest shareholder.) By pumping up the company's bank and debenture obligations and at the same time insisting on maximum dividend returns, Argus was progressively bleeding Massey dry.

One of the enduring mysteries is what held the Massey management back from acting in the interests of the majority of its non-Argus shareholders. While Phillips was running Massey the company's interests were automatically dovetailed to coincide with Argus's fiscal aspirations. During most of Thornbrough's twenty-two-year presidency this seemed to be equally true. Though nothing was written down, the unspoken contract appears to have been that McDougald would allow Thornbrough to run the Massey operations entirely as he wanted—provided that he allowed McDougald freedom in setting dividends. In a confidential report dated July 15, 1978, Sir Monty Prichard, then no longer head of Massey's Perkins subsidiary, described Thornbrough in his relationship to Argus as "a man of *their* choice from whom they were evermore to demand and receive complete loyalty, even to the extent of obsequiousness."

That Thornbrough stayed in the Massey presidency for more than two decades was attributable in part to his managerial skill as well as ability to undercut would-be replacements. Every time McDougald happened to mention the need for an orderly succession, he was told by Thornbrough that no one was qualified or available.

McDougald's interest in Massey affairs, apart from courting dukes for the board, was highly eccentric. At one point he ordered Wallace Main, the company's vice-president for administration, to sell off Massey's large experimental farm near Toronto to his developer friend John Prusac. Main sold it instead to the highest bidder. McDougald was furious, not only because Prusac had been bypassed but because he had structured the original deal to go through Cecil Hedstrom, his sister-in-law, who was now out her commission. McDougald instructed Thornbrough to fire Main; Thornbrough instead froze his salary. (Black regards Main as "the Captain Dreyfus of Massey—an innocent and courageous man victimized by those around him"—and eventually made up his full vice-presidential remuneration.)

The crisis at Massey first came to the public's attention on March 10,

1978, when Thornbrough stood up in front of the company's annual meeting and announced a first-quarter loss of $38.8 million, temporary plant shutdowns, and the possible liquidation of several manufacturing facilities. That same day, the authoritative Dominion Bond Rating Service slashed Massey's credit rating. Dividends had been suspended a month before; reports of revenue losses were flooding in from every division; currency exchange rates had turned against the company. All of Massey's poison pigeons had suddenly come home to roost. "I kept Bud fully informed," Thornbrough remembers, "and the day before the meeting, I took my senior executives down to New York to meet with our bankers. Bud, who was then very ill at Palm Beach, wanted to know precisely what was going on. He wasn't supposed to talk on the telephone, so I used to call his wife, Jim, and give her messages. But the evening of the annual meeting, she left the phone for a moment and Bud's voice came on. We must have talked for twenty minutes. He told me that he was going to croak one of these days, that he had only half a heart left, but that he was keen to live and wanted to save Massey. It was our last conversation."

Five days later, McDougald was dead.

Most Massey executives mourned their chairman's passing because he had at least provided them with a sense of style that had endowed the company with a touch of grandeur. More thoughtful observers were shocked by the virtual certainty that had McDougald survived another six months, Massey would have been bankrupt. "Bud was a great benefactor of mine and was very kind to me," Black later mused, "but his true brilliance was as a kind of asexual Cagliostro, a man who had everyone believing he was a supremely capable executive when it was all an absolutely brilliant con job.* When that first resounding cry that the emperor has no clothes came out with Massey's 1978 first-quarter figures, Bud, with his impeccable sense of timing, conveniently died. He

---

*Count Alessandro Cagliostro was the assumed name of the notorious Italian adventurer and impostor Giuseppe Balsamo, who was born in Palermo, Sicily, on June 2, 1743. Among his many adventures was the Diamond Necklace Affair (1783–85) involving Marie Antoinette, Cardinal de Rohan, and an adventuress, Countess de Lamotte. Partly by means of the queen's forged signature, Rohan was induced to purchase for her an £85,000 necklace originally made for Mme du Barry. Rohan gave the necklace to the countess, who was to give it to the queen, but the countess sold it to an English jeweller and shared the money with Cagliostro. Meanwhile, the jeweller who had sold the necklace sent his bill to the queen, who denied all knowledge of it. A great scandal ensued. A highly cultured rogue, Cagliostro was imprisoned in the Bastille, escaped, visited England, and was imprisoned in the Fleet. On emerging, he went to Rome, where he was arrested and condemned to death. His sentence was commuted to life imprisonment in the fortress of San Leone, where he died in 1795.

knew the jig was up. And all those people who had been sitting around rubbing their hands, glad that Bud was on the hot seat, were disappointed. He was never on the hot seat. We gave him a big funeral and he became 'John A. McDougald, Legendary Financier.' I'm all for Bud — but you have to realize the essence of his genius."

CONRAD BLACK MOVED TO MASSEY on August 16, 1978, settling into the chairman's quarters in the Sun Life Building on University Avenue. The space had been unoccupied for fourteen years — since the death of Col. Eric Phillips. The office was grand, with its ten windows, gold-brocade curtains, a huge oak desk, and an illuminated globe of the world. "It's positively papal," Black boasted.

Bay Street wags were amusing one another with the riddle: "What's the difference between Massey-Ferguson and the *Titanic*?" (*Answer:* "Different bankers.") The quip didn't do justice to Massey's true situation, which was more closely analogous to bailing out a still majestic but wallowing *Titanic* with a soup ladle. Black had been persuaded to transfer himself to the Massey offices by the company's bankers, who believed his presence would provide psychological succour to its strained debt position. A group of U.S. bankers, led by Citibank of New York, had informed Black that if drastic measures were not taken immediately, the American banking group would not renew its line of credit, setting off a cascading effect that would have pushed Massey into insolvency. He presented a façade of determined calm. "There are few genuinely great companies in Canada. Massey is one of them. As such, it is worthy of prodigious effort," he told the *Financial Post*. "Only an act of God — a 20 per cent prime lending rate or complete collapse of the North American agricultural or labour markets — could sink Massey now. Meanwhile, the disbelievers, waiting like Madame Defarge for the guillotine to fall, have done us a favour by depressing the stock."

In private, he joked about "the procession of shaky-kneed and sweaty-palmed lenders" trooping in to inquire anxiously about the status of their loans, and mused about the situation in which he found himself. "I have tried to point out that Argus has other purposes besides being a milch cow for Massey," he said. "But almost nobody grasps the exact motivation of my activities. I hold the balanced view that, being such a great old company, Massey deserves some kind of effort before just being kissed off. On the other hand, there are certain dangers inherent in getting too personally involved. All the forces of envy are waiting to tar me with the brush of a fiasco wholly created by other people."

Ironically, Argus's investment was a tenth of what the Commerce had in Massey. Nine foreign banks all had more. Yet most of Massey's 277 lenders treated Black as if Argus represented a majority, if not 100 per cent, of the company. "We were in default on every covenant; the company was in a shambles," Black recalls. "Logically, Massey should probably have gone bust years ago. But some things defy all laws of economics and nature – like bumblebees."

Within weeks of Black's takeover, Massey announced the largest annual loss of any Canadian corporation in history: $256.7 million in U.S. dollars. Black kicked Thornbrough upstairs to the newly created deputy-chairmanship and on September 8 named his friend Victor Rice president. "The situation was so desperate we didn't have time to fish around for anybody on the outside," Black later explained. "What we needed was not a textbook, business-school approach but a broken-field runner. I knew Victor fairly well by then. He is a man of such high intelligence and such fanatical ambition that to succeed he wouldn't fail to implement absolutely draconian measures (which I was advocating myself) – the only way to save the company from literally falling apart."

Rice is an impatient man who makes quick rabbit-like gestures with his hands and nose when he speaks. He moved in with a vengeance. He replaced fifteen of Massey's twenty-one vice-presidents, closed seven plants (which had employed 12,000 people), and even saved about $30,000 annually by eliminating interoffice memos with executives' names printed on them. Expense accounts were trimmed mercilessly. In May 1978, John Staiger, Massey's senior corporate vice-president, had issued a memo calling for the elimination of expense-account luxuries. That July he attended a management committee meeting in London and for his ten-day journey handed in an expense account of £2,000, including £30 three days running for newspapers, books, and periodicals. Black inspected the tallies when he became chairman and Staiger, by then over retirement age, left shortly afterwards.

Then Black moved in his ultimate deterrent: David Radler was appointed vice-chairman of the executive committee. He became auditor-general of the whole operation, exercising his tough cost-saving instincts. Black placed his own appointees on the board and promptly dropped Alex Barron, his recent nemesis from the Argus takeover. ("I asked a skill-testing question of two Massey directors, Page Wadsworth and Trumbull Warren, namely: 'Do you think that a certain prominent Canadian businessman named Alex Ethelred Barron should be re-elected a director of this company?' When they both said no, I said: 'You two and I have just been appointed as the board's nominating committee." And that was how Barron took leave of Massey.)

Black's euphoria in those initial months was shared by Victor Rice.

The two men particularly enjoyed teasing Massey vice-presidents about the plethora of grandiloquent titles that had sprouted at the company's head office—especially designations referring to officers in relation to various parts of the globe, such as "Vice-President in charge of Africa," and so on. At one point, Rice proclaimed himself President of the World—and the only way Black could top him was by appointing himself Interplanetary Chairman. Outsiders unwittingly added to the contest. The *Globe and Mail's Report on Business* named Black its 1978 Man of the Year, describing him as "a powerful and unpredictable force" in Canada's business world.

Black was always careful to dissociate his own future from Massey's long-term prospects, but that was not the public perception. Massey's difficulties, rooted in specific problems, were gradually becoming abstract in the sense that a sea of red ink seemed to drown even the best of initiatives. For 1979, Massey showed a net profit of $36.9 million (U.S.), and the turnaround made cheerful headlines, but a closer reading of the figures revealed that all but $18 million of the income jump was due to currency gains. The result was hardly an impressive return on $3 billion in sales, especially when the company was paying out $1 million every working day in interest on its bank loans.

Despite its horrendous undercapitalization and inherent weaknesses, Massey had one great asset: a worldwide distribution system that could be used for other products, such as, say, cars and trucks. Victor Rice hoped he could pull together ten merchant bankers willing to risk $50 million each to save the company. This would have had the beneficial result of injecting some badly needed equity financing while at the same time perpetuating him and his team in office because there would have been no single shareholder dominant enough to put in his own management team. Rice searched the world's financial markets for prospective partners but found no takers. At that time, the world's money managers could place their funds in energy companies for an easy 20-per-cent return, and Massey couldn't hope to match that.

Enter Sir Siegmund Warburg.* The German-born investment special-

---

*A member of one of the leading Hamburg banking families of pre-Hitler Germany, Siegmund Warburg was born in 1902, arrived in Britain as a refugee in 1933, and launched his merchant bank, S.G. Warburg & Co. Ltd., in 1946. An adviser to several British prime ministers and a confidant of a diverse group of world leaders, he became a controversial force in the City. (He quotes a comment by a rival City merchant banker, presumably a ten o'clock starter: "Know this fellow Siegmund Warburg? Starts in the office at *eight* o'clock in the morning.") He tangled with established City houses like Morgan Grenfell, Lazard Brothers, and Hambros, and came out on top in the great 1958–59 battle for control of British Aluminium Co. Ltd. on the side of the Reynolds Metals Company of the United States and its British ally, Tube Investments Ltd. (He had suggested Tube to Reynolds as a suitable British partner.) He was knighted in 1966 and as an elder statesman of international finance

ist, then seventy-six, had established one of London's most successful modern merchant banks, with clients such as British Petroleum, the Royal Dutch–Shell group, Unilever, and Trusthouse Forte. His worldwide network of seventy-five prime contacts included Henry Kissinger and the late Anwar Sadat. Warburg had been active in Canada for years through his personal representative, A.G.S. "Tony" Griffin, and through Peter Stormonth Darling, one of the London bank's most enlightened executives, who had also become a formidable expert in Canadian finance. In September 1978, William Wilder, former head of Wood Gundy and now an energy company executive, brought Warburg and Darling around to meet Black at 10 Toronto Street. After some initial sparring it turned out that the British bankers wanted Black to front a

---

now spends much of his time in Switzerland, in a house at Blonay that commands a spectacular view of Lake Geneva. He belongs to the Alsterufer branch of the Warburg family (named from the street on which an earlier Siegmund lived). The other branch, descendants of Moritz Warburg, are known as the Mittelweg Warburgs from Moritz's address of 17 Mittelweg. The Mittelwegs—who carried the middle initial M (for Moritz)—have included Paul M., who married Nina Loeb of the New York banking family of Kuhn, Loeb; Felix M., who married Frieda Schiff, daughter of Jacob Schiff (1847–1920), head of Kuhn, Loeb; and Max M., Fritz M., and Erich M., partners in the Hamburg banking house of M.M. Warburg. Sir Siegmund's London firm has in recent years been among the most profitable of the seventeen merchant banks that make up the London Accepting Houses Committee, with assets greater than those of Lazard Brothers, N.M. Rothschild & Sons, or Baring Brothers. It has affiliates in Germany, Switzerland, Luxembourg, and France, has its own offices in New York and Tokyo, is a partner (with a French associate, Banque Paribas) in Warburg Paribas Becker of New York and Chicago, and was a founder shareholder in the Edmonton-based Canadian Commercial Bank. Warburg established a Canadian presence in 1953 through Triarch Corp. Ltd., a Toronto-based financial house formed by a group that included S.G. Warburg & Co., Glyn Mills & Co., Helbert Wagg & Co. Ltd. and Kuhn Loeb (he was a London partner of the Wall Street house, founded in 1867 and then headed by his kinsmen John M. Schiff and Frederick M. Warburg, from the early 1950s to the end of 1964). Triarch's president was Tony Griffin, who stayed with the firm till his retirement as chairman in 1976; the vice-president was Donald C. Meek, who became head of a similar Toronto operation called Merafin Corp. Ltd. In 1967 Triarch was the key firm in returning control of John Labatt Ltd. to Canada from Milwaukee, where it had resided after the 1964 acquisition by Jos. Schlitz Brewing Co. The London house has managed more issues for Canadian borrowers in the Eurobond market than any other bank, having raised more than U.S. $10 billion for Canadian issuers including most of the provinces and all of the Big Five banks. It has been financial adviser to the Alberta Treasury and such major Canadian companies as Consolidated-Bathurst Inc., Harlequin Enterprises Ltd., Moore Corp. Ltd., PanCanadian Petroleum Ltd., Ranger Oil Ltd., and the Royal Bank. It engineered a classic reverse takeover that gave Roy Thomson control of the Kemsley newspaper chain in Britain and guided the Thomson North Sea oil revenue to Canada. Consumers' Gas Co. paid the Warburg firm more than $1 million for advice on its takeover of Home Oil Co. Ltd. Sir Siegmund's son, George, left the firm in 1962 and is with the Colonial Bank in Connecticut, and the operating head is David Scholey, whom Warburg says he considers an adopted son and whose wife is Sandra Drew, daughter of the late George Drew, Tory leader in Canada from 1948 to 1956 and former premier of Ontario.

foreign takeover of Massey for one of their European clients. "I told Sir Siegmund," Black says, "that we were not in the business of fronting anything, that Massey still had a substantial chance of being saved, a turnaround which would make the Weston and Eaton's situations, with which I was somewhat familiar, look like chicken-feed." Black ended that interview with the comment, "We've got to make the effort and fight it out. Either we are Massey's controlling shareholders or we're out—and that's that."

But the feelers continued. Warburg's European client turned out to be none other than West Germany's giant Volkswagenwerk AG, and on October 31, 1979, one of its top executives (Friedrich Thomee), who was in Toronto to view the Tutankhamen exhibit, met Black and Page Wadsworth, the former Commerce chairman and a Massey director. He made a tentative offer for 51 per cent of Massey, but Black said that he wasn't interested in selling shares. "The only price we could legitimately ask for our position," he said, "is much less than I think it will be worth, and I remind you that Volkswagen was not in much better shape a few years ago than Massey is now."

No formal offer was ever made, but Sir Siegmund kept nibbling at the edges and would occasionally telephone Conrad from his Swiss hideaway to suggest gently that it was time for the Commerce board to pull the plug on Massey, or less gently protest the fact that "Victor Rice's overly optimistic projections are still being taken seriously by some European bankers." Bill Wilder maintains that Volkswagen really *was* genuinely interested in a deal. "If they had put in a half-billion dollars," he says, "that would have been the making of Massey. But Conrad never let them in the front door."

"I don't know precisely why the Volkswagen deal was turned down," says Michael Cochrane, who was Massey's vice-president of planning and business development. "Black should probably have let it go forward, but in defence of Conrad he has a strong sense of Canadian history and a sense of fairness which would have made it difficult for him to go through with it."

Cochrane and several other Massey executives were advising Black to pack his bags and leave while the going was good, especially during the summer of 1979, when Massey's first-half profits (at $53.8 million) were on a temporary upswing. Instead, Black dug himself in deeper. In an interview with Irvin Lutsky of the *Toronto Star* published on August 24, 1979, he declared that Argus was preparing to put $100 million into Massey as part of a preferred share refinancing plan. He insisted that unless Argus put its dollars on the line first, other underwriters would not invest in the firm, hinting that a mysterious "offshore buyer" was prepared to take a significant slice of the new offering.

Massey was continuing to suffer from serious internal management problems. Its top executives divided themselves into "doves" (who thought that current operational moves were adequate to turn the company around) and "hawks" (who believed that much more radical cost-cutting would be required). Rice appointed a study group charged with reorganizing his management team and suggesting more drastic expense reductions. Just before Rice left for a badly needed holiday in Sri Lanka, he saw the group's report and specifically ordered that it not be shown to Black until his return. Black had heard rumblings of such a document and asked to see a copy. When he read its recommendations, he got very excited and demanded that they be implemented immediately. He called in Massey's top executives. "From now on," Black thundered, "I'm taking much closer control of day-to-day operations. I'm no longer going to be a bird in a gilded cage around here!" He threatened to fire Rice at least twice, but not much happened. During a private meeting with his executives at the University of Toronto's Hart House after his return from Asia, the Massey president warned his people never to speak to Black or David Radler without first checking with him.

By the end of February 1980, Massey's affairs seemed to have improved a little, at least enough to prompt Black to play host at a York Club dinner to celebrate his conviction that dividend payments on preferred stock would be resumed by year's end. At the annual meeting of shareholders, Rice boasted that Massey had achieved the largest financial turnaround in any one year of any company in Canadian history. True or not, it was a fact that Rice's energetic canvassing of the free world's financial communities had produced new loans of $580 million from 212 banks. At the York Club dinner, Russell Harrison, chairman of the Commerce (which had faithfully carried Massey through its worst moments), snorted to a friend: "*Now* they invite the other bankers!"

In the next few weeks, as if by the trick of an apocalyptic deity, the company's hopes were dashed through a combination of unexpected events. President Jimmy Carter's recent embargo on U.S. grain shipments to the Soviet Union had robbed American farmers of their buying power; the dollar had started to fall dramatically on world currency markets while the British pound had begun a sharp climb—a combination that played havoc with Massey's internal price structure. Worst of all, interest rates kept zooming. The cost of servicing Massey's swollen bank debt was multiplying beyond endurance. Farm machinery sales in North America, already low, dropped by a third in March 1980 and by nearly half in April. Even the weather conspired against the firm when the U.S. cornbelt was hit by drought.

Despite such horrendous problems, Black confided on April 28 in a private letter to Robert Anderson, president of the Hanna Mining Company in Cleveland: "The fact that ill-considered management decisions and bad luck led it to the brink of insolvency must not obscure the enormous opportunity presented by this company whose acute state of undercapitalization has made it possible for us to buy real and absolute control of it so comparatively inexpensively while being hailed as saviours as we do." Speaking to Irvin Lutsky of the *Toronto Star* on May 15, 1980, he described the situation as "a fantastic opportunity" and grandly declared: "We took a roller-coaster ride all the way down with Massey and we plan to ride it all the way back up."

Eight days later, he resigned as the company's chairman and chief executive officer.

THE MASSEY BOARD MEETING on May 23 was one of the most dramatic in the company's not uncolourful history. After dealing with routine items, Conrad stood up to give an accounting of his stewardship. Even the company's official board minutes could not completely bleach out the emotions of the occasion:

> The chairman stated that there now was involved a question of strategy in connection with his own position and those of Argus Corporation and of the Canadian Imperial Bank of Commerce in relation to the company. He commented that there had been a widespread view that the position of Argus had been a restraining influence on the company's ability to attract new equity. While Argus continues to plan to participate in refinancing, it does not wish to be responsible for all the present equity requirements of the company and has made this position clear privately and publicly on many occasions. Notwithstanding this position and the many repetitions of it, some lenders, especially in the United States, and certain elements of the financial community in Canada and elsewhere, have chosen to persist in the belief that the so-called Argus group was inexorably and open-endedly committed to Massey-Ferguson. Mr. Black felt that he had an obligation to all interested parties to disabuse them of these misconceptions.

Black went on to report that the Commerce's executive committee had deferred to June 5 its decision on whether to grant Massey further credit, warning directors that the bank might wish to take back receivables in return for further loans. He described his own position as "becoming ambiguous," pointing out that Argus had ten times as much money invested in Norcen Energy Resources as in Massey. Then he dropped his bombshell, which was duly recorded in the meeting's official minutes:

The Canadian Imperial Bank of Commerce has indicated its desire to talk to the federal government on the matter of Massey-Ferguson's financial condition. Mr. Black felt that such a meeting was premature and had intervened to prevent it taking place. However, if such a meeting was objectively in the company's best interests, then Argus Corporation should not stand in the way. Argus would not, however, under any circumstances accept to be viewed as part of any request for assistance from the federal government. He stated that it was very important that it be realized that the Argus group was a potential key participant in a refinancing group and not a prospective petitioner for assistance. Mr. Black stated that he had therefore come to the conclusion, for many reasons, that it was timely to de-emphasize his own role and that of Argus Corporation in connection with the company. Such a move was being made, however, without any reduction in interest of either himself or Argus Corporation in the company. He expressed his opinion that such a move would be in Massey-Ferguson's best interests as it would serve notice on prospective investors that Argus was not an obstacle to their taking a substantial position; it would enable Mr. Rice to speak more authoritatively on behalf of Massey-Ferguson to prospective investors; and it would lend greater credibility and weight to the Argus group's declared preparedness to invest in a new Massey-Ferguson equity issue under certain conditions.

He stated that, in the circumstances, he wished to revert to the position of chairman of the executive committee, which had been occupied in the past by former Argus chairmen, E.P. Taylor and J.A. McDougald, and he recommended that Mr. Rice be appointed chief executive officer of the company and, on a temporary basis, chairman of the board, which position would ultimately be occupied by the nominee of whoever leads a comprehensive refinancing.

Black's abrupt departure from the Massey chairmanship shook the financial community. No matter how much he protested that he was, after all, staying on as both a director and major shareholder and that he was merely establishing a *cordon sanitaire* between Massey and Argus, investment analysts interpreted his change of status as a vote of no confidence in Massey's future. The company's stock, which in the best of times had been regarded as a mature cyclical and boring investment, hit new depths.

Later, musing about that last exit from Brooklyn, Black expanded on the reasons for his decision: "I wasn't going to sit around there while the third-quarter earnings came in. The greatest service I could perform for that company was to get into a position where any investment that Argus made in Massey would be clearly seen to be disinterested. And not be construed by the other shareholders as my availing myself of their resources to bail out a company that didn't really deserve it.... My objective at Massey all along was to get the operating improvement in the company to intersect with its cash requirements in a way that would enable us to take real, not façade, control of a refinanced Massey at a bargain-basement price, and be hailed as saviours for doing it. But as soon as the British pound shot up, interest rates went through the roof, and the U.S. farm equipment market collapsed, it was just no dice. There was no way Massey was going to make it on the original scenario. So, like Marshal Joffre after the failure of Plan 17, just prior to the first battle of the Marne, I devised a new strategy, which was to get the money in before the earnings could be improved. I knew I had to get out. I couldn't sit there, because it would look as if I were taking the money of whoever was participating on our side and refinancing merely to bail myself out. I also wanted to send the lenders the message that *they* were on the hook, and I wasn't."

Less than two months after his resignation, as part of his Argus reorganization, Black quietly wrote down to zero the value of the holding company's investment in Massey, which at its height had been worth $32 million. ("Our downside risk is absolutely nothing, but our upside opportunity is still enormous. Words like downside and upside offend me culturally, but sometimes they're useful.")

Although he had cited Massey's requests for financial help from Ottawa as one of the main reasons for his resignation as company chairman, Black had in fact met Herb Gray, Minister of Industry, Trade, and Commerce, two months earlier to discuss the guidelines of such assistance. The March 23 meeting was followed by a long letter in which Conrad suggested that Ottawa's bail-out of Chrysler's Canadian operations should include a new diesel engine plant that could be shared by both the troubled companies. The scheme called for the federal government to invest $100 million in a preferred issue of Massey, in return for which Argus would put in a further $200 million. Gray acknowledged the letter without agreeing to its contents, so Black dispatched follow-up missives on July 4 and August 27, repeating his intention of remaining a major participant in any Massey refinancing and requesting "favourable noises" from Ottawa endorsing his approach.* Black told Gray that he had been in touch with Joe Clark, the Conservative leader, and that there would be no opposition from that quarter. "I can assure you," he wrote, adopting a tough tone, "that we in the Argus group, in contemplating the fate of Massey-Ferguson, will not be motivated by any questions of nostalgia, nor will we accept any heritage of continuing responsibility for this company in which we have a trivial investment that we have publicly written off as having no worth, and which was mismanaged in an era when none of us had any connection with nor influence upon it whatever."

Speaking to Deborah McGregor of the *Financial Times of Canada* on the same day, Black for the first time openly betrayed signs of desperation. "I don't care whether the money comes from Ottawa, Queen's Park, or the Ayatollah Khomeini," he said, "as long as the package is big enough to provide the proper refinancing." When she asked about a rumour that Argus-owned Dominion Stores was about to sell off its Quebec stores and funnel the proceeds into cash-starved Massey, Black shot back, "That's absolute horseshit. It's hysterical to suggest that we would steal money from Dominion and hurl it at Massey."

In a final letter to Gray, mailed three weeks later, Black could no longer contain his anger. "I would be remiss," he wrote, "if I did not mention reports that elements of the Cabinet and senior civil service in Ottawa would be well-disposed to assist Massey-Ferguson only if 'Black crawls up the steps of Parliament and begs.' ... I need not dwell again on all the effort Argus Corporation and I personally have made to help Massey through this inherited crisis despite our prodigious lack of enthusiasm and complete blamelessness for it. Under absolutely no circumstances will we inflict further embarrassment upon ourselves than we have already done by maintaining some appearance of solidarity between Massey-Ferguson and ourselves, which is all that has kept Massey afloat for the last two years while its operations have been so impressively streamlined."

In a private conversation with Cabinet secretary Michael Pitfield, Black reiterated his stand: "If you guys want to say 'under no circumstances will the government put a nickel into Massey, that's not what

---

*For the full text of the Gray/Black correspondence, see Appendix C.

we're here for, and it's not our responsibility'—if you say that, you'll not get a word of criticism from me. But one hour later, we'll say the same."

At this point, the nation's press turned sharply against Black, blaming him for most of Massey's troubles and ridiculing the notion of any federal aid. "The idea of a handout to Argus Corporation to save its biggest loser is distasteful in the extreme," wrote Christopher Young in a typical sally published by the Ottawa *Citizen*. "Talk about corporate welfare bums!"

By September, Massey was facing another cash crunch, as reflected in Standard & Poor's lowering of the company's credit rating. The firm's labour force was being reduced from 68,000 to 44,000. Factory space of ten million square feet had been shut down. But nothing seemed to help. At the September 11 directors' meeting, Black tentatively presented the extreme scenario that would have honoured obligations to Canadian, American, and British banks but which in effect invited bankers of other nations to take over local assets and write off their loans.

From Thornbrough came the unexpected argument that Massey had too long been under the domination of the Bank of Commerce, and that it would be a smart move to open negotiations with the Royal to take over the loans. "Al," Black replied, trying to hold his temper, "for one hour this morning Russ Harrison [chairman of the Commerce] was preparing his directors for a possible loss of $100 million on the Massey loan. Do you think the Royal got to be the most profitable bank in the country by taking on loans like this?"

At the time, the Commerce's Massey obligation was the largest unsecured commercial loan in the world. The bank's directors approved the $100-million-loss provision, driving down the Commerce's profit by $14 million for the year, which made it the only one of the Big Five to report a lower net in 1980. Harrison felt very nervous about his position at Massey and started to bypass Black to discuss corporate affairs directly with Rice. At the same time, Argus shareholders were pressing Black not to invest the company's funds in the floundering farm implement firm. Everyone agreed that refinancing was essential, but an impasse had been reached on how it could be brought about. Argus was prepared to make a further investment only if the bankers relaxed their terms; the bankers would make no concessions until Massey could guarantee a fresh influx of cash; government support was not politically practical as long as Argus remained Massey's dominant shareholder. "It was," Black pontificated afterwards, "a state of affairs that had become a Gordian knot and required a clarification as decisive as Alexander's."

On October 2, 1980, Conrad acted. Whispers from Germany that morning had indicated that the Dresdner Bank was about to call its $10-million Massey loan—which could have started a stampede of creditors fighting over Massey's picked-over carcass. In Ottawa, the powerful Economic Development Committee of the Cabinet was about to decide government policy on the Massey predicament. Victor Rice was off in Des Moines, trying to bludgeon farmers into buying his tractors. He was called to a phone and spent the next five hours hanging at the end of a long-distance hook-up with Black, trying to deal with Conrad's dramatic move earlier that morning: all of the Argus directors had resigned from the Massey board and its holding of three million shares was being donated to Massey's pension funds.

PRESSURE HAD BEEN BUILDING inside Argus to jettison its troublesome Massey investment for some months. The holding company's board had empowered its executive committee to make the final decision. (It consisted of the two Black brothers, David Radler, Hal Jackman, Fred Eaton, and Dixon Chant, Argus's executive vice-president.) Monte was in England at the time; Fred Eaton learned of the decision from Bill Harris, chairman of Barclays Bank of Canada, who in turn had heard it on a radio news bulletin; Hal Jackman claims he was told that Argus would retain an option on the stock that had been donated to the pension funds. (Jackman was so anxious to resign from Massey that he sent his resignation over to the Argus offices in the custody of two commissionaires—just in case one of them had a heart attack on the way.) Radler stayed in Vancouver, but he had left a resignation behind in Chant's desk, dated May 16. The giveaway seems to have been worked out by Black and Chant. Its effect was to make Massey the world's largest employee-controlled company, but the real power had now slipped to the banks. The next day, Russ Harrison of the Commerce phoned Victor Rice to inquire pointedly: "How's *my business* doing?"

Derek Hayes, Massey's corporate secretary, was leaving Massey at about this time to take a parallel position at Shell Canada. Black heard about the shift and phoned him up. "You and I," he declared grandly, echoing the famous signal of Vice-Admiral Frank Fletcher during the Battle of Midway, "are transferring our flags to more seaworthy ships."

Public reaction to the Argus "gift" was anything but kind. "Conrad Black's unexpected extrication from the Massey scene was a stroke of corporate genius," wrote John Belanger in the *Toronto Sun*, "but anyone who imputes noble motives to the man or his henchmen is making a serious mistake. Noble he ain't; smart he is." The *Sun* attacked Black's actions in an editorial so vicious that he threatened to sue. To calm him down, publisher Douglas Creighton agreed to run his unedited reply, which read in part: "For the record (not that the *Sun* is a newspaper of record for anyone who doesn't suffer from lip-strain after ten seconds of silent reading) the *Sun*'s theory that we should mortgage all the assets of our other companies, which are all prospering and have hundreds of thousands of other shareholders, to bail Massey out of a mess that none of us had any hand in creating, is too asinine to merit further reply...."

"I am amazed," Black publicly declared, "by the number of so-called financial experts who are luxuriating in the view that I am some sort of punch-drunk prizefighter on the ropes. Well, screw them."

In private, his thoughts weren't much different. "Not to wax overly philosophical," he waxed, "in any significant career in the history of the world, except for maybe Alexander the Great, there are setbacks. In seeking victory one must sometimes accept the possibility of defeat. I'm coming perilously close to sounding like Richard Nixon the day he resigned when he was quoting Teddy Roosevelt, but the fact is that Massey was bust when I took it over and I couldn't possibly end up with a worse situation. Meantime, I've distracted my opposition and multiplied the worth of Ravelston seven times. Massey was a trivial investment and an inherited problem, lent importance only by the fact that it is such a great old company.

"With a stunning lack of originality," Black continued, warming up to his subject, "some people have leapt on this thing as a way of showing that Black is a flash-in-the-pan. They say I staked everything on Massey, as if I could have staked everything on matters that no individual in the world could influence—interest and exchange rates, the Iranian Revolution, stuff like that. That will just not fly. I can document every minute I was an officer of that company. Historically, nobody is going to hang this one on me. All those pent-up forces of envy and disbelief finally showed their true colours instead of masquerading in the deceitful fashion they have used since I took over at Argus. It has replaced the view of me as a whiz kid, which I have always found to be at best tasteless, with some kind of image of durability in survivorship despite rough shocks—the sudden clash of battle and the long-drawn-out trials of vigilance, that sort of thing. It is terribly important, particularly for someone who is supposedly a leader of the Establishment, that such a person not just come upon his success as a Sir Galahad but have his ups and downs."

Mesmerized by the persona he was creating, Black contended that "there is something about the Canadian mentality that cannot stand an unbroken string of successes, unless it comes after a long life or after evident ordeal. No one begrudged Terry Fox getting the Order of Canada and no one boos any more when E.P. Taylor wins the Queen's Plate. But present Canadians with too much success too soon and it's just unbearable. That's how it works in this country."

Not an inconsiderable consolation was that Argus's donation to the Massey pension funds of its three million shares represented no real financial drain. It allowed Black to claim $39 million as a capital tax loss, which by law can be taken back one year. Having made a profit on its sale of Domtar shares to MacMillan Bloedel, Argus was thus able to recover the $7.4 million it had paid in taxes on that transaction and still retain a $9.2-million tax benefit on future deals.

By the end of 1980, Massey was reporting a $199-million loss, with its Australian operations in receivership. During the following six months Victor Rice mounted a valiant $715-million refinancing effort which at least temporarily salvaged the situation. Some $200 million in guarantees from the Ontario and federal governments facilitated the eventual refinancing, but the company's long-term future remained in doubt.

On October 28, 1981, John Turner, a Massey director, gave a dinner for Toronto's financial community to which Black was invited. Rice made an eloquent speech about his ordeal, and of the three individuals he singled out for special mention in keeping the company alive, one was Black. They toasted each other and went home.

The most enduring reminder of Black's own ordeal is a startling painting that hangs in his Argus office, depicting the Massey dealership at Arras in France. The artist has caught the eerie green glow of war, portraying the farm implement dealer's burnt-out buildings gutted by the gunfire of 1918. A column of weary soldiers marches by, towing a fieldpiece. It is a scene straight from Hell.

This was the canvas Conrad defiantly tucked under his arm as he was walking out of his chairman's office at Massey for the last time. "I'll be goddamned," he told Rice, "if I'm leaving here with nothing to show for it. I'm taking this, and if you want to invoice me for it, go ahead!"

He never did get a bill. But occasionally Conrad recalls those hard days at Massey, particularly his memorable exit carrying that strange painting out of its haunted offices. "It was," he shrugs wryly, "like grabbing a deckchair while jumping off a sinking ship."

CHAPTER SEVEN

A Random Walk through the Mind of Conrad Black

*Even if Conrad is unexpectedly attuned to other
people's sensitivities, he has trouble differentiating
between knowing and feeling, between solitude and
loneliness, between repeating Toronto Club bons mots
and forcing the lock of his true emotions.*

Conrad Black's most impressive quality is his memory. The
uncanny ability with which he can recall at will almost anything
he has read, seen, or experienced is a daunting natural gift, like a
singer's perfect pitch or a tightrope-walker's sense of balance. There is
apparent in every aspect of his discourse a portentous ability for remembering obscure facts and fussy details. He has occasionally dazzled
visitors with such bravura sleights-of-mind as rhyming off the names
and tonnages of every ship in the Spanish Armada, reconstructing John
Diefenbaker's 1957 Cabinet, or reeling out daily casualty reports on
both sides at the bloody siege of Leningrad.

But more often he will resurrect details of historical incidents,
thoughts, and examples like a pop-archaeologist, evaluating the depth
of other people's knowledge by sifting for clues in their reactions to his
flights of recall. He is also possessed by an alarmingly active Proustian
tendency to judge current events through parallel historical perspectives.

Each of his acquaintances and associates has his own favourite list
that Black has at some time dredged up from his memory store,
including the salary of each of Sterling's six hundred employees; the
winners (by constituency names) of Quebec's federal M.P.s since Confederation; the latest ranking of cardinals in the Vatican's Byzantine
pecking order; and the fact that Spencer Perceval was the only British
prime minister to have been assassinated in office.

John Finlay, one of Conrad's Hollinger associates, recalls a dinner
they had at the York Club with Pierre Gousseland, the French-born

chairman of Amax, a giant U.S. metal extracting firm. "Conrad absolutely dazzled him," says Finlay, "by going through France's five republics in perfectly fluent French, not just by dates but by individual ministers, their accomplishments and downfalls. This fellow just sat back and listened, spellbound. But after dinner Gousseland had to leave, and we withdrew to the club's drawing room with an Englishman who was the Amax senior vice-president of finance. When it turned out he had served aboard a Royal Navy battle cruiser, Conrad started to go through the British fleet, gun by gun, inch by inch. At one point they were talking about a particularly tense period during the Second World War and Conrad demanded, 'Where were you when that took place?' The Englishman said, 'August, 1943? I can't remember.' So Conrad asked him, 'What ship were you on?' As soon as he found out it had been HMS *Renown*, Black shrugged and said, 'Oh well, you must have been stationed in Gibraltar.' The fellow just wilted."

Jonathan Birks, the most interesting of the carriage-trade store's Inheritors, recalls determining to test his friend's memory. Birks had just finished reading a book on the Bonapartes and, with the volume's family chart before him, telephoned Conrad on the spur of the moment. "Since I had just finished the book and had the Bonaparte family tree in front of me," Birks said, "I figured there was no way I couldn't remember more about Napoleon than he did. So I coyly started in on the subject of Bonaparte, where his family came from, which prince had married what princess, and stuff like that. Within twenty minutes, he had exhausted my chart. Obviously talking off the cuff, he went on for another half hour, not only reciting what each man had done but how his later absence would affect the history of the Austro-Hungarian Empire. It was a very humiliating experience."

Peter White, one of Black's original partners in the Sterling newspaper chain, recalls a similar incident when they were both living in Knowlton and a relative from Britain who had served as captain of a Royal Navy cruiser dropped in for a visit. "The subject of some battle that had taken place in the theatre of war that my uncle had been in came up and Conrad said, oh yes, such and such ships were in that engagement, weren't they? Uncle Hank disagreed and named the battle line he thought had fought that long-ago day. But Conrad was adamant. 'I don't think you're right, sir,' he maintained. They looked it up. Of course, Conrad turned out to be right and my uncle, the naval captain, turned out to be wrong. The longer you know him, the more often you come across this ability of Conrad's to drag up events, dates, and conversations. He can probably remember every telephone number any of his friends ever had."

Nick Auf der Maur, Conrad's Montreal friend, spent most of the 1960s enlisting himself in various radical causes, including the setting up of a Cuban press operation in Canada. He recalls, "I recruited this Argentinian guy I knew to be office manager of their Montreal bureau, and when the head of the Cuban press agency was in town I asked them if they'd like to have dinner with a real live capitalist press baron. I'd built up Conrad as the owner of a big chain of newspapers, and the Cuban was quite enthralled by the whole idea. We were chatting away, and at one point Conrad went to the washroom. So I said, 'You know, Mr. Black is quite knowledgeable about your part of the world. Just ask him what he knows about the Argentinian Navy, for example.' So when he came back, the Argentinian asked him about naval activities surrounding the time of Juan Perón's overthrow. Conrad promptly proceeded not only to reel off the entire fleet and the names of every ship's captain but also where each vessel was manoeuvring on the day of Perón's ouster. The two Latin Americans just sat there stunned that this weird guy in an Italian restaurant in Montreal in 1971 could recite precisely what had happened sixteen years before off Buenos Aires in the Rio de la Plata."

Brian McKenna, another Montreal friend, recalls sitting in on arguments Conrad had with Patrick Brown, who had covered the Vietnam War for the CBC, was married to a Vietnamese, and had spent years boning up on that strife-torn country's post-colonial history. "Conrad would hold forth not just on the complex politics of Saigon but he knew the home provinces where each of the various players came from and the details of their political circumstances. It was," McKenna remembers, "just as if he were discussing the parish politics of east-end Montreal."

When Scott Abbott, sports editor of the *Sherbrooke Daily Record*, spontaneously challenged Conrad to recite the final major league baseball standings for 1953, he spun them off in reverse order, giving the won-lost record of each team, and making only one mistake. (Abbott vividly recalls his first meeting with Conrad: "He greeted me by saying, 'I understand you're an American presidential history buff.' When I allowed that I could name all the U.S. presidents with the dates of their administrations, he shot back: 'Yes, but can you do it backwards in thirty seconds?' I gather he could, but I didn't ask.")

The late Igor Kaplan, Conrad's lawyer, had a similar experience when he invited Black to his house during a visit of his European-born mother. "They were discussing the politics of the Weimar Republic when she casually mentioned tht it was too bad Gustav Stresemann, the foreign minister of the Weimar Republic, had died so suddenly. Conrad enthusiastically agreed, but reminded her that he'd been responsible for almost destroying the Treaty of Locarno. Mother was flabbergasted. 'My God, I'd forgotten that,' she said. 'I was about seventeen when Stresemann came to power. Today there are very few of *my* contemporaries who would remember him because Hitler was the most dominating name in German politics, which makes it even more remarkable that Conrad, who was not even born then, would know details of what the man had been trying to achieve.'"

Kaplan's explanation for Black's phenomenal memory was that Conrad listens and reads with as much energy as most people use for speaking and acting: "When you're talking to him, Conrad looks directly at you, he never glances away, and he never appears ready to interrupt or answer you." Brian Stewart, a friend from Black's university days, says that when Conrad is reading, "there's an almost physical sense of concentration that comes over his face. His brows get furrowed – it's as if he were burning up each page."

It is a mental feat implanted during his youth by the habits of Conrad's family. "He used to challenge his father on general questions a lot," Stewart recalls. "I was quite interested in bullfighting at the time, and even though Conrad had told me that his father knew nothing about it, I asked George Black who he thought the greatest bullfighter of all had been. He was damned if he was going to admit he wasn't sure. He must have sat there and thought for ten solid minutes before he said: 'I have it: Manolete, of course.' It was a good answer, and I vividly remember the two of them, father and son, continually challenging each other on some pretty obscure stuff."

PHYSICALLY, IT IS HIS EYES that are Black's most compelling feature. When he gets bored, they grow as blank as the gaze of a Las Vegas croupier – but during negotiations on percentage spreads, they glint with Cromwellian intensity. Their colour is a matter of minor dispute. "I think they're hazel," he himself says. "I'm not sure. Even Sir Nevile Henderson in his memoirs refers to Adolf Hitler's eyes as being surprisingly blue, so blue one could become quite lyrical about them if one were a woman. Hitler, of course, had brown eyes. And Henderson's embassy wasn't very successful, in any case." (In fact, Black's eyes are periwinkle-grey, a hue found mostly inside gun muzzles.)

His body language can be deafening. Anger lends primitive cadence to his limb movements as he paces his office like a puma in heat. "He has a natural knack of demonstrating personal power which in a negotiating situation is a tremendous asset," noted Igor Kaplan. "People pick up the vibrations of that power subconsciously from the way he moves and listens. It's very subtle, but it works."

Black has a highly disquieting impact on most businessmen. A fellow Bank of Commerce director, for example, claims that at one executive committee meeting during which Argus's financial affairs were being discussed, "the boardroom reverberated with Conrad's absence."

When he is thinking out the repercussions of a major business move, Black's face clenches like a fist from the effort of trying to turn his brain into a computer that will accurately assess the downside risks of the proposition he is testing. His concentration is diluted by the occasional gleam of mischief, as if he were a paratroop colonel in a former African dependency who has hit on the notion of selling TV rights to his takeover of the local palace.

Once having made a decision, he relaxes into his more customary mode of a middleweight pugilist gone soft. Six feet tall and pudgy-shouldered, he carries himself as awkwardly as if he were crossing a pond of freshly formed ice. In repose, he makes steeples of his fingers and speculates upon the edicts of the universe. He listens to anyone who doesn't bore him to distraction so intently that the echoes of comprehension are visible on his face. "He is intensely verbal," *Fortune* noted in a 1979 profile, "speaking in measured cadences and spinning out long sentences that in the end—on the very brink of disintegration—he somehow manages to salvage."

Black's pomposity can grow tiresome, so that one expects him to describe the Air Canada shuttle between Toronto and Montreal as "a miracle of heavier-than-air locomotion." He reels in his sentences like dancing swordfish; makes up words ("dowagerish"); hones his insults ("I warn you, this man is an insufferable paltroon"); loves to coin epigrams slightly out of plumb ("Nelson Skalbania would be less of a gambler if he actually *had* $100 million"); and concocts pithy quotes ("Now that we've proven we're no good at playing hockey competitively in this country any more, takeovers have become the great Canadian sport"). He loves to show off his knowledge. "Andreotti is interesting," he will declare to a roomful of Establishmentarians who think he is about to glorify the exploits of some newly arrived Neapolitan chef. "Andreotti was possibly the most intelligent head of government in the West. Ironically enough, Italy hasn't been administered with any degree of efficiency or consistency since the early middle Roman Empire—yet it has staged a heroic feat of parliamentarianism."

Not for Conrad any *esprit d'escalier*, the belated *bon mot* that comes to mind as one is descending the stairs after a party. The quip is off his tongue with enviable timing.

173

He is a highly complicated character, perhaps best caught in comparisons with painters and composers. Hippolyte Loiseau, the French essayist, once complained that Mozart was the only person who really understood him. With Conrad, it would take Mahler. His mental gymnastics can be best comprehended as a subject appropriate to the pointillism of Georges Seurat. The nineteenth-century French neo-impressionist imbued his paintings with an inner glow through the use of minute brushstrokes, meaningless by themselves but startling in their combination.

This aura of multidimensional complexity, which Black does little to discourage, is an attempt to create his own brand of immunity. Despite the half-dozen scrapbooks of clippings he has kept to document his exploits and his willingness to talk on any subject at the drop of a split infinitive, he has dug a deep moat to protect his inner self. As an amateur historian he knows the importance of creating a vacuum around himself, of generating that quality of romantic remoteness that sets any society's memorable figures apart from their lesser cousins.

Through all the speculation about his modes and motives, Conrad remains the prisoner of his own cool reason, closed up as a snail. Despite the avalanche of public praise and invective, he is desperately protective of his home and family, trying to insulate his wife and children from the intrusions of the curious and the covetous. He gives at the office.

CONRAD BLACK UNDERSTANDS LIFE as a tangle of ambiguities and realizes that even the best theories eventually collapse into detail. He is a fatalist, believing that people's destinies are always more fascinating than their day-to-day reactions. He subscribes to the exquisitely sad comment by the seventeenth-century French satiric moralist Jean de La Bruyère, who wrote that "life is a tragedy for those who feel, and a comedy for those who think." He finds it difficult to believe in redemption, in clean slates, or in atonement – because every act must have its consequences, which have to be understood and absorbed. His arrogance is intellectual, not egotistical, and the difference is that he has the historian's sense of perspective.

What makes him interesting is that he follows the strong existential streak in his nature. It leads him beyond mundane preoccupations to the invention of new challenges, then rising to meet them – even if, as in the attempt to rescue Massey, he destroys himself a little in the process.

A random walk through the mind of Conrad Black is no effortless journey.

He may well be the only businessman in Canadian history who

deserves to be taken seriously when he confesses: "Hal Jackman and I agree that we're basically more Nietzschean than Hegelian."

The Protestant work ethic may be his Holy Grail (in the sense that "achieving" is not a dirty word), but Conrad aims both higher (by nominating himself as the chief animator of Canada's new proprietor class) and lower (by observing the whole scene as something of a game in which all he really wants is to be better at it than the current set of players).

He has trouble working out any form of understandable motivation for himself, returning always to his pride in not having inherited all his money and his contempt for rich men's sons who consume their resources. "I'm rich and I'm not ashamed of being wealthy," he keeps repeating, as if the words were some verbal amulet to ward off the plague. "Why should I be? I made all my money fairly."

This is hardly an epiphany to warm the soul, and even if Conrad is unexpectedly attuned to other people's sensitivities, he has trouble differentiating between knowing and feeling, between solitude and loneliness, between repeating Toronto Club *bons mots* and forcing the lock of his true emotions.

The upper-class family traditions in which he was raised allowed him few chances to wrestle with reality, but that hasn't robbed him of yearnings or the desire to argue with the universe. The ethics he has evolved, however far removed they may be from the more ordinary pursuits of the less-blessed majority, at least have been derived not from intellectual assimilation but out of deliberate thought and experience. If Conrad defends his perceptions, both political and economic, with a dash of savagery, it is because he recognizes that impulses opposed to his own could quickly destroy the values four generations of Blacks have been trying to protect.

"I act from intuition," Black told a friend in the spring of 1982, "and my intuition tells me at the moment that just as a squirrel is good at putting up acorns, chestnuts, or whatever the hell squirrels collect, this is the time to build up one's reserves and get into a solid material condition. I don't want to sound pseudo-biblical, but there is a time to assemble and organize your assets, if you are a so-called man of means as I am judged to be, and a time to—if not dissipate them—commit them."

MOST CANADIAN BUSINESSMEN are about as introspective as lion tamers. That minority of thoughtful executives who somehow manage to juggle their ideals and ambitions tend to be Rhodes-scholar types, affecting upper-class Anglicanism, mid-Atlantic accents, and a strain of transient piety to sustain their compromised view of life. Conrad Black is different. A conservative to the core of his being, he has what Nick Auf der Maur calls "this weird little egalitarian streak. He's insufferable with people he thinks are stupid, dull, or a waste of time. But if somebody's interesting or if he thinks he can glean some unfathomable mystery of a current trend in society, he can be quite charming. I've introduced him to people in bars where he'd get the idea he might learn about the workings of twentieth-century depraved minds, or something, and he'd sit there for hours asking questions like a crown prosecutor, trying to find out exactly what's up."

But Black has trouble connecting with ordinary people in everyday situations, as if he suffered from psychic jet lag. There is in his bearing Jehovian pride that tends to complicate the simplest of human exchanges. He suffers from what the French call *l'orgueil*—an untranslatable quality of the thirst to play God that implies its possessor is seldom wrong and never regretful. "I may make mistakes," Conrad cheerfully admits, "but at the moment I can't think of any."

When a close friend asked Black, then at the height of his infatuation with French Canada's social evolution, "If you're so interested in politics, why don't you run for premier of Quebec?" Conrad thought it over for a moment. Then he replied, "Quebec's not ready for me. Maybe Spain."

Franco aside, the riposte was an uncharacteristic oversimplification. Black's view of the political process is far more comprehensive than his wisecrack implied. Among the new generation of Canada's Establishment, Black is one of the few with the wit and the intellect to sort his beliefs and prejudices into some kind of credible philosophical context. "Because intellectuals...dominate the power of the word, the conservative philosophy of capitalists has made a very poor showing in the recent history of ideas," he maintains. Whenever businessmen have tried to defend themselves with words, "they have tended to bellow ultra-right clichés like wounded dinosaurs, much to the amusement of the intellectual left. John Stuart Mill labelled the Conservative party in England the 'stupid party'; the truth is that until recently conservative ideas were so poorly articulated that they simply weren't taken seriously." No redneck reactionary, Conrad places himself firmly in the stream of neo-conservatism, alongside Bernard-Henri Lévy, Daniel Bell, Norman Podhoretz, and Irving Kristol.

In the autumn of 1979, when Kristol spoke in Toronto at an Insurance Bureau of Canada banquet, Black gave the introduction and told of the visit to Canada of their friend and fellow-traveller, William F. Buckley, Jr. "He came here to debate with David Lewis, the former leader of our New Democratic Party," Conrad said, "and when he arrived at Toronto

Airport the immigration officer asked, 'What is the purpose of your visit?'

"Buckley countered, 'To desocialize Canada.'

"With the usual phlegmatic manner of those airport people, the officer responded not at all to that, but moved on to ask what would be the duration of the visit.

"'Twenty-four hours,' Buckley smoothly replied."*

Conrad Black's ideological roots stretch back to the stern political doctrines of Great Britain's Whigs—the land-owning families who held power in eighteenth-century England under the early Georges, mixing their reliance on individual enterprise with such touches of reform as the belief in a constitutional monarchy instead of divine-right absolutism. Whiggism developed in the United States in the early nineteenth century, uniting some eastern capitalists, southern plantation owners, and pragmatic predecessors of the Republicans. "There is a bit of the Whig in me," Black admits, "but I tend to be more conservative than those people, not really believing in their style of Jeffersonian free-thinking. I'm also more of a humanist. I'm offended at Jefferson, for example, sitting there at Monticello with all his slaves, agonizing over whether to free them, talking about how the tree of liberty must be refreshed from time to time with the blood of patriots and tyrants. There are some areas of non-identification for me in that, but there's some truth in it, too."

Black retains a clear notion about the separation of private wealth and public authority but insists that the accumulated forces of the political right and left arrived at an impasse more than a decade ago. "This," he pronounces, "is a position that both conservative and socialist Hegelians can recognize as requiring a synthesis. The indecision...of our society...is traceable to the profound schism between those who would unite nostalgia, common sense, and the power of the individual to recapture some of the past, and those who would complete the socialization of our society. The Soviet Union has achieved great gains in the past few years, not because it's a dynamic or creative or even productive society—it's none of these—but because it possesses a national consensus undisturbed by societal contradictions that strike to the very core of public policy."

At a time when most Canadian tycoons feel that if Ottawa politicians could organize it, there would be a bounty on businessmen's scalps, Conrad's convoluted chatter has a soothing effect—even if few of the

---

*During his introductory remarks at the banquet, which was being held in the CPR-owned Royal York Hotel, the fire alarm suddenly went off. When it was eventually subdued, Black improvised: "I knew the waiters were NDP, but I'm disappointed in Ian Sinclair." The audience loved it.

177

Toronto Club regulars privy to his musings have much idea of what he is talking about.

Black interrupts his theory-spinning with another thought: "Perhaps we're all waiting for a new Karl Marx to emerge from the reading room of the British Museum with the canons of a new order, reconciling the more popular elements of capitalism and socialism." Then he adds: "While we await that event, those of us who are preoccupied with both commerce and the humanities may reflect on the curious unevenness of our blessings. We still have the wealthiest and most creative society in the history of the world, but never have relations between the commercial and cultural leadership weighed more heavily. The businessman tends to think that the government person, elected or otherwise, is either a sleazy politician or an officious, intermeddling bureaucrat. The government person tends to regard the businessman as an absolute dullard … an avaricious booby advancing forward like a bear to a honey pot, with no interest but gluttony. A mutual reduction of suspicions would be a good thing."

One of the more interesting private exchanges in this escalating confrontation between Canada's public and private sectors took place in the spring of 1981, following a private Toronto luncheon attended by both Black and Michael Pitfield, Clerk of the Privy Council and Secretary to the Trudeau Cabinet. On May 12, the Argus chairman penned a lengthy epistle to the Ottawa mandarin generally credited with being Trudeau's guru-in-residence:

Dear Michael:

The…luncheon on Friday was a useful one, and if, as you indicated, such business-government contacts may recur and multiply, a few reflections might be helpful. These are entirely personal and make no pretense to being representative.

I am sure everyone appreciates the implacable and complex nature of inflation as a problem and the unique jurisdictional difficulties that the Canadian federal system imposes upon the central government. I am also certain, however, that most Canadians, and certainly most members of the financial community, do not believe that, in fighting inflation, the federal government has shown the requisite degree of restraint, frugality or even psychological mobilization. From the Prime Minister's unforgotten comment about having wrestled inflation to the mat to your own disparagements of President Reagan's budget-cutting, the possibly inaccurate impression has been allowed to subsist that those who lead the federal government consider themselves responsible for a social and political climate that is (as you pointed out) stable and prosperous compared to less favoured countries, and that the over-indulged Canadian public is the slothful and ungrateful author of its own woes.

Thus, on Friday, there was the singular insinuation that the "explosion" in executive compensation after the removal of anti-inflation controls was a wellspring of renascent inflation when, in fact, even if there was such a phenomenon, it was practically irrelevant. Similarly, the wager you offered that Mrs. Thatcher would not only be defeated, but would lead the British Conservative Party to oblivion as she did so – and your persistent assimilation of corporate growth to restraint of competition may have reconfirmed suspicions that your familiar notion of countervailing forces is, inter alia, a Neo-Hegelian pretext for unlimited government interference in the private sector. (Incidentally, I accept your bet on Mrs. Thatcher. I think she will probably be re-elected and it is much more likely that the Labour Party will vanish than that the Conservative Party will.)

It may, in the circumstances, have been difficult for some to consider your references to the National Energy Program as the most moderate of many alternatives that were considered, the suscitation of the nauseating concept of a 10 per cent limit on corporate shareholdings in industries far removed from banking, and your own protestations to profound attachment to the business community as anything more substantial than rather disingenuous posturings.

Lest you should doubt it, I am a centralist, a believer in a mixed economy, in a taxation-based restraint on inflation and in FIRA. (I don't agree with Gordon Gray's comments on this subject. No self-respecting country can tolerate the extent of foreign control of strategic industries that we have endured, and the early economic growth of the United States was financed by debt rather than equity capital.) I support the federal government's constitutional initiative and the espoused objectives and many of the specific dispositions of the National Energy Program.

Just as you believe that it is vital in the continuing independentist debate in Quebec to gain the constitutional changes the federal government is now seeking (and I agree with you), the repatriation of much of Canadian industry, apart from being desirable in itself, would also be extremely useful in coping with the nationalistic Quebec argument that Canada is only an Anglo-American branch plant, and in endowing all Canadians with a greater sense of traditional economic identity. I have undoubtedly bored you and some of your colleagues with my championship of the view that in this and several other respects the aspirations of the federal government and the more enlightened and important elements of the business community could be confluent.

There have been many changes, in personalities, attitudes and circumstances, in the last few years in the Toronto financial community, and a more constructive relationship between that community and Ottawa is now possible. I have always been careful not to imply that I thought there was any equivalence between the Toronto Club and the Privy Council. Nor am I unmindful of the political attractiveness and humorous possibilities of ignoring, baiting or even discriminating against the proverbial Toronto Establishment. Such a policy, apart from being a squandered opportunity, would be, to say the least, unstatesmanlike. (If my memory is accurate, there was no federal Liberal Minister from Toronto in nearly thirty years prior to the elevation of Paul Hellyer in 1957. You should, in fairness, remember that few Toronto businessmen have known the federal government as a powerful collaborator in a great enterprise, as the corresponding people in Montreal have known it in the long federalist debate in Quebec.)

Obviously the federal government and the Toronto business community can continue to coexist more or less satisfactorily in a state of reciprocal suspicion. However, if the federal government does have some serious notion of the dynamic of capital and does believe in some plausible version of an incentive system (and neither of these points emerged with particular clarity from your remarks on Friday), then a closer rapport between the federal government and the Toronto business community, insusceptible to allegations of unseemly collusion or truckling to special interests, is possible and desirable.

I do not wish to seem an importuning and sanctimonious busybody, but if there is anything reasonable I can do to help produce such an improved business-government relationship, in the uncontroversial national interest, I would be happy to pursue it.

I passed on your good wishes to Shirley, who fully reciprocates them to you and Nancy, as do I.

Yours sincerely,

Conrad M. Black.

Not to be outdone, Pitfield shot back this riposte:

Dear Conrad:

It was a delight to read your letter of May 12. Shades of Lord Beaverbrook and Grattan O'Leary! I haven't been for twenty years on the receiving end of such firm and sweeping assertions—each containing a kernel of truth surrounded by a thick and highly debatable shell.

Of all your remarks that I might contest, two that I feel I must clarify are with regard to what I said concerning President Reagan's budget-cutting and Mrs. Thatcher's program. On the former, my statement was that Mr. Reagan's budget-cutting was no more in relation to his economy than what Mr. Trudeau's government did in Canada in 1977, and not yet as much as was done in 1978 and in 1979 and, of course, on the tax reduction side, we have done more year by year than Reagan ever dreamed of doing! As regards his overall policy mix, I think it is a long-shot but I wish him well. In relation to Mrs. Thatcher's program, I said that it could not but be highly divisive in an already polarized and class-conscious society. Consequently I see a dim future for both the Conservative and the Labour Parties, and fear Britain may be in for a period in which a third group has the balance of power—not a happy situation in the Parliamentary form of government.

For the rest, it is fascinating to hear what one thought one said played back by another in terms of what he thought he heard. Your judgements in this regard I respect. I know you do not expect me to accept them. In fact, I would hope that neither of us is as extreme or as uncompromising as you suggest. To the contrary, I suspect that we and our colleagues are men of goodwill trying to make the best of a murky situation; that we are fallible and imperfect, but not intent on disparaging, deceiving, insinuating, posturing, ignoring, baiting, discriminating or truckling.

On the basis that this is so, I hope that we will soon meet again. I think discussion between us and our colleagues would indeed be extremely fruitful and I look forward to it.

Yours sincerely,

Michael

BLACK CAN (AND DOES) GO ON FOR HOURS drawing out analogies, both defending capitalism's achievements and condemning its less-attractive byproducts. "When I noted several years ago at Christmas-time," he says, "that Walter Cronkite's newscast was sponsored in part by an electric denture-cleaning device, I had a profound conviction that the trajectory of this society simply could not continue." He warms to his subject: "We have called upon our entire work force to maintain traditional bourgeois standards of artisanship, thrift, and respect for the work ethic while on the job. And they are encouraged after hours to transform themselves from economic Jekyll to Hyde, becoming profligate and consumptive spenders and swingers, to maintain the system at a breakneck pace of production and self-indulgence." At least in public, Black exalts the puritan ethic ("frugality, sobriety, diligence, self-abnegation, piety and sexual conservatism") and condemns its decline: "Gradually before my eyes – and I came late as an onlooker – the spirit of sacrifice and self-help, under the incitements of the consumption economy and the trucklings of the political community, gave way to a demand for luxury and leisure. Equality, not just civil but economic equality, became more important to our society than liberty. It was not just…a revolution of rising expectations and, therefore, of prearranged disappointments, but of entitlements, of a whole population righteously believing it could effortlessly receive what elemental arithmetic assured could not be sufficiently supplied. It would have been astonishing, given the banality and compulsiveness of much of this, if the entire institutional structure of our society hadn't been sorely tested, especially with the added pressures of the Vietnam War."

It is when he dons the cloak of a Cold War gladiator that Black becomes least obscure. He is particularly upset by what he views as Europe's reluctance to shoulder its appropriate share of Western defence. "The Europeans had been conditioned by the inanities of the Carter era," he expounds, "…to believe that the United States would foot the bill for an adequate Western security in exchange for the benign condescensions and tutelages of the wise European beneficiaries. They do not really want the United States to be stronger than is necessary to maintain a modest level of deterrence in Western Europe, and the determination of the present administration to re-establish American strategic strength, apart from being welcome in itself, should, with a little statesmanship, have a salubrious effect on relations with Europe…. Europe is going to have to choose between genuine self-strengthening or real trustworthiness and constancy as an ally, or Finlandization. I would be reassured if American diplomacy were in the hands of more consistent people than at present but…am gratified by Reagan's latest initiative. With discretion and sensitivity, I still think the United States can conduct Europe to a more exalted destiny than self-righteous passivity. In this respect, our greatest ally is the illimitable vanity of the Europeans themselves."

Although Black likes to parade himself as an ideological Renaissance Man, open to the winds of thought from any direction, the character into which he fits best is that of a Canadian William F. Buckley, Jr.* For example: "I'm terribly impatient with that New York-Washington group of small-l liberals who fail to recognize the increasing danger to our civilization. By 'civilization' I'm not referring to whether corporate income taxes are 40 per cent or 60 per cent. I mean that which fundamentally differentiates North American society from others. These people are so full of good intentions, so talented and admirable, yet they have the utmost difficulty in recognizing the danger of our position. Their absolute smugness, their 'there'll-always-be-an-England' feeling, their fanatical determination not to believe that there's a strategic threat of great proportions and that the United States simply has to maintain a much more plausible state of military deterrence, is a case of badly misplaced altruism. To me, the United States before Ronald Reagan represented the most precipitate decline of the relevance of any major country since the fall of France in 1940."

In the spring of 1981, Conrad attended the annual Bilderberg Conference, a private gabfest that usually brings together the free world's most influential citizens, including David Rockefeller and Henry Kissinger. He was gratified to be thanked by Jeane Kirkpatrick, the U.S. ambassador to the United Nations, for his championing of the Reagan Administration's foreign policy. "As my last intervention at the conference," he boasts, "I said that I thought Ronald Reagan was going to re-establish the United States as unquestionably the greatest economic and military power in the world, which is what it should be."

Later the same year, when Black and his wife, Shirley, put on an entertainment at the Art Gallery of Ontario for Andy Warhol, who had

---

*In the summer of 1973, when *Saturday Night* was in one of its periodic financial slumps, Black, who by then had acquired his chain of small newspapers, wrote to Buckley for advice on the publishing business:

"I take the liberty of writing to you on behalf of many members of the journalistic, academic, and business communities of this country who wish to convert an existing Canadian magazine into a conveyance for views at some variance with the tired porridge of ideological normalcy in vogue here as in the USA.

"In order to understand better what we are getting into, we would be very appreciative if you could afford us a brief interview in the course of the summer which would touch upon the difficulties you have faced, especially financially, at the *National Review*. We are aware of the lack in Canada of serious editorial talent of an appropriate political coloration. The leaders of this nascent enterprise, including the undersigned, are aware also of the precarious economic prospects of such a project.

"We are, however, people of some means as well as of some conviction, and unless faced by an insuperable economic barrier, intend to persevere with our plans, to execution. Financial support and editorial contributions have been arranged in a measure sufficient to justify the final preparative stages.

"It is in that context that we would like some advice from you as we will at least partially emulate your example at the *National Review*."

just completed painting a portrait of Conrad, one of the attending guests was Thomas O. Enders, U.S. Assistant Secretary of State for Inter-American Affairs. An old friend of the Blacks' from his term as American ambassador to Canada, Enders was at the time masterminding the U.S. response to the militarily escalating situation in El Salvador and had been involved with the Cambodian bombings during the Vietnam War. In his brief remarks to the gathering, Conrad complained that Enders hadn't taken his advice on how to conduct the war in Southeast Asia, to which Gaetana, Enders's outspoken wife, yelled out: "If Tom had, the war would have lasted even longer!"

The point was never resolved, but Black had been advocating early mining of Haiphong harbour and a general escalation of hostilities against the North "instead of having all those American draftees slogging around the jungles of South Vietnam." His hawkish attitude is probably best exemplified by his half-serious suggestion to the artist who painted a fresco of summer clouds on the ceiling of his Palm Beach breakfast room that she include the depiction of a B-52 in mid-mission. "My attitude towards America in the sixties," he says, "is a little like de Gaulle's when he visited Stalingrad. His guide, who was a Russian colonel, took him to the heights above Stalingrad to point out the ebb and flow of the battle that had devastated the city, and de Gaulle said, 'What a great people!'

"The guide said, 'You mean the Russians?'

"And de Gaulle replied, 'No, the Germans, to have reached the banks of the Volga.'

"While I don't mean to subscribe to the often implied malicious falsehood that there was anything in the slightest national-socialistic about what the United States was doing...to have this tremendous tumult in their own country, wage war in Vietnam, and dominate the world commercially and culturally, all at the same time, was an enormous feat of the prodigious creativity of the American people."

He is violently opposed to anti-Americanism in any form. "It is disgusting, and it is vile," he wrote to a member of the Progressive Conservative Opposition on February 1, 1973. "It is fashionable and is fostered to the maximum degree possible by such instruments of public suasion as the CBC, *The Toronto Star, The Montreal Star, Maclean's* and *Saturday Night.*"

Probably his strongest pro-American sentiments were expressed in a long personal letter, dated August 27, 1981, to Tom Axworthy, then principal secretary to Pierre Trudeau:

Dear Tom:

Thank you for sending me a copy of the Prime Minister's address on Canadian Foreign Policy, which he delivered in the House of Commons on June 15.

I would like to make a couple of comments on Soviet-American relations, the European Alliance and this North-South question.

While the Prime Minister summarized the Afghanistan outrage in suitable terms, I felt that I detected in his remarks occasional indications of a notion of equivalence in the behaviour of the USSR and the USA. I know that this is not his opinion and, in the abstract, some useful comparisons might be drawn between the foreign policy conduct of those two countries and no good purpose is served by raining excessive acerbities upon the Russians. However, I would caution you in the most strenuous terms against reposing any confidence in the idea of "a basic compatibility of interests between the two countries" or any endorsement of the rightfulness of the USSR's assertion of "no less right than its rival to be heard about problems in any corner of the globe." Anything that seeks to reduce or dissimulate a recognition of the extreme danger that the USSR poses to our Western civilization, with all of the values and freedoms that the Prime Minister so accurately describes in the early part of his remarks, will not be helpful to the achievement of the objectives that he outlines....

Conrad M. Black

BLACK'S MOST FERVENT FORAYS INTO DIPLOMACY occurred in 1973 when he was trying to pump a few original foreign policy initiatives into Claude Wagner, then the Tories' external affairs critic. In one nine-page briefing paper sent in February 1973, he sounded off on half a dozen issues, including the then controversial cod war. "As I understand it," he wrote, "the breeding grounds, in international waters, are being fished out, by gluttonous foreigners. A strong stand here would satisfy both the conservationist-ecologists and the nationalists and would seem the only way to preserve the resource. If the countries fishing the spawning-grounds are unwilling to impose a voluntary quota system, retaliate, by naval harassment of the fishing vessels from countries that are not militarily daunting (Scandinavians) and by other forms of retaliation against any that are (I don't know if the Soviets are involved here or not). An immense fuss could be made in the UN about this, where we would win some kudos by our example of abstinence and conservation-mindedness. Demand to know why the government is not pressing this

185

more energetically. Quote from Cabot on the profusion of cod in the 16th century; evoke the carrier pigeon and other extinct species."

BLACK PREFERS TIDINESS in human affairs above all else. He yearns for order. The countries he admires run on time. It's the *results* that matter, not the manner in which political power is exercised. That's why his admiration of Napoleon, for example, is expressed not so much in terms of battlefield victories as by recounting the rise in France's health and literacy rates during the Bonaparte regime. Criticism of Maurice Duplessis's autocratic rule is countered by Black's remonstrations about the miles of highway paved and the number of kilowatts added during his time in office.

His short list of political heroes illustrates Black's propensity for seeing history as determined not by mass movements or the struggle of ecopolitical forces but by wilful acts of eccentric leaders, royal whim, and sets of confluent intrigues. He has scant confidence in the perfectibility of man and no faith at all in the perfection of doctrine. But he does hold fast in support of authoritarian figures who were unafraid to proclaim the grandeur of their dreams: politicians and conquerors who launched themselves on impossible missions and survived.

He has a weakness for grand gestures. "There is something in the belated recognition of greatness that gives me a vicarious pleasure," he confides. "For example, André Malraux writes of going to see Charles de Gaulle at Colombey-les-deux-Églises when he was in political exile. He had refused his premier's pension and only had his retirement income as a two-star general, which wasn't particularly great. Although de Gaulle liked wine, most of his supply had gone off, and when he opened a bottle it turned out to be vinegared. Being de Gaulle, he betrayed no dismay; he was determined to drink the vinegar and pretend it was all right. So he offered the bottle and said, 'Malraux, you take wine, I believe.'

"Malraux replied, 'Not in your house, *mon général*.'

"Of course, only two years after that, de Gaulle was back in the Élysée Palace and could have any vintage he wanted. Similarly, Sigmund Freud on his seventieth birthday was honoured with a special plaque by the Vienna Academy of Arts and Sciences, the same body that had earlier thrown him out as a quack. He declined the Academy's invitation to appear and receive it. Thomas Mann, who had written the citation, arrived at his house and read it to him. It had a line something like: 'More significant by far than the continued applause of one's longtime adherents is the long and unjustly withheld credit of one's former adversaries.'"

Conrad's admiration for acts of vindication is reflected in the proximity of a large bronze bust of Marshal Ferdinand Foch that sits on the windowsill of his Argus office. "I've always been impressed with him," explains Black, "not really for his talents as a general but with his determination. As a young student at the Jesuit seminary of Saint-Clément in Metz, he was writing his graduating exams in 1871 when the sound of the German guns announced that Metz had become part of the German empire. He saw Napoleon III being driven through the town in his carriage, sick, having been defeated at Sedan. It was forty-seven years later, as a French marshal and Commander-in-Chief of the Allied Forces in the First World War, that he re-entered Metz, and on November 11, 1918, his conditions for an armistice were accepted [at Compiègne]."

Black truly admires only Mackenzie King among Canadian politicians. "He sincerely believed he was the instrument of divine providence—and people who can talk themselves into such a preposterous notion or slide into such a self-image without at the same time becoming other-worldly in their day-to-day activities are vested with quite powerful self-management." He gives Pierre Trudeau mixed notices, and Joe Clark no notice at all. (This didn't prevent him from predicting the success of Clark's campaign. During the 1976 Conservative leadership convention, Black worked for Claude Wagner and lent some support to Brian Mulroney, but as early as Thursday noon—when most other observers were still calling for either Wagner or Mulroney to win—he told Brian McKenna of CBC's "the fifth estate" that Joe Clark would squeak in on the Sunday ballot, which was precisely what happened.)

Black bestows considerable credit on Trudeau as a national leader not afraid to swim against history's currents. At the same time, he vigorously condemns the Liberal prime minister's economic policies and regards the use of the War Measures Act in 1970 as his major positive achievement. "The greatest problem with Trudeau as statesman," he says, "is not that he's a subversive or that he's arrogant, or any of the other things his critics accuse him of. It's that he's so unoriginal. I've read everything he ever wrote in his days as editor of *Cité Libre*. It's a mishmash of in-jokes and conceited little asides. Occasionally there's an elegant phrase but never once anything that was original. Never. From what I gather, this man really sincerely believes that the Department of Regional Economic Expansion, for example, is a great step forward instead of being, of course, as it is, just a plastering-over of the squandering of billions of dollars on the friends of the Liberal party. I personally don't have any great objection to the patronage system; but I do object to the profligate waste of public money, and particularly so when it's represented as a brilliant new page in the annals of political reform."

True to his admiration for historical figures who fail to achieve their destinies, Black did write one friendly private letter to Trudeau just after the Liberal leader's 1979 election defeat.

Dear Mr. Trudeau:

I am taking the liberty of writing to you to offer a word of encouragement at this extraordinary moment in the history of our country and in the evolution of your own career. My motive is not any presumption that such sentiments are necessary, but my hope is that you will find this a refreshing expression of a widespread sentiment.

All Canadians must be grateful to you for what you have achieved for them in the past. And most will be hopeful that, whatever the future may hold, you will still be available, as General de Gaulle said of Georges Pompidou in 1968, "dans la réserve de la nation."

The following excerpt from a letter written by Cardinal Villeneuve to Maurice Duplessis, following the latter's defeat in 1939, may have some applicability in these circumstances:

"La balance du succès a renversé ses plateaux. Ça ne change rien à ce que vous étiez hier, une homme avec des défauts et des remarquables qualités d'esprit et de coeur, un fond d'idées saines, des aptitudes au gouvernement, un homme d'Etat... Malgré les apparences et malgré les déboires qui peuvent s'ajouter encore, qui sait si l'avenir ne vous réserve point de nouveau le pouvoir. Et vous y reviendriez avec la sagesse que donne l'épreuve."*

My best wishes to you.

Conrad M. Black

Trudeau, then Leader of the Opposition, replied almost immediately:

*"Fortunes have been reversed. But that does not change the man you were yesterday, a man with faults but also remarkable qualities of heart and mind, a fount of sound ideas, of aptitudes for government, a statesman... In spite of the appearances and in spite of the setbacks that may yet occur, who knows if the future does not reserve to you a return to power and you would come back to it with the strength adversity can give."

Dear Mr. Black,

I have played many roles in my time, but none were as delightfully unexpected as playing Duplessis to your Villeneuve.

As his biographer, you are undoubtedly aware that poor Maurice will feel even hotter than his environment when he finds out that words of encouragement sent to him have now been addressed to one of his former tormentors.

In turn, may I encourage you in your recent efforts to lend credibility to the intellectual right. I realize it's an uphill battle, but the reward is worth the struggle. The reward, of course, is that every able conservative who has seriously applied his mind to his philosophy has eventually and inevitably turned into a liberal.

Facetiousness aside, I appreciate your thoughtful message. It was very kind of you to send it.

Yours sincerely, and best personal regards,

P.E. Trudeau

Despite this cordial exchange, Black objected fiercely to the Trudeau administration's 1981 budget ("catastrophic, an absolute disaster"). In contrast, Black has been one of only half a dozen Canadian businessmen who have supported at least the principle of Canadianization enunciated in the Liberals' National Energy Program. "I don't have any problem with the putative objectives of Canadianization," he says. "Things could not have continued the way they were. It's a legitimate issue. But if this turns out to be a carefully orchestrated verbal façade for the strangulation of the industry, a kind of socio-economic first step toward virtual nationalization of one of the country's most important economic sectors, then it could be extremely serious, very harmful to us—and it won't work either constitutionally or economically. You're going to get not only a loss of the mega-projects but a monstrous disincentive to production. The feds are favouring all these drilling funds so there will be plenty of exploration going on, but they never produce very much. These drilling funds just exist to siphon off the highly taxed income of dentists and doctors. In one sense, you've got to appreciate Ottawa's professionalism. They've selected their adversaries carefully: the blue-eyed sheiks of Alberta and the fat cats of Bay Street—nobody is going to cry any tears for us. There is really no point in calling Trudeau a Hitler. Any reply has to be a lot more subtle than that."

Black has become distinctly unenthusiastic about placing his personal investments in Canada and is quietly shifting part of his private fortune into U.S. real estate. "Canada," he contends, "has always functioned awkwardly, because it is an accidental country. It…owes its physical existence to a delineation of spheres of influence in North America between the British and the Americans following the War of 1812, and the subsequent extension of the frontier to the Pacific Coast. Canada has really had three *raisons d'être*...: the British connection, clearly a factor of declining importance; the assimilationist fears of the French, which have led to independentist sentiments in Quebec rather than to any bracing federalism; and a diffuse hostility to the United States. No state institutions, no overriding Canadian interest have ever existed to bring these different tendencies together.... We did not arise from any heroic revolution or statesmanship of our own."

PERHAPS IT HAS BEEN THIS DISILLUSIONMENT with the underlying meanness of the Canadian political process that has sent Conrad outside the country in his continuing search for heroes. When he was very young and very much more liberal in his thinking, he would drive his father to distraction by playing, over and over again, late at night and at full volume, a recording of Franklin Delano Roosevelt's 1936 Madison Square Garden speech in which he vilified American businessmen, shouting, "These forces are unanimous in their hate for me! And I welcome their hate!" as the huge crowd roared its approval. One day it was suggested forcefully that for the benefit of a continuing father-son relationship, it ought to be the last time Roosevelt's voice would come booming through the Black household at 2 a.m.

What Conrad admired about FDR was not only his anti-Nazi crusade or domestic statesmanship but also how he could be such a patrician yet understand the people so well; how he could be so devious in the name of exalted causes.

De Gaulle and Napoleon remain two of Conrad's favourites, and he will use any excuse to repeat long passages from both men's writings and communiqués. But most of his idols are Americans, going back to Abraham Lincoln. "He conducted four battles at once: the war between the states, the war with the radical Congress, the war with his wife, who was a mental case, and the war with his own doubts about himself."

Conrad's favourite historical quotation, which was also frequently cited by Maurice Duplessis, is from one of Lincoln's addresses: "You cannot bring about prosperity by discouraging thrift. You cannot strengthen the weak by weakening the strong. You cannot help the wage-earner by pulling down the wage-payer. You cannot help the poor by destroying the rich. You cannot establish sound security on borrowed money. You cannot build character and courage by taking away man's initiative and independence. You cannot help men permanently by doing for them what they could do for themselves."

Conrad was also fond of Harry Truman. He was more offended by Richard Nixon's banality than by his evil. "Nixon's problem was basically psychological and he deserves the compassion due to sick people. He was sleazy, tasteless, and neurotic, but I thought he had one partially redeeming virtue: he had the mind of a foreigner. While he spoke in idealistic terms, he knew that it was all a bunch of bunk, that the world just wanted to steal America's money and use it. I don't find Adolf Hitler a frequent source of quotations, but he had this one truly great line that he uttered in his private train when he was leaving France in July 1940 after his one and only visit to Paris. This was in that movie *The Sorrow and the Pity* – it's just the announcer saying it, we don't have Hitler's voice for it, and for all I know it may have been invented by these Communist French movie producers…it's not in Bartlett's *Quotations* or anything like that. He was sitting in his car while they changed engines when some people on the platform recognized the Führer and started to applaud. He said to his companions: 'Look at them, the French, they're trying to pick my pocket. They don't realize I'm the greatest pickpocket in Europe.' Nixon was a little like that, but in a much more exalted way. He was canalized to purposes that were objectively admirable. His paranoia, I felt, was almost endearing when he summarily ordered Kissinger to submit the entire State Department to lie detector tests."

Henry Kissinger has always been a particular favourite. Black was pleased when Fred Eaton gave him an autographed copy of the Kissinger White House memoirs as a Christmas present in 1979 – even though he prefers to peruse Kissinger's book on the Congress of Vienna. Black invited Kissinger to an off-the-record seminar (over lunch at Truffles in the Four Seasons Hotel on May 22, 1980) with a couple of hundred of Canada's most important executives. The departing guests were treated to the sight of Kissinger and Black climbing into the back of a tug-sized Cadillac limousine, its hood symbol a gold eagle devouring a snake, its licence plate ominously numbered WAR 010.*

But his sentimental choice, the only major American political figure he has publicly defended, is Lyndon Baines Johnson. "I felt a real sympathy for him because of the merciless attacks upon him that drove

*A reference not to Kissinger's state of mind but to one of Black's holding companies, Warspite Corp. – named after HMS *Warspite*, a British battleship (laid down in October 1912, launched in November 1913, and completed in March 1915), and 10 Toronto Street, the address of Argus's headquarters.

him out of office and because of what I thought to be a tremendously statesmanlike stance that he, as a wealthy white Southerner, took toward civil rights and the issue of poverty in general."

Black first encountered Johnson during the 1964 Democratic National Convention at Atlantic City. His friend Peter White (then executive assistant to Forestry Minister Maurice Sauvé, who belonged to the U.S–Canada Interparliamentary Association) had two tickets to the convention's VIP section. Sauvé couldn't leave Ottawa, so White arranged for Black and Brian Stewart, a CBC National News reporter, to go instead. "Conrad went absolutely to the wire with LBJ," Stewart remembers. "It sounds a little histrionic now, but he felt that everything he believed in politically was under assault, and he couldn't enter a discussion anywhere without getting into a screaming match, which happened frequently. Conrad fervently subscribed to the domino theory. He was convinced that the war wasn't being correctly reported by the media and that the Americans had a perfectly legitimate right, in fact a duty, to defend Vietnam, the same way they would defend Europe."

On August 25, 1969, a few weeks after Black and his partners had purchased the *Sherbrooke Daily Record*, Conrad cleared out six columns of advertising to make room for a lengthy accolade he had written marking Johnson's sixty-first birthday. Headlined "A Year After Chicago: Homage to LBJ," the article was a prolonged tirade against the former president's many critics, including Norman Mailer ("the bedraggled warhorse of American blowhardism"); Stewart Alsop ("one of the more torrential snivellers of the American press"); Jesse Unruh ("the mere gross appearance of this man indicates that he has had his front feet in the trough long enough"); and "the cavernously pontifical" Walter Lippmann. Black's obsequious tribute ended with this emotional paragraph: "Johnson's abdication, like that of Cincinnatus, was a classic example of the voluntary surrender of great power, a very dramatic act in history, as in the theatre. All knew that a titan had passed whose like would not be seen again. His talents, his ego, his compassion, determination and capacity for work, were like his services to the nation and his much-caricatured ears, very prominent."

The information officer of the U.S. consulate-general in Montreal sent the eulogy to Johnson, whose long-time crony, Congressman J.J. (Jake) Pickle of Austin, Texas, read it into the *Congressional Record*. A year later, Black decided to view Vietnam for himself and asked Pickle to help facilitate his tour. The Congressman had been so delighted to discover an articulate supporter of the Southeast Asian war that he brought Black's trip to the personal attention of William P. Rogers, then U.S. Secretary of State. "When I arrived at the gate of the U.S.

embassy in Saigon and announced my name," Conrad remembers, "the sentry on duty stood bolt upright as only a Marine can and barked into a telephone, 'Mr. Black is here!' It was like the meeting of Stanley and Livingstone. After a few moments, someone came running down the hall, waving a telegram from the Secretary of State, representing me as a personal friend of LBJ's."

The U.S. ambassador arranged for Black to interview Nguyen Van Thieu, then president of Vietnam, whose awareness of the circulation and editorial clout of the *Sherbrooke Daily Record* must have been somewhat sketchy. He chose the occasion to reveal, for the first time, that he intended to run for re-election, that he planned to discipline his generals involved in black market operations and outlined, in some detail, the complicity of the Kennedy administration in the overthrow of President Ngo Dinh Diem in 1963.

"I liked Thieu," Conrad recalls. "I described him as the Daniel Johnson of the Orient. He showed me around the palace. He was obviously a bit of a rascal, but I admired his courage. My interview turned out to be one of the biggest news stories of the war." (After being published first in Sherbrooke, the Thieu story made front-page news in the *New York Times* and *Le Monde* in Paris, eventually reaching a world-wide audience.)

Black lived out his Vietnamese tour in Saigon's Caravelle Hotel. "I'd have my dinner on the roof," he says. "The Caravelle really had an excellent cuisine. You'd see in the distance planes dropping flares that turned night into day. Then I'd go down to my room and see, *live* by satellite from Dodger Stadium, the latest baseball game. During the day I'd go out to Tan Son, then one of the world's busiest airports, watch six Phantom-5s take off abreast, then be invited to hop on a B-52 and fly out to the Cambodian border or something. It was surrealistic."

"Somewhat to his embarrassment," Brian Stewart says, "Conrad came back to announce that the war was as good as over. '*We've won it,*' he kept saying. What he didn't anticipate was the collapse of American resolve, and that absolutely shook him. He came out of the Vietnam era somewhat battered and certainly exhausted by the whole debate."

BLACK'S RELATIONSHIP WITH THE PRESS is reminiscent of Jean-Luc Godard's comment about the Gallic temperament: that the essence of the French character is not to reveal but to withhold. Conrad's sense of friends and enemies within the media is powerful and extremely ambivalent. He enjoys his high profile, yet every six months or so proclaims that he is going permanently underground, refusing to acknowledge even routine press queries. Friends in Montreal remember a New Year's Eve party when he announced that he was going to become a celebrity—the William F. Buckley, Jr., of Canada. And as one of them says, he did, "Suddenly Conrad was a force to be reckoned with, becoming one of those quotable people who flow naturally into CBC radio and TV panels."

Exposed to unwanted press coverage as both subject and object, he vehemently protests against such attention—yet he has deliberately created a public persona of precisely the man he wants to be, realizing that anonymity and a sense of style are not always compatible. Unlike most people, who cross their Hush Puppies and in silent supplication ask themselves, "Who in God's name am I?" Conrad is one of those rare fortunates on good terms with himself. His ego doesn't leak. He is not obsessed with the search for his identity, already knowing precisely who he is and quite content to exist within the tumult of his own making. He believes that no matter what his legion of detractors may say or think, the currency of his life is valued on an immutable standard, with no discounts or bargain days.

Although Black remains anxious to feed the chimeras of his own legend, he genuinely longs for privacy. He seldom achieves it. Even on his wedding night, reporters were camped outside his bedroom window until four in the morning. Asked, as he frequently is, "Are you *the* Conrad Black?" he will reply, "No. I am *a* Conrad Black."

As a symbol of wealth and power, Conrad finds himself the target of some unusual pleas. One autumn evening in 1981, for instance, the Blacks' front doorbell rang and there, as if from a tableau in a Victorian melodrama, was a bundled-up baby girl. In a sixteen-page letter pinned to the swaddling clothes, her parents recounted how they had come upon hard times and asked the Blacks to adopt their daughter and give her the upbringing she deserved. (The child's parents eventually reclaimed their offspring.)

Whenever he can manage it, Black escapes with his wife, Shirley, to one of Toronto's more obscure ethnic restaurants or goes shopping with her in the Dominion Store at Don Mills Plaza. Even there they are almost always recognized. Once, just to get away from it all, the Blacks decided to take a lightning holiday in Hawaii. At every stop along the way somebody spotted them, but finally they reached the safety of the Royal Hawaiian Hotel. They sprinted happily down to the ocean. A split second after they had settled into their beach chairs with that first deep sigh of sunny relaxation, a man on the next chaise longue held out a hairy paw and said, "Hi, Conrad." He turned out to be a debenture dealer from Greenshields, hustling Dome preferreds.

Before gaining the Argus crown, he encouraged the beatification of his achievements, testing the arc of his authority, trying to impress his elders. Once safely ensconced in power, he revolted against the notion of having been created by any force except his own brilliance and savagely turned on his former boosters. In a private letter to the editor of the *Globe and Mail* complaining about an article written by Hugh Anderson in *Report on Business*, Black wrote: "I do express my gratitude to Hugh Anderson for attacking my 'whiz-kid reputation.' This is certainly not my self-image nor a role I ever aspired to, and is a spontaneous fabrication of the media, including Anderson himself."

Black feels himself unfairly attacked, particularly in accusations that he cynically abandoned the floundering ship in October 1980 when he abruptly wrote off three million shares of Massey-Ferguson and severed Argus's thirty-five-year connection with the troubled agricultural implement firm. "There is nothing," he complains with ill-concealed bitterness, "that so offends public consciousness in this country as an unbroken series of successes. The Canadian mentality simply can't abide it. The suggestion that I somehow bombed out as a businessman because Massey didn't fly is just not credible. All the serious judges think my performance at Massey was absolutely brilliant and that if I am to be faulted at all, it is for having spent the time I did over there. I always felt it was worth it, because if it hadn't been for me that company would have gone bust two years before, and every knowledgeable person realizes it."

Canada's business press, at least when it first discovered him, gave Black the kind of raves usually reserved for movie-fan tabloids. "Business watches the progress of Conrad M. Black with awe," gushed *Executive* magazine. "He has made one fortune, inherited another, written a major book and snatched the ring of power from strong and sophisticated protagonists at Argus." Ken Waxman, who wrote a glowing profile of him in *Quest* magazine, put forth Conrad's often repeated claim to being a self-made man. "But anyone who looks on Black's lineage and wealth and dismisses him as just another overprivileged plutocrat, will have missed the whole essence of the man," Waxman observed. "For by using his own inventiveness and intelligence, he has created a reputation for himself in the business and academic worlds; a reputation he believes owes little or nothing to his inherited wealth."

At about the same time, Black became the darling of the U.S. financial writers searching North America's attic for nuggets of interesting copy. "If Conrad Black had been operating in New York or Chicago when he made the bold series of moves that elevated him to the presidency of Argus Corp., his name would be instantly recognizable to American businessmen," reported *Fortune*. "Yet Black's achievement is considerable. He has a tight grip on one of the key levers of corporate power in Canada."

While Black does admire a very few individual journalists, he despises their profession. "My experience of the working press," he says, "is that they're a very degenerate group. There is a terrible incidence of alcoholism and drug abuse. The mental stability of large elements of the press is more open to question than that of many other comparable groups in society. A number of them are ignorant, lazy, opinionated, intellectually dishonest, and inadequately supervised.

"The individual journalist, if he has any panache or talent, becomes something of a celebrity. Much of his social life is built up on the press-circuit: bars, hangers-on, media groupies, the stifling and depraved gossip of the degenerate little media community, and the fawning of unfulfilled women, boys, and hucksters.... Journalism tends to attract the sort of person who settles whimsically on it as a calling or comes to it after disappointments elsewhere, because of the relative ease of entry to the field. These people, discouraged and purposeless, are easily influenced by their angrier colleagues. It is by inadvertence, inexperience, the investigative nature of the press, the antithetical role of the employee, and the negligence of the employer, and not by any organized subversion, that the press veered away from being a mirror to society, and became a perverse sort of irregular and often disloyal opposition."

Black blames this sad state of the journalist's craft on the decline of resident media proprietors, who might have been eccentric and curmudgeonly in character but at least ran their own shops. "With the rise of the chains," he says, "the publisher has become a local coordinator and functionary, answerable to his absentee employer on economic matters, with a mandate to ensure that the journalistic content is sufficiently anodyne to avoid disputes with advertisers, sufficiently formless to avoid strikes in the newsrooms. The proprietors take relatively little interest in the journalistic aspects of the business. Lord Thomson of Fleet may be the greatest businessman in the history of the media; he was, on balance, an indifferent publisher. The successors to Joseph E. Atkinson, J.W. McConnell, Jacob Nicol, Pamphille Du Tremblay, Max Bell, Victor Sifton, Michael Wardell, and both John Bassetts are comparatively pallid and equivocal. (Brigadier R.S. Malone...of the *Globe and Mail* is a conspicuous exception.)"

CONRAD BLACK LIKES TO REFER TO HIMSELF variously as a historian, an ideologist, or (quoting the *Toronto Star* with a smirk) a "Metro mogul." What he really prides himself on is being a proprietor.

Although he seems taken up with a selfish crusade to aggrandize his already considerable personal assets, Black thinks of himself essentially as a historian, the profession he listed on his licence application when he married Shirley Walters in 1978. He recognizes no basic conflict in the eternal dilemma that separates academics (even fleeting ones like himself), who seek truth, from businessmen, who chase dollars. "It all depends," he insists, "on how good an intellectual you are. The keen mind can develop a rationale for almost anything. Financial prominence can be accommodated to grand designs extending well beyond the frontiers of mundane commerce."

"One doesn't want to sound pretentious or superficial," Black proclaims, sounding a bit of both, "but I continue to be perplexed at the erosion of conviction and the gradual descent of our society into moral torpor. I'm reduced to reading Oswald Spengler, whose theme is that the decline of civilization is as likely as the turning of autumn leaves. Still, the emergence in the West of a renascent intellectual right – rigorous and articulate – has been a long time coming. It has been followed, as such developments usually are, by a move to the right in the politics of Britain and the United States. The re-emphasis of the importance of the *proprietor* in the Canadian business scene is part of this same trend."

Here is the very essence of Conrad Black's motivating philosophy. He numbers himself among that brave band of entrepreneurial giants who are waging a holy war to keep the idea of major proprietorships alive in a time when the public sector is engulfing every form of human endeavour: "The tendency to bureaucratize the business world is, if anything, more dangerous than the same process in government. Self-perpetuating managements, not effectively accountable to their shareholders, are a real danger to our system. I don't intend to be an absolute proprietor, some swashbuckling buccaneer of the 1980s, but I do believe that proprietorships are better run because the motivation is greater. When it's *your* money, you run things better than when it isn't. Every cent wasted comes eventually from your own pocket. The great thing about all this takeover-itis going on is that eventually all the major companies in this country will have an identifiable proprietory group."

Black's emphasis on personal ownership (reinforced by the successes of Galen Weston, Fred Eaton, Ken Thomson, Charles Bronfman, Doug Bassett, Ted Rogers, and their fellow Inheritors) has led him to dismiss the earnest strivings of the country's managerial class. "The stupefying lack of imagination of most Canadian business leaders just amazes me," he pouts. "Worst of all are the professional managers.

There are exceptions, but most of them are no thundering balls of fire." Conrad admires Ian Sinclair, who put together Canadian Pacific Enterprises, but he has, at least on one occasion, diluted his assessment. "Sinclair is full of what you might call endearing posturings," Black told a friend, "but he has no style whatsoever. His suits don't fit."

Black's infatuation with thinking of himself as a proprietor may well be rooted in his achievement of tucking ownership of the Argus group of companies so firmly under his wing. Commenting on the steel-trap grip he holds over his business empire, he once told an inquiring TV interviewer, "Short of death, imprisonment, or demonstrable insanity, I'd say we were in a pretty good position."

CHAPTER EIGHT

Wintering on the Gold Coast

*"Conrad is an aristocrat; he definitely does not think of
himself as just another common man. So why
shouldn't he consort with his fellow aristocrats?"*
—Peter White

B etween Christmas and spring, when late-April breezes finally
melt the slush of the Toronto winter, Conrad Black and his
family mysteriously vanish from the Canadian business and
social scene. Their seasonal pilgrimage, which occupies fully a third of
each year, takes them to the golden littoral of the southern U.S. east
coast, the American Establishment's ultimate pit stop—Palm Beach,
Florida.

Situated at the ocean terminus of Okeechobee Boulevard, which runs
east off Interstate 95, Palm Beach is an island twelve miles long and half
a mile wide formed by the two inlets of Lake Worth. It's connected to
the mainland by four lift-bridges, but the true distance from the Florida
most visitors encounter is very much greater than these modest spans
would indicate.

"Out there" are the tourist bayous of Fort Lauderdale, Pompano
Beach, and Miami, with their forests of condos and those cute cottages
ringed by fences Robinson Crusoe might have constructed. They come
every winter, the Canadian snowbirds and their American counterparts,
soaking up the sun, frequenting shops as specialized as Mr. Bidet and
drug stores that advertise free blood pressure tests alongside rhinestone-
butterfly sunglasses. Here, too, are the vulpine, sexually charged men
who arrive self-consciously alone in their electric-blue leisure suits with
built-in Instamatics. They gravitate from steak house to dimly lit piano
bar, sloshing back shots of bourbon and gripping drinks with ragged-
cuticle fingers on which pinkie rings are conspicuous only by their
absence. Their taste knows no season. They come south to spread a little
joy. Swaggering through the Florida nights, they search for nubile
"stews" who might accommodate their desires, but they seldom find
any. The flight attendants and their sisters wallow in funky fantasies of

their own: fluffing up their bangs, tucking themselves into maillots two sizes too small, holding out until they're discovered and become up-wardly mobile soap stars.

At another level, Florida is a war zone, its resentful Hispanic exiles bent on reducing the state's resident WASPs to a besieged ethnic minority. The *Miami Herald* regularly front-pages reports about saboteurs "sent from Cuba to destabilize Florida." (It is not a very tough assignment.) A sheet that bills itself as the *Terrorist Intelligence Report* claims that Fidel Castro is trading Soviet-made AK-47 assault rifles for cocaine from Central America, funnelling the drug into Southern Florida, and making himself a personal fortune in the process.

Be that as it may, Dade County around Miami, centre of the state's $10-billion drug import trade, recorded a 1981 rate of 1.6 murders a day—a considerable underestimate, because most victims have never been found. "Look at these swampy fields around the county," says Robert Murphy, chief of the Miami homicide bureau. "If the bodies lying out there could all jump up and yell at once, it would sound like the goddamned Dolphins had scored a touchdown."

EXCEPT FOR SHARING THE SAME BENIGN CLIMATE, Palm Beach is a universe removed from all that. "There has been no violent crime in the history of Palm Beach," Black points out. "There are break-ins occa-sionally, but in case of a serious burglary they just lift the causeways and catch the guy."

In other parts of Florida, having money may create enemies and even be a threat to your life; in Palm Beach, wealth is converted into pleasure—at a highly favourable rate of exchange. It may well be the most assiduously zoned community on earth. Local bylaws forbid hot-dog and hamburger stands, laundromats, billboards, neon signs, aluminum siding, hippies, funeral parlours, and hospitals; the dead and dying are discreetly carted across the causeway to West Palm. The privileged citizens who inhabit this immaculate and hermetically sealed-off roost of modern U.S. capitalism have a highly individualistic way of responding to events. In the mid-seventies, when the east coast of Florida was being fouled by oil slicks, Palm Beachers convinced them-selves that this was no ordinary ecological problem but rather the work of Communist sympathizers among the crews of passing merchant ships who were deliberately flushing their fuel tanks to pollute the winter capital of American free enterprise.

The gesture might have been appropriate.

During the early months of 1982, nine million Americans were out of work, the U.S. business failure index was up a traumatic 45 per cent, and fears of economic catastrophe haunted the land. Carolyn Grant Whittey, a columnist in the *Palm Beach Social Pictorial*, nonetheless gushed: "Between going to Hialeah to attend the glamorous races, going to all the parties and various balls, and getting to polo and all that excitement, there's just no time to be bored these days is there darlings? I am thoroughly convinced no one ever stays home in Palm Beach." Except for pushing their own shopping carts around the Publix Supermarket on Sunset Avenue (instead of asking the family chauffeur to do it for them), the matrons of Palm Beach did not feel much effect of the economic slowdown. Publix's shelves reflected their mood by stocking eleven kinds of English marmalade and regularly selling out the Romanov caviar ($13.69 for two ounces) and Dom Perignon ($69.99 a bottle).

Recessions, in this realm, are economic phenomena that happen to other people in other places. Most Palm Beachers are the heirs or possessors of fortunes too massive, too cleverly diversified, and much too carefully husbanded to be affected by mere swings in the business cycle. "About the worst that can happen," wrote Tom Buckley in the *New York Times Magazine*, "is that for a year or two they may have to live on the interest rather than the interest on the interest." Money still counts in Palm Beach—though society is much more open than it used to be when the Phippses, Wideners, Munns, Stotesburys, and Marjorie Merriweather Post dominated the winter season. The current social pecking order is no longer established solely through monetary supremacy. Titled Europeans have been all the rage; the Marchese Pucci, Countess Monique de Boisrouvray, and Arndt Krupp von Bohlen und Halbach, the forty-four-year-old heir to the German munitions empire who employs twenty-seven servants in a Palm Beach villa he recently renovated for $2.5 million, are high on the society-column rosters.

Palm Beach is one of the last places on earth where there still exists a true social season. Invitation lists to the annual cycle of house parties and fancy-dress balls delineate an individual's status, and social-climbing seems to be the favourite indoor sport. The late Arthur Somers Roche, an American millionaire who spent most of his life in Palm Beach, once appeared at an Everglades Club costume party dressed as a social-climber—with a ladder up his back. Its four rungs were lettered, in ascending order, "Common People," "People," "Nice People" and "Right People." Parties aren't quite as extravagant as they used to be. In 1938, Pepsodent heir Kenneth Smith held an all-night dance, expressing his appreciation by presenting each of the orchestra's musicians with a new car. As late as 1971, Countess Margaret "Migi" Willaumetz arranged a surprise party for Mop, her thirteen-year-old Yorkshire terrier; it was attended by twenty of the island's most presentable pooches.* Much of the town's social life is centred on the chukkas at the nearby 12,000-acre Palm Beach Polo and Country Club, whose notable guests have included both the late Duke of Windsor and the current Prince of Wales.

As in most other habitats of the thoroughly rich, careful lines of demarcation are preserved between new and old money. The newly minted tycoons and their flashy women wear Lilly Pulitzer prints, play tennis adroitly, attempt polo, and buy long limousines, beamy yachts, and opulent mansions. But none of it works very well. No matter how hard they try, they still tend to exhibit etiquette instead of manners, call butlers by their first names, put their initials on car licence plates, and use credit cards instead of personal cheques.

If there is one indisputable mark of old money in Palm Beach, it is the daily parade of the daughters of established wealth along Worth Avenue, the main shopping complex of lanes and courtyards. The women have somehow uncannily contrived to standardize their appearance: they nearly all resemble the finalists in a national Dina Merrill look-alike contest. Some still play court tennis, an adaptation of the *jeu de paume* originated by the kings of France, with its sagging net and loose raquettes, and regale one another with Palm Beach gossip. ("After poor Philip died, his servants put him into the walk-in freezer and went right on collecting their wages. They'd still be doing it today if the people at the bank hadn't caught on when they tried to give themselves a raise.") Their prevailing ethic is probably best summed up by the wife of Stephen "Laddie" Sanford, who once told a friend, "I have been blessed with one of the most beautiful homes in the world. I look out through the window on the ocean—and I can't help feeling it's mine."

CONRAD BLACK WAS INTRODUCED TO PALM BEACH in 1969. He had been to Cuba as an observer of Fidel Castro's tenth anniversary in power, had hated it, and took up Bud McDougald's invitation to visit the Palm Beach mansion the Argus godfather then occupied across the road from his sister-in-law, Doris Phillips. "I've never been back to Cuba, but I have often returned here," says Black. "Palm Beach isn't everyone's cup of tea. Some people are offended by the extreme opulence, but I find it sort of entertaining. A couple of seasons ago I was

---

*Graduates (*summa cum bone*), no doubt, from the Sir Charles School of Dog Training, which specializes in teaching "proper decorum." Dogs aren't the only Palm Beach pets. One of the Palm Beach du Ponts imported tame iguanas from Cuba and trained them to stand at attention whenever he called them with a special whistle.

standing at the corner of Worth Avenue and County Road when I heard two slight *rumplings*. I turned around and saw that a Silver Cloud II had been struck in the fender by a Phantom V—which had come to such an abrupt stop that a Silver Shadow had bumped into *it*. So you had three Rollses stuck together. It was hilarious."

From the winter of 1978 onward, Black rented the Palm Beach house of Neil McKinnon, the late chairman of the Canadian Imperial Bank of Commerce; then he purchased the Federalist mansion of John R. Drexel III, a descendant of the Philadelphia banking family.*

During the four months of his annual southern sojourn, which is interrupted by frequent flights to Toronto, Conrad works at losing weight by bicycling ten miles a day along Lake Worth. In the course of these rambles he hatches his corporate manoeuvres, such as the notion of investing in the Hanna Mining Company of Cleveland. "I'm not all that social down here," he says. "I bring in my own guests, ride my bicycle, swim, and read. If you wanted to spend every night going to some goddamned fund-raising function at the Breakers, you could—but that's not why I'm here. The only campaign to which I ever contributed was the Reagan-for-President fund."

He is increasingly fascinated by Palm Beach's eccentrics. "The great realtor in town is my friend Parker Bryant. He has an assistant who is in charge of opening people's houses in the late autumn, taking down the shutters, and stuff like that. I talked to him one day and discovered he was Sir Alastair Ewing, a retired admiral in the Royal Navy and last

---

*Because of his unbounded admiration for Douglas MacArthur, Conrad has propagated an apocryphal story that the general proposed to Louise Cromwell Brooks in the garden of the Blacks' Palm Beach house. The mansion is built on a property once owned by E.T. Stotesbury, MacArthur's father-in-law and a partner second only to J.P. himself in the J.P. Morgan banking house. Black's claim to the contrary, there is no evidence that MacArthur, then a brigadier-general of forty-two, courted his wife-to-be in that particular garden in 1922. His bride was the divorced wife of Walter Brooks, Jr., and stepdaughter of Edward Townsend Stotesbury (1849–1938), a Civil War drummer boy who had climbed to wealth with Drexel and Company in Philadelphia (he told Bar Harbor cronies in August 1929 that he'd just reached a lifetime goal—$100 million—and he died at eighty-nine after a routine day at the office). One of E.T.'s two stepsons, James H.R. Cromwell, was divorced in 1929 from Delphine Dodge, daughter of the Detroit car magnate Horace Dodge. Six years later Jimmy Cromwell married Doris Duke, known as the richest girl in the world. The tobacco heiress and Cromwell, named U.S. minister to Canada by President Franklin Roosevelt in 1940, were divorced in 1947, and her next husband was the Dominican playboy Porfirio Rubirosa. Louise divorced MacArthur in 1929 on the grounds of non-support, and the next year became the wife of Lionel Atwill, the British-born onetime matinee idol. One of Atwill's four marriages, it ended in divorce. Louise's next husband was Alf Heiberg, a U.S. Marine Corps bandmaster. The general's second wife was Jean Marie Faircloth of Murfreesboro, Tenn., whom he married in 1937 and who, with their only child, Arthur, survived him on his death in 1964 at the age of eighty-four.

captain of HMS *Vanguard* [the last British battleship, scrapped in 1960]. We had a great old chat."

What most intrigues Black—and every other visitor to Palm Beach—is its collection of bizarre houses. This is home as art form. Rich Americans and wealthy émigrés from an increasingly socialist Europe have realized their architectural fantasies—concocting Moorish castles, Venetian palazzos, Cotswold manor houses, Mexican haciendas, mixtures of Regency and Gingerbread, Disneyland-Cinderella, Palladian Revival, Pyranees Monastic, and Nouveau Riche Divine. Gated mansions half-hidden behind meticulously trimmed ficus hedges are ringed by lawns as smooth as broadloom. Addison Mizner, who designed many of the most magnificent of these retreats from reality (including the Black house), specialized in baroque carved wooden ceilings, Spanish tiled floors, splashing fountains, colonnaded archways, winding staircases (which occasionally lead nowhere), and wide foyers that open into elaborately decorated ballrooms.

The state religion of Palm Beach is interior decorating. The local phone book lists 195 decorators, two of them specialists in furnishing yacht staterooms. "I'm a nest-builder by instinct, and there is nothing I would rather do than decorate a house," says Mary Lee Fairbanks, wife of the charismatic Sir Douglas and a Palm Beach resident since the Second World War.

A drive through the town's main drag is like leafing through *Who's Who*, with houses that have belonged to Estée Lauder, Samuel Newhouse, Rose Kennedy, Earl E.T. Smith, the last American ambassador to Cuba, and various branches of such well-known American plutocratic families as the du Ponts, Guests, Vanderbilts, Kelloggs, Armours, Sanfords, and Pulitzers.* Canadians who make Palm Beach their winter home include Paul Desmarais (chairman of Power Corp.),

*Perhaps the resort's most confirmed workaholic was Robert R. Young, known as the daring young man of Wall Street for his successful speculation during the market crash of 1929. Chairman of the New York Central and former chairman of the Chesapeake & Ohio Railway, he was sixty when he killed himself with a shotgun in the third-floor billiard room of his oceanfront mansion, The Towers, in January 1958. On the morning of his death the financier—who during his successful battle for control of the Central in 1954 had said he would look after the interests of small shareholders (he called them Aunt Janes)—received a letter that began: "Mr. Young, I loved you and trusted you. You betrayed me. You did not do what you said you would do. I own ten shares of Central stock, and it represents a great deal of money to me...." It was the only letter he opened that day from the number that had arrived in the mail. The Towers was the former southern base of Atwater Kent, the radio manufacturer and rival of E.T. Stotesbury for the social leadership of both Bar Harbor and Palm Beach. Young's northern base was Newport, where a David portrait of Napoleon graced his library.

204

Saidye Bronfman (Sam's widow), Gerald Bronfman (Harry's son), Robert Campeau (Ottawa developer), Lawrence Freiman (former owner of the Ottawa department store), Robert Cummings (Montreal financier), Jack Reitman (president of the Montreal ladies'-wear chain), George Mara (Toronto wine importer and industrialist), Beverley Matthews (senior partner of McCarthy & McCarthy), and Signy Eaton (John David's widow). A recent Canadian visitor to the Blacks was Emmett Cardinal Carter of Toronto. During the winter in 1982 Conrad gave him a tour of Palm Beach, at the end of which he inquired of the churchman: "Well, Your Eminence, does this conform with your vision of paradise as closely as it does with mine?" To which Carter replied: "Yes, I think so – if you would just change the helicopters to angels."

Worth Avenue, where they shop, easily rivals London's Bond Street, New York's Fifth Avenue, or Rome's Via Condotti. As well as boasting the world's only Gucci supermarket and stores that sell everything from hand-carved ebony hummingbird feeders to matched ornamental artichoke poachers, the Avenue has a special appeal to Conrad. He has found a shop that sells historical autographs. He already has a Churchill, a Franklin Roosevelt, a Truman, and a General MacArthur – as well as one of the thirty original abdication letters signed by Edward VIII.

Worth Avenue has so many art galleries they've taken to specializing. Heaton's, for example, sells only portraits of animals; La Galerie Jean Bousquet hangs seascapes; Jaro's shows Yugoslav naives; Joan Gillespie exhibits "original little whimseys." The most enterprising among local art dealers is probably Wally Findlay, who buys Monets and Renoirs and hires imitators by the hour to copy the masterpieces. "He puts the real thing up for a million dollars or so," observes Conrad, "then exhibits the duplicates for $30,000 – and when people come in they gladly buy the copies, a bargain by contrast. It's at once magnificent and an outrage."

Many Palm Beachers store their most valuable paintings, jewellery and other treasures in the vast vaults of the First National Bank, of which Clark Gable was once chairman. The modest institution, with a 1981 net income of $5.3 million, is the only bank in North America which pays no interest on its deposits. This device exempts it from having to report any individual's cash holdings to Washington, allowing its clients to shield their fortunes from the prying eyes of the Internal Revenue Service.

The First National, founded in 1927, is one of the community's best-known landmarks. Its vaults hold three thousand mink stoles, stacked cases of rare wines, gold and silver objects, gun collections and, once, even a Yale University racing shell. The sure sign of a gala evening in Palm Beach is the appearance of an armed minuteman on the bank's roof to provide emergency protection for revellers who wish to return their jewels to the vaults after midnight.

Palm Beach was established in the 1890s by Henry Morrison Flagler, one of John D. Rockefeller's original partners in Standard Oil. Flagler populated the island by extending his Florida East Coast Railway south from Jacksonville and erecting the giant hotel Royal Poinciana, which with its 1,600 rooms and eight miles of corridors was then the largest wooden structure in the world. He later built the even more magnificent Breakers Hotel and formed a partnership with Col. Edward R. Bradley. (The latter opened the Beach Club, which became one of America's most luxurious gambling casinos.) Flagler's energy and imagination rapidly turned Palm Beach into a favourite winter resort for such diverse figures as John Jacob Astor III, President Warren G. Harding, William Randolph Hearst, and Paris Singer, the sewing-machine heir. It was Singer (on the rebound from an ill-fated liaison with Isadora Duncan) who encouraged the self-styled architect Addison Mizner to create a number of the town's bizarre mansions. The two men eventually co-operated in creating the Everglades Club. With its famous sliding roof that opens over the dance floor on starry nights, the Everglades shares with the Bath and Tennis Club the distinction of being the community's most exclusive watering hole.*

"There is a completely antediluvian system of segregation around here," Black claims. "I asked Charles Wrightsman about it one day, and he said that Palm Beach 'is really three societies. You have the sort of vulgar, "shiny-sheet" set,† the people who are at the fancy balls all the time, who eat in restaurants and apply for club memberships. Then above that you have the Club People, who are proud of their status—and at the top are families like the Fairbanks who really just can't be bothered with all that stuff.' As Wrightsman put it, 'The Bath and

*Smallest of the local establishments is the Palm Beach Country Club at the northern end of town. Its membership is almost entirely Jewish, although Rose Kennedy, now ninety-two, still keeps up her dues. In *The Last Resorts*, Cleveland Amory tells the story of a Jewish gentleman trying to register at the Breakers and being informed that while not actually restricted, the hotel catered primarily to a Christian clientele. The visitor promptly went to another hotel, calling himself a Christian, only to be told that its clientele was primarily Jewish. Fed up with Palm Beach protocol, the would-be guest exclaimed: "Well, I'll be a son of a bitch." The desk clerk immediately countered: "If you can prove that, I can get you in anywhere."

†The *Palm Beach Daily News*, which, because it's printed on glossy stock, lets no ink rub off on readers who peruse its pages during breakfast in bed.

Tennis was started by phonies and it has been run by punks ever since.* The Everglades has slipped a lot too. I've been a member for fifty years and I haven't set foot in it for twenty-five.'"

Charles Bierer Wrightsman and his wife, Jaynie, have become the Blacks' chief mentors in Conrad's intended invasion of the U.S. business world. It is a formidable link. Now in his late eighties, Wrightsman made his original fortune with the Standard Oil Company of Kansas but probably became better known as a philanthropist and collector of *objets d'art*. His condominium on New York's Fifth Avenue has a *parquet de Versailles* floor under a Savonnerie carpet (originally woven for the grand gallery of the Louvre to the order of Louis XIV) and twenty pairs of priceless Meissen birds. The Wrightsmans used to spend their summers aboard the 680-ton *Radiant II* (which required a crew of twenty-three), cruising the Mediterranean with such guests as Jackie Kennedy and her sister, Lee Radziwill; Hervé Alphand, France's former ambassador to Washington, and his wife, Nicole, a *Time* cover girl; Lord Harlech, who was British ambassador to the United States in Jack Kennedy's time in the White House; Brazil's former finance minister and ambassador to Washington, Walter Moreira Sales; Gérald van der Kemp, the curator of Versailles; the late Roland Redmond, longtime president of the Metropolitan Museum of Art; and the director of the National Gallery in Washington, John Walker, and his wife, the former Lady Margaret Drummond, a daughter of the 16th Earl of Perth.

The Blacks refuse to discuss the Wrightsman collection, but their Palm Beach house is believed to contain $25 million in art treasures. It has a seventy-by-forty-foot pool (salt water, kept at a constant 90° F) which, when anyone swims, is constantly flanked by uniformed waiters carrying drinks and other necessities on silver trays. Departing guests who chance to glance backward as they drive out of the Wrightsman estate might notice yardmen raking the driveway gravel after them so that no unsightly tracks spoil the estate's perfection. "Charles is unbelievable," says Black. "The great expectation of his life is that somebody will try to break into his house. I pity the person who tries it.... By the

---

*The Everglades was founded by Singer and Mizner, and its membership was restricted to their friends. In 1925, E.T. Stotesbury and E.F. Hutton (then married to Marjorie Merriweather Post) objected to such tyranny. They founded the Bath and Tennis as a countervailing institution and promptly proceeded to run it just as despotically. When Paul Desmarais made his grab for Argus in 1975, Bud McDougald managed to get him temporarily blackballed at the Everglades. Mrs. McDougald has been attempting to keep Conrad from joining, but the barrier is about to fall because Black has the backing of Page Hufty, a former McDougald confidant and one of Palm Beach's most powerful social arbiters.

way, I once complained to Wrightsman that Jimmy Carter was the worst president since Warren Harding. He disagreed. 'I *knew* Harding,' he told me, 'and he wasn't this bad.'"

Wrightsman and his fellow Palm Beachers consider Conrad Black a snowbird worth watching. In spite of themselves, they are mesmerized by his financial knowledge, his phenomenal memory—and the fact that he is half their age. Especially in the Florida of the 1980s, where the rich find themselves living a precarious existence within a soft-putty culture that seems on the brink of apocalyptic change, Black is a welcome *wunderkind*. "He has never liked Canadian winters and enjoys the contacts he makes down there," says his partner Peter White. "He loves meeting America's gentry. Conrad is an aristocrat; he definitely does not think of himself as just another common man. So why shouldn't he consort with his fellow aristocrats?"

CHAPTER NINE

Mandate from Heaven

*"In this organization, the emperors, not
the praetorian guard, make the decisions."*
—Conrad Black

Squeezed between the Bacchus Cellar and the penitentiary-style head office of Excelsior Life on a nondescript block in downtown Toronto is the Argus building where Black spends most of his days. "Be it ever so humble," he quips, "at least we're owners. It's good not to have a landlord, and highly agreeable not to pay any rent."

Decorated with window boxes overflowing with white petunias and pink geraniums, the Argus headquarters at 10 Toronto Street looks like a movie-set version of a British merchant bank on lower Threadneedle. Its Doric columns, silk wall-coverings, Georgian mouldings, and crystal chandeliers create the appropriate ambiance for the hush of money. Erected in 1852 as Toronto's main post office, the building was purchased and refurbished by E.P. Taylor and his partners in 1959 for $750,000. Black has since put in a further million dollars to create Canada's most elegant—and most secure—corporate head office. It is the only building on Toronto Street whose sidewalk is unobstructed by parking meters.

At first glance, the free-standing two-storey structure appears vulnerable, with only a pair of kindly commissionaires on duty and no other visible protection. But closer inspection reveals that every pane of glass in the building is bulletproof and that there are hidden security devices in the most unexpected corners. Callers can get in only if buzzed through both sets of entrance doors by the commissionaires in the anteroom, who keep a list of expected visitors. It's only when Peggy Kennedy, the downstairs receptionist, receives the proper signal that she pushes the button that electronically opens the inner front door.

Inside, glass has been used to produce some extraordinary effects. Most of the reflecting surfaces are peach mirrors, which make the visitor appear tanned and rested, if slightly out of focus. "Peach mirrors," explains Peter Cotton, the building's most recent decorator, "build confidence, making people feel as if they had just come back from a weekend in Palm Beach." (In the original design, Cotton had included a blush-endowing pink bulb for the elevator, but it was too much. The Argus elevator, which runs up only one floor, is panelled with pressure-treated mahogany and has naval-bronze railings.)

Cotton used his decorating knowhow—he also did Toronto's Brick Shirt House, Toby's Goodeats, and the Chocolate Fantasies stores—to give the entire building a mood of vespers at twilight, insulating its occupants from the world that lurks outside the muffling fabric of its drawn draperies. Each of Argus's three main offices reflects the character of its occupant. According to Cotton's analysis, the Argus partners can be characterized as representing the *hunter* who goes out and captures the prey (Conrad); the *farmer* who cultivates and preserves existing stock (Monte); and the *shepherd* who looks after the other two (Argus executive vice-president Dixon Chant). Chant's office resembles that of a shepherd/bank chairman, with such pastoral touches as a framed copy of the cheque for $65 million paid to Paul Desmarais for his Argus stock in November 1978. Monte's quarters are airy and light powder-blue, designed to make him feel as if he were sitting in his light powder-blue Cadillac or in a Palm Beach living room. Conrad's office is dominated by its paintings: two A.Y. Jacksons, a Pilot, a Colville, and the sketch of Maurice Duplessis presented to the Quebec premier by the Union Nationale caucus in Quebec City on the anniversary of his thirtieth year in politics. The room is unpretentious but authoritative, with scattered books, corporate documents, and a tape recorder at the ready, loaded with the transcript of a speech about the excesses of Keynesianism.

Offices on the main floor house the balance of the Argus staff of a dozen employees, chief among them Harry Edmison, the resident economist. A knowledgeable and canny former research specialist with Wood Gundy who spent the Second World War in E.P. Taylor's Ottawa, he has been with the company since 1946. Conrad Black's hyper appointment schedule is choreographed by the immensely capable and super-discreet Joan Avirovic.

There is also a chauffeurs' waiting room that has a card table, colour TV, and separate ventilation, in case they should smoke. The upstairs dining room looks like an alcove in some exquisitely furnished private club, its walls dripping rust velvet, its furnishings in various subdued tones of sandalwood. Coffee is borne in on silver trays with china that has a Romanesque band (white with navy and gold); there are golden tongs for the sugar cubes.

The building's most impressive area is the main-floor boardroom. Its three shades of muted green blend ever so soothingly, a counterpoint to the gilt-frame mirrors sculptured with golden eagles, perched ominously, watchfully—Napoleon, deciding the matters of empire, would be at ease in such a room. "You can hide emotionally in space like that," claims Cotton, its designer. "We put wooden floors down and cheery area rugs to make the boardroom look a little less quiet. Wood sort of helps splash the noise around a bit."

Black's emphasis on gracious decor is a throwback to established Argus traditions. "We always had around this company a certain reputation for being stylists," he maintains. "I remember as a youngster that the only people around who had any panache—and Toronto was really a tank town then—were the Argus group, particularly the talents they had aside from business itself. E.P. Taylor was a sportsman and promoter of ideas—a builder. Lyford Cay in the Bahamas is a place in which not many Canadians have set foot, one created by Taylor from a tropical wilderness. It is, I would guess, surpassed only by Palm Beach as a popular winter resort for well-to-do people, at least on the eastern seaboard. Bud McDougald was more of a society figure: patron saint of the Toronto Club, confidant of all sorts of incredible people, pillar of the clubs in Palm Beach, New York, London, and so on—a legendary figure in his milieu. Wally McCutcheon was better known for his foray into government and did at least make the effort, very rare among industrialists, to try that transition. Col. Eric Phillips was justly recognized not only as a great industrialist but as a prodigious intellect, largely because of his lengthy chairmanship of the governing body of the University of Toronto in days when the chairman was a much more visible and influential person in the operation of the university than has subsequently been the case. So in the sense of endeavouring to be something other than only a businessman, I feel I'm following their example."

Despite such nostalgic links, during his brief tenure as Argus chairman, Black has carried out the holding company's almost total de-McDougaldization. The Argus portfolio has been re-oriented not only in the nature of its holdings (with the Massey, Domtar, and Noranda positions gone, and Norcen and Hanna added) but in that the governing philosophy of the closed-end investment trust has been turned upside down. Instead of having only minority holdings and depending on the moral suasion of the partners to keep satellite companies in line, Black has consolidated majority or overwhelming control positions in the Argus outposts and is rapidly turning the fleet of companies into a monolithic proprietorship. Equally significant has been Black's move to protect Argus's taxable income by turning the dormant conglomerate into an active operating company, most of whose revenues have found their way into tax-sheltered activities. In fact, following the reorganization that took place after his purchase in the spring of 1982 of a dominant minority share in Hanna Mining Company of Cleveland, Ohio, Black all but wound up Argus Corporation itself, a corporate shell no longer useful for his purposes.

Black's magisterial office manners tend to put off visiting executives who arrive unprepared for a papal audience. In most official encounters, he exudes an almost Nietzschean intelligence that makes him an insufferable companion and an invaluable partner. "Much of Conrad's charm is a private affair," says one long-time business acquaintance. "In his everyday corporate encounters, he can come across as a nasty son of a bitch." Espousing a contrary view is Roy MacLaren, the Liberal member of Parliament and one of the group that took over and rejuvenated *Canadian Business* in 1977, who knows Black well. "Conrad is, above all, a gentleman, extremely sensitive to other people's feelings, practising the infinite courtesies," he says. "Of course, anyone in his employ who has demonstrated incompetence isn't likely to be around for very long."

"What makes Conrad so exceptional," says Ron Graham, an author and former senior CBC-TV producer, "is that he has never at any time taken the predictable way out of a situation. On every deal that comes along, he seems to be telling himself, okay, I know how to do this safely – but let's do it creatively, even if it means trouble. What's extraordinary is that just when you think you've got him figured out, he'll do something completely unexpected, probably surprising himself in the process."

Graham is the first to admit that Black's behaviour is inconsistent, exhibiting many unexpected kindnesses. In the autumn of 1978, after he had conquered Argus and returned from his honeymoon, Conrad threw a bash for several hundred friends at Toronto's York Club. "We chatted a bit, and the receiving line behind me kept getting longer. 'Stand beside me for a moment – I want to talk to you some more,'" Graham recalls Black's insisting. "So I went through the receiving line again. Second time around, he told me to go back, that he wanted to have yet another word with me. I obediently started through the line a third time and, with tongue in cheek, asked if I could leave yet. He told me not to – and the whole scene got to be a running joke between us.

"But at the end of the evening I complained, 'Now you've done it. You've humiliated me in public. And I'm the last person left here.'

"Ferreting out the fact that I was staying at the Windsor Arms, he offered to give me a ride. As I was getting out of the car he said, 'I was teasing back there, and if I in any way embarrassed you, I apologize.' I was astounded, but I took the apology in the spirit in which it was given. Here was a sensitivity I'd heard about but had never really experienced. There are a lot of little kind things he's done that he didn't have to do."

One element in this unexpected side of Black is how extremely sensitive he is to criticism from any source, and the parallel capacity he retains to be delighted. "One night," his Vancouver-based Argus partner David Radler remembers, "Conrad phoned and fretted, 'I think Jimmy Pattison doesn't like us.' I asked him why.

"'Maybe it's because we're trying to buy one of his companies,' came the reply.

"The following week Conrad called again and was crackling with delight: 'Jimmy just sent me a big smoked salmon in the mail! He may not like you, but he does like me.'" Pattison, a Vancouver entrepreneur whose sunny nature is his trademark, was making it clear that he loved *all* the Argus partners – and wasn't interested in the deal anyway.

With another member of the business Establishment Black's relations were less euphoric on at least one occasion. When Charles Bronfman, the Canadian head of Seagram's, asked the Argus chairman for a pledge to purchase a million dollars' worth of Israeli bonds, Black immediately agreed – if the Expo owner would transfer the broadcasting franchise for his baseball team to CJAD, the Argus-owned Montreal radio station. "CFCF kept the Expo broadcasting rights, so I'm not exactly falling over my feet to buy Charles's bonds," he later told a friend.

Argus's long-term aspirations and more immediate objectives are formulated inside Black's head, but he does consult most of his partners on major decisions. This is done only marginally through the traditional medium of board meetings. Argus directors gather formally only four times a year, mainly to declare dividends. The eighteen-member Argus board has a seven-member executive committee, which in turn has a four-member quorum, allowing Black and his immediate retinue to guide things their own way.* The Argus empire's dominant board has become that of Ravelston (because it is the only one where every director is a partner), but it hardly ever meets. As the accompanying chart indicates, the Argus partners have been dispersed throughout the holding company's corporate stable to constitute Black's intelligence and control network.

"In this organization," Black boasts, "the emperors, not the praetorian guard, make the decisions." There are few surrogates within the Argus orbit. It's Black who makes the final judgements, though he does

---

*For a table showing the Argus succession, see Appendix D.

DOMINION STORES LTD.

*G. Montegu Black
*Chairman of the Board and
Chairman of the Executive
Committee*

*Allen C. Jackson
*President and Chief
Executive Officer*

Lewis H.M. Ayre
*Conrad M. Black
*Thomas G. Bolton
*Dixon S. Chant
Pierre P. Daigle
Glen W. Davis
Hon. Clarence L. Gosse
Hon. W. John McKeag
André Monast
Beryl Plumptre
Ronald T. Riley
Trumbull Warren

The Directorate

**LABRADOR MINING AND
EXPLORATION CO. LTD.**

P.C. Finlay
Chairman of the Board

Conrad M. Black
Vice-Chairman of the Board

C. Bruce Ross
*President and Chief
Executive Officer*

G. Montegu Black
Executive Vice-President

Dixon S. Chant
Executive Vice-President

Robert F. Anderson
Maurice Archer
Lewis H.M. Ayre
Edward G. Battle
Edmund C. Bovey
Charles G. Cowan
David M. Dunlap
John R. Finlay
Richard Geren
M. Brian Mulroney
C.E. Nickels, Jr.
Peter G. White

*Peter White is vice-president; Cowan
is secretary; Wendell F. White is
treasurer but not a director.*

**ARGUS
CORPORATION LTD.**

*Conrad M. Black
*Chairman of the Board,
Chairman of the Executive
Committee*

*G. Montegu Black
*President and Chief
Executive Officer*

*Dixon S. Chant
Executive Vice-President

Douglas G. Bassett
Edward G. Battle
Thomas G. Bolton
Glen W. Davis
*Fredrik S. Eaton
Harry H. Edmison
John R. Finlay
*H.N.R. Jackman
H.T. McCurdy
D.A. McIntosh
*F. David Radler
Ronald T. Riley
C. Bruce Ross
Trumbull Warren
Peter G. White

**NORCEN ENERGY
RESOURCES LTD.**

*Conrad M. Black
*Chairman of the Board and
Chairman of the Executive
Committee*

*Edward G. Battle
*President and Chief
Executive Officer*

Donald D. Barkwell
Douglas G. Bassett
*G. Montegu Black
*Edmund C. Bovey
*Dixon S. Chant
*E. Jacques Courtois
Robert Després
Fredrik S. Eaton
John R. Finlay
P.C. Finlay
*Edward A. Galvin
Frederick A.M. Huycke
J. Louis Lebel
Richey B. Love
Hon. W. John McKeag
F. David Radler
C. Bruce Ross
Barbara J. Sparrow
John R. Yarnell

*The two other officers, not directors,
are William T. Kilbourne, vice-president
administration and secretary, and Alick
S.G. Duguid, treasurer.*

All are of Toronto except Radler
(Vancouver), Riley (Montreal),
Warren (Hamilton), and White
(London, Ont.); Eaton, Finlay,
Jackman, and Radler are also vice-
presidents of the company. Edmison,
the secretary of Argus, is also
secretary of Ravelston Corp.; the
other officer of Argus and Ravelston
is Wendell F. White, a chartered
accountant, who is treasurer of both
but not a director.

*Members of the Executive Committee

This chart is dated May 1982, before
changes were made in the membership of the Argus Executive Committee, which rose to seven from six.

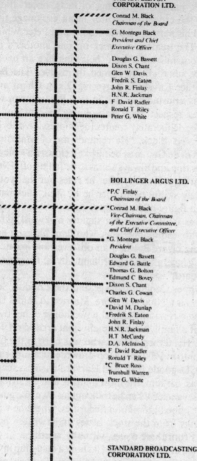

THE RAVELSTON CORPORATION LTD.

Conrad M. Black
Chairman of the Board

G. Montegu Black
*President and Chief
Executive Officer*

Douglas G. Bassett
Dixon S. Chant
Glen W Davis
Fredrik S. Eaton
John R. Finlay
H.N.R. Jackman
F David Radler
Ronald T Riley
Peter G. White

Chant is executive vice-president;
Finlay is vice-president; Harry H.
Edmison is secretary and Wendell
F White is treasurer; Edmison and
White are not directors.

HOLLINGER ARGUS LTD.

*P.C Finlay
Chairman of the Board

*Conrad M. Black
*Vice-Chairman, Chairman
of the Executive Committee,
and Chief Executive Officer*

*G. Montegu Black
President

Douglas G. Bassett
Edward G. Battle
Thomas G. Bolton
*Edmund C Bovey
*Dixon S. Chant
*Charles G. Cowan
Glen W Davis
*David M. Dunlap
*Fredrik S. Eaton
John R. Finlay
H.N.R. Jackman
H.T. McCurdy
D.A. McIntosh
F David Radler
Ronald T Riley
*C Bruce Ross
Trumbull Warren
Peter G. White

Chant and Ross are executive vice-
presidents; Ross is also general
manager; Cowan is secretary; the
other officer is Wendell F. White,
treasurer of Hollinger Argus, Argus
Corp., Labrador Mining and
Exploration, and Hollinger North
Shore Exploration, who is not a
director

STANDARD BROADCASTING CORPORATION LTD.

*G. Montegu Black
Chairman of the Board

*H.T. McCurdy
*President and Chief
Executive Officer*

*Dixon S. Chant
*Chairman of the
Executive Committee*

*Conrad M. Black
G. Allan Burton
Pierre P. Daigle
Jacques J. Giasson
Donald H. Hartford
*H.N.R. Jackman
W. Leo Knowlton
Richard R. Moody
M. Brian Mulroney
Lawrence M. Nichols
John R. Storar

Nichols, executive vice-president of
Standard, is president of subsidiary
Bushnell Communications Ltd.,
Ottawa; Hartford, senior vice-
president, is head of the radio
division and president of
subsidiaries CFRB Ltd. and CJAD
Inc.; Storar is chairman of
Standard Broadcasting Corp.
(U.K.) Ltd.; Moody is president of
Standard Broadcast Sales Co. Ltd.

canvass his partners, juxtaposing strings of facts, observations, and opinions, as would the crown prosecutor in an espionage trial. His brother, Monte, and his partners David Radler and Peter White are in on every decision. The quartet can pick up one another's pulse of understanding without missing a beat, behaving like an exotic rock group in three-piece suits who've named themselves The Board of Directors. Of the other Ravelston partners, Dixon Chant and Fred Eaton are constantly consulted, but it is H.N.R. Jackman who has earned Black's highest respect. "Hal is absolutely brilliant, and it's part of his cunning that he deliberately creates the impression of being a bit of a stumblebum," says Black. "He reminds me of Malcolm Muggeridge's description of de Gaulle as being like a clown on a bicycle who comes into the circus ring and always seems to be falling off. Everybody laughs and points at him. It's only after he rides out that you realize what a consummately skilful performer he is. Well, Jackman is still widely regarded as a figure of fun, a three-time political loser for the federal Conservatives in Rosedale,* a slightly awkward, giraffe-like fellow physically, with odd mannerisms, who flaps his great eyebrows and blows on his big cigar. But he's an observer and participant of extraordinary intelligence, absolutely brilliant – by far the greatest intellect on the Argus board."

A graduate of Upper Canada College and the London School of Economics, Jackman is all that and more. Married to James Duncan's daughter Maruja, who is an intellectual powerhouse in her own right, he is a descendant of a family of sea captains that arrived on Toronto's shores in the 1850s. His father, Harry, who was born in the Cabbagetown district of Toronto in 1900, had a top-drawer education (University of Toronto Schools, Osgoode Hall, and Harvard business school), but the stock market was, for him, the most alluring and enduring field of study. He was only seventeen when he took out his own margin account and at twenty-eight joined Dominion Securities, where he was put in charge of the leavings from the stock issues underwritten by the big investment house. From these issues, virtually worthless in the early 1930s, Harry Jackman and later his son Hal built a blue-chip investment portfolio and a major Canadian financial empire. The key investment companies are Debenture and Securities Corporation of Canada and Dominion and Anglo Investment Corporation Ltd. (assets of $60

*Rosedale was the seat his father, Henry Rutherford (Harry) Jackman, held from 1940 to 1949; the N.R. in Hal's initials refers to his grandfather Newton Rowell, Chief Justice of Ontario and chairman of the Royal Commission on Dominion-Provincial Relations in the late 1930s.

million in 1980). Its insurance operations (Empire Life Insurance Company and Dominion of Canada General Insurance Company) are held by E-L Financial Corporation Ltd. The Jackman family controls Victoria & Grey Trustco Ltd., the country's fourth-largest trust company (more than $3.75 billion in assets in 1981), and has a major holding in Algoma Central Railway, one of Canada's biggest transportation operations. Hal Jackman lives an unusually modest and unpretentious existence, travelling to most parts of Toronto by subway – particularly after his 1974 Oldsmobile was towed out of the Argus parking lot because the commissionaire on duty thought the wreck could not possibly belong to a company director.

In his political incarnation, Jackman remains a grey eminence and fund-raiser. During the 1980 Conservative convention that debated Joe Clark's leadership, Jackman was so vociferous in his support – waving his coat in the air and leading the Clark cheering section – that at the next Argus board meeting, Black proposed a mock resolution censuring Jackman for "bringing embarrassment and disrepute to our association" by the spectacle he put on at the Tory slugfest.

Apart from politics, Jackman's main hobby is playing war games with the several thousand toy soldiers in his basement, including entire battalions of meticulously painted French *chasseurs*, Austrian *schutzen*, and Prussian *landwehrmänner*. Black and Jackman often face off to recreate the battles of Waterloo, Austerlitz, and other famous engagements, not always managing to maintain their calm. "I remember once moving my men across a river," Black recalls, "and Hal's saying, 'You can't do that.'

"'Why not?'

"'You are leaving your artillery unprotected.'

"'Well, so what?'

"'You just can't *do* it, Conrad.'

"'What do you mean, I can't do it? I've just done it. And I'm about to win this battle. So don't tell me I can't do it.'

"'You have violated every law of war!'

"'That's neither here nor there, Hal. You have just been defeated.'"

Hal Jackman first bought into Argus during the early sixties, mainly as an investment, and eventually increased his holdings to 9 per cent. McDougald asked Jackman to join the board during the Paul Desmarais raid in 1975. "It was a little like being knighted," Jackman recalls. "I was taken to the Toronto Club, lectured on the glories of keeping pure the Everglades Club membership in Palm Beach, on how important it was to keep the Jews out of boxes at the Royal Winter Fair, and all of this awful religious stuff which, I'm sure, he was only doing for effect.... We weren't really interested in selling our shares to Desmarais anyway, because the price wasn't right."

On June 6, 1979, when Black traded a 12.24 per cent interest in Ravelston for Jackman's Argus holdings* at the same inflated value he had paid for the widows' shares, Hal sent his friend Conrad the lines delivered by Brutus to Cassius in Shakespeare's *Julius Caesar* — in effect pledging his support, provided that he was told precisely what was going on:

> That you do love me, I am nothing jealous.
> What you would work me to, I have some aim.

While Jackman definitely ranks as one of the key decision-makers in the Ravelston/Argus group, nothing within the Black organization happens by chance or without a complicated series of test runs on future projections. The process is somewhat akin to a chess game, in the sense that each step is made only after the implications of the next ten moves are analysed. "Conrad," says Brian Mulroney of the Iron Ore Company of Canada, in which the Blacks have a major shareholding, "has a magnificent capacity for conceptualization. If I look out a window, I'll see a tree. He might see a paper mill. He can put together the pieces of any corporate puzzle."

Black's favourite saying is "A dime for a dollar," which means that either an investment isn't worth even ten cents and should never be touched, or it's worth going all the way. Another is "The money is in the deal" — that if any deal is interesting, the money can always be found. His decisions seem brash and perverse but are usually analysed to death and are always run past Argus's team of legal advisers and tax experts.

As well as P.C. Finlay, his son, John, Donald McIntosh, and Charles Cowan, who sit on Argus boards, Black's counsel include Geoffrey Skerrett, Doug Berlis, Alan Bell, and John Turner ("Conrad's got to feel comfortable with you before he asks you to waltz, but I guess he feels easy with me and needs some outside strength"). Argus's main auditor is Jack Boultbee at Coopers & Lybrand.

IN ANY ASSESSMENT OF THE ARGUS POWER STRUCTURE, one name is usually left out because few outsiders know precisely what George Montegu Black III really does.

---

*Jackman raised the Ravelston holding to 16 per cent by buying, through E-L Financial, a further 3.76 per cent. In the summer of 1982 he reduced the holding to 4.7 per cent by selling the rest to the Blacks.

Four years older than his brother, very different in temperament, intellectual depth, and approach to life, Monte is a very special kind of alter ego. Instead of indulging in the flights of imagery and grandiloquence that characterize Conrad's discourse and behaviour, Monte has a plain and unaffected manner. His fire-hydrant-sized cigars, his girth and strut mark him as a cartoonist's dream capitalist. He describes his politics as being "far to the right – way over the horizon for most people" and believes there should be no income or indirect taxes. ("If the rich want a rich car, they should pay taxes for it at the source, so there wouldn't be any need for all those people in Ottawa. The guy who sells you a car should fill out the form and take in the money – 40 per cent on a Cadillac, or 5 per cent on a Volkswagen.")

Mainly preoccupied with the executive direction of Dominion Stores and Standard Broadcasting, he is an equal partner in all Conrad's investments, though there is a clear understanding between the brothers about who is Numero Uno. "There is a great misconception about Monte's role," the late Igor Kaplan, the Blacks' lawyer, pointed out. "Perhaps more than anyone else, I know how much Conrad relies on Monte. He wouldn't have any hesitation, if he were to go into politics, for example, to put everything into a blind trust managed by his brother. He's very smart, no intellectual, no great reader, but a superb analyst. You give him a financial statement on a prospective deal and he won't just split hairs: he'll grind them, he'll make *powder* out of them."

"Our strength," says Monte of his relationship with Conrad, "is that we are very different. What turns us on is different: how we spend our time, both inside and outside the office, is different – and that's good because you cover more ground that way. I view my strength as being able to get along with almost anybody. You've got to be honest with people, to say what you think, and at the same time be yourself – not feel above or below them. The combination of Conrad and myself covers most of the business facets – which is the strength of our partnership."

Intimates of the family describe Conrad as the one who plunges ahead and Monte as his sea anchor, question-asker, and chief resident buffer. "I fancy myself more as an operator of companies than as a deal-maker," Monte says, "but I love to watch the way Conrad's mind works. I can keep up. I don't have to take too much of a back seat – but he's quite startling, the way he goes about it. He gets moving so fast that he sometimes tends to leave a gap between the horse and the leg."

Montegu's upbringing was far more conventional than that of his brother. He attended Upper Canada College and Trinity College School, where he won colours in cricket, football, and hockey. His scholastic ambitions ran so low that he had to finish Grade 13 at York Mills Collegiate, and after he had a brief fling at the University of Western

219

Ontario, his education petered out altogether. He went to work as a junior analyst in Montreal for Brian Heward, a stockbroker friend of his father's. "I learned a lot," he recalls, "but in the basic fabric of the Blacks there is this nagging streak that says you really don't want to work for anybody else. After nearly six years, a number of senior partners at Jones Heward had died, yet control of the firm had not changed."

In October 1968, he was flying to Bermuda with David Knight, an old TCS friend whose grandfather and father had acquired control of a Bay Street mining investment house called Draper Dobie. "This plane was a Viscount and first class was at the back," Monte recalls. "Our families took up the whole section, except for Stan Randall (then an Ontario Cabinet minister), and we were trying to talk business. David was determined to turn Draper around, give it a real research department, and make it a reasonable company. So I told him: 'Your search is over. Look no further. For 25 per cent of the company and $25,000 a year, I'm yours.'

"He said: 'Sold.'"

In February 1976, Monte Black, who had been president of the firm since 1972, bought most of Knight's holdings. He had transformed it into a respectable boutique operation in the early seventies and pioneered a remarkably innovative computer unit, still in use, capable of crunching the historical spreads and prices of active stocks at a glance. But what made Draper Dobie count was the lunches the Black boys gave in its panelled dining room. For $14,000 they converted an office into a reasonable facsimile of what they thought an executive lunching area should look like, furnishing it with leftover Portuguese pine from the Art Shoppe, hired a part-time cook, and began to throw daily receptions—sometimes for breakfast, lunch, *and* dinner—which instantly established their reputation as fun hosts, if not fiscal geniuses. "We used to serve six-course meals with five wines, tapering off with port, cigars, and brandy," Monte says. "We entertained John Robarts a couple of times and just about everybody else. Bud McDougald once said he'd come, but decided at the last minute to eat at the Toronto Club instead."

By 1977, the economies of scale had caught up with Draper Dobie; Monte began negotiating with McDougald's old firm, Dominion Securities, for a merger, which turned out to be a takeover. The elder Black brother became vice-president in charge of DS's international operations, and it was from there that he moved on to Argus.

Monte Black is a happy man. He runs two of Argus's chief operations, travels as he pleases, and caters to his every whim. He drives a customized Cadillac, water-skis, goes to horse shows, owns summer houses in

Muskoka and Caledon, and handles his private investments through a company called Trachrannont. His chief indulgence is his collection of a dozen antique boats, including a forty-foot Ditchburn cabin cruiser called the *Glenelder* built of Honduras mahogany.

He shuns the limelight, insisting that Conrad is the family's leader – and lightning rod. Yet he has been an integral part of each of the many convoluted deals that have transformed Argus into an attention-riveting conglomerate.

THE SUM OF THOSE MACHINATIONS – not the original Argus takeover – has given the Blacks both their personal fortune and the reputation for being too clever by half. Watching Conrad Black make the deals that have expanded and consolidated the Argus business empire has been like witnessing an over-sophisticated jazz dance – a performance that's graceful and innovative at one level, yet shocking to the fastidious and amusing to the detached at another. He has behaved as though he held a mandate from heaven to do as he pleased. He has been tough and ruthless, his iron discipline suffering from little metal fatigue. Black is proud of having fought the corporate wars with detached competence under pressure, even if the battle itself has always been of more interest to him than its outcome. Once triumphant, he has refused to share the spoils with the vanquished and has delighted in making his corporate victims twitch.

Favourable opinions of Black's performance range from the admiring expletives of John Turner ("Conrad has a mind of genius proportions – and more important, he's got balls!") to the more sedate description by John Bassett, former publisher of the *Toronto Telegram*: "I know of nobody of my or his generation who possesses the same remarkable combination of intellectual interest and aggressive drive in business."

Others view him as the ravenous predator of Canada's Establishment. "I am not," says Stephen Jarislowsky, a leading Montreal money manager, "overly entranced by Conrad Black. He made a great number of fast moves because he didn't have enough money to get himself into the picture, and some of his behaviour has been relatively ruthless. His is basically a predatory activity."

Jarislowsky and his fellow critics condemn Black for what they say is his single-minded rush to convert Argus into a proprietorship that would mainly benefit its owners. He has achieved this by staging a series of corporate reorganizations and takeovers that hardly anyone outside his immediate circle of partners could follow. "His manoeuvres," wrote *Canadian Business*, "make Pac-Man look like a Pritikin dieter."

Certainly, Black has engaged his talents in Argus's consolidation and expansion with Napoleonic zeal. "Conrad once gave me a personal assessment of himself and near the top of his list of desirable qualities was strategic attention to detail," says his Argus partner Peter White. "He referred me to Napoleon's orders of battle, told me how Bonaparte used to keep four secretaries working at once, and, without revisions, would send the missives off to his marshals—knowing that every single element of an upcoming campaign had been planned ahead. Conrad has the same sort of ability to anticipate events."

When Black took over Argus in the early summer of 1978, he was hailed as having won great power and that position of corporate unassailability all good capitalists dream about. In fact, the company he had captured turned out to be something of a paper tiger, and his ownership position of its key asset, the 23-per-cent share it held in Hollinger, was so vulnerable that, as he confided to a friend at the time, "we were half a dozen phone calls away from being out on the street. There were five other blocks of Hollinger that together had more shares than we did."

Not only Hollinger (then carried on Argus's books at $1.5 million, though it was turning in $40 million a year in pre-tax royalties) but all the other Argus satellite companies—except the relatively small Standard Broadcasting—were similarly exposed. His capture of control over Ravelston had given Black and his immediate partners about 20 per cent of Argus's equity (and about 60 per cent of its votes), but what Argus, in turn, actually *owned* was not very impressive. Apart from its vulnerable Hollinger stake, there was a 16-per-cent minority holding in the troubled Massey-Ferguson, an 18-per-cent non-control bite of Domtar, the Montreal chemical/paper company, and 23 per cent of the unexciting Dominion Stores. "Argus was desperately short of cash, and everything was stacked up in a way that assured stagnation," Black complained to one of his lawyers at the time. "It was designed exclusively to enable Bud McDougald and some of his fellow directors to strut around the Toronto Club and similar socio-economic venues, convincing everybody they were owners when in fact they weren't."

On July 15, 1978, the day after Black's wedding, he sat down with Monte, Peter White, and David Radler beside the swimming pool of his Toronto house to plot a collective way out of this dilemma and become in fact the secure and wealthy proprietors most outsiders believed they already were.

At that poolside confab, many of the major moves that would take place in the next four years were debated and settled. The agenda included decisions to jettison Argus's non-control holdings in Domtar and Noranda at some point; to get into the Canadian energy business (though Norcen was not yet perceived as the eventual vehicle for this move); and, most important of all, to transform Argus into an operating instead of a holding company with *majority* rather than merely effective control over its various investments. This was the most far-reaching decision made that day because from it flowed the aggressive Argus grab for assets, which would become the target of so much criticism. What Black and his partners were determined to achieve was total freedom for themselves in the reshuffling of Argus's portfolio, an objective that could be realized only if they held absolute control of the assets involved – and could keep the process away from the scrutiny of independent-minded boards of directors. Under McDougald, who hated governments and all their works, Argus was structured, to minimize taxes, as the beneficiary of dividends from its network of investments. This didn't advance Black's strategy of floating large bank loans to repay the cash he had spent acquiring Argus, and subsequently to finance its reorganization. He needed a substantial operating income against which to write off interest payments. That was why, over the next forty-two months, Black turned the Argus portfolio inside out, using the cash generated by the companies themselves to expand his hold over them. The process was probably best described in a confidential memo he sent his partners in Ravelston on January 25, 1982: "For three-and-a-half years we have pursued the policy of maximizing Ravelston's underlying equity while upgrading and fine-tuning assets to improve our ultimate return on that equity. This policy led over that time to what was probably the greatest compression of corporate dealing in Canadian history."

It was indeed.

THE INSTRUMENT USED to perpetuate the Black brothers' personal hold over the Argus assets was their grandfather's company, Western Dominion Investment, which was incorporated in 1911. The Black family retained a minority interest in Western Dominion from the founding until 1923, when they acquired control.* Western Dominion's

---

*Harold Sidney Harmsworth (1868–1940), 1st Viscount Rothermere, was the first head of Western Dominion. He was a younger brother of the ebullient Alfred Harmsworth (1865–1922), Viscount Northcliffe, virtual creator of the British popular press through his skill at making journalism both lively and profitable. Harold, a shy man, was a principal architect of the Harmsworth family's fortunes and once estimated his own wealth at £20 million. The Harmsworths' publishing business was the largest in the world and at one time or another they owned a major part of the British national press, including the *Evening News, Daily Mail, Daily Mirror,*

main asset* is the 51-per-cent control block it holds in Ravelston, which in turn has 97 per cent of the Argus voting stock and a 52-per-cent share of Dominion Stores. As the accompanying chart indicates, the food chain is the incongruous owner of a new company called Hollinger Argus, which became the repository for 67 per cent of Labrador Mining—which has as its main assets a controlling slice (36 per cent) of Norcen (which in turn holds 20 per cent of Labrador).

When Black first took over Argus, the only major outside shareholder was Paul Desmarais of Power Corporation, who had taken a run at the company by purchasing E.P. Taylor's stock and making a takeover bid in the open market. He had collected 25.6 per cent of Argus's common shares and 59 per cent of its non-voting Class C preferreds but had never been granted a seat on its board because, as Bruce Matthews, Argus executive vice-president at the time, observed, "there really wasn't room for a fellow as *energetic* as Paul in the Argus picture."

Robert Scrivener had first brought Desmarais and Black together at the 1978 Hollinger Dinner. The two men stayed up drinking until two o'clock in the morning and struck a deal under which the Power chairman sold off his Argus shares to Ravelston without having to absorb any loss. The ostensible selling price was $80.5 million—but figuring out precisely what had taken place, as in all other Black deals, was about as frustrating as attempting to solve Rubik's Cube underwater while trying to outwit a pack of sharks.† Black's recapture of the

---

Sunday Pictorial, Sunday Dispatch, and *The Times.* Western Dominion, based in Winnipeg, was established to make property investments in the Canadian west. The successive heads of WDI since Rothermere have been Blacks—G.M., his son, George, and George's son Conrad. The lawyer who incorporated the company was Charles Stewart Tupper, who in 1915 succeeded to the baronetcy of his grandfather, one of the Fathers of Confederation and briefly Prime Minister of Canada.

---

*The Black brothers bought the interest of their cousin Ron Riley in Western Dominion Investment for $4 million. Their only remaining partners are David Radler and Peter White, each of whom owns 12 per cent of WDI. The senior partners in Ravelston are Glen Davis (16 per cent), Ron Riley (10 per cent), Hal Jackman (4.7 per cent), and Fred Eaton (4 per cent). Dixon Chant, Douglas Bassett, and John Finlay have 1 per cent each. Conrad Black has owned his shares of Western Dominion through a series of personal trusts named after the British battleships *Warspite, Ramillies* and *Iron Duke.*

---

†The transaction, finalized in November 1978, was broken down into $65 million cash, with the balance in promissory notes. The money came from the Commerce and the Toronto-Dominion at half of prime plus one; instead of floating a straight loan, the banks received term-preferred shares in a newly created subsidiary of Ravelston called 89211 Canada Ltd. The yield was lower than the usual interest rate, but because dividends paid by one Canadian corporation to another were not taxable, the percentage was enough to service the debt.

The Black Empire

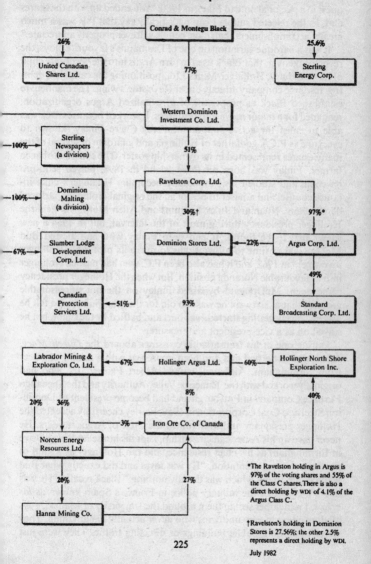

Conrad & Montegu Black

26% — United Canadian Shares Ltd.

25.6% — Sterling Energy Corp.

77% — Western Dominion Investment Co. Ltd.

51% — Ravelston Corp. Ltd.

Sterling Newspapers (a division) ←100%

Dominion Malting (a division) ←100%

Slumber Lodge Development Corp. Ltd. ←67%

Canadian Protection Services Ltd. ←51%

30%† — Dominion Stores Ltd. ←22%— Argus Corp. Ltd. ←97%*

49% — Standard Broadcasting Corp. Ltd.

93% — Hollinger Argus Ltd.

67% — Labrador Mining & Exploration Co. Ltd.

60% — Hollinger North Shore Exploration Inc.

20% 36% Labrador Mining & Exploration Co. Ltd.

8% — Iron Ore Co. of Canada

3% — Norcen Energy Resources Ltd.

40%

20% — Hanna Mining Co.

27%

*The Ravelston holding in Argus is 97% of the voting shares and 55% of the Class C shares. There is also a direct holding by WDI of 4.1% of the Argus Class C.

†Ravelston's holding in Dominion Stores is 27.56%; the other 2.5% represents a direct holding by WDI.

July 1982

225

Desmarais holding was described by *Fortune* as "a breathtaking bit of financial wizardry." Desmarais gave his assessment of the Argus conquest in a personal note to Black in 1980: "You ended up with the shares and, as the rejected suitor, I can realistically say that this was a much greater accomplishment than most people will ever properly appreciate."

It was a baroque variation on one of Desmarais's favourite ploys, the reverse takeover, that Black used to turn Argus into the corporate child of its subsidiary, Hollinger Mines Ltd., positioning the cash-rich, debt-free resource company directly under Ravelston's wing. The manoeuvre established Black as proprietor of a revitalized Argus organization, realigned for a major move into resources. It worked because Black was able to enlist the active support of Percy Claire Finlay (known to everyone as P.C.), godfather of Hollinger and guardian of several of the many estates represented in its ownership roster. The son of a tobacco farmer, Finlay was born on Pelee Island in 1898, played semi-pro baseball, and studied law, eventually becoming Hollinger's chief in-house counsel and adviser to nearly all the original Hollinger partners' descendants. Noah and Jules Timmins and Allen McMartin held the Hollinger presidency during most of the interval, but in 1964 a new leader had to be found. It had been Finlay who had alerted Bud McDougald in time to allow Argus to make its profitable Hollinger investment in 1962, and it had also been P.C. who had pushed Hollinger into its favourable Noranda position. But when the Hollinger presidency came open, McDougald bypassed Finlay on the not unreasonable grounds that at sixty-six he was too old for the job. Finlay, who felt he was just nicely getting started, was hurt and baffled by the slight, but he stayed on as a vice-president and treasurer.

During one of his transatlantic crossings aboard the *Queen Mary*, Allen McMartin had met and been impressed with a mining engineer from Birmingham, Alabama, named Albert Fairley, Jr., who had originally worked with the Tennessee Valley Authority and the Shenango Furnace Company in Pittsburgh and had become president of Dominion Steel and Coal Corporation in 1959. Fairley cheerfully accepted the Hollinger presidency and soon joined the circle of Argus insiders. He never gave up his American citizenship, kept his house on Ridge Drive in Birmingham as his chief residence, and ran Hollinger as a kind of northern mineral plantation. "He was loyal and did exactly what Bud wanted him to do, which was usually nothing," Black recalls. "He was like a member of the military police in Franco's Spain known as *los grisos*. I remember seeing them around the University of Madrid, guys all dressed up in grey uniforms who never actually *did* anything. They weren't guarding public buildings or directing traffic. They were just there. When I asked what they did, I was told, 'Nothing. There are three hundred thousand of them; they are armed to the teeth and they have been standing there since 1939. They are just waiting, in case Franco should ever need them.' That's what Fairley was like. He didn't actually do much, but if Bud had ever needed him he would certainly have swung into line."

When in Toronto Fairley lived in an apartment in the Manulife Centre, where he also kept his Cadillac, but he spent much of his time going to Alabama and back.* He became a director of the Canadian Imperial Bank of Commerce and, in one of the more bizarre twists of personal loyalty, disqualified himself in 1979 from voting on Brascan's application for a $700-million loan to purchase control of F.W. Woolworth on the grounds that he had a conflict of interest because he was an American citizen.

Finlay never took Fairley very seriously. A grand old man, P.C. is able to turn on at will either a beatific smile or worry lines that make his face look like the prow of a foundering ship. The Hollinger veteran had always felt quite secure in the knowledge that he had in his desk unlimited and irrevocable power of attorney for estates that controlled nearly 15 per cent of the company's stock. The heirs of all but one of the partners of the original Hollinger gold mine incorporated in 1910 – Noah and Henry Timmins, Duncan and John McMartin, and David Dunlap – have employed Finlay's firm as their legal or financial advisers. (The exception was John McMartin, who married Mary McDougald, a sister of Duncan McDougald, Bud's father. McMartin transferred the care of his financial affairs to Crown Trust.) Finlay weathered at least fourteen McMartin family divorces.†

*The car was eventually inherited by P.C. Finlay, who doesn't believe in paying good money to get it cleaned. His guests are startled, whenever it starts raining, to see Finlay making a dash for the garage and backing his car out for a free wash.

†The two main lines of the McMartin family are those of Duncan (who died in 1914) and John (1918). The brothers left a collection of heirs now scattered mainly outside Canada. Of Duncan's three children, only Allen remains; he lives in Bermuda and has two sons, Duncan Cameron and Allen Bruce. His brother and sister both died there – Melba Van Buren in 1947 and Duncan in 1979. Melba was married three times; her daughter, also Melba and married three times (she is now Mrs. George Lubovitch), lives in Liechtenstein. The younger Melba's half-brother, Wallace McMartin Orr, lives in Spain. Duncan was married five times; he left a daughter, Marcia, by Pauline, his second-last wife, and a son, Duncan Roy, by Hilda, the wife who survived him. The cigarillo-smoking Hilda lives in Bermuda. The children of John and Mary (née McDougald) McMartin are all dead. The only son, John Bruce (Jack), died in Montreal in 1944. The daughters were Grace, Jean, Rita, and Frances. The John McMartin family relied heavily for financial advice on John A. (Bud) McDougald, Mary McMartin's nephew, and he was associated with the

227

Shortly after Black took over Argus, rumours began to circulate on Bay Street that financiers Harold Crang and John C. Turner were planning to take over Hollinger. (It was a rich plum to covet: for instance, in 1979 alone its interest in the Iron Ore Company of Canada had produced a royalty income of $44 million.) The hold of Argus, with less than a quarter of Hollinger's stock, was tenuous in the extreme, so that almost as soon as Black moved into the chairman's office he began trying to consolidate his grip. He already had an additional 8 per cent of the company sewn up through his control of Crown Trust and persuaded Finlay to negotiate "put" arrangements with his Hollinger heirs. P.C. did have trouble bringing some of the heirs into line. One of them, the widow of D. Moffat Dunlap, who had married Harold Crang,* showed reluctance to sign over the first call on her 245,000 Hollinger shares requested by Black.

family's Hollinger and Crown Trust holdings. Grace became the wife of Dr. Joseph Gilhooly, an Ottawa eye-ear-nose specialist and sportsman; their big summer house at the end of Meach Lake, near Ottawa, is one of the landmarks of the area; they left no children. Jean, who became Mrs. Joe Mulford and lived in Virginia and New York, left a daughter, Olga, who married a Dutchman and lives in the Netherlands. Rita, successively Mrs. LeMay and Mrs. Floyd-Jones, lived in the Adirondacks in upstate New York (her parents had bought a place at Saranac Lake in 1906) and left two children, Peter LeMay and Barbara Howley, both of Saranac Lake. Frances died without children. The McMartin family's lifestyles have provided some memorable footnotes to Canadian corporate history. The senior John McMartin spent $70,000 decorating the dining-room ceiling of his summer house in Cornwall, Ontario, with a five-foot-wide frieze depicting a lakeside scene. It had real bulrushes gummed against the plaster and stuffed flying ducks impaled on invisible wires. His son Jack used to march into Montreal bars and with his walking stick smash every bottle behind the counter. Weary bartenders let him enjoy himself, because they knew they could charge him a flat $1,000 fee per performance. His cousin Melba once bought a sixty-four-carat diamond the size of a man's thumb join, but only wore its paste imitation. When her brother Duncan was an RCAF instructor near Calgary during the Second World War, one Friday the pay failed to arrive and he wrote a cheque to cover the station's payroll.

*Harold Crang's first wife was Dorothy Ritchie, one of the four daughters of Harold F. Ritchie, a Toronto manufacturers' agent and entrepreneur known as Carload Ritchie because he had a reputation for never selling anything in less-than-carload lots. The other daughters—Kathleen, Pauline, and Antoinette (Tony)—became, respectively, Mrs. Thomas W. Gilmour, Mrs. Beverley Matthews, and Mrs. Charles Gundy. Kay Gilmour was a leading figure in the St. John Ambulance Brigade and was with the organization in Britain while her husband was serving as a captain in the Royal Canadian Artillery. Tom Gilmour worked with his father-in-law's firm, which was later sold to Beecham Group Ltd., and his wife became a Dame Grand Cross of the Order of St. John; they both died in 1980. After the death of Dorothy, Crang married Peggy, the widow of D. Moffat Dunlap, son of one of the five original Hollinger partners. She had a daughter, Donalda (Mrs. Richard Robarts), and two sons, David and Moffat; David is a director of Hollinger Argus and other companies in the Hollinger group and of Crown Trust Co. Moffat, a noted equestrian

228

"Well, Mr. Finlay," she said at the crucial moment during the negotiations, "I am being advised by my sons and my lawyer not to approve this document. Can you give me one good reason why I should sign?"

"Yes," came the reply. "You and your late husband and your late father-in-law's estate have prospered by following my advice for fifty-four years, and this is no time to change."

"That's good enough for me."

P.C. had delivered again.

At Hollinger's board meeting in January 1979, Black rewarded his ally by proposing that Finlay replace Fairley in the Hollinger presidency. P.C., who was then a sprightly eighty, allowed that this was only fit and proper – provided, of course, that he was given a twenty-year, renewable contract. At the Hollinger Dinner that followed he poked gentle fun at Conrad and Monte, comparing the Black brothers to the Ringling brothers and Joyce Brothers – chiding Conrad for paying attention to Milton Friedman, whom he equated with Milton Berle.

WHILE BLACK WAS EXPANDING his Argus holdings, he had to keep looking over his shoulder at the considerable debt load accumulated in his drive for power. He had paid $9.2 million for each block of Ravelston shares owned by the McDougald and Phillips estates and had forked out $1.6 million for General Matthews's small but strategic 3.9 per cent interest. Max Meighen's shares had cost a further $11.8 million. All these purchases placed a premium valuation equal to nearly twice the liquidating value of the stock. The total price for the 77.6 per cent of Ravelston purchased from these sources was $31.8 million.

On November 1, 1978, when the price for Meighen's Ravelston shares was being negotiated, Alex Barron had turned very tough very quickly. "This is Wednesday," he'd told Monte Black. "You've got until Friday afternoon at three o'clock to agree to pay us $42.50.... Don't

---

who has his own realty firm, was formerly married to Margaret Humphrey, daughter of the late Gilbert Watts (Bud) Humphrey, head of Hanna Mining Co. of Cleveland. Pauline Matthews died in 1967, and three years later her husband, a senior partner in the big Toronto law firm McCarthy & McCarthy, married a widow, Kathleen Woods, a daughter of Edwin G. Baker, one of Toronto's leading businessmen as chairman of Moore Corp. Ltd., president of Canada Life Assurance Co., and a director of Inco, Stelco, and the CPR. In 1978 Bev Matthews married for a third time; his bride was Phyllis, widow of Neil McKinnon, chairman of the Commerce. Tony Gundy's husband, a pillar of the financial structure as chairman of Wood Gundy, the investment house co-founded by his father, Harry, died in 1978. Harold Crang's brokerage firm, J.H. Crang & Co., which he founded in 1929, became Crang & Ostiguy Inc. after a 1972 merger and in 1977 lost its name after merging with Greenshields Inc.

phone me with a lesser bid. If the decision isn't made by Friday, then we'll go to court and I don't give a damn if it takes five years and five million dollars, we'll fight to the end of the road. *That's* the price, and *that's* all I have to say." And the Blacks had agreed.

To spread the risk and attract worthy associates, the Blacks laid off $17.6 millions' worth of Ravelston stock on their partners – Davis, Jackman, Riley, Eaton, Chant, and Bassett – keeping a majority for themselves. But the debt load kept growing, and the brothers quickly decided to carry out their plan to sell the 18 per cent held in Domtar.

Conrad Black and Alex D. Hamilton, the operating chief of Domtar, had joined the Argus board on the same day back in 1976, but had never grown close. A professional executive who had put in a long apprenticeship in the pulp-and-paper industry in Quebec, Ontario, and British Columbia, Hamilton set out to treat the Blacks as ordinary shareholders. Max Meighen, chairman of Domtar's executive committee, threw out hints that Black had finally met his match, as if the contest for Argus had been some kind of physical joust: that Hamilton did whitewater canoeing; that he went skiing in the Bugaboos; that his father lived to be in his nineties; that he wasn't going to be pushed around.

On July 27, 1978, the Black brothers called on Hamilton in his Montreal head office. He was cordial but made no motion of inviting either of them or any other member of Argus's new slate onto his board. Hamilton pointedly indicated that he no longer regarded Domtar as part of the Argus stable by objecting to the $30,000 his company was expected to contribute annually toward the upkeep of Argus's head office at 10 Toronto Street. After they had left Hamilton's office and were standing in the elevator, Conrad said to Monte, "Well, that's it. This isn't for us. We'll never get control of this place. We've got to beat the bushes and get somebody to buy our Domtar stock."

During the next four months, the Domtar shares were offered to Brascan and four other companies, but it was Page Wadsworth, a former chairman of the Commerce and a director of MacMillan Bloedel Ltd., who recommended their purchase by the West Coast forest-products giant. Domtar's executives were unaware of the specifics, but after hearing the rumours, Hamilton telephoned Conrad Black at 5:30 p.m. on December 20 to inquire whether any action affecting Domtar had been taken by the Argus board, because the Montreal paper company was holding a directors' meeting the following day. After sparring with Hamilton for a while, Black said that Argus had decided to sell its Domtar block to MacMillan Bloedel that very afternoon for $27 a share and that the Vancouver company was planning a public bid to raise its holding to 51 per cent. Hamilton immediately telephoned Barron, the chairman of his board, who rushed to Montreal in a chartered jet. The following day, Domtar directors jolted Canada's corporate world by announcing a retaliatory takeover run at MacMillan Bloedel.*

ARGUS'S PROFIT-TAKING OF $37 MILLION on the Domtar stock sale was just one small victory in corporate manoeuvres that included:

Bow Valley Industries. Tipped off by Don Early and Bud Willis of Greenshields that the Seaman brothers wanted to sell out, Black, through Hollinger, decided to bid for control of this $400-million Calgary-based energy company, with uranium deposits in Saskatchewan as well as oil properties in the Beaufort, the North Sea, and Abu Dhabi. The initial purchase of 1.85 million treasury shares at $22 each was negotiated on a handshake by Daryl K. (Doc) Seaman and Black in the latter's office at Massey-Ferguson, but as the stock began its climb to $60, the Alberta oilman advised Black that his board wouldn't approve the deal. One factor in the change of heart is thought to have been pressure from the Montreal-based Bronfmans, who held half a million Bow Valley shares and didn't want another dominant stockholder on the scene. "These oil and gas people," Black complained at the time, "are no joy to deal with. They've completely lost touch with such normal disciplines of commerce as price/earnings ratios."

Standard Broadcasting. In June 1979 the Black brothers purchased a $2.25-million block of Standard stock to push their ownership position over 50 per cent, at the same time expanding the company's broadcasting operations to Italy. With holdings in seventeen communications enterprises in the United Kingdom and new Canadian outlets in Ottawa and St. Catharines, this Argus subsidiary hummed along like a neat, well-oiled money machine.

*This offer was followed by yet another bid for MacMillan Bloedel from its largest shareholder, Canadian Pacific Investments Ltd., whose chairman, Ian Sinclair, was told by Premier Bill Bennett that takeovers by outsiders of British Columbia's biggest company were not acceptable. Control of MacBlo subsequently passed to Noranda, and control of Noranda in turn was bought by Brascade Resources Inc., a partnership formed in 1981 by the Bronfman-controlled Brascan Ltd. (holding 70 per cent) and Caisse de Dépôt et Placement du Québec (30 per cent). Meanwhile (in the summer of 1979) MacBlo sold its Domtar block to the Caisse at $27 a share (the same price MacBlo paid to get it from Argus in December 1978), and by the summer of 1981 the Caisse, together with another provincial investment agency, Société Générale de Financement du Québec, owned 42 per cent of Domtar.

Noranda Mines. Although a major Noranda amalgamation had trimmed the 11-per-cent stake tucked into Hollinger, Black remained Noranda's largest shareholder. He kept perusing lists of the company's stockholders to invent a takeover scenario. On January 9, 1979, Alf Powis, the Noranda chairman, wrote to Black confirming plans to appoint him to the Noranda board at $10,000 in director's fees for its four meetings a year. A month later Black accepted, noting that he might move his stock position to 15 or 20 per cent in the future. Powis objected, pointing out that such a move "would be widely interpreted as a bid for control," and immediately issued treasury shares to cut the value of the Argus holding. In a letter to Powis on March 13, Black declined to have his options restricted, and suggested to the Noranda chairman that they "maintain the informal arrangement that you and I agreed upon on January 4, after John Turner's dinner for Peter Lougheed... if we are planning any change of course, I shall call you, and perhaps if Noranda is about to do anything startling, somebody could advise us before the newspapers do. Obviously in the circumstances, it would not be appropriate for me to become a director of Noranda and I must decline your invitation, but I am grateful to you and your colleagues for having made it. Noranda need have nothing to fear from us."

Six months later Black abruptly sold off the Noranda stock (carried on the Hollinger books at $15.00 a share) at the equivalent of $64.50 a share to Trevor Eyton of Brascan, triggering the Bronfman-controlled company's successful Noranda takeover.

Hollinger Argus Ltd. As part of his move to reduce debt and consolidate his hold over Hollinger's cash flow, Black transformed the mining company into the group's main operating vehicle, creating an income flow against which to write off Argus's interest charges, salaries, and other expenses.* At a shareholders' meeting, Herbert Beswick, who had held Hollinger stock for forty-three years, objected, but the move was approved with little fuss. Hugh Anderson wryly pointed out in the *Globe and Mail*'s *Report on Business*: "As at each stage in the complicated operation, the minority shareholders will not have the assistance of independent valuations of the assets that are being moved around, or of expert outside opinions certifying the fairness of the transactions.

---

*The massive reorganization, completed in the summer of 1979, involved the acquisition by Hollinger of the controlling interest in Argus from Ravelston, in return for $51.7 million in cash and 900,000 Hollinger treasury shares. Upon the deal's completion, Ravelston controlled 43.5 per cent of Hollinger, which in turn owned 77 per cent of Argus, while part of the cash was used to pay off the $15-million promissory note held by Desmarais on the Argus buyback.

Canadian law does not require them to be furnished in these circumstances and the managements of the companies involved have chosen not to do so."

Crown Trust. After the company had served its purpose in the acquisition of Argus, Black began shopping around for a buyer to take Crown Trust off his hands. His prime prospect was Reuben Cohen, the financier from Moncton, N.B., who had missed out in the original deal with the John McMartin estate and by then owned 32 per cent of the company's stock. Cohen and his partner, Leonard Ellen of Montreal, had visited Black in Palm Beach in January 1979, and the Argus chairman had told them that although he was not actively planning to auction off the block, he would accept the highest offer. The Maritimer's suggestion of $41.50 a share struck Black as eminently fair, and he promised to warn Cohen if a more generous bid were received.

David Radler, the Argus associate who had become Crown's chairman, saw unrealized potential in the trust company and began to sound out western investors including Israel Harold Asper, the energetic head of Winnipeg's CanWest Capital Corporation. At a cookout on June 23, 1979, in Igor Kaplan's Harbour Square condominium on the Toronto waterfront, everyone got giggly from an overdose of chicken teriyaki and *sake,* and in mid-party, Asper and the Argus tribe reached tentative agreement for CanWest to buy Crown Trust at $44 a share.*

Just before the $17.7-million sale was finalized by Asper in Black's Massey office, Kaplan excused himself, murmuring, "I have to call Monte," implying that he had to ask the elder Black brother's permission. Instead, this was an arranged, last-minute message to Cohen, tipping him off to the higher offer. Cohen didn't believe Crown was worth that much and stuck with his $41.50 bid. Crown went to CanWest, and the Black brood realized a profit of $4 million simply for having held onto the trust company for a year.

FP Publications Ltd. On October 9, 1979, Black dispatched a letter by messenger to Brig. Richard S. Malone, then chairman of FP Publications, the country's second-largest newspaper chain, bidding $100 million for the lot. The missive ended with a characteristic call to arms: "My ambition is not to be a busybody or an interloper but (if I may put

---

*The accompanying transfer of the Commerce's key 9.9-per-cent holding later became the object of a $5-million lawsuit brought by Cohen, in which he claimed that the bank should have taken his minority status into account —particularly because he had been trying to buy the same block since 1977 and the bank was holding his shares as collateral.

this without being self-righteous) to help, with incumbent shareholders, to be a restorative influence in this company whose newspapers are so central to the history and future of Canada." The eight-newspaper chain had 1,448 voting and about two million equity shares, divided unevenly among heirs of four estates (Victor Sifton, his son, John W. Sifton, Max Bell, and J.W. McConnell). The other major shareholder was R. Howard Webster, the Montreal financier and chairman of FP's Toronto newspaper, the *Globe and Mail*, with 22.5 per cent of the voting shares and 20.6 per cent of the equity class. Malone, who had managed newspapers for both Victor Sifton and John Sifton, held 7.5 per cent of the voting shares. The only common strain among the partners was their incompatibility. Their infrequent get-togethers resembled nothing so much as a badly staged Eugene O'Neill play about family feuds and dark doings in the front parlour. At one point, the late Armagh Price, aunt of Victor John, the fourteen-year-old heir of John W. Sifton who was due to inherit 22.5 per cent of FP's voting shares on his twenty-fifth birthday, told Deborah Dowling of the *Financial Post*, "I have no objections to Mr. Black and I am willing to work with the man—but not with the present top management of FP, who have kept me and other members of the family in the dark for an extremely long period of time." Other members of the FP family were less comfortable about associating themselves with Black and his partners—John Bassett, chairman of Baton Broadcasting, George Gardiner, president of Gardiner, Watson, a Toronto investment firm, and Fred Eaton. When *Globe* publisher Roy Megarry, anxious to maintain the independence he enjoyed while Webster was a major shareholder in FP, appeared in his newsroom on November 30, 1979, and confirmed rumours of a takeover bid by the Black team, he set off a move by employees to buy the paper. (About 850 of them signed a petition favouring the plan.) Black dismissed Megarry's performance as "indiscreet and amateurish—we are not the ravaging dragon trying to defile the virgin *Globe and Mail*." But the intercession achieved the objective of flushing out higher counter-bids, and the chain was eventually sold to Ken Thomson for $165 million.

Norcen Energy Resources Ltd. With Black's characteristic regard for military analogies, it was code-named Operation Catapult. The exercise's designation was chosen to emphasize that this was to be a new-style investment that would propel Argus out of its low-margin, slightly humdrum traditions into the exciting energy field—a way to convert those dull but valuable Iron Ore royalties into control of a powerful, contemporary energy company. Placed in charge of the search for such a paragon of Canadian capitalism were John R. Finlay (P.C.'s son, a lawyer and investment analyst), Charles Bruce Ross (executive vice-president of Hollinger), and David M. Dunlap (the Hollinger heir and director). They began by leafing through a handbook of Canadian resource companies, investigating the likelihood of being able to nab either Consumers' Gas or Home Oil, but kept coming back to Norcen. Established in 1954 as Northern Ontario Natural Gas Company Ltd.,* a gas distributor that left a historic bribery case in its wake as it progressed through Northern Ontario, the company merged with Canadian Industrial Gas & Oil Ltd. in 1975, crowning an extraordinary series of CIGOL takeovers involving two *wunderkinder* of the 1960s, Paul Desmarais and Maurice F. Strong. Norcen had expanded under the inspired guidance of Edmund C. Bovey and Edward G. Battle into one of the top Canadian-owned energy companies, combining gas distribution systems with oil pipelines in Manitoba and Saskatchewan and dozens of oil and gas properties on four continents – all growing at a compounded annual rate of more than 20 per cent, producing an unobstructed cash flow from its natural resources division of more than $200 million a year. One reason Finlay's resource committee thought that Norcen might be a suitable takeover target was that Hollinger's tradition-minded shareholders – as well as most of Canada's investment community – still thought of the company as the prosaic gas utility it had been, instead of the high-flying energy conglomerate it had become.

On December 6, 1979, Black, through Labrador Mining & Exploration Company Ltd., managed to pick up the 9-per-cent slice of Norcen's stock Gordon Securities Ltd. had accumulated as an investment for Brascan in the second-largest single block purchase ($64.2 million) on record at the Toronto Stock Exchange. Bovey, the Norcen chairman, who had been hearing rumours about his company's takeover for more than a year, was nervous about the interloper's identity – being especially concerned that the Bronfmans or Steve Roman of Denison Mines might take a run at it. "I calculated that Ed was one of those guys who would be at his office by nine o'clock in the morning, which I rarely am," Black recalls. "So at nine exactly, CFRB time [on December 7], I phoned his office and the receptionist answered. I asked, 'Is Mr. Bovey there, please?'

"And she said, 'No, I'm afraid he isn't, may I give him a message?'

"So I identified myself and told her I had something important to tell him. I got halfway through the word important when she said, 'Mr. Bovey is right here, sir.'

---

*NONG changed its name in 1965 to Northern & Central Gas Co. Ltd. and became Northern & Central Gas Corp. Ltd. in 1968.

"Ed picked up the phone, and without a hello or good morning, said, 'I hope it's you!' He couldn't have been more co-operative, unlike Alf Powis, who had this self-image that he couldn't have anybody like me around." Three days later, Labrador's chairman, P.C. Finlay, revealed to Paul Taylor of the *Globe and Mail* that Labrador was the $64-million purchaser of Norcen stock. "We have no plans at the moment to buy more shares," he said, adding a couple of days later that his company did not plan to seek an active role in Norcen's management. Bovey cheerfully told the *Financial Times of Canada* that it was all a friendly development. "This is not a takeover bid, but an investment," he said. "And when someone invests, we take it as a vote of confidence."

A few days later, Labrador Mining prepared a tender offer for 7.2 million Norcen shares at $40 each, which was announced on January 16, 1980. At this point, the Norcen directors rebelled. Black had not treated their company as a long-term investment —and the price he was offering was well below Norcen's existing asset value of $53.

The Norcen board would neither recommend nor reject the Labrador offer, although the directors said that they would not turn in their shares. (When Black, who was in Palm Beach, phoned Paul Desmarais to ask how he should deal with the recalcitrant directors, the Power chairman snapped: "Fire the whole damn bunch of them!") Black did nothing; but two weeks later, in a stunning rebuke to the Norcen directors, investors resolved the dilemma by massively oversubscribing to Black's offer. "It sure beats the grocery business," he told a friend, all but levitating behind his desk.

At that year's Hollinger Dinner, P.C. Finlay joked about how the Argus chairman had become an oilman. "Conrad went to the dentist the other day," Finlay quipped, "and ordered him to drill. When the dentist said he could see no cavities, Conrad told him, 'Drill anyway. I feel lucky today…'"

WITHIN HALF A YEAR of the Norcen takeover, Black was busy concocting yet another of his corporate fruitcakes, one that would have prompted Norcen to finance its own takeover. The scheme, as outlined to the Ontario Securities Commission, called for eight steps.*

*1. Labrador Mining transfers its iron ore and other resource assets, valued at $170 million, to a new company (Norelab Mining Resources Ltd.) in exchange for common shares of Norelab.
2. Norcen acquires 3,435,294 shares of Hollinger Argus (58.8 per cent of the issued shares) from Ravelston and certain associated companies at $68.50 a share for $235,318,000, payable $119,043,000 in cash with the balance accounted for by the issuance of common shares (at $38.17 each) or preferred shares of Norcen.

The real purpose of the intended switch was to increase the net worth of Ravelston to $160 million from $60 million and shelter the Iron Ore royalties in East Coast oil drilling. "Mr. Black," noted Jack Stacey, an analyst for Moss, Lawson & Company Ltd. of Toronto, "has effectively put a lid on Norcen's price. There really aren't enough numbers yet to evaluate the deal, but I still have a gut feeling it is being done to the advantage of Ravelston. The basic question is: who dictates Norcen policy—Conrad Black or management?"

Black was determined to roll over assets worth $4.6 billion with no tax liabilities in yet another internal reverse takeover at a time when such ploys were increasingly coming under scrutiny to protect minority shareholders. Members of the Ontario Securities Commission raised questions, but Black claimed to have satisfied them. "I pacified the OSC and Henry Knowles [the Commission's chairman]," he said, "as if I were on a pilgrimage to Canossa to see the Pope and stood outside the window in the snow.* While I didn't humble myself to *that* extent, I think they were a little flattered that I went there at all. It was more consideration than they really deserved in view of some of the outrageous stances they were taking. I cleared the air, gave them a good explanation of this whole deal, and we reached complete accord."

Nevertheless, on November 11, 1980, Black abruptly cancelled the massive corporate restructuring, blaming the effect of Ottawa's new budget and energy policies for Norcen's inability to handle the added

3. New Ravelston (a fresh company to be incorporated by the Ravelston group) acquires 2,677,677 common shares of Labrador Mining (66.9 per cent of the issued shares) from Hollinger Argus at $81.00 a share for a total of $216,891,830, payable $76,757,642 in cash with the balance of $140,134,188 being in the form of preferred shares in New Ravelston.

4. Norcen offers to purchase up to 7,500,000 of its own common shares at $38.17 cash a share.

5. Labrador transfers up to 1,500,000 common shares of Norcen to Norelab at $38.17 a share, payable in cash.

6. The Norcen common shares acquired by Ravelston would be transferred to Norelab at $38.17 share, payable by the issuance of $116,275,000 of preferred shares of Norelab.

7. Norcen acquires all of the issued shares of Norelab from Labrador Mining for $170,000,000, payable by issuing to Labrador Mining 4,453,759 common shares of Norcen valued at $38.17 a share.

8. Norcen makes an offer to purchase all shares of Hollinger Argus it does not already own at $68.50 a share, payable in cash and preferred shares of Norcen.

*Canossa was the Italian castle noted as the scene of the penance of Henry IV, head of the Holy Roman Empire, before Pope Gregory VII in January 1077 to seek a lifting of the excommunication imposed on the emperor for his interference in church affairs. Henry is reported to have stood in the snow for three days outside the castle before Gregory granted him absolution.

debt burden. Bay Street's verdict was a dramatic price drop in the Argus-associated companies, indicating that despite the criticism that the shuffle had attracted, minority investors thought it would have benefited their holdings. Black himself remained philosophical about the withdrawal. "It will appease the lobby of the envious and the destructive, so they'll get off my back for a while," he told a friend. "It's a little like feeding the piranhas before you cross the Amazon."

Five months later, Ed Bovey, the Norcen chairman, who during twenty-three years' service had marched his company from assets of $17 million to $1 billion, decided to retire. Although Bovey was happy with the Argus takeover and agreed to stay on the board, he was concerned about the future of the magnificent art collection he had amassed for the company. The canvases were so valuable that Norcen became one of the few Canadian companies to appoint its own curator, a lively lady named Cecelia Davies. Black assured Bovey that he had nothing to worry about. "After all," he told the departing chairman, "I first heard about Norcen through your bloody paintings."

Dominion Stores Ltd. Ever since it was established in 1919, Dominion Stores had been an unspectacularly successful food merchandiser, its annual reports featuring plump cabbages, lean sides of beef, and ecstatic housewives posing beside tin mountains of canned corn. Under the guidance of unusually able successive chief executive officers – Thomas G. McCormack, Thomas G. Bolton, and Allen C. Jackson – sales grew to nearly $3 billion. Nothing much changed during the first two years of the Blacks' stewardship. Then, in the last days of 1980, the company suddenly sold off its eighty-seven Quebec-based stores for $100 million to Provigo Inc., the Montreal-based food chain run by Pierre Lessard, the province's most interesting young executive. The deal set off yet another mongrelization of the Argus portfolio. This time, in a $260-million reorganization, the staid food company was made a mining conglomerate overnight, becoming the controlling unit for Hollinger Argus, which itself had been a hybrid consolidation of dissimilar Argus assets.* "Dominion Stores could work for a thousand years selling radishes and tomatoes and never get a deal like this!" boasted Black. That was true enough, but the food chain's investors took a different view; word of the

---

*This latest log-rolling exercise called for Hollinger Argus to pay out as a dividend its holding of Argus stock on the basis of 0.2775 Argus common and 0.8352 Class C shares for each Hollinger share, while Dominion Stores made an offer for all Hollinger shares at $14 in cash plus 1¼ Dominion common shares for each Hollinger share. This device was so complicated that the filing prospectus to outline the relevant details took ninety-one pages of small type.

shuffle depressed Dominion to a three-year low. Diane Francis summed up the source of the financial community's jitters in the *Toronto Star*: "It's said that Conrad and Montegu—born to the wealth of their late father, George, a key partner in Argus—are, after all, a rich man's sons playing around with the public companies they control as though they were toy soldiers."

Instead of greeting Black's newest wrinkle as yet another triumph of his fiscal alchemy, most investors felt that he had gone too far in his obsessive quest for financial independence. The net effect of the transaction was to transfer $48 million in cash to Ravelston. "With a mixture of pomposity and paranoia that has become familiar," commented Hugh Anderson, who had moved from the *Globe and Mail* to the Montreal *Gazette*, "young Conrad Black has allowed that not everybody in the business world is wildly enthusiastic about his manoeuvre. Montreal stockbroker Dominik Dlouhy, head of Maison Placements, expresses a common and reasonable view that this kind of major move should be subject to approval from shareholders: 'What we should have is a special meeting to consider it, and the Argus people should not use their voting power to push it through. It's not required legally. But it would be a reassuring gesture.' What about it, Conrad?"

Black dismissed these and other pointed queries with the rejoinder that "these people are demagogues of the marketplace without a stake in anything." He went on to plead guilty to an accusation yet to be made: "The only charge that anyone can level against us is one of insufficient generosity to ourselves, and I suppose we are prepared to be judged [on that basis]."

BY THE CONCLUSION of the Dominion Stores deal, Conrad Black's private wealth had swelled exponentially in one of the most remarkable acts of personal fortune-building in Canadian history.

Money and power on that scale can be assessed only by the size of the offers they attract. In the spring of 1981, on his way home from Palm Beach, Black had some very special passengers on his Argus jet. Paul Reichmann, the co-owner of the $7-billion real estate conglomerate Olympia & York, had gone down to pick up his mother, Renée, and wife, Lea, from their wintering quarters at the Fontainebleau Hotel in Miami Beach. They accepted Black's offer of a ride north to Toronto—making that journey the first one in which any Argus aircraft had served kosher meals. During the trip, Reichmann informally offered Black $200 million for control of his Argus empire.

Black casually declined and continued rolling over his companies, with Ravelston bidding to buy the outstanding Argus stock at $9.27 a share. Typical of Black's corporate manner was the Argus annual meeting on May 26, 1982. Only seven weeks earlier Black had launched a $210-million bid for control of the Hanna Mining Company. Of the thirty or so people in attendance, few were outside shareholders, and not one of them asked the Argus chairman a single question.

The Argus partners have traditionally challenged one another on the speed with which they could handle these yearly love-ins with shareholders, timing themselves and then trying to beat their own records. (Thirteen minutes from the opening to the closing gavel at Canadian Breweries' 1955 annual meeting was E. P. Taylor's Personal Best.)

After his 1982 annual meeting, Black boasted that he had wrapped up all the official Argus business in fourteen minutes—missing Bud McDougald's record by only one minute.

CHAPTER TEN

Hard-Hearted Hanna

*"For years I wondered what the difference
between Canada and the United States really was —
apart from Quebec and the monarchy. Now
I know. This is a very gentle place, and that's
a real hardball league down there."*

—Conrad Black

It was as glittering a gathering as the Union Club in Cleveland had seen in many a season.

There was Nathan Williams Pearson, chief financial adviser to Paul Mellon of the Pittsburgh industrial family. The names of a few U.S. dynasties are more familiar (the Rockefellers, du Ponts, Fords) and others are equally rich (the Lykeses of New Orleans and Tampa and the Pews of Philadelphia), but the Mellons, who are dominant in half a dozen major corporations (Gulf Oil and Aluminum Company of America among them), are in a class by themselves (Paul Mellon's sister, Ailsa Mellon Bruce, left an estate of $570,748,725 in 1969). George Arthur Stinson, former chairman of National Steel Corporation and a senior statesman of the industry, was in attendance, as were Charles Ames (head of Acme-Cleveland Corporation) and William Boeschenstein (chairman of Owens-Corning Fiberglas).

What these men have in common is that they are all directors of the Hanna Mining Company, the world's second-largest iron-ore producer — which until relatively recently was a clubby, family-dominated concern. Four Hanna relatives — George Humphrey II, George Kirkham II, William Moore, and R.L. (Tim) Ireland III — have seats on the board, representing a significant shareholding in the company. They were there, too, except for Kirkham, who was fishing in Alaska. Equally imposing (though not present) were two of Hanna's prominent partners: Peter Grace (of the New York mercantile family enterprise, which collected 1981 revenues of $6.5 billion) and Stephen Bechtel, Jr. (a former Hanna director and head of the San Francisco-based master builders, which had billings of $11.4 billion in 1981 while transforming the world's landscape).*

Talk among this distinguished group—bolstered by half a dozen of Hanna's executives led by Robert F. Anderson, the mining company's crusty chairman—was mainly of a guest who had not yet arrived: Conrad Black. They had just spent four months vainly beating off the attempts of the Canadian entrepreneur and takeover artist to become Hanna's dominant shareholder. The corporate donnybrook had been one of the bloodiest ever carried on across the 49th Parallel, fought with knees to the groin by both sides. The Americans had hired a cadre of forty lawyers to throw the book at Black, accusing him of, among other things, "fraudulent and manipulative conduct" and "a pattern of racketeering." They put him on the stand for four days, down in the Cleveland federal courthouse, trying to break his will and change his story.

Black had clawed back just as savagely and been bloodied in the process. If the Argus chairman had ever entertained any doubts that by reaching for Hanna he was challenging the very core of the American Establishment, they were dispelled by the astonishing spectacle of five of Wall Street's most prestigious investment bankers, including Morgan Stanley, Salomon Brothers, and First Boston Corporation, sidestepping the chance to become financial advisers to Norcen Energy Resources, Black's takeover vehicle.

But that was all blood under the bridge now, as the American business honchos nervously awaited their guest. What riled them most, though no one was impolite enough to say it aloud, was the affront to their belief that an elite must remain impervious to the efforts of anyone who tries to buy his way into it. Yet here was this upstart Canadian (still in his thirties, for God's sake) who had just paid U.S.$130 million to become Hanna's dominant shareholder. In the process, he had bailed the company out of debt. It was too much. This was definitely not an evening these Hanna gentry were anticipating with much pleasure, particularly since the very next day the company would report earnings for the first half of 1982 down to 23 cents a share from $3.50 for the similar period of the previous year.

For Black, the occasion had a hidden irony of its own. It was to Cleveland that his father, George Montegu Black, Jr., had been dis-

*Bechtel's Canadian assignments have included the Interprovincial and Trans Mountain oil pipelines, the Westcoast Transmission and Alberta-California gas lines, the Churchill Falls hydro-electric operation in Labrador, the Syncrude oil-sands plant (and the Alsands project, dropped in May 1982), and Hydro-Québec's giant James Bay power scheme. The only outside director of the Canadian subsidiary is John Turner, the former finance minister.

242

patched in 1948 to superintend the recovery of the leaky U.S. operations of E.P. Taylor's Canadian Breweries. The elder Black had been placed in command of a rundown plant that had once turned out Peerless motor cars and was then supplying the United States with Carling's Red Cap Ale; it had been losing $40,000 a week, largely because of problems involved in the switch to the newly introduced non-returnable bottle. He stabilized the affairs of the brewery there, averting financial disaster, and had often been a guest at the Union Club in his year of commuting between Toronto and Cleveland but was not asked to join. No one had thrown a club reception for *him* at which he was to be the star turn.

Conrad finally arrived, accompanied by his brother, Monte, and Edward Battle, president of Norcen, the Hollinger Argus subsidiary about to take the Hanna investment under its wing. The assembled company shuffled uneasily as introductions were completed and the formal dinner on August 3 got under way. Then Anderson said a few gracious words about Hanna's new era, the tough fight they'd had, and his hopes regarding the visiting Canadians' future contributions.

Black stood up. He began slowly, describing first the flight from Toronto aboard Norcen's Sabreliner, how they had been reading Hanna's financial results on the way down and had asked one another who had suggested they buy into Hanna in the first place—that maybe the best thing would be to order the pilot to turn around and head right back to Toronto. The American directors took this semi-jocular introduction with visible scepticism, shifting uncomfortably in their seats.

Then Black looked straight at Anderson and deadpanned: "Seriously, Bob, I'm delighted to be in Cleveland and say a few words…"

Long pause.

"…*without being under oath."*

The group broke into belly-pumping laughter. He had them hooked. It would be all right.

"I'm a little curious," Black went on, "that my optimism about this great country isn't completely shared. I was somewhat mystified by some of the gloomy talk around the dinner table, until I found out that George Stinson was a Democrat!"

Again, just the right note, received with bourbon-accented guffaws. The Union Club, after all, is a hallowed hall of Midwestern Republicanism, and the company's father figure, Marcus Alonzo Hanna (1837–1904), had been the creator of the GOP's electoral machine. Cleveland itself, Black seemed to sense, is a repository of large wealth whose conservative custodians have been schooled in circumspect ways of hiding their true worth.

MARK HANNA, A CONTEMPORARY and friend of another Cleveland businessman named John D. Rockefeller, had successfully managed the 1896 presidential campaign of William McKinley, a fellow Ohioan. Appointed and then elected a U.S. senator, he became the power behind the throne and directed McKinley's 1900 campaign. After McKinley's assassination by an anarchist at the Buffalo exposition in 1901, Hanna became a backstage influence on the new president, Theodore Roosevelt. The Hannas formed marital and business alliances with many other wealthy U.S. clans, and they brought into the family company George M. Humphrey, a Michigan lawyer who was to become rich and powerful in his own right.

In many ways, Cleveland is really Hanna City — its principal legitimate theatre, two hospitals, a downtown park, and a school (not to mention a barbershop, funeral parlour, and parking lot) all bear the Hanna name. The company itself sprang from two roots — the grocery and commission agency established in 1852 by Dr. Leonard Hanna, Mark's father, and the enterprises launched in the early 1840s by Daniel P. Rhodes, a Vermonter who had gone into the coal and iron ore business in Ohio and who became Mark's father-in-law in 1864. Three years later, after the loss of a Hanna steamer in a Detroit River collision, Mark joined Dan Rhodes in the newly formed Rhodes & Company, which was reorganized in 1885 as M.A. Hanna & Company, a partnership.* This was succeeded in 1922 by the M.A. Hanna Company (without the ampersand), which wound itself up in 1965 in a $648-million distribution to its shareholders. Out of this came the present Hanna Mining Company, whose name is deceptive: it's a good deal more than *mining*. Hanna is involved in mining and shipping iron ore in the United States and Canada, mining and petrochemicals in Brazil, operates the only integrated U.S. nickel producer (with a mine and smelter in Oregon), and has a silicon smelter near Wenatchee, Washington. It owns a dozen bulk carriers in the Great Lakes–St. Lawrence Seaway trade, a subsidiary in Bermuda that manages ten insurance companies, has major coal holdings in Colorado, Pennsylvania, Kentucky, West Virginia, and Vir-

*In a parallel to the founding of the fortunes from the Hollinger Mine in Ontario, Dan Rhodes became involved in the iron ore of the Mesabi by grubstaking prospectors. He shipped them supplies aboard his own vessel, and started to pick up mining claims from customers who couldn't pay. Mark Hanna, who'd joined him in 1867, put four new ships — all painted black — into service in 1874. They became known as the Black Line. Dan Rhodes's son, James Ford Rhodes (1848–1927), dropped out of the business in 1885 and turned to what he'd wanted to do all along. The seven volumes of his monumental *History of the United States from the Compromise of 1850*, covering the twenty-seven years to 1877, appeared between 1893 and 1906. His *History of the Civil War* earned him a Pulitzer Prize in 1918.

ginia, a U.S. oil and gas exploration company, and minority interests in oil and gas producers in Canada and the North Sea.

After a split among the Hanna heirs in 1915, Mark's branch ended up with such properties as the *Cleveland News* and Hanna Building Corporation, which held valuable Cleveland real estate. The family links to Hanna Mining are through the descendants of Mark's brothers, Howard Melville and Leonard Colton.*

What Conrad Black didn't say that evening at the Union Club – and what didn't really *need* saying – was that his arrival on the scene marked the end of the historical dominance of the Hanna and Humphrey descendants in Cleveland's corporate pecking order. "They just didn't understand that it wasn't a game any more," Black later told a friend. "They just didn't understand that all those years of theorizing about what to do with dad's and granddad's company and all those sorts of business-school scenarios were at an end. They were now dealing with real people whose pens were hovering over their chequebooks and who had takeover bids in their briefcases. I'm not referring to myself, because I don't have a briefcase. But Battle does."

Black's approach to the Hanna takeover was based, as are all his

---

*A chart of the Hanna and Humphrey descendants would fill pages, but the links of some Hanna Mining directors include: **R.L. Ireland III**, who's known as Tim, a brother-in-law of the late Gilbert Watts (Bud) Humphrey and a grandson of the Robert Livingston Ireland (1867–1928) who married Kate Hanna, niece of M.A. and third daughter of H.M. Tim Ireland is a partner in Brown Brothers Harriman & Co., private bankers, and his sister Kate is one of the bank's half-dozen limited partners, along with Averell Harriman. BBH has been described as the oldest (established 1818) and largest private bank in North America, and the only large U.S. commercial bank owned and operated by a partnership rather than a corporation. The partners still work at rolltop desks in the panelled Partners' Room at the Wall Street counting house. Tim's sister Louise is the widow of one Hanna chairman (Bud Humphrey), the daughter-in-law of another (George M. Humphrey), and the mother of a Hanna vice-president and director (**George M. Humphrey II**). Bud's sister Pamela was the widow of H.M. (Bud) Hanna III (a grandnephew of M.A.) when she married **Royal Firman II** (they were divorced in 1970). H.M. III's sister Kate married Warren Bicknell, Jr. (a former Hanna director), and their daughter Kate married **George D. Kirkham II**, a Cleveland stockbroker. (Kirkham is a senior partner in the firm of Prescott, Ball & Turben, whose chairman is John Butler, who married Bud Humphrey's other sister, Carol.) A fellow member of the Hanna board is **William Henry Moore**, retired chairman of Bankers Trust Company in New York; Moore is a trustee of the Vincent Astor Foundation and a director of blue-chip corporations like IBM, American Can, and Nabisco Brands. His mother was Fanny, whose brother, Leonard C. Hanna, Jr., had the good fortune to buy into IBM in the 1920s when the stock was trading at $2. A man of artistic inclinations who favoured New York over Cleveland as a place to live, Leonard gave away an estimated $93 million before his death in 1957 and left an estate of $30 million. He still had 29,550 shares of IBM, then trading at $295 a share. A bachelor, he was the last member of the Hanna board to bear the Hanna surname.

corporate manoeuvres, on military history. Instead of dipping into the Napoleonic canon, this time he resurrected Israel's strategy during the Yom Kippur War in 1973: "At the outset, Israel assumed there was no problem; even though they had intelligence reports of Egyptian preparations, the Israelis just didn't believe them. They got themselves into a desperate condition but eventually made a great comeback—encircling the Egyptian Third Army, negotiating about providing water for its soldiers squatting there in the desert. The comparison with Hanna was that once we got our expedited appeal, the opposition had to settle. I would be surprised if they didn't put a somewhat Sadatesque coloration on it."

On a less grandiose level, Black admits he was playing Russian roulette with all the chambers loaded. "For years I wondered what the difference between Canada and the United States really was—apart from the French Canadians and the monarchy," he confessed to a Canadian friend. "Now I know. This is a very gentle place, and that's a real hardball league down there."

ROBERT ANDERSON, THE HANNA CHAIRMAN, who became Black's chief opponent, is the first non-family head of the company. A gruff, no-nonsense mining engineer who started with Hanna as a pit foreman in the Mesabi Range of Minnesota, Anderson is a supremely able administrator who locks the executive-suite door if his managers are more than a minute late. He is a hard-rock Lutheran who also believes in balanced budgets, *domestic* steel manufacturing, and boasts that he liked jelly beans *before* Ronald Reagan made them a mandatory snack for loyal Republicans. He enjoys fishing for salmon in Labrador and hunts blue-winged teal in the Lake Erie marshes. But his idea of a really good time is watching, from his thirty-sixth-floor eyrie, lake freighters eeling their way up the crooked Cuyahoga River to unload ore for the steel mills of Ohio and Pennsylvania. Hanna is his life, and he fought like a tiger to keep the company out of alien hands.

Anderson had been attracted to Hanna by George Humphrey, then its president, who later served as Secretary of the Treasury in the Eisenhower administration. It was George's son, Gilbert Watts (Bud) Humphrey, who first introduced Hanna Mining to Black's horizon. The two men met in the spring of 1978 when Conrad joined the board of Massey-Ferguson, on which Humphrey was the only American apart from Al Thornbrough, the deputy chairman. In January 1979 Humphrey invited Black to Cleveland for dinner at the Union Club. The then newly minted Argus chairman told the American executive that he

246

regarded Hanna as his natural American ally, and that he hoped "to get a little something going in the U.S. of A." To which Humphrey replied, "When you're ready, come and talk to me." Black was touring a Dominion Stores warehouse in June 1979 when he telephoned Humphrey to explain one of his upcoming Argus stock shuffles that would affect the Iron Ore Company of Canada, in which they were partners. The Hanna head used the occasion to complain about the state of the American steel industry. "I remember my father telling me," Humphrey told Black, "that what this industry needs is a couple of high-priced funerals." Two days later, Bud Humphrey died suddenly on the golf course, and Bob Anderson took over.

After a 1980 Iron Ore Company meeting in Cleveland, Black dropped in to see Bud's elder son, George Humphrey II, at his Hanna office. The young heir, according to Black, "spoke in terms of great bitterness and vituperativeness about the treatment that he and his family had received, since his father had died, at the hands of Hanna management." Black suggested that they might make common cause in keeping the notion of family proprietorship alive in Hanna. They agreed to meet for dinner at Humphrey's house in Gates Mills on August 12, when a similar discussion ensued. The subject was to be continued in talks with various members of the Humphrey family over the next year and a half.

Probably the most interesting encounter was with Louise Humphrey, George's mother—another widow of a man named Bud. They met at New York's Lincoln Center in April 1981, when she arranged for Black to sit next to her at a white-tie dinner at the Metropolitan Opera, of which she is a benefactor-patron. "We had a rather extended conversation, which she quite swiftly turned to matters of business," Black recalls. "She was extremely critical of the way Hanna was being run. She asked me to keep in touch with her son George, and I floated very gingerly before her the idea of whether, if we bought some shares, that would be regarded as a friendly or unfriendly thing by her family...and she said they would be delighted if we bought some shares." Mrs. Humphrey also confided her concern about the careers of her sons, George and Watts, the latter a vice-president of National Steel Corporation, in which Hanna holds a major interest.

Four months later, Black called George at his summer place in Maine to say that his interest in Hanna was keener than ever, but George told him his situation had changed and that he was committed to management. Two days later, on August 17, after he had spoken to Tim Ireland, George phoned Black to say that if the Argus chairman wanted to buy into Hanna he should deal with management.

Black's next conversation with Mrs. Humphrey came about with the assistance of her Toronto-based daughter, Margaret, whose first husband was Moffat Dunlap, the Hollinger heir. When Black asked Margaret at a philanthropic function whether she thought her mother would mind his calling to inquire what the Humphrey family's collective attitude might be toward his heightened interest in Hanna, she agreed to find out. In November Black reached Mrs. Humphrey at a property she owns at Miccosukee, Georgia, on the Florida border, and she arranged for him to meet her younger son, Watts.

As a result of what he still interpreted as the Humphreys' encouraging noises, Black nosed Norcen into a starting Hanna position with purchases totalling about 55,000 shares (for U.S. $2 million) in the Cleveland company in August 1981. At the end of the month, Ed Battle established a secret $20-million credit line with the Canadian Imperial Bank of Commerce to cover the acquisition of 4.9 per cent of Hanna's shares. (The transaction was so confidential that it was identified only by an account number, and Battle instructed the bank not to deliver any notices of the agreement to the company's offices.) On September 9, the Norcen executive committee met to approve the plan, which temporarily limited purchases to the 4.9 threshold – a significant step because under U.S. stock regulations a holding of more than 5 per cent in a publicly traded company must be revealed and the ultimate reason for the investment stated.

The minutes of that meeting – attended by the Black brothers, Battle, Edward Galvin, Edmund Bovey, Dixon Chant, and William T. Kilbourne (Norcen's corporate secretary and administrative vice-president) – became the central document in Hanna's legal assault on Conrad's eventual takeover bid. The actual minute of the meeting referring to the original purchase reads: "Mr. Battle stated that the company, subsequent to telephone contact with the members of the executive committee, had initiated through stock market transactions the acquisition of a 4.9-per-cent stock interest in a U.S. company listed on the New York Stock Exchange with the ultimate purpose of acquiring a 51-per-cent interest at a later date." Under questioning during the court case that followed, Battle and a Hanna lawyer confirmed the purpose of the purchase in the following exchange:

Q. Well, the point is, you had already determined that you were embarking on a program to eventually acquire a 51-per-cent position in Hanna at a later date, had you not?

A. Yes.

Q. And that is what you explained to the executive committee on September 9th of 1981; is that correct?

A. That is correct.

Q. At the meeting of September 9, 1981, and I am speaking of the meeting of the executive committee, you did explain to members of the executive committee present that the 4.9-per-cent stock interest was made with the ultimate purpose of acquiring a 51-per-cent position at a later date, did you not?

A. I did.

In his own testimony, Kilbourne, a Yale-educated economist-lawyer and former U.S. Navy flier, stated that at least three directors opposed the move to pass the 4.9 threshold: Galvin, because he didn't know enough about Hanna's prospects; Chant, because he neither wanted to upset Hanna's existing management nor to expand investment in the mining industry; and Montegu Black, because he didn't want to go up to 51 per cent. The Hanna thrust was approved without a vote, and under subsequent questioning Conrad admitted that, given the proper timing and circumstances, Norcen's long-term objective of acquiring control of Hanna was confirmed at that meeting. In private, he would claim that the Norcen minute really was ambiguous and that the Hanna lawyers had "hideously and grotesquely misinterpreted" its meaning. On a more philosophical plane, instead of musing on Napoleon as he usually does, he retreated to repeating an observation Charles de Gaulle made when he left for England after the fall of France in 1940. "Once that minute surfaced," Conrad confided, "my immediate reaction was that quote from de Gaulle: 'It has begun as badly as it could, and therefore it must continue.'"

Internally, Norcen preserved the secrecy of the stock play that followed by giving both companies code names; Norcen referred to itself as "Prince" and to Hanna as "Maiden" – reluctant though she proved to be.

On October 28, James Connacher, the reclusive head of Gordon Securities, which specializes in block trades, called Black to report that about 575,000 Hanna shares were available at U.S. $37 each. (By this time Norcen had a 2.5-per-cent holding, and this block purchase would boost the percentage to 8.8.) Given the go-ahead, Connacher made the buy. Black tried to notify Anderson in Cleveland, but he was away checking his company's ventures in Brazil. Carl Nickels, one of Hanna's two executive vice-presidents, who had already been informed that a large buy order was going through the market, was on the phone to Brian Mulroney, president of the Iron Ore Company, asking who the buyer might be. "It's either Brascan or the Black interests – and you should hope it's the Blacks," was the reply. When a secretary handed Nickels a note that Black was on the other line, the Hanna executive drew the obvious conclusion. Switching calls, he demanded, "What the hell are you doing, Conrad?" Black turned uncharacteristically obse-quious, explaining that he was "an absolutely friendly buyer with no sinister motives" and that if Hanna's board became publicly upset with his purchase he would back away. Finding himself not particularly impressed by the explanation, Nickels immediately requested Goldman Sachs, Hanna's New York investment advisers, to run a profile on Black. That evening, Conrad called Mulroney (a friend from his Quebec days), requesting that he assure his confrères on the Hanna board that Black "didn't have cloven feet and wear horns." Mulroney undertook that delicate task but warned Black that in Hanna circles he was perceived as "a paper purchaser, not a builder or job creator."

The next morning, George Humphrey (whose bitter complaints about Hanna management a year earlier had originally aroused Black's interest) contacted the Argus chairman from an airport phone booth. He told Conrad that he intended to inform Anderson of their previous conversations and that he welcomed the Norcen purchase "as long as we're not blindsided, and I'm sure we won't be." The football term (signifying the downfall of a quarterback who, with arm poised to throw the ball to a pass receiver, presents a blind side to his opponents) left Conrad, whose interest in sports is defiantly minimal, totally baffled.

His puzzlement dissolved a few days later, as the result of a Hanna management meeting called by Anderson, who had returned to Cleve-land from Brazil. At a Saturday emergency session the Hanna inside directors were warned by three senior representatives of Goldman Sachs that "most of the transactions in which Black had been involved appeared to be principally designed and structured for his personal enrichment, as opposed to the primary benefit of the shareholders, minority or otherwise." The meeting lasted four hours and, flying home that evening, Mulroney felt a deep sense of foreboding about the struggle that was to come. At a formal board meeting on November 3, Hanna's directors heard out a more detailed Goldman Sachs condem-nation and unanimously decided that Black was a plague inside their house—and that they wanted him out, even as a minority investor, as soon as possible. The following afternoon, Black and Battle jetted to Cleveland to meet Anderson and Nickels at the Sheraton-Hopkins Hotel. It was a rocky confrontation, with the Hanna and Argus head men trying to face each other down. The gloves were off. Anderson virtually ordered Black to "peel off" his stock. Black refused.

One exchange during that bitter meeting deserves to be preserved in the aspic of some future collection of great moments in Canadian capitalism. When Nickels, who has the eagle look of a Marine Corps colonel permanently on manoeuvres, queried the Argus chairman on his corporate performance, Black flashed his tabby-cat smile and, pointing to his pocket, mused, "Two hundred million dollars isn't bad."

THE DOCUMENT NORCEN FILED with the U.S. Securities and Exchange Commission on November 9, 1981, claimed that the purpose of its share purchase was "to acquire an investment position in Hanna." This statement was drafted at least four times, following Black's instructions to make the filing "as short and antiseptic as possible." The SEC declaration had the effect of depressing Hanna's stock on the New York Exchange by U.S.$8 over the next five months, down to $26 at the end of March 1982. Having been officially informed that Black was content to treat Hanna as a passive holding, investors assumed there would be no takeover bid to drive share prices upward. (It was the contention of Hanna lawyers in the subsequent court case that the SEC filing constituted deliberate misrepresentation: "…the market was maintained at an artificially low level…thus enabling Norcen to announce a tender offer at a price which appeared to be a substantial premium over market." Black offered U.S.$45 a share for Hanna's stock, which was assigned an appraised value of U.S.$74 a share in Norcen's internal documents.)

On December 21 Black journeyed to Sewickley, an exurb of Pittsburgh, to see Watts, who described his brother George as "obviously a candidate to be the head of Hanna." Black's Christmastide suggestion for some sort of shareholders' trust involving the Hanna-Humphrey families and the Mellon interests was brought forward as a New Year's plan for a Norcen tender offer for Hanna shares, with the Humphreys taking part through a share purchase agreement. The Humphreys were code-named "the Z family" when Norcen put the finishing touches on its draft of the tender offer in January.

Ed Battle was "ready to go" when he joined Monte for presentation of the Norcen plan to Watts Humphrey at a meeting on Friday, February 5. After warning his brother that "the Blacks were planning to take control of Hanna Mining Company in some way," Watts phoned Monte Black on Monday morning to say no. By this time Conrad, who had been mesmerized by the tantalizing possibility of a grand alliance with the American Establishment (as represented by the Hanna board of directors), was fully committed to his move.

At a Toronto meeting with Anderson on February 16, 1982, Black expressed a desire to buy 20 per cent of Hanna, so that he could equity-account the investment in his Norcen balance sheets. The Clevelander hung tough but suggested there might be room for negotiating a swap of Black's holdings for Hanna's investment in Labrador Mining & Exploration.*

By the first week of March, Black had negotiated a $400-million credit line with the Commerce for the Hanna bid. After the failure of a peace mission to Palm Beach, where Anderson presented Black with a formal swap offer for Labrador, the Hanna board dug in for the expected assault. Word of Black's bid was beginning to seep out. Bill Mulholland, chairman of the Bank of Montreal, mentioned to Mulroney on the telephone, "I hear our friend Conrad is making goo-goo eyes at Hanna."

On Friday, April 2, back at the Sheraton-Hopkins in Cleveland, Monte Black and Ed Battle delivered a salvo at Anderson and Nickels. "I am here today to tell you," declared Battle, "that on Monday morning the board of directors of Norcen has authorized me to go for a tender offer for 51 per cent of the Hanna Mining stock." The only way to head off the threat, Battle warned, was for Hanna to agree that Norcen could hold 30 per cent of its stock – and that as part of such an arrangement the Canadian company would be allocated five seats on an enlarged, eighteen-member Hanna board, with the vote of 80 per cent of the directors required for all major decisions. In other words, Norcen would hold veto power over Hanna. Battle ended his harangue with a terse ultimatum: Norcen's private jet was due to leave for Toronto from Cleveland's Hopkins airport at 7:15 that evening. Unless Anderson accepted his terms by then, the takeover bid would be launched on Monday.

Anderson, who felt that a gun had been put to his head, won a brief reprieve when Monte Black and Battle agreed to return to Cleveland on Sunday to resume discussions. On Saturday, Anderson phoned Conrad Black in Palm Beach and urged the Argus chairman to fly to Cleveland to hammer out a settlement in a face-to-face session. Conrad declined, even though Anderson offered to send a Hanna plane to pick him up.

At the Sunday meeting in Cleveland, Anderson offered a counter-proposal: a 20-per-cent holding in Hanna with Norcen buying 11.2 per cent in newly issued Hanna shares to add to its 8.8-per-cent stake;

*This is the company that owns the Newfoundland portion of the properties being mined by Iron Ore Company of Canada. Some 67 per cent of its shares were held by Hollinger Argus, and 20 per cent by Hanna. P.C. Finlay, Labrador Mining's chairman, is its dominating influence. Brian Mulroney remembers attending his first Labrador board meeting when Finlay produced a document for the directors to read. "Now," he said, "I want you to look this over very carefully. It's our annual report." Bud Humphrey, then Hanna's chairman, demanded, "When is it going to press?" To which P.C. unabashedly replied, "It went yesterday."

agreement that the Norcen holding would stay at 20 per cent for ten years; and the purchase by Norcen of Hanna's Labrador shares. Battle threw the proposal back at Anderson, dismissing it with the comment, "I'm not even going to bother with these agreements because they are completely unacceptable. They are not what we want."

Monte Black chimed in, "You have moved so far from our position that there is nothing here to negotiate."

Before the markets opened on the morning of April 5, Norcen, taking aim at a 51-per-cent control position in Hanna, fired its U.S.$171-million tender offer for 3.8 million shares at $45. (Hanna's stock, which had been selling in the $26-$27 range, jumped to $31.875 on the last day of trading before the Norcen takeover announcement.)

Anderson came storming into the public ring, denouncing the Canadian snowbirds as corporate vultures. Conrad Black and his associates "have demonstrated repeatedly and convincingly over recent years that their first interest is in serving themselves and not the remaining public stockholders," he roared. "They do not appear to have the financial strength or the management expertise to make an important contribution to this company." More to the point, Anderson's lawyers had been working through the night preparing to file suit in Cleveland's U.S. District Court for a restraining order against Norcen preventing the Canadian company from transmitting its offer to Hanna shareholders. It was quickly granted and the scene was set for the Norcen/Hanna legal confrontation. The court hearing on Hanna's application for a preliminary injunction, unusual to Canadians in the bitterness of the invective it produced and the juicy details revealed in its testimony, served as the jousting ground for the legal talent assembled by Norcen and the Hanna team headed by Dick Pogue.

For the Wall Street and Cleveland lawyers who acted for the Norcen side it was just another case. For Pogue, it was very much more than that.

Jones, Day, Reavis & Pogue, where Richard W. Pogue is a senior partner, is not just another legal factory. It is the fifth-largest law firm in the United States, with more than 300 lawyers, and its partners charge $260 an hour; Pogue's own roster of clients includes General Motors, Westinghouse, B.F. Goodrich, and Dow Corning. A veteran of the takeover wars (Mobil/Marathon/U.S. Steel), Pogue is a self-possessed Midwesterner who peers at petitioners over half-moon glasses, advances opinions in a friendly drawl, and is about as casual as a coiled cobra. Cleveland is a way of life to him. He can recount in detail how his city grew, how the iron ore, coming down the lakes from Minnesota, and the coal, being hauled up from West Virginia and Kentucky, were joined here to create one of the industrialized world's great steel manufacturing centres. For him, the intrusion of Conrad Black represented not just an unwanted outsider at the gates, but an *Easterner*, a product of the Wall Street mentality that relies on legalese instead of facts. Two other lawyers (Patrick McCartan and John Strauch) carried out the cross-examination for Hanna, but it was Pogue who formulated the strategy for the counterattack against Black's takeover bid.

The Hanna lawyers bore in relentlessly at the April hearing on the Canadian company's executive committee minutes of September 9, 1981, which showed intent to win 51 per cent of Hanna, an intent kept secret while Norcen publicly stated that its 8.8-per-cent holding in the Cleveland company was an investment position only, and made plans for its takeover tender offer of April 5, 1982. They accused Norcen officers, including Black, of fraud and racketeering, charging that the original SEC filing and press release early in November 1981 were "wilfully, intentionally, and materially false in concealing and misrepresenting Norcen's true purpose and intentions." When the minutes of Norcen's September 9 meeting were discovered, Pat McCartan pounced on them. "Bob," McCartan advised the Hanna chief, "we've just found the show-stopper."

Summarizing their case, the Hanna lawyer claimed that the Black/Battle testimony provided "a chilling insight into Norcen's plans for Hanna if and when it gets control (i.e. extraordinary dividends, asset liquidation, and the like)." George Humphrey, whose meetings with Conrad in 1980 had been the takeoff point for the Blacks' move into Hanna, testified: "I would do anything in my power to keep Conrad Black or any of his associates from owning even so much as one share of this company."

"They set out to have us absolutely hammered by the judge in a manner so extreme that no appeal court could quarrel with his findings," Black later observed. "But at the end of my testimony, the judge had me irto his chambers and said that in his twenty years on the bench, I was tne finest witness he'd ever had, and that whatever his verdict, it would not reflect adversely on my efforts."

The judge, a Greek-American named John M. Manos, is a Republican who trained as a metallurgical engineer and who relaxes by reading Sophocles and Euripides. As he had ruled in the case of Mobil Corporation's controversial bid for Marathon Oil Company in 1981, Manos, in the Norcen-Hanna case, granted a preliminary injunction against the defendant takeover artists on June 11, 1982. Finding the Canadian company's construction of the record "strained and unpersuasive," Manos said the evidence supported Hanna's contention that Norcen's repeated misrepresentations of its intention to acquire control of Hanna and the purchase of 575,000 shares of Hanna stock on October 28, 1981, were "manipulative violations" of the U.S. Securities and Exchange Act.

Undeterred, Black immediately launched an appeal. Even though the ruling had gone against him, Black continued to condemn Hanna's "absolutely unabashed character assassination" and praised the judge for rising above it, pointing out that Manos had made no adverse comments on his credibility. "At no point," Black boasted, "does he suggest for an instant that there's anything basically wrong with us, that we are unworthy of conducting commerce in the U.S. That was, for me, by far the most important aspect of this case." With characteristic understatement, the Argus chairman then laid out his prospects. "I have not gone this far to stop now," said he. "They are not invulnerable. Half the Humphrey family still wants to sell its stock and Hanna is not going to be able to make enough money this year to pay the chairman's salary!" In the end, Black signed a "consent decree" with the SEC that admitted no wrongdoing while undertaking to refrain from any future violations of U.S. securities regulations, and a federal court in Cincinnati granted him an expedited appeal of the Manos judgement.

A separate investigation was being carried on by an officer in the Toronto police department's fraud squad who had seized legal documents relating to the Hanna offer. According to the police search warrant, the information sought was "evidence in respect to the commission, suspected commission or intended commission of an offence against the Criminal Code, to wit, forgery, contrary to section 324(1) and uttering contrary to section 326(1) of the Criminal Code of Canada in that during the months of October, November, and December, 1981, Norcen Energy Resources Ltd. published and circulated an issuer bid report which was false in that it failed to disclose a material change proposed by its acquisiton of the Hanna Mining Co."* At the same time, the Ontario Securities Commission was maintaining a watching brief on the proceedings in the United States.

Black stoutly continued to fend off all his accusers and their charges.

---

*Section 324(1) of the Criminal Code reads: "Every one commits forgery who makes a false document, knowing it to be false, with intent (a) that it should in any way be used or acted upon as genuine, to the prejudice of any one whether within Canada or not, or (b) that some person should be induced, by the belief that it is genuine, to do or to refrain from doing anything, whether within Canada or not." Section 326(1) reads: "Every one who knowing that a document is forged, (a) uses, deals with, or acts upon it, or (b) causes or attempts to cause any person to use, deal with, or act upon it, as if the document were genuine, is guilty of an indictable offence and is liable to imprisonment for fourteen years."

Although Norcen's request for an expedited appeal from the Manos judgement had been granted, the U.S. Court of Appeals in Cincinnati had yet to hear it. Brian Mulroney, who accurately described his own position as being "the jam in the sandwich," now began to play an active role as peacemaker and eventually brought Black and Anderson together for a secret exploratory session at the Bristol Place Hotel, near Toronto airport. At a later meeting (on June 29 in the Hanna apartment in New York's Carlton House), the two chairmen agreed on a ceasefire, approved by their lawyers a few days later.

Resolution of the impasse was swift, as a merciful fog of amnesia engulfed the former combatants. The day after the settlement, Bob Anderson sent a huge bouquet of lilies to Conrad Black's wife, Shirley. On a conference call among the two company chairmen and Dick Pogue, Hanna's legal eagle, Black was kidding around a bit, deferring to Anderson, at one point pledging his freshly coined allegiance with the comment: "You're my chairman now, Bob..." Pogue cut in to exult: "...and I'm your lawyer!" Conrad turned a bit icy in his reply. "Well," he conceded, "you're one of them, Dick."

At the end of the day—and especially after his performance that night at the Union Club—Black had climbed the first and hardest rung on his way into full-fledged membership in the American business Establishment. "It's an Establishment board," he said of his Hanna investment, "and that was all part of the rationale for our move—our entrée into the U.S. and our association with the Mellons, the Bechtels and the Graces."

The actual settlement ran along lines similar to the Hanna compromise offer Ed Battle had thrown back at Anderson while issuing his ultimatum in Cleveland on April 2. It called for Norcen to purchase 1.25 million Hanna treasury shares (at U.S.$45 each), raising its holding to 20 per cent for an eight-year standstill period, with the two Black brothers and Battle becoming Hanna directors. Conrad would join the executive committee. As part of its $90-million deal Norcen purchased Hanna's 20-per-cent interest in Labrador Mining & Exploration and its 40-per-cent stake in Hollinger North Shore Exploration—thus doubling its share in the royalty-producing Iron Ore Company. The truce was a standoff, yet it proved to be one of those rare deals that benefited both sides. The injection of U.S.$90 million into its treasury enabled Hanna to wipe out virtually all its long-term debt. For Black, it meant that he could equity-account his Hanna investment, tax-shelter his Iron Ore earnings and, best of all, complete the Argus shuffle he had started four years earlier.

By the late summer of 1982 precise details of the Argus reorganization had yet to emerge, but the possibilities included a follow-up offer for the

13 per cent of Labrador stock held by minority public shareholders (required under Ontario's securities legislation), an offer for the 7 per cent of Hollinger Argus still on the market, sale of the assets of Dominion Stores, and completion of the move to privatize Argus itself. (At the end of July, Ravelston closed a bid to bring in the outstanding Argus common shares, raising the Ravelston holding to 97 per cent in that class.) Ravelston's increased holding in Argus gave it 52 per cent of Dominion Stores, which in turn held 93 per cent of the Hollinger Argus package, which included the Black group's investment in Norcen, Hanna, Labrador Mining, and the Iron Ore Company. "...Argus itself," wrote Richard Spence, associate editor of the *Financial Times of Canada*, about the impending changes, "is being shunted aside in one of the last shuffles of reorganization. A few more changes will be needed but effectively the old Argus is dead, an anachronism belonging to other men in another time."

At the conclusion of the Hanna incursion, resting on his laurels for a bit, Black allowed that, having spent the past four years designing a position for himself that he would enjoy and for which he felt an aptitude, he had been inordinately successful in his quest. "This," he said, sweeping his hands to indicate the tendrils of power flowing out of his office at 10 Toronto Street, "in fairness, is not a bad job."

Despite his smug mood, the battle for hard-hearted Hanna had come close to denting Black's reputation within the hallowed circles of the Canadian Establishment. "I saw the first glimmerings of the Massey-Ferguson thing again," he told a friend on the day before the news of the settlement became public. "The jackals and piranhas smelled blood. They thought they had me, that I was about to go up the chimney in a puff of smoke. I'm speaking here not in any spirit of paranoia but in recognition of the mentality of our fellow citizens – the ghoulish fascination with presenting an agonizing replay of the supposed possibility that I had committed crimes and might be charged with them – that sort of thing.

"I never had any fears how it was going to end up," he contended. "It's all atmospherics in the United States. They never believed a goddamn word of all that bunk about racketeering. But some of our more credulous and Boy-Scoutish locals sure believed it."

Having won his spurs within the American Establishment, Conrad Black closed that particular phase of his corporate evolution with a shrug and a wink. "It takes a while to debrief Canadians on how these things are done down there."

CHAPTER ELEVEN

Keeping Up with Conrad

*Taking pains to deliver a subliminal message that only
one in a thousand visitors to his house would even
vaguely appreciate defines Black's style.*

Conrad Black's ascendancy within the Canadian Establishment
can be explained partly because he is so acutely aware of what is
happening in the country and world at large. He avidly studies
the forces that bestow and rob institutions of their authority. This is in
marked contrast to the practices of most surviving members of Canada's
Establishment, many of whom are out of touch with prevailing realities.
They sponsor seminars and attend testimonial dinners to applaud one
another's assurances. The merchant princes of the Renaissance thought
the ornamental carvings on castle cannons would help them escape the
ravages of war. Similarly, a number of Canadian business leaders
continue to imagine that their chief contribution to life (apart from
making themselves rich and comfortable) remains the preservation of
civility in human affairs. They pretend to themselves that they are
carrying the colonizers' burden, trying to tame the savages – whether
these challengers to their authority are fiery separatists from Quebec,
pushy deputy ministers from Ottawa, or steely-eyed Yanks busy nabbing
the country's most valuable resources. Because they believe so implicitly
in themselves and their mission, members of the Establishment's round
table are seldom able to distinguish between the public interest and their
own. In the process, power is draining out of them like blood through
dead men's shoes.

Having examined and documented the manipulative techniques of
the late Maurice Duplessis, Black understands power and how it can
best be protected. He is an expert on French-Canadian nationalism –
and has, incidentally, sold off the Quebec-based assets of Sterling,
Dominion Stores, and Norcen. At the same time, he is close to the
powers that be in Washington, where he is on intimate terms with *two*
former directors of the Central Intelligence Agency and with Thomas
O. Enders, former ambassador to Canada and currently Assistant

Secretary of State for Inter-American Affairs. He knew the late David Bruce, ambassador *extraordinaire*. He is friendly with Henry Kissinger, Malcolm Muggeridge, Andrew Knight (editor of the *Economist*), Marietta Tree (who's been called the salonkeeper to the liberal wing of the Democrats), and Leopold Rothschild, and claims Sir Siegmund Warburg as his most influential financial mentor. At home, such Ottawa luminaries as Michael Pitfield, Clerk of the Privy Council, and Energy Minister Marc Lalonde are in regular contact with him, even at his winter retreat in Palm Beach.

This concern for keeping in constant touch with the flux of change in the real world differentiates Black from his Argus predecessors, who believed that what happened outside the sooty walls of the Toronto Club was bound to be of only marginal significance. At the club itself, the lunching spot once permanently reserved for the late Bud McDougald (whether or not he was in town) has now become known as "the chairman's table," being occupied by whoever happens to be senior member on the premises that day. With most of the younger action-guys having moved on to the better kitchen and more sophisticated ambiance of Winston's, going to the Toronto Club has become a bit like having lunch at Madame Tussaud's. Most of its tables are occupied by decathlon bores, equally dull whether they are expatiating on politics, economics, religion, or sex. Black, who has belonged to the club for seventeen years, lunches as frequently at Winston's but is increasingly using his private dining room at the Argus offices on Toronto Street.

Perhaps it is partly because McDougald was so devoted an Anglophile that Black has become concerned with monarchy* and with such aristocratic irrelevancies as having his friend the Duke of Norfolk officially approve a special family coat of arms. It consists of an eagle and a lion holding a big blue book over a shield that features two fleurs-de-lis, two sheaves of wheat, and a plumb-line crossed with an anchor. (The nautical heraldry salutes Conrad's first ancestor to set foot in Canada, Malachi Salter, a Boston-born seaman who settled in Halifax about 1749 and became a leading Nova Scotia entrepreneur.) His motto is a Latin rendering of the title and first line of a poem by

---

*The former Argus panjandrums maintained strong links with royalty. During McDougald's reign at Argus, whenever the Queen, Prince Philip, or any member of the royal family visited Toronto, he or she would inevitably be put up at Bud's. In late 1974, when Princess Anne and her husband, Capt. Mark Phillips, officiated at the opening of the Royal Agricultural Winter Fair, they stayed at the McDougalds' place, attended an afternoon reception at E.P. Taylor's horse-breeding farm near Oshawa, and dined with Doris Phillips (no relation), widow of another Argus partner. In the same tradition, Black has been sounded out by the office of Ontario's Lieutenant-Governor to play host for future royal visits to the Toronto area.

Arthur Hugh Clough–"Say Not the Struggle Nought Availeth"–a favourite quotation of Conrad's father's, most memorably used by Winston Churchill in a message of congratulation to Franklin Delano Roosevelt on his 1940 re-election. (Bud McDougald's motto was much more to the point: *Vincere vel Mori*–"Conquer or Die.") During his visits to London, Black stays at Claridge's Hotel, one floor above the permanent suite the great Bud occupied there. (Black maintains his own vintage Rolls-Royce in London.)

Another link with his predecessor is Black's penchant for collecting automobiles. He has yet to reach McDougald's conspicuous record of maintaining the country's only thirty-car garage to house his vintage models, but he does boast an even dozen–four Cadillacs, three Rolls-Royces, two Mercedes, two Lincoln Continentals, and a Packard in a pear tree. Each has mounted on its hood a six-carat gold-plated eagle killing a snake. This is an unofficial Argus crest McDougald thought up to symbolize Paul Desmarais's ill-fated attempt to take over his empire. Conrad adopted the imagery, substituting his principal adversary, Max Meighen, for Desmarais. He may well be the only driver heading down Toronto's Don Valley most mornings who, instead of playing music on his sound system, is listening to tapes of speeches by General of the Army Douglas MacArthur. He talks glowingly of his military hero as "perhaps the last really great conservative spokesman in the Anglo-Saxon world."

With his brother, Monte, Black purchased most of the fleet of wooden boats belonging to the late Nelson Davis, including the fifty-five-foot *Ravelston*, which he describes as being "as graceful as the old *Mauretania* coming down Southampton Water." His most valuable corporate possession, however, is his new executive jet. The $15-million transoceanic Canadair Challenger, one of four aircraft owned by Sugra Ltd. ("Argus" spelled backward), has been decorated to resemble a flying version of the company's Toronto Street headquarters. It is the only corporate aircraft in captivity with a cabin that has a mahogany floor, leather armchairs, oak panelling, and Group of Seven paintings with softly glowing picture lights above them.

Black extends the notion that elegance is a prerequisite to life even to the way he dresses. In his biography of Duplessis, Black characterized the former Quebec premier as having "a terribly Flaubertian view of the world...believing...that a gentleman could allow himself almost no informality..." and described with relish the politician's precise manner of dress ("his elegant suits and fine cuffs, his detestation of rumpled clothes"). Black might have been depicting himself. There is nothing democratically dishevelled about him. In his pinstriped uniform he is almost a parody of a British merchant banker done up correctly by Benson's of Savile Row; he stops just short of having a gold pocket-watch with fob attached. (In fact, Black buys all his suits at a substantial director's discount in the Pine Room of Eaton's downtown Toronto store. Ilie Dumitru, the resident tailor, drops into the Argus offices for fittings.)

Again like Duplessis who "after his years at the Seminary...took no participatory interest in any sport except croquet," Conrad takes to the game that has been described as combining "elements of chess, billiards, golf, and war." Ideally played on summer evenings by the glow of Chinese lanterns, croquet appeals to Black because of "the sort of Oscar Wilde absurdity of it...like a Monet painting with the women in their long lace dresses and the men in their wing collars, and so on, batting away at the balls." His cousin Ronald T. Riley remembers once taking his bride, the former Jessie Fulcher, to the Black house. "Jessie is a devastating croquet player," Riley says, "but she had some trouble with Conrad on that pitch behind their house—a terrible place to play a set." Black's own best moments in the sport were his games with Brig. Richard Sankey Malone, then president of the FP chain of newspapers, which Black was hoping to buy. The two men played many matches, but when the deal fell through, Argus partner David Radler ruefully commented that Conrad had "wasted five years of croquet games with Malone."

It isn't that Black loves croquet so much as that he despises other sports with rare passion. "I don't take a great deal of pleasure in monitoring my own muscle tone and things like that," he says. "I am very suspicious of the whole underlying psychology of activities like jogging. All those people running around look to me like the faces that you'd see in depictions of the ecstasy of St. Teresa—it's as if they had been pierced by spears or something."

Black's chief diversion is reading. He laps up books at the rate of several a week and is such a print addict that he can't abandon even a longstanding surface-mail subscription David Radler once gave him to the *Jerusalem Post*. He has slugged his way through the collected thoughts of Hegel and Spengler's *The Decline of the West*, enjoys lighter works by S.J. Perelman and William Manchester—and remembers most of what he reads.

THERE IS AN ELEMENT OF SUMMONING COURTIERS to account even in the most casual of Black's invitations. In any gathering of what passes for Canada's *beau monde*, behaviour and speech patterns alter imperceptibly as Conrad drifts into the room, checking out the lay of the land. People steal glances at him, playing a little too hard at appearing casual, unexpectedly finding themselves making exaggerated hand gestures. It is as if they had bagged some unusual big-game specimen that had the power to rattle their teeth.

What makes his peers distinctly uncomfortable is that Black aspires to become not so much the Establishment's leader as its messiah. He declares himself much too impatient to join the sequestered ranks of his less flamboyant Establishment colleagues and makes little attempt to disguise his intended ascendancy. "I am not," he demurs, "going to pull an Adlai Stevenson and ask that this cup pass from me – though it is not a distinction I have particularly sought."

While Black readily subscribes to the sanctity of great wealth, he remains convinced that many of his corporate contemporaries have succeeded by inadvertence instead of by their own efforts, and that only proprietors (like himself) are worthy of forming a true elite. "It has always seemed to me," he says, "that the *real* Establishment in this country should be a handful of owners and a group of extremely capable managers so self-assured as to *behave* like owners, plus a battery of some lawyers and heads of large accounting firms and discreet stockbrokers who serve them well and with whom they are comfortable. The core of the actual Establishment ought to be this relatively small number of actual proprietors whose companies are on the move."

The owners within Black's definition are very different from the corporate mandarins who run many Canadian firms. The professional manager loses his prestige (and often his job) on the downside of an investment, but doesn't make much personal profit on an upswing. The ambitious proprietor's capital gain becomes his life. To be a proprietor is to be a possessor of the power that counts – the authority, as Bertrand Russell once noted, to produce intended effects. In this context, Black has become the natural leader and spokesman for a surprisingly influential group of bosses' sons pushing against the confines of a shrinking economy. "Though very rich, they are not coupon-clippers or passive managers," Alexander Ross wrote in *Canadian Business*. "They are aggressive entrepreneurs, operating at high levels of magnitude their fathers only dreamed of, working with the sort of feverish urgency that only the up-and-coming are supposed to possess, working hard to control their companies – perhaps because they know that the alternative is to have their companies control them."

It is the members of this group of owners that Shirley and Conrad Black consider their true friends. As well as his brother, Monte, and

Argus partners and their wives David and Rona Radler and Peter and Mary White, the Blacks' circle includes:

Douglas and Susan Bassett. Dougie (as he is known by nearly everyone) carries his life in his hands like a placard, waving opinions, ambitions, and convictions at benign and hostile passersby with infectious charm and terrier friendliness. In the process he has significantly expanded his father's communications empire and become a major Establishment player. "We're great believers in friendly hands," he says of his relationship with Black, "—great believers in working together as a unit. There's great strength in that." Bassett is as close to Black as any of the Argus partners, and his father, John, and stepmother, Isabel, are also members of the Black set.

Galen and Hilary Weston. Guiding light of the fiscal restoration that turned his father's empire into a profit position (160 companies with 1981 sales of $7.4 billion), Galen is the most international of Toronto's young Inheritors. He plays polo with the Prince of Wales, recently purchased Fort Belvedere (the eighteenth-century folly where Edward VIII signed the documents of abdication), and jets around the world tending his corporate interests. His wife (the former Hilary Frayne) is the Canadian Establishment's reigning beauty.

Fredrik and Nicky Eaton. "Fred," says Black, "is a prodigious reader, a much more academic person than most of the other so-called Inheritors. He's got a fair amount of panache and lives like a wealthy and unabashed proprietor." The Eatons are among Canada's few genuine merchant aristocrats, and even though they try to live ordinary lives, it never quite works. (Fred's younger brother Thor, who attended Forest Hill Collegiate before switching to Upper Canada College, was once heard earnestly complaining that he was the only kid in his class who hadn't had a *bar mitzvah*.) In charge of the family business since 1977, Fred has revitalized the operation (with a 1980 net estimated at $60 million) and is closely involved with Black, who also sits on the department store's key operations committee.

Ken and Marilyn Thomson. Probably the country's only billionaire, Thomson still occasionally suffers from being known as "Young Ken," simply because his father was such a powerful presence. It's a silly epithet: Thomson is due to celebrate his sixtieth birthday on September 1, 1983, and his business ventures have overshadowed his father's deals in both scope and daring. Black and Thomson operate a mutual admiration society with strictly limited membership.

Albert and Ada Reichmann. They are members of the legendary clan of Austro-Hungarian Jews who came to Canada via Tangier in the mid-fifties, a family admired by Black as Canada's most impressive group of entrepreneurs. (At the 1982 Hollinger dinner, Black placed Albert at the table of honour between John Turner and Jacques Courtois, the Montreal lawyer who is Thor Eaton's father-in-law.) During directors' meetings at the Canadian Imperial Bank of Commerce (which in the spring of 1982 had only two loans of more than a billion dollars outstanding—to Jack Gallagher's Dome Petroleum and the Reichmanns' Olympia & York Developments), Black occasionally finds himself defending the reclusive developers' interests. "I know how hard it is for some people here to believe," he is reported to have said at one Commerce meeting, "that some guys with full beards who speak English like the Marx brothers imitating Kaiser Wilhelm, wear thin lapels, black ties and unusual headgear could actually be worth a loan of this size. Well, they *are*—and of the two loans being discussed, we're focusing on the wrong one. What we're running here is a business, not the Toronto Club."

John and Geills Turner. One of Black's chief legal advisers ("John is sensitive to what'll fly") and considered by Toronto's business community to be the prime-minister-in-waiting, Turner has transcended his allegiance to Pierre Trudeau's Liberal party by viewing it not as an ideological condition but as a state of impatience with the way things are. His wife, Geills, is a god-daughter of George Black's.

Tom and Sonja Bata. Joint rulers of the giant shoe empire, they are the Blacks' Toronto neighbours. The two families occasionally enjoy a joint barbecue—cosy and close, even though their backyards measure roughly seventeen acres.

Ted and Loretta Rogers. By combining the flash of a riverboat gambler with workaholism, basic street-smarts and impeccable connections, Ted Rogers has corralled the world's largest cable TV network and turned a small inheritance into a major fortune. His wife is the capable daughter of Lord and Lady Martonmere of Bermuda and Nassau.

Latham and Paddy Ann Burns. Chairman of Burns Fry Ltd., one of Bay Street's large investment houses noted for the shrewdness of its leadership, Burns says, "I am quite in awe of Conrad's knowledge and memory. We were together recently and, when I had to make a call, he reeled off my three telephone numbers. Even *I* have trouble coming up with that." Paddy Ann Burns is one of the Toronto Establishment's more spirited and interesting members. "If present trends continue," says Latham, "Conrad may try to re-orient the system toward free enterprise by moving into politics, or he might get bored and move his activities to another country."

Leighton and Brenda McCarthy. The head of one of Toronto's most active boutique investment houses, Leighton is a classic self-confident Establishment type. He was in Grade 2 with Conrad, and the two have remained good friends ever since.

Philippe and Nan-b de Gaspé Beaubien. Everybody's favourite French-Canadian aristocrats, the Beaubiens (he runs the Canadian edition of *TV Guide* and a growing network of radio stations) have involuntarily conquered Toronto society. The former mayor of Expo 67, Philippe is the first Québécois to carve out a significant communications empire—and personal power base—within English Canada.

Jonathan and Maria Birks. One of the Establishment's more thoughtful Inheritors, the jewellery chain heir holds views on Conrad that border on hero worship. "He's the freshest thing that's come along," Jonathan says. "It's just great for people of my age group to see someone who's not afraid to say, 'Goddamn it, keep your head up high and, if you believe in something, *say* you believe in it, and don't be afraid of criticism—go out and do it, and do it well.' There's a Renaissance aspect about Conrad which translates as a calling he feels to establish himself and leave a permanent mark."

Glen and Mary Alice Davis. A former history professor at the University of Manitoba, Glen is the most unlikely-looking member of the Canadian Establishment. Slightly wall-eyed, with jug ears, he still sports the brush cut he adopted to thwart the attempts of his father, Nelson, to make him a member of the Toronto Club. (Nelson kept telling Glen, "As soon as you have a decent haircut, I'll put you up for the Toronto Club"—which was why the son never let his hair grow in, even a little. He once appeared at Phoenix airport on a visit to his father at his winter home wearing a peaked cap facing backwards, which was the most daring form of rebellion he could dream up, and always insisted on wearing a trick tie clip that contained a ballpoint pen.) His theory that the club would never admit anybody with an adolescent brush cut collapsed when Black put him up anyway, and no one dared object. Glen runs the empire of medium-sized private companies founded by his late father and keeps very much to himself. "I admit," says Black, "that Glen is a terribly implausible character, but he is actually quite intelligent and has a hundred million bucks."

Irving and Gail Gerstein. President of Peoples Jewellers, a political Conservative activist and Young Presidents' Organization booster, Gerstein is a third-generation Inheritor who runs the country's second-biggest chain of jewellers. The proud owner of a Finnish-built Swann yacht, he is plugged into the international elite and loves to entertain such people as Donald Zale from Dallas, who commands the world's largest jewellery operation.

Roy and Lee MacLaren. This Liberal member of Parliament practises politics with class, and understands the subtleties of power. "I see no sign that power is corrupting Conrad," says Roy, "not only because Shirley's there with him but also because he has a healthy sense of humour that will prevent him from ever exaggerating his own sense of authority."

Ron and Jessie Riley. "Conrad," says his cousin Ron, who is a senior vice-president of Canadian Pacific, "wants to leave an imprint on history – that's his prime motivation. He has a lifelong belief in heroes, particularly business leaders of the Taylor/McDougald variety, and is determined to emulate them."

Others who don't fit into the proprietor-class category but who are comfortably within the Black social circle include Ed and Peg Bovey (he's a former chairman of Norcen and a Hollinger Argus director); Murray and Barbara Frum (he is a super-successful real estate investor; she is Barbara Frum); Julian and Anna Porter (he is Toronto's best libel lawyer, she the country's best book editor); Jeremy and Jean Riley (the most intellectual of the Rileys, he is a former principal of Stanstead College in the Eastern Townships, now taking a Ph.D. in education; she is a granddaughter of Louis St. Laurent, the former prime mininster, and known in Toronto society as "a super lady"); Jim Coutts (the former prime ministerial adviser, now consultant to Black on a monthly retainer fee); Donald and Mary Early (she's Toronto society's adjudicator; he hangs his shingle at Greenshields); Michael and Kelly Meighen; Brian and Mila Mulroney; and His Eminence G. Emmett Cardinal Carter (Archbishop of Toronto). While he despises most journalists on sight and sound, Black is friendly with Brian Stewart, the CBC's prime Ottawa

TV commentator, and Larry Zolf, the network's caustic wit. He also seasonally wishes Barbara Amiel, chic neo-conservative associate editor of the *Toronto Sun*, "an ideologically uplifting Christmas."

Powerful in their own right, most members of the Blacks' circle expend extraordinary energy assessing Conrad's every move, analysing the texture of his thoughts and outbursts, trying to guess which way he'll jump next. They behave as if part of their own *karma* were linked to his future.

Inside the Blacks' entourage, it has become *de rigueur* to live as if economic recessions and psychic downturns didn't exist. No one follows this creed with more conspicuous grandeur than Black himself. Its most visible outcropping is the house he recently had built for himself on a tree-lined lane where Toronto fades off into drowsy suburbs. Erected on the property where his father's house once stood, the magnificent dwelling, which weighs in at about $3 million, boasts 25,000 square feet of exquisite workmanship. It became a major construction site while being built, with twenty bricklayers and six roofers busy at one time. Its deliberate grandeur (copper cupola and all) ranks the residence as a minor Georgian palace. One of the fireplaces has a handcarved surround by Grinling Gibbons, the famous British craftsman responsible for much of the decorative work at Blenheim Palace, Hampton Court, and St. Paul's Cathedral.

The designer of record of the house was the late Lord Llewelyn-Davies. The Cambridge-trained architect, whose wife was also made a life peer and became Labour's chief whip in the House of Lords, rebuilt the Stock Exchange in London and planned much of modern downtown Teheran. The architects who saw it through to reality were Thierry Despont of New York and John Parkin of Toronto. "Conrad originally told me he had in mind building a Canadian Versailles," says Parkin. "The house is very symmetrical, very composed, a scholarly kind of dwelling. It has a three-storey elliptical library wing with a cupola modelled on St. Peter's. The library's prominence is symbolic of the man's sheer literacy, indicative of the fact that he doesn't choose to make an ass of himself by devoting his spare time to activities like jogging. It was great working with him because Conrad understands an architectural plan the way he reads a balance sheet. The house is elegant but not grandiose, with everything, just everything, in its proper place."

The mansion was decorated by Shirley Black with Neal McGinnis and Mimi Kemble, both of Palm Beach, acting as consultants. Its furnishings create a Jamesian ambiance that owes more to *Brideshead Revisited* than Canadian Quaint. It will serve well as an appropriate stage-setting for Conrad's famous soirées—entertainments he mounts so that he can attend parties with people he really enjoys.

Here, too, will hang the canvases he has commissioned from Eldred Clark Johnson, a Palm Beach artist who has painted several maritime scenes for him. One depicts two great ocean liners passing each other in New York harbour just before the outbreak of the Second World War. "You have the *Europa* with the Swastika on her stern against the shimmering skyline of Manhattan with all it symbolized for the people arriving from the continent, including Bertolt Brecht and Albert Einstein," Black explains. "The *Normandie*, the most magnificent of all the pre-war liners, is making her way out of New York, symbolic of the France that was about to crumble. That ship, of course, later died quite prematurely in a fire on the New York waterfront and was replaced as flagship of the French Line by the *Europa*, renamed *Liberté*, which was awarded to France as a war prize. It's an allegory, but I suppose it will be a bit obscure for most people."

Taking pains to deliver a subliminal message that only one in a thousand visitors to his house would even vaguely appreciate defines Black's style. That exquisitely honed sense of appropriateness is his predominant characteristic. "Style," as defined in the 1981 book *Doing It With Style* by Quentin Crisp and Donald Carroll, "is an idiom which arises spontaneously from one's personality but which is deliberately maintained. To put it another way: to be a stylist is to be yourself, but on purpose."

That's Conrad.

Epilogue

*If Conrad Black didn't exist, he would
invent himself. His critics claim he has.*

Since Conrad Black long ago surpassed himself as a subarctic Horatio Alger character—attaining a position and wealth to which most private-sector achievers aspire only as a lifelong ambition—his future is an open question. It is highly improbable that he would judge the buffeting he received for his abrupt departure from Massey and bumpy bid for Hanna as cause enough to retreat from the corporate wars, though at least one family member, his cousin Jeremy Riley, thinks so. "I saw Pierre Berton on television talking about his youth in the Yukon," Riley says. "He described how the people had come over the Chilkoot Pass, dragging a ton of equipment to the mountain peak, charging up and down until they got all their stuff together at the top. Berton talked about some of the old guys in Whitehorse when he was a kid who had accomplished nothing except to get to that point. I sometimes wonder whether Conrad might already have achieved his ambition and that he will retire early, like his father. He doesn't really do a lot to look after the body in which his brain reposes."

Peter White, Black's Argus partner, disagrees: "Conrad has this constant dilemma which will probably never leave him: how best to capitalize on his talents. He knows perfectly well that it would be unworthy of him simply to have a career as a businessman. His great problem is that he's more intelligent than 99 per cent of the people with whom he comes in contact and at least at the beginning didn't make much of an attempt to hide it."

Black doesn't have too serious a career dilemma. But there will come a time when merely multiplying his dollar-holdings will lose its fascination. He talks vaguely about eventually pursuing other book projects, but most of the speculation among his contemporaries puts him in some as yet undefined political function.

Nick Auf der Maur (his Montreal friend): "If Conrad had only been born in seventeenth-century France, he wouldn't be a bloody merchant prince. He'd be out there as adviser to the Sun King, and he'd be damn good at it."

The late *Igor Kaplan* (his lawyer): "I'd bet, say thirty to one, that he'll be Prime Minister of Canada one day. Why not?"

David Smith, M.P. (his Liberal pal): "He'd love to buy a Senate seat. I don't think you can buy senatorships any more, but he'd just love it."

Larry Zolf (his favourite humourist): "Conrad could get elected, even as a Marxist-Communist. As a politician, he's a natural with that charm and easy-going boyish nature. He's got the grace."

Ron Graham (his CBC producer): "Black has the makings of a fascinating but not very pleasant politician."

Donald Early (his investment adviser): "Conrad would make an excellent politician. This country, unfortunately, isn't quite ready for him. He might make a good dictator, but that doesn't seem to be a popular form of government these days."

Jonathan Birks (his friend): "He would never just become a back-bencher. He'd run to be Number One. But Canada may be too small to offer him enough challenge in the long run."

John Bosley, M.P. (his Conservative pal): "Offer him the prime ministership, guarantee him a seat, and tell him he doesn't have to do anything except govern — and he'd do that very well."

Monte Black (his brother): "We were sitting around on March 15, 1978, to discover that Bud McDougald, our leader, was dead. So the merry-go-round started whistling. You stick out your fingers, grab the brass ring, and see where it leads you. Who knows what the future will bring?"

Laurier LaPierre (his former professor): "I don't think Conrad wants to be prime minister, but he really *does* want to be the power behind the throne and feels his money will buy him that. I don't think he will handle very well being thwarted or being denied that kind of role, and I don't think he will use his authority wisely. He is one of the few people I know for whom attaining power is an all-consuming goal. What Lord Acton meant in his famous epigram is that absolute power corrupts absolutely because there is no room for love. Once Conrad has finished consolidating his economic environment, he will attempt to create a significant political environment for himself. In the James Bond and John le Carré stories, there is always some weird genius who has a nuclear bomb and is threatening to use it to sanctify mankind. Conrad is like that: he will apply his economic clout politically to repress what he considers the moral wrongs of the world."

PLUGGED INTO THE INVISIBLE CONDUITS of influence that give contour to the country's economy, Black readily admits he may be a child of history – though he claims no divine intervention. His career has progressed through a series of carefully planned and meticulously executed moves. But he does not feel entirely exempt from the forces of destiny. "It is important to maintain some sort of conviction," he purrs, "the feeling that you are predestined to certain opportunities. It takes a great deal of discernment to realize what's possible and what isn't – to impose oneself on a situation, to tolerate people who in the final analysis are not sympathetic to your cause. There is an intuitive, almost metaphysical, process involved in judging whether something is really possible – and if it *is*, whether it's worth it."

Black eschews any political ambitions ascribed to him, though he has publicly declared he isn't interested "in any electoral position except that of prime minister." He would probably move into public life only if he had more confidence in the country's political institutions, if he felt he could use his office to organize society better, or if his conservative ideological stance became more widely acceptable. "I don't romanticize political life," he says. "I would find it a rather disagreeable experience, having all my neighbours vote against me and that kind of stuff. Who needs it? I occasionally rebel against the thought of being just another grubby businessman, but I wouldn't necessarily conceive that politics is the place to betake myself." Black's only current political involvement has been to hire as his private consultant Jim Coutts.

Acutely conscious that Canadians remain unable to approve of precocious success, Conrad is determined to transfer at least some of his activities outside the country and turn the Black group into a "diversified major enterprise carrying the name of Canada to the four corners of the earth." The Hanna purchase is only his first tentative step into the major leagues of the American Establishment.

IF CONRAD BLACK DIDN'T EXIST, he would invent himself. His critics claim he has. There certainly is a decidedly theatrical bent to his actions and pretensions, the realization that all great stage performances depend on their cumulative effect and that an individual's public worth is made up equally of reality and sorcery. Black may well be the ultimate method actor. Even if the role he has chosen to play is himself, it is a character constantly in flux, progressing through a series of incarnations that test the limits of his circumstance. What makes this alchemy interesting is that Black behaves as though he had been granted carte blanche to fulfil his self-imposed destiny.

He is smugly content with his achievement of having stirred into life Argus's "antediluvian hodge-podge of somnolent companies" and believes he has not held power long enough to be a candidate for corruption. "I'm quite happy with the trajectory of my career," he allows, "but I'm a great believer in not becoming hypnotized by the rhythm of one's own advancement. I have always felt it was the compulsive element in Napoleon that drew him into greater and greater undertakings, until he was bound to fail."

A mixture of calculation and boldness, naturalness and artifice, Black is obsessed with being at the centre of things, knowing the movers and shapers, being aware precisely who is disposing of authority in the power exchanges that colour his world. Not the least of his fortitudes is his capacity for self-glorification. He is not particularly attracted to modesty for its own sake and loves to inhale the fumes of flattery, whatever their source. Busy building corporate and private monuments to himself with the easy assumption of entitlement, he has never suffered the humiliation of being asked to wait in the anterooms of money and feels little if any ambivalence about being rich.

BECAUSE HE IS STILL TWO YEARS SHORT of his fortieth birthday (and behaves, as Brascan president Trevor Eyton once noted, "as though he were either seventeen or seventy"), Conrad Black is occasionally dismissed by his elders as an upstart unworthy of bearing the mantle of his legendary Argus predecessors. "A good many people," he admits, "are astonished and outraged that someone of my tender age should be in the position I'm in."

The problem Black faces is that, because of their own advanced chronology and circumstances, the widening circle of his detractors and supporters tends to view him as a finished product. He is still far removed from that state of grace and has yet to pick his favourite role model—not being certain whether he wants to be another Howard Hughes, another Napoleon Bonaparte, or both.

Each new experience provides the bounce that helps determine Black's ultimate direction. He describes his career so far as an avocational version of the expanding-funnel offence conceived by B.H. Liddell Hart, the British military strategist. "I keep advancing," he says, "like a platoon of men through a forest, parallel lines moving in various directions—and whenever there is a breakthrough, I try to exploit it."

In the cradle of his imagery, in the sweep of his ambition and the potential he possesses for good and evil, he is very different from his fellow commercial princes. There is an existential quest for power in this walking brain of a man that appears to defy customary boundaries. He is out there making the deals, mesmerizing himself with the cadence of his rhetoric, bicycling the lonely winter path along Lake Worth or brooding in the hush of his Georgian study, folding himself in and out of his cars, yachts, jets—pursuing his string of intuitive leaps—and loving every minute of it.

His run has just begun.

The very model of The Establishment Man, Conrad Black is the sum of all he longs to accomplish. "I sometimes feel," he muses, "like Spencer Tracy's description of himself—that I'm one of those people things happen to…"

Conrad Black

Appendices

Appendices

Appendix A

This is the text of the crucial agreement signed by the major Argus shareholders on May 30, 1969, which transferred control of the holding company dominated by E. P. Taylor to a finely balanced partnership of Maxwell Meighen, John A. McDougald, the estate of Col. Eric Phillips, George Black, and Maj.-Gen. Bruce Matthews. Its purpose was to remove E. P. Taylor from the helm of the closed-end investment trust he had founded in 1945.

THIS AGREEMENT made the 30th day of May, 1969.

BETWEEN:

John A. McDougald   of The Municipality of Metropolitan Toronto,

PARTY OF THE FIRST PART;

A. Bruce Matthews   of The Municipality of Metropolitan Toronto,

PARTY OF THE SECOND PAR

Canadian General Investments Limited, a Company incorporated under
the Laws of the Province of Ontario,

PARTY OF THE THIRD PART;

Third Canadian General Investment Trust Limited, a Company incorporated under the Laws of Canada,

PARTY OF THE FOURTH PAR

Maxwell C.G. Meighen   of The Municipality of Metropolitan Toronto,

PARTY OF THE FIFTH PART;

Western Dominion Investment Company Limited, a Company incorporated
under the Laws of the Province of Manitoba,

PARTY OF THE SIXTH PART;

George Montagu [*sic*] Black, Jr.   of The Municipality of Metropolitan Toronto,

PARTY OF THE SEVENTH PAI

Grew Limited, a Company incorporated under the Laws of the
Province of Ontario,

PARTY OF THE EIGHTH PAR

AND

Doris Delano Phillips   of The Municipality of Metropolitan
                                          Toronto,

PARTY OF THE NINTH PART

WHEREAS the parties hereto own all the issued Preference
shares (herein referred to as the "Preference shares") and all the issued
Common shares (herein referred to as the "Common shares") in the
capital stock of The Ravelston Corporation Limited (hereinafter called
the "Company"), a company incorporated as a Private Company under
The Corporations Act of Ontario, and the individuals who are parties
hereto are all of the directors of the Company, and the parties hereto are
desirous of declaring the terms and conditions on which the said
Preference shares and the said Common shares shall be held and of
controlling the transfer of such shares as hereinafter provided;

NOW THEREFORE THIS AGREEMENT WITNESSETH
that, in consideration of the premises and of the mutual covenants and
agreements herein contained and for other good and valuable consider-
ations, each of the parties hereto covenants and agrees with each of the
other parties hereto as follows:

1. No Preference shares and no Common shares of the Company
shall be transferred without either (a) the previous express sanction of
the directors of the Company expressed either by a resolution passed at
a meeting of the board of directors by the affirmative vote of a majority
of all the directors of the Company or by an instrument or instruments
in writing signed by a majority of all the directors of the Company; or
(b) the previous express sanction of the shareholders of the Company
expressed either by a resolution passed by the affirmative vote of
holders of at least fifty-one per cent (51%) of the Common shares of the
Company for the time being outstanding, at a meeting of the holders of
such Common shares or by an instrument or instruments in writing
signed by the holders of at least fifty-one per cent (51%) of such
outstanding Common shares.

2. Nothing herein contained shall prevent the legal personal representative or representatives of a deceased shareholder from becoming
registered as a shareholder or shareholders in respect of any share or

shares held by such deceased shareholder at the time of his death or prevent the transfer of any share or shares to a person required to qualify such person as a director of the Company upon his appointment or election as a director, such legal personal representative or representatives of such deceased shareholder and any such director to become a party to this Agreement; and nothing herein contained shall prevent the hypothecation or pledge of any shares by any shareholder to a Canadian chartered bank by way of security for any moneys borrowed by such shareholder, but any such bank shall as to any further transfer be bound by all the provisions hereof, including the restrictions on transfer set forth in clause 1 hereof, and the holder of shares who shall have transferred the same or any of them to such chartered bank by way of security only shall be and be deemed to be the holder of such shares within the meaning of this Agreement.

3. Any holder of Preference shares and any holder of Common shares desirous of selling any or all of the shares held by such shareholder (hereinafter called the "Voluntary Transferor", which expression shall include the legal personal representative or representatives of a deceased shareholder, the committee or tutor of a mentally incompetent shareholder, the trustee of a bankrupt shareholder, or the liquidator of a corporation shareholder) may give a notice in writing (hereinafter called a "Voluntary Transfer Notice") to the Company and to all other shareholders of the Company (hereinafter in this clause 3 referred to as the "offeree shareholders") stating that such Voluntary Transferor desires and offers to sell to such offeree shareholders of the Company, or to persons or corporations designated by them, the Preference and Common shares in the capital of the Company specified in such notice, at the purchase price per Preference share and the purchase price per Common share to be determined by the Auditors of the Company as the value thereof, on the basis hereinafter set forth, as of the last day of the month next preceding the month in which such Voluntary Transfer Notice is given, provided that if less than all of the shares of the Voluntary Transferor are so specified in such notice, such notice shall specify both Preference and Common shares and the number of Common shares so offered shall bear the same proportion (as nearly as may be) to the number of Preference shares so offered as the number of all Common shares held by the Voluntary Transferor bears to the number of all Preference shares held by the Voluntary Transferor; and upon the giving of such Voluntary Transfer Notice such offeree shareholders of the Company shall have the right at such time not later than six months after the giving of such Voluntary Transfer Notice as the offeree shareholders of the Company may decide to accept such offer and to purchase

and pay for the Preference and Common shares of the Company covered by such Voluntary Transfer Notice at the respective prices per share to be determined by the Auditors of the Company as hereinafter provided (or at such other prices as may be agreed upon between the Voluntary Transferor and the offeree shareholders) or to procure other persons or corporations to purchase and pay for such shares at the prices aforesaid, the purchase price for all of said shares so offered to be paid without interest against delivery of certificates for such shares duly endorsed in blank for transfer; and unless otherwise agreed as between themselves, the offeree shareholders shall be entitled to purchase and pay for the said Preference and Common shares (other than shares purchased by persons or corporations designated by the offeree shareholders as aforesaid) in the same proportions respectively as the offeree shareholders then hold Preference and Common shares, respectively, in the capital of the Company; provided that if within the six-month period aforesaid the offeree shareholders have not exercised their right to purchase and have not purchased, or procured other persons or corporations to purchase, the said Preference and Common shares offered to them by the Voluntary Transferor, the Voluntary Transferor shall have the right at any time within two months after the expiration of the said six-month period by notice in writing to the Company and to the offeree shareholders to require the offeree shareholders to take and to join with the Voluntary Transferor in taking all such proceedings, and to sign all such consents and to exercise all such voting powers as directors and/or shareholders of the Company to dissolve the Company, to distribute its assets ratably among its shareholders according to their rights and interests in the Company, and to surrender the Charter of the Company, and for such purpose to enter into such agreement with the Company and to authorize the making of such application to the Lieutenant Governor of Ontario as may be necessary or desirable.

4. If the holders of at least fifty-one per cent (51%) of the Preference shares and of at least fifty-one per cent (51%) of the Common shares of the Company at any time outstanding so require by notice in writing (herein referred to as a "Compulsory Transfer Notice") to any shareholder (including the legal personal representative or representatives of a deceased shareholder, the committee or tutor of a mentally incompetent shareholder, the trustee of a bankrupt shareholder, or the liquidator of a corporation shareholder) the shareholder to whom such Compulsory Transfer Notice is given (herein referred to as the "Forced Transferor") shall be bound to sell to the shareholders of the Company who are signatories to such Compulsory Transfer Notice (hereinafter in this clause referred to as the "purchasing shareholders"), or to persons

and/or corporations designated by them, all (but not less than all, unless the Forced Transferor and the purchasing shareholders otherwise agree) of the Preference and Common shares held by such Forced Transferor in the capital of the Company at the purchase price per Preference share and the purchase price per Common share to be determined by the Auditors of the Company as the value thereof, on the basis hereinafter set forth, as of the last day of the month next preceding the month in which such Compulsory Transfer Notice is given; and upon the giving of such Compulsory Transfer Notice the Forced Transferor shall be bound to sell to such purchasing shareholders, or to persons and/or corporations designated by them, all (or such lesser part as may be agreed upon as aforesaid) of the Preference shares and Common shares in the capital of the Company held by such Forced Transferor at the said respective prices per share to be determined by the Auditors of the Company as hereinafter set forth, and the said purchasing shareholders (as hereinbefore in this clause 4 defined) shall be irrevocably bound, jointly and severally, to purchase and pay for such shares, or procure other persons or corporations to purchase and pay for such shares, at such respective prices, the purchase price for all of such shares to be paid, without interest, at such time not later than six months after the giving of such Compulsory Transfer Notice as the purchasing shareholders of the Company may decide, against delivery of certificates for such shares duly endorsed in blank for transfer; and unless otherwise agreed as between themselves, such purchasing shareholders shall be entitled and bound to purchase and pay for the said Preference and Common shares to be purchased (except the shares to be purchased by other persons or corporations designated by the purchasing shareholders) in the same proportions, respectively, as such purchasing shareholders then hold Preference and Common shares, respectively, in the capital of the Company.

5. (1) The dividends, if any, upon any Preference and/or Common shares sold pursuant to a Voluntary Transfer Notice under the provisions of clause 3 hereof which are declared subsequent to the date of acceptance of the offer of sale of such shares thereof by a Voluntary Transferor but prior to the date of payment of the purchase price of such shares shall, when paid, belong to the Voluntary Transferor;

(2) the dividends, if any, upon any Preference and/or Common shares of the Company sold pursuant to a Compulsory Transfer Notice under the provisions of clause 4 hereof which are declared subsequent to the date of the giving of such Compulsory Transfer Notice but prior to the date of payment of the purchase price of such share shall, when paid, belong to the Forced Transferor.

6. (1) Upon the giving of a Voluntary Transfer Notice under the provisions of clause 3 hereof or a Compulsory Transfer Notice under the provisions of clause 4 hereof the parties hereto shall cause the Auditors of the Company to determine the respective values (which shall constitute the respective sale prices) for the purposes of this Agreement, of the Preference shares and Common shares of the Company, such determination to be made as of the last day of the month next preceding the month in which such Voluntary Transfer Notice or Compulsory Transfer Notice, as the case may be, is given, and such respective values shall be determined on the following basis:

(a) In determining the value of Preference shares and Common shares sold pursuant to a Voluntary Transfer Notice under the provisions of clause 3 hereof all assets of the Company, including all shares owned by the Company, shall be valued by the Auditors at their market value.

(b) In determining the value of Preference shares and Common shares sold pursuant to a Compulsory Transfer Notice under the provisions of clause 4 hereof, such portion of the assets of the Company as consist of common shares of Argus Corporation Limited shall be valued by the Auditors at their market value or their break-up value, whichever is greater, and all other assets of the Company shall be valued by the Auditors at their market value.

(c) For the purposes of subsections (a) and (b) of this subclause (1) of this clause 6, the Auditors in determining the market value of any shares owned by the Company may be guided by, but shall not necessarily be bound by, the closing price or quotation for such shares (if listed on any Stock Exchange) on the day as of which such market value is to be determined, and if not so listed, or in the absence of any such price or quotation, may, in their discretion, base their determination of such market value on such other financial reports, data and information as may be available to them.

(d) In determining the value of Preference shares and Common shares sold either pursuant to a Voluntary Transfer Notice under the provisions of clause 3 hereof or pursuant to a Compulsory Transfer Notice under the provisions of clause 4 hereof the value of the Preference shares shall not exceed their par value and the value of the Common shares shall not be less than One Cent per share.

(e) The goodwill of the business of the Company shall be valued at One Dollar.

(2) Nothwithstanding anything contained in clause 4 and in this clause 6 of this Agreement:

(a) If within one year after the completion of the purchase of and payment for any Preference and Common shares of the Company purchased from a Forced Transferor pursuant to a Compulsory Transfer Notice as provided in clause 4 hereof, the Company shall sell any of the common shares of Argus Corporation Limited owned by it at a price in excess of the greater of their market value or their break-up value (as determined by the Auditors of the Company for the purpose of fixing the purchase price of the Preference and Common shares of the Company purchased from such Forced Transferor as aforementioned) each shareholder who purchased any of such shares from such Forced Transferor shall thereupon pay to such Forced Transferor such additional amount (as determined by the Auditors of the Company) as the Forced Transferor would have been entitled to receive from such shareholder if at the time of such forced transfer the common shares of Argus Corporation Limited then owned by the Company had been valued at the sale price thereof subsequently received by the Company as aforesaid.

(b) If within one year after the completion of the purchase of and payment for any Preference and Common shares of the Company purchased from a Forced Transferor pursuant to a Compulsory Transfer Notice as provided in clause 4 hereof, any shareholders of the Company shall sell in the aggregate a majority in number of the outstanding Preference shares and/or Common shares in the capital of the Company at a price or prices in excess of the respective purchase prices paid by any shareholders of the Company to such Forced Transferor, the shareholders of the Company who purchased such Preference and Common shares of the Company from such Forced Transferor shall forthwith pay to such Forced Transferor an additional amount in respect of each share so purchased equal to the amount of such excess.

(3) In determining the respective values of the Preference shares and Common shares of the Company in accordance with the provisions of subclause (1) of this clause 6 and in determining the amount payable to a Forced Transferor under the provisions of subclause (2) of this clause 6 the Auditors shall be acting as experts and not as arbitrators, and accordingly the provisions of The Arbitrations Act shall not apply, and the determination by the Auditors of such respective values and of such amount shall be final and binding upon all parties concerned.

7. So long as any party hereto continues to hold any Common shares in the capital of the Company, all of the other persons and corporations now or hereafter parties hereto will, at all meetings of shareholders of the Company at which directors of the Company are to be elected, vote or cause to be voted either in person or by proxy, as the case may be, all of the shares in the capital of the Company now or at any time hereafter held by them to secure the continuance in office and the election from

time to time as a director of the Company of such party if an individual, or the nominee of such party if a corporation, or, in the case of the death of such party, of the nominee of the legal personal representatives of such party; provided that the corporations which are Parties hereto of the Third and Fourth Parts shall be entitled jointly to only one such nominee director, and provided further that for the purpose of this clause 6 the Party of the Ninth Part is presently the nominee of the Party of the Eighth Part, the Party of the Seventh Part is presently the nominee of the Party of the Sixth Part, and the Party of the Fifth Part is presently the joint nominee of the Parties of the Third and Fourth Parts.

8. Any person or corporation not an original party to this Agreement who becomes the transferee of any shares in the capital of the Company pursuant to the terms of this Agreement shall sign this Agreement and thereby become a party hereto and be bound by the terms hereof.

9. Subject to the provisions restricting the transfer of shares contained in the letters patent or supplementary letters patent (if any) of the Company, any of the terms and provisions herein contained may be altered, added to or modified in such manner and to such extent as may be agreed upon in writing by persons or corporations from time to time parties hereto holding in the aggregate not less than seventy-five per cent (75%) of the issued and outstanding Preference shares and not less than seventy-five per cent (75%) of the issued and outstanding Common shares of the Company, and any such alteration, addition or modification shall be binding upon all persons and corporations from time to time parties to this Agreement.

10. A reference to this Agreement shall be endorsed on all certificates for Preference shares and Common shares issued by the Company to or owned by any of the parties hereto.

11. Any notice required or authorized to be given or served under any of the provisions of this Agreement may be given by delivering the same personally to the party or parties to whom the same is addressed or by mailing the same in a prepaid registered letter addressed to such party or parties at their usual place of business or abode. Such notice, if delivered, shall be effective on the date on which delivery is effected and, if mailed, on the date on which it would reach the person to whom it is addressed in the ordinary course of post.

12. This Agreement shall be binding upon all persons and corporations now or hereafter signatories hereto irrespective of any changes in their respective holdings of shares in the capital of the Company or of any changes in the parties to this Agreement. Each such signatory shall

as a shareholder, director or otherwise take such action and cause the Company and the Auditors of the Company to take such action as may be requisite to implement the provisions hereof.

13. This Agreement shall enure to the benefit of and be binding upon the heirs, executors, administrators, successors and assigns, or other legal representatives of the parties hereto.

Appendix B

This is the text of the controversial agreement signed in Palm Beach on May 15, 1978, by which Conrad Black was able to capture control of Ravelston Corporation, and through it Argus Corporation, from the widows of two of its partners, Col. Eric Phillips and John A. McDougald.

THIS AGREEMENT dated the 15th day of May, 1978

BETWEEN: CROWN TRUST COMPANY, DORIS DELANO
                 PHILLIPS and DIXON S. CHANT, surviving
                 Executors and Trustees of the Estate of W. Eric
                 Phillips, deceased,
                 (hereinafter called the "Phillips Trustees")
                             OF THE FIRST PART;

            –and–

                 DORIS DELANO PHILLIPS,
                 (hereinafter called "Mrs. Phillips")
                          OF THE SECOND PART;

            –and–

                 W.E.P. INVESTMENTS LIMITED,
                 (hereinafter called "W.E.P.")
                          OF THE THIRD PART;

            –and–

                 DIXON S. CHANT,
                 (hereinafter called "Chant")
                          OF THE FOURTH PART;

            –and–

                 HEDLEY MAUDE McDOUGALD, DORIS
                 DELANO PHILLIPS and CROWN TRUST
                 COMPANY, Executors and Trustees of the Estate of
                 John Angus McDougald, deceased,
                 (hereinafter called the "McDougald Trustees")
                         OF THE FIFTH PART;

            –and–

HEDLEY MAUDE McDOUGALD,
(hereinafter called "Mrs. McDougald")
OF THE SIXTH PART;

–and–

WESTERN DOMINION INVESTMENT
COMPANY LIMITED,
(hereinafter called "Western Dominion")
OF THE SEVENTH PART;

–and–

CONRAD M. BLACK and GEORGE MONTEGU
BLACK III,
(hereinafter collectively called "Black")
OF THE EIGHTH PART;

The parties hereto mutually agree as follows:

1.(a) In this Agreement, unless the contrary intention appears, the following words and phrases have the respective meanings hereinafter set forth:

(i) "Phillips Interests" shall mean the percentage interest in the issue capital of The Ravelston Corporation Limited (hereinafter called the "Company") held in the aggregate by the Parties of the First, Second, Third and Fourth Parts;

(ii) "McDougald Interests" shall mean the percentage interest in the issued capital of the Company held in the aggregate by the Parties of the Fifth and Sixth Parts;

(iii) "Black Interests" shall mean the percentage interest in the issued capital of the Company held in the aggregate by the Parties of the Seventh and Eighth Parts;

(iv) "Directions of the Parties Hereto" shall mean the directions given by or on behalf of the Phillips Interests, the McDougald Interests and the Black Interests, provided that in case of any difference of opinion among such Interests a majority of such Interests (which shall include the Phillips Interests and the McDougald Interests) shall govern.

(b) For the purposes of this Agreement:

(i) Any nomination, appointment, notice, consent, approval, decision or direction to be made or given by or on behalf of the Phillips Interests shall be sufficiently made or given if made or given by the Phillips Trustees;

(ii) Any nomination, appointment, notice, consent, approval, decision or direction to be made or given by or on behalf of the McDougald Interests shall be sufficiently made or given if made or given by the McDougald Trustees;

(iii) Any nomination, appointment, notice, consent, approval, decision or direction to be made or given by or on behalf of the Black Interests shall be sufficiently made or given if made or given by Conrad M. Black or, failing him, by George Montegu Black III.

2. This Agreement will remain in force for a term of ten (10) years from the date hereof and shall be binding upon the successors and assigns of W.E.P. and Western Dominion. In the event of the death or retirement of any of the Phillips Trustees or the McDougald Trustees, this Agreement shall enure to the benefit of and be binding upon the remaining Trustees and any successor trustees of the respective Estates of W. Eric Phillips, deceased, and John Angus McDougald, deceased. In the event of the death of Mrs. Phillips, Mrs. McDougald, Dixon S. Chant, Conrad M. Black or George Montegu Black III, this Agreement shall enure to the benefit of and be binding upon her or his respective personal representative. In this Agreement the term "personal representative" shall include executors, administrators and trustees.

3. While this Agreement remains in force:

(a) None of the Parties hereto will sell, transfer, pledge, hypothecate or otherwise dispose of or encumber any shares held by them in the capital of the Company, except with the written consent of the Phillips Interests, the McDougald Interests and the Black Interests.

(b) The Parties hereto will at all meetings of shareholders of the Company, either in person or by proxy, as the case may be, vote or cause to be voted all shares in the capital of the Company now or at any time hereafter held by them, in accordance with the Directions of the Parties Hereto on every by-law, resolution, matter or question submitted for consideration at all such meetings and, without limiting the generality of the foregoing, will, at all meetings at which directors of the Company are to be elected, vote or cause to be voted all said shares in accordance with the Directions of the Parties Hereto for the election and re-election from time to time as directors of the Company of the following:

(i) Three persons nominated collectively by the Phillips Interests and the McDougald Interests; and

(ii) one person nominated by the Black Interests; and, where action by the shareholders is taken by way of consent or confirmation in writing instead of at a general meeting of shareholders, the Parties Hereto will similarly act in accordance with the Directions of the Parties Hereto in giving or withholding such consents and confirmations.

(c) The Parties of the First, Second, Third and Fourth Parts, as representatives of the Phillips Interests, the Parties of the Fifth and Sixth Parts as representatives of the McDougald Interests, and the Parties of the Seventh and Eighth Parts, as representatives of the Black Interests, will cause their respective nominee directors to vote at all meetings of directors of the Company in accordance with the Directions of the Parties Hereto.

(d) The Parties of the First, Second, Third and Fourth Parts, representing the Phillips Interests, will at all meetings of shareholders of the Company vote or cause to be voted all of the shares in the capital of the Company now or at any time hereafter held by the Phillips Interests in accordance with the Directions of the Parties Hereto, and will from time to time by prior instruments in writing appoint such person or persons as nominees of the Phillips Interests to vote for and on behalf of the Phillips Interests at any or all meetings of shareholders of the Company.

(e) The Parties of the Fifth and Sixth Parts, representing the McDougald Interests, will at all meetings of shareholders of the Company vote or cause to be voted all of the shares in the capital of the Company now or at any time hereafter held by the McDougald Interests in accordance with the Directions of the Parties Hereto, and will from time to time by prior instruments in writing appoint such person or persons as nominees of the McDougald Interests to vote for and on behalf of the McDougald Interests at any or all meetings of shareholders of the Company.

(f) The Parties of the Seventh and Eighth Parts, representing the Black Interests, will at all meetings of shareholders of the Company vote or cause to be voted all of the shares in the capital of the Company now or at any time hereafter held by the Black Interests in accordance with the Directions of the Parties Hereto, and will from time to time by prior instruments in writing appoint such person or persons as nominees of the Black Interests to vote for and on behalf of the Black Interests at any or all meetings of shareholders of the Company.

(g) A reference to this Agreement shall be endorsed upon, or a copy of this Agreement shall be attached to, the share certificates representing the shares in the capital of the Company held by each of the Parties hereto.

4. The Parties of the First, Second, Third and Fourth Parts, as representatives of the Phillips Interests, and the Parties of the Fifth and Sixth Parts, as representatives of the McDougald Interests, hereby agree to join with the Parties of the Seventh and Eighth Parts, representing the Black Interests, in giving a Compulsory Transfer Notice to one or all of the remaining shareholders of the Company, pursuant to the provisions of Clause 4 of the Agreement made the 30th day of May, 1969, between John Angus McDougald, A. Bruce Matthews, Canadian General Investments Limited, Third Canadian General Investment Trust Limited, Maxwell C.G. Meighen, Western Dominion Investment Company Limited, George Montegu Black, Jr., Grew Limited (now W.E.P. Investments Limited) and Doris Delano Phillips. The date upon which such Compulsory Transfer Notice shall be given shall be determined by the representatives of the Black Interests, and such determination shall be final and binding upon such Interests. Any such Compulsory Transfer Notice shall designate that the purchasing shareholders shall be the Party of the Seventh Part or such person and/or corporation designated by the Party of the Seventh Part.

The Parties of the Seventh and Eighth Parts, representing the Black Interests, hereby agree to save harmless and indemnify the Parties of the First, Second, Third and Fourth Parts, as representatives of the Phillips Interests, and the Parties of the Fifth and Sixth Parts, as representatives of the McDougald Interests, from and against all claims and demands, damages, loss, costs, charges and expenses which the Phillips Interests and the McDougald Interests may sustain or incur or be liable for by reason of the failure on the part of the Party of the Seventh Part or such person and/or corporation designated by the Party of the Seventh Part to purchase and pay for the shares in the capital of the Company pursuant to such Compulsory Transfer Notice.

5. If any provision of this Agreement is illegal or unenforceable, it shall be considered separate and severable from the remaining provisions of this Agreement, which shall remain in force and be binding as though the said provision had never been included.

Appendix C

These four private letters written by Conrad Black during the 1980 financial crunch at Massey-Ferguson to Herbert Gray, Minister of Industry, Trade and Commerce, were influential in helping to gain the agricultural implement firm a temporary reprieve.

Argus Corporation
Limited
10 Toronto Street
Toronto, Canada
M5C 2B7

March 24, 1980.

CONRAD M. BLACK
Chairman

The Honourable Herbert E. Gray, P.C., M.P.,
Minister of Industry, Trade and Commerce,
333 West Block,
Parliament Buildings,
OTTAWA, Ontario,
K1A 0A7.

Private and
Confidential

Dear Herb:

Following the conversation last evening between you and Victor Rice and myself, I would like to summarize the diesel project as we envision it.

Without miring us in the recent history of Massey-Ferguson, you and your colleagues would be aware that it is Canada's greatest international manufacturing company, does business in almost every country in the world and that, in many countries, it is the principal popular representative of Canada. On a unit basis, it is, and has been for some years, the largest producer of tractors and of diesel engines in the world.

At the time that Victor and I entered upon our present functions at Massey-Ferguson in the summer of 1978, it was most of the way through a year that produced a loss of $262 million (U.S.). The former management had financed a good deal of expansion, that subsequently proved to be injudicious, on issues of debt rather than equity; and to take advantage of the historically low value of the British pound compared to the U.S. and Canadian dollar, it perpetuated the state of affairs in which the engines, axles and transmissions of the great majority of our North American tractors and combine harvesters were produced in the United Kingdom and in France. The combination of the deterioration of several of our divisions, a sharp reversal in foreign exchange patterns and sky-rocketing interest rates brought this company to within sight of insolvency. I assumed the chairmanship when our international lending community, comprised of more than 200 banks, made it known that if drastic measures were not taken, they could not assure us of the availability of credit; and Massey-Ferguson could have been broken up into national units and disposed of, thus, presumably, paying off the creditors but leaving

continued ....

295

The Honourable Herbert E. Gray, P.C., M.P.   March 24, 1980.

nothing for the shareholders and eliminating this great and historic company.

Since then, we have succeeded in disposing of virtually all of our unprofitable divisions, we will have reduced our international man-power from 67,000 to about 46,000 this year (very few of these reduc-tions having occurred in Canada, I am happy to report), and we have taken about $200 million on an annualized basis out of cost structure. At the same time, there have been major product improvements, consider-able marketing efforts, and the nearly cataclysmic year of 1978 was succeeded by a $37 million profit last year, and we expect a much more substantial profit this year. We have, at the same time, substantially re-Canadianized Massey-Ferguson, are moving the North American head-quarters back from the United States to Canada and have ensured that, while no less an international company than in the past, it is centrally directed by Canadians resident in Canada.

We have reached the point where it is appropriate and possible to re-finance the company and to replace large quantities of debt, now requiring on average more than 20% annual rates of interest, with equity yielding approximately half that percentage. While this procedure, which I may assure you has not been an easy one, has been in progress at Massey-Ferguson, the so-called Argus Group, which is Massey-Ferguson's largest shareholder, has undergone an almost equally startling transformation and is now able (which was not the case two years ago) to come very materially to Massey-Ferguson's assistance in such a re-financing. As I have said to you on two occasions by telephone, we must, however, be mind-ful of our limitations; and while we can participate in a re-financing that will clearly re-establish Massey-Ferguson as a sound corporation with a solid equity base and operating performance, we are not able at the same time to provide capital resources necessary to create a North American engine facility and, thus, liberate ourselves from the vagaries of the tumultuous international exchange patterns.

This brings us to our present project. It is very ironic that this company, with its licencees and affiliates, produced more than half a million diesel engines last year, but none in Canada and very few in the United States, and those in an uneconomical plant that we have since closed. Our thought was that, if in whatever assistance the Federal Government might consider for Chrysler Corporation in Canada, there could be accom-modated a facility for converting the blocks of gasoline automobile engines to diesel engines and a facility for producing diesel engines for agricul-tural and some other purposes, the following results would be achieved.

continued ....

The Honourable Herbert E. Gray, P.C., M.P.   March 24, 1980.

The actual facility would be lent a diversity and a prominence that no single-purpose plant of Chrysler Corporation could now reasonably aspire to. Whatever happened to Chrysler Corporation, and I don't mean to imply that I am being negative about its future, the dieselization and diesel aspects of this facility would be a permanent source of employment and export possibilities, starting with, but by no means confined to, our own purchases for our tractors.

Secondly, Canada would finally be in the diesel business, which has an extremely promising future and in which a Canadian company is an acknowledged world leader. In addition to supplying Chrysler's own future needs for automotive diesel engines, such a facility as we envision could sell to Ford, International Harvester, etc. in a way that an exclusively Chrysler plant could not. We have been very large suppliers to Chrysler and to Ford in various locations around the world for some years.

Thirdly, this project would enable us to take advantage of the present pattern of foreign exchange, which would be particularly welcome after the terrible erosion of profits that we have suffered in the last several years by the rise of the pound and the decline of the U.S. and Canadian dollars.

Fourthly, since it is our objective and intention to strengthen our position in the large tractor market in the United States and perhaps to repatriate certain Canadian-based assets in that field, this could be a particularly promising source of exports for Canada.

Fifthly, in addition to giving whatever assistance you may eventually make in favour of Chrysler a much more positive character, it would also, I submit, be a particularly fruitful combination of public sector and private sector resources in a venture that would be wholly and greatly to the benefit of this country, far beyond improving the prospects of a subsidiary of a foreign-owned automobile company.

As I have already remarked, it is not possible at this time for Massey-Ferguson to be re-financed and to embark on such an extensive capital programme as this diesel facility would require as a free-standing project. If, however, and this is what we are suggesting, the Government were able to facilitate a comparatively modest participation in our re-financing, amounting to no more than half of what we, ourselves, in the so-called Argus Group would invest in the company, and if the Government could provide the encouragement necessary to Chrysler to co-operate with our project, we could provide the expertise necessary to install these dieselization and diesel capabilities. We envision the Federal Government or any of its agents or

continued ....

The Honourable Herbert E. Gray, P.C., M.P.   March 24, 1980.

affiliates, including the Canada Development Corporation, investing $100 million in a preferred share issue of Massey-Ferguson. We, for our part, in the Argus Group, would undertake to invest $200 million in Massey-Ferguson, and I believe that it would be possible to convert bank debt to equity and underwrite further equity issues totalling from $100-250 million more. With this injection, Massey-Ferguson's debt:equity ratio would advance from its present precarious 2.3:1 to approximately .75:1, and the earnings, as applicable to the common shares, would improve by more than $50 million.

We would have the means to accelerate our programmes of increased market penetration, while effectively Canadianizing ourselves, and we would provide the expertise necessary to create this diesel facility according to the highest international standards.

As we have explained to you in confidence, we have already gone to considerable lengths to establish a foundation for third party sales, including our discussions with Daimler-Benz in regard to their North American diesel requirements, and the possibility of acquiring other companies in the farm machinery business and rationalizing production of power trains, trucks and rotary combines. A former government made substantial grants to White Motor Company for technological assistance in developing the rotary combine, and there has been much talk of assistance to Deutz, a Germany company interested in entering the diesel field in Quebec. Without disparaging those initiatives, I believe that what we are envisioning will be of infinitely more benefit to this country and of much greater economic consequences to the North American market.

I want to emphasize that such an arrangement as I have described would make the Government immune to any charge of simply bailing out a faltering company, and by investing twice as much as the Government or its affiliates would be called upon to invest in Massey-Ferguson, we would be equally irreproachable of the charge of maintaining ourselves in business through a Government dole. I need hardly add that Hollinger Argus Limited, its principals and its affiliated companies would never be a party to such an arrangement if it consisted of seeking Government assistance on an uneconomic or unsound investment basis. We would put our money on the line and collaborate with you and others in the creation of a great Canadian enterprise.

I know also that I need not add what a positive effect such a project would have on the climate of business-government relations throughout this country. I can also envision many incidental benefits,

continued ....

The Honourable Herbert E. Gray, P.C., M.P.   March 24, 1980.

including reducing perceived inequalities in the Auto Pact and increasing
the percentage of Canadian ownership in Massey-Ferguson from approximately
55% to about 80%.

    We would be pleased to amplify our proposals at your convenience,
and we are satisfied that this project contains the potential of very
great benefit to our country.

Yours sincerely,

Conrad M. Black,
Chairman of the Executive Committee,
HOLLINGER ARGUS LIMITED.

CMB/jea

Hollinger Argus Limited
10 Toronto Street
Toronto, Canada
M5C 2B7

CONRAD M. BLACK
CHAIRMAN OF THE EXECUTIVE COMMITTEE

July 4, 1980.

The Honourable Herbert E. Gray, P.C., M.P.,
Minister of Industry, Trade and Commerce,
333 West Block,
Parliament Buildings,
OTTAWA, Ontario,
K1A 0A7.

Dear Herb:

I want to summarize the status of Massey-Ferguson and of the project involving that company, which could be of interest to the federal Government, and also set out the relationship between Massey-Ferguson and the so-called Argus group as it has evolved. I need not stress the size of Massey-Ferguson nor its importance as a representative of Canada in virtually every country in the world, nor its place in Canadian history and current economic life. However, a bit of history would be germane.

Argus Corporation became the largest shareholder of Massey-Harris, as it then was called, in the immediate post-war era but had little to say in the management of the company until 1956, when a serious dispute arose with the then Chief Executive Officer, Mr. James S. Duncan, over skyrocketing inventories and a misjudgement of the company's potential in what had become primarily a replacement market in the principal Western countries. From 1956 to 1964, Massey-Ferguson was effectively directed by Colonel W. E. Phillips, Chairman of Argus Corporation and of the governing body of the University of Toronto. Colonel Phillips was an outstanding industrialist, who cleaned up Massey's operations and restored it to a healthy condition. He and his Argus colleagues exercised an influence at Massey-Ferguson that vastly exceeded the approximately 12% voting interest that Argus had in Massey-Ferguson's equity.

When Colonel Phillips died in December 1964, the non-correspondence of view between his two principal associates, J. A. McDougald and E. P. Taylor, escalated and created a schism in the Argus group that effectively stifled corporate initiative until Mr. Taylor sold his large Argus shareholding to interests headed by Paul G. Desmarais of Montreal in 1975. Mr. McDougald and Mr. Taylor were each unwilling to entrust to the other the authority that Colonel Phillips had exercised at Massey-Ferguson. In this comparative vacuum, Massey-Ferguson's management was left to

Continued ......

300

The Honourable Herbert E. Gray, P.C., M.P.   July 4, 1980.

a group of Americans who had great ambitions for the company and personally possessed both integrity and intelligence, but who gradually
became the prisoners of their dreams. In the comparative absence of
an ultimately effective Argus influence, Massey-Ferguson temporarily
ceased to be, for practical purposes, a Canadian company and committed
some extremely serious errors. The most significant of these were:

1) Failure to participate seriously in the large tractor market in
North America (over 100 h.p.). This was clearly the part of the farm
equipment market that was destined to be the fastest-growing and was
favoured by a higher margin; and Massey-Ferguson avoided this sector of
the market until it finally produced in the middle 1970's a large tractor
that was afflicted by severe technical misjudgements and gave the company
a disastrous reputation for product unreliability.

2) Massey-Ferguson embarked upon a very ambitious programme in the construction machinery field, especially in Germany. The whole project was
both ill-considered and untimely. It did not have the distribution for
such products, it did not have the technical or financial strength to com-
pete seriously with such companies as Caterpillar, and it concentrated
its investment in Germany where the rising value of the Deutschemark
made it virtually impossible to export profitably. The whole venture
cost Massey-Ferguson approximately $250 million.

3) It perpetuated the assembling of tractors in North America composed
largely of components from its European factories. Tractors ostensibly
made in Detroit and combine harvesters manufactured in Brantford had
engines manufactured in the U.K. and, in the case of tractors, axles and
transmissions from either the U.K. or France. While there were certain
advantages to this procedure in days when the Canadian and U.S. dollars
were very strong compared to the British and French currencies, Massey-
Ferguson's management failed to grasp the implications of all of the
economic and political forces that have in recent years entirely reversed
the relationship between North American and Western European currencies.
This enormous additional manufacturing cost imposes a severe competitive
disadvantage in North American and world export markets.

4) When it set about developing a North American engine facility, it
settled upon an oversized factory in Canton, Ohio, which never operated
at more than 30% capacity, is now closed and unsold, and has already
cost Massey-Ferguson more than $100 million in losses.

5) Virtually all of Massey-Ferguson's ambitions of expansion throughout
the world were financed by bank borrowing and floating rate loans, which

continued ....

The Honourable Herbert E. Gray, P.C., M.P.   July 4, 1980.

have not been accompanied by acceptable levels of profitability that
would build up retained earnings in the company and have, in these recent
years of very high interest rates, been a severe and destabilizing impedi-
ment.

6)   The Massey-Ferguson management presided over and tolerated a completely unacceptable and noncompetitive degree of inefficiency and general
corporate slothfulness, which may be illustrated by the fact that at the
beginning of 1978, Massey-Ferguson had approximately 78% of the sales of
Deere and Company (John Deere) and approximately 115% of Deere's number
of employees. Massey-Ferguson failed to adjust to an era of freer trade
and found itself with many more factories in many more countries than
were justifiable. Although its distribution and penetration were excellent
in the peripheral markets of the world, it was hamstrung by a complicated
and obsolete procedure of shipping components all around the world for re-
assembly closer to the point of sale. In this process, it dangerously
weakened its position in the home markets of Canada and the United States
where, in recent years, sales have been close to a billion dollars Canadian
but profits have been sparse and infrequent.

       I could continue in this vein at great length but the foregoing is,
for our purposes, an adequate résumé of the principal strategic errors
committed by Massey-Ferguson's management without the benefit of what
would have been a steadying and realistically Canadian direction from the
principal shareholder. In my opinion, neither Mr. Taylor nor Mr. McDougald,
whatever may be said about them, would have failed to stop and reverse
most of these grievously mistaken policies, had either been prepared to
accord the other the authority to do so.

       With this background, you will appreciate that the so-called Argus
group, as it has been reconstituted in the two years since Mr. McDougald's
death, does not accept any obligatory responsibility for Massey-Ferguson.
Our total historic investment in Massey-Ferguson is $36 million, now
valued at precisely zero. This is hardly a material or relevant investment,
neither to us, given our nearly one billion dollars invested in other
industries, nor to Massey-Ferguson, itself, a company with approximately
1.8 billion dollars of short-term debt and $800 million of long-term debt.

       The Argus group, however, was the only conceivable focal point of any
strength or credibility proximate to Massey-Ferguson when the latter company reaped the whirlwind in 1978 and produced a loss of $262 million U.S.
Successive groups of U.S. lenders came to see me in the summer of 1978,
following the assumption of control of Argus Corporation by my associates
and myself after the death of Mr. McDougald in March of that year. I

continued ......

The Honourable Herbert E. Gray, P.C., M.P.   July 4, 1980.

was advised that if drastic measures were not taken at Massey-Ferguson, the
international lending community would withhold its support, causing Massey-
Ferguson to be broken up into national units and disposed of by individual
receivers in virtually every significant country in the non-communist world.
This fate will probably be unavoidable next year unless Massey-Ferguson is
refinanced, and would be catastrophic not only for the company, itself, but
for the credibility of Canada in the world.

My objectives were to assure that the operational performance of Massey-
Ferguson was improved to the point where the company could be refinanced;
to convert Argus's position from one of apparent open-ended involvement in
Massey-Ferguson, whatever might happen to worldwide interest and exchange
rates and farm equipment markets; and to engineer a metamorphosis at Argus
Corporation, itself, from its former enfeebled and sclerotic condition as
a passive holding company to a serious resource-oriented industrial enterprise, capable of coming materially to Massey's assistance, were it to
choose to do so.

All of these objectives have now been achieved. Without dwelling too
much on the first point, I would only mention that in the past two years,
Massey-Ferguson has disposed of 10 million square feet of factory space
and by next year, will have reduced its number of employees from 68,000 to
44,000. At the same time, production would have increased significantly
had market conditions not recently necessitated the temporary closure of a
number of factories. Our recovery strategy was to build upon an operating
improvement a reasonably orthodox public refinancing and, by the autumn of
1979, a five-firm underwriting group, after the most extensive research in
the history of Canadian corporate finance, declared that Massey-Ferguson
was eminently financeable in normal economic circumstances, and our $262
million loss in 1978 became a $37 million profit in 1979.

Unfortunately, as you are as aware as I am, economic circumstances
ceased to be normal, interest rates soared, the British pound soared in
relationship to the U.S. and Canadian dollars and farm equipment markets in
the United States collapsed. We were, therefore, obligated to reverse our
strategy entirely and attempt to refinance Massey-Ferguson in order to produce satisfactory results instead of awaiting satisfactory results to enable
the refinancing.

The collapse of the United States farm equipment market, which has
caused all of the manufacturers to shut their factories or suspend production, will, as all observers have recognized, have a very negative
impact upon Massey's third quarter results which should be published at
the end of August. It is not going to be possible to rely upon a conventional public underwriting to assist in the refinancing of Massey until the
operational results are unambiguously successful over a sustained period.
Massey-Ferguson is already encountering, in regard to private placements,

continued .....

The Honourable Herbert E. Gray, P.C., M.P.   July 4, 1980.

both the natural timidity of capital and the greed of industrial elements
that might naturally be interested in participating in a refinanced Massey-
Ferguson but cannot resist the temptation of awaiting a possible insolvency
in order to buy selectively among its assets at greatly discounted prices.

The accompanying material clearly indicates that with an infusion of
capital and conversion of debt into equity totalling $400 million, even at
dividend rates and terms of convertibility highly advantageous to a potential investor, Massey-Ferguson would be solidly and profitably self-
sustaining. I have, accordingly, come to the tentative conclusion that
some serious prospect of refinancing should accompany the third quarter
results in order to prevent hysteria sweeping the lending and financial
communities. Since neither the public nor any particular private interest
can be looked to by Massey-Ferguson as a potential investor in these circumstances, we must envision a refinancing based upon the Canadian Imperial
Bank of Commerce and ourselves.

As I mentioned earlier, we felt that it was essential, in order to
impart a sense of realism to the international lending community, which has
collectively advanced almost two billion dollars to Massey-Ferguson, nearly
65% of that in the manufacturing rather than the finance companies, to disa-
buse them of any notion that the so-called Argus group was prepared to
insulate Massey-Ferguson from the whole range of uncontrollable circumstances
that have beset it. For that reason and in order to lend greater credibility
to any investment that we do ultimately make in Massey-Ferguson, I have gone
to some lengths to establish a cordon sanitaire between Massey and Argus.
I am no longer an officer of Massey and we officially value our investment
in that company, as has been publicized in the last few days, at zero, but
this does not imply any abandonment of interest by us in Massey-Ferguson.

Indeed, all of the company's major problems, in particular those of
manufacturing inefficiency and product quality, have been successfully
addressed, except for undercapitalization and continued overseas sourcing
of diesel engines. These two elements leave the company helplessly vulnerable to the vagaries of interest and exchange rates. In order to assure
not only survival but a very optimistic future, a refinancing should include
both a recapitalization and at least the beginnings of a North American
diesel facility.

As I wrote to you in my letter of March 24, I believe that it is possible for us to refinance Massey-Ferguson if there is evidence of a reduction of Massey's dependence upon an overseas source for engines. It is in
this area, on a project basis and not as any sort of bail-out of the company as a whole, that the collaboration of the public sector would be most
valuable to Massey and most helpful to the national interest. It is ironic

continued .....

The Honourable Herbert E. Gray, P.C., M.P.   July 4, 1980.

that this company, which with its licensees and affiliates, produced more than half a million diesel engines last year, has no diesel facilities in North America. Here is an industry with a very promising future, where a Canadian-owned company is one of the acknowledged world leaders, and yet, where Canada has no position at all.

There is potential for gradually transferring the core of Massey's diesel engine business, including a great deal of research and development, to this country and thus establish Canada finally in this industry in a position where it can take advantage of the relationship between the Canadian and U.S. dollars. There have already been extensive discussions between Massey-Ferguson personnel and representatives of your Department on a technical basis, which I need not duplicate here; but the concept is to work towards a modest facility, first, assembling dieselized automobile engines and gradually bringing in research facilities and full production to the Q.14 and Q.16 engines with agricultural and vehicular applications, respectively.

In addition, as Massey is an acknowledged world leader in alternative fuel use and research in lower octane fuels, almost all of its continuing activities in these areas could be concentrated in this country. I have spoken at some lengths with Premier Davis about this and he has authorized me to describe him as sympathetic to the proposal and favourably disposed to respond to it. What we have in mind would consist of Government encouragement at both levels, strictly on a project basis, to an enterprise, that would be indisputably to the country's benefit and need not be any more controversial than previous incentives to other companies, including Ford and Stelco, were.

The President of Massey-Ferguson, Mr. Rice, who is chiefly responsible for the operational improvement within the company, will be in touch with you shortly with a view to pursuing these discussions to a successful conclusion before the end of August. With a serious expression of support, even one stopping well short of an outright commitment, from the federal and provincial Governments on this project and, of course, conditional upon the Governments being satisfied that it would be an important economic benefit to Canada and an endeavour that Massey-Ferguson was financially and technologically capable of achieving, I believe that a simultaneous successful reorganization of Massey-Ferguson's capital structure could be carried out and led by the Bank of Commerce and ourselves.

I do not mean, and have no right or intention to imply, that it is the responsibility of Ottawa and Queen's Park to create a more favourable climate for the fulfillment of Massey-Ferguson's capital needs, nor could we co-exist with the idea that the Argus group is, itself, asking for Government assistance, especially on an uneconomical basis. What we are envisioning

continued ....

The Honourable Herbert E. Gray, P.C., M.P.   July 4, 1980.

here is the application of long-established federal and provincial Government policies to assist new industries of conspicuous economic benefit so as to coincide with the definitive and orderly reorganization of the debt and equity structure of Massey-Ferguson.

The Chairman of the Canadian Imperial Bank of Commerce, of which I am also a director, Mr. Harrison, has read my letter to you of March 24 and expressed his support for that concept. He has authorized me to write that his bank, which is presently loaning Massey-Ferguson $295 million U.S. and obviously stands to lose a great deal should there be no resolution of the impending cash insufficiency at Massey-Ferguson, is prepared to participate in a conversion of debt to equity, provided the total of the infusion and conversion is sufficient to put Massey-Ferguson clearly on a sound foundation. I would be prepared to recommend to my associates and shareholders an investment in Massey-Ferguson on approximately the same conditions as those that the Bank of Commerce would seek, though our investment would be of a somewhat different nature, as it would come from a prospective common shareholder rather than from a converting lender.

If there were the evidence of official support for some variation of this diesel project that I have mentioned, in addition to the tangible support of Massey-Ferguson's principal historic shareholder and largest lender, I believe it would be possible to reorganize the vast relationship with its other bankers, moving short-term debt to long-term debt, and removing some of the uncertainties of interest rate fluctuations to enable Massey to plan and borrow, and generally administer itself in a continuous and orthodox manner.

I need not dwell once again upon the incidental benefits to the climate of business/Government relations and in such areas as reducing the perceived inequalities in the Auto Pact and accelerating re-Canadianization of Massey-Ferguson. As a Member of Parliament from Windsor, you would be particularly sensitive to the benefits that this project could bestow upon that area. It is an unsatisfactory and potentially dangerous condition to have this most famous and international Canadian manufacturing company, known and respected throughout the world, continue indefinitely in this perilous state. It is also unnatural, as the company, by any normal criteria, is sound, efficient, financeable, and remains as it has been for many years, pre-eminent in many principal sectors and geographic regions in the farm equipment and diesel engine industries.

Although our companies have practically no financial stake in Massey-Ferguson and accept no responsibility for the temporary deterioration of that company's condition, we would be prepared, in co-operation with those financial institutions and jurisdictions that do have an important stake

continued ....

The Honourable Herbert E. Gray, P.C., M.P.   July 4, 1980.

in Massey-Ferguson and its future, to help in resurrecting it as a great
international company. What we are proposing is economically sustainable,
politically unassailable and entirely consonant with the national interests
and good international reputation of this country.

                                        Yours sincerely,

                                        Conrad M. Black.

CMB/jea
Encls.

Hollinger Argus Limited
10 Toronto Street
Toronto, Canada
M5C 2B7

CONRAD M. BLACK
CHAIRMAN OF THE EXECUTIVE COMMITTEE

August 27, 1980.

The Honourable Herbert E. Gray, P.C., M.P.,
Minister of Industry, Trade and Commerce,
333 West Block,
Parliament Buildings,
OTTAWA, Ontario,
K1A 0A7.

Dear Herb:

As discussions regarding Massey-Ferguson have been intensive recently and circumstances require some important decisions in these matters quite soon, I thought it appropriate to update you on my own activities and observations.

A very detailed examination of Massey-Ferguson's options by the Canadian Imperial Bank of Commerce has confirmed the findings of other studies, including those of the underwriting group and ourselves, that Massey is essentially sound, and with any sort of normal debt:equity ratio, would be stronger than any other company in the industry in the world except John Deere and, possibly, International Harvester. My continued discussions with representative international, financial spokesmen, in particular, Sir Siegmund Warburg, convince me more firmly than ever that if Massey were partially relieved of this Sisyphean burden of debt:equity imbalance traceable to the misjudgments of yesteryear, it could collaborate profitably in consolidation of the international farm equipment and diesel industries.

Despite these optimistic horizons, the acute cash shortages, exacerbated by market conditions that have had a heavy impact upon all of Massey's competitors, including John Deere, and by the current jittery climate among Massey's lenders, have lent the September 4 date a particular significance. As I foresaw in my letter to you of July 4, the third quarter results, like those of all other companies in the industry, will be poor; and, if the announcement of those results is not accompanied by any reference to relief of the debt:equity imbalance, a cascade of loan calls and a general default, followed by the dissolution of Massey-Ferguson in a maze of national receiverships, will, as I also foresaw in my previous letters, be practically unavoidable.

continued .....

The Honourable Herbert E. Gray, P.C., M.P.   August 27, 1980.

Since it is universally agreed that this fate would be both tragic and completely unnecessary, I want you to know what we in the so-called Argus group are prepared to do to avoid it. You will appreciate the delicacy of our position. I have been criticized recently in the financial press (in my opinion, completely unjustly) for failing to take the small investor totally into my confidence about our future corporate reorganization plans. None of our companies presently enjoys any significant cash surplus, though all of them (I naturally exclude Massey-Ferguson from this category) are having excellent years. Accordingly, any undertaking that we might make to participate in a Massey refinancing is a promise to brave what will undoubtedly be extensive skepticism and alarm in the borrowing of large amounts of money by public companies to be reinvested in a rather speculative venture. As you know, we accept no responsibility for Massey-Ferguson's present condition, and, indeed, press a modest claim to much of the credit for the operating improvement that has been wrought in that company in the last two years and which all have recognized.

Notwithstanding the risks inherent in a large investment in Massey-Ferguson at this time, including extreme structural, disclosure and share-holder relations problems, I am prepared to undertake on behalf of our companies on a best efforts basis, but with reasonable confidence of success, to raise and invest in Massey-Ferguson up to $150 million. Any such invest-ment would have to be conditional upon a total equity package, including conversions of debt, of $600 million and upon agreement amongst the parties on certain elemental questions of management and upon assurances that the international lending community would thereafter maintain a composed and supportive attitude, including reasonable concessions about the terms and rates of its loans to Massey-Ferguson.

I believe that the Canadian Imperial Bank of Commerce would be prepared to convert $150 million of debt to equity, and perhaps as much as $200 million. On the pre-condition of such heavy commitments by the Bank of Commerce and ourselves, the underwriting group believes, but is not prepared to guarantee, that it could find up to $100 million on a more or less orthodox rights issue. I have met with representatives of the Government of Ontario, includ-ing Premier Davis, and Mr. Harrison, Chairman of the Canadian Imperial Bank of Commerce, and I will be meeting with the Premier on Friday morning to endeavour to work out a common front and to bring Massey-Ferguson as close as we reasonably can to the over-all figure of $600 million, which we agree would have to be attained to give this investment an acceptable risk: reward ratio.

There have been by Massey-Ferguson management and by me many initiatives designed to explore more traditional possibilities of investment. Within

continued ....

Canada, they have been uniformly unavailing. Those companies with extensive resources, such as Canadian Pacific and Seagrams, are not interested in anything so apparently risky. Other companies less wealthy are undeterred by the risk but have insufficient resources to be helpful, or are prepared to be helpful only for a quid pro quo from elsewhere in our corporate group, particularly Norcen Energy Resources Limited, to which I could not, in fairness to the shareholders of that company, accede. Potential international sources of investment are, as I predicted in my last letter, so mesmerized by the prospects of Massey's insolvency and subsequent purchase of its assets from the receivers that they have produced no serious proposals, though there is no shortage of offers to buy Massey-Ferguson's best assets at a fraction of their real value. Bits and pieces of additional equity might be possible to find among lenders (apart from Canadian Imperial Bank of Commerce), suppliers and a few corporate friends, but the arithmetic still indicates that, without an additional ingredient, the company will fall short of its $600 million objective.

I am aware of Bob Johnstone's opinion that this refinancing can be handled without recourse to the federal Government, but I do not share that opinion. Without, at the very least, an expression of support from Ottawa, even one, as I wrote to you in July, "stopping well short of an outright commitment," or, as I put it in my meeting with Bob Johnstone on August 14, "favourable noises," I doubt that any announcement that the Bank and ourselves, even if joined by the provincial Government, might make, would do more than produce a febrile suspension of two or three months.

As I have repeatedly stated, any federal or provincial Government encouragement to Massey-Ferguson could be on a project basis, envisioning the long-delayed establishment in this country of some serious diesel facility and, thus, contribute simultaneously to the resolution of Massey-Ferguson's two great strategic problems -- hopeless vulnerability to interest rate and currency fluctuations caused by its catastrophic debt:equity ratio and its dependency on a foreign source of engines, albeit a subsidiary.

I have, on a discreet and hypothetical basis, spoken to Joe Clark and Mike Wilson about this subject and I don't think that they would oppose such an initiative.

In any case, it is not for me to evaluate the political implications of this question, though I will try to be as helpful as I can; but I can assure you that we in the Argus group, in contemplating the fate of Massey-Ferguson, will not be motivated by any questions of nostalgia, nor will we accept any heritage of continuing responsibility for this company in which we have a trivial investment that we have publicly written off as having no worth, and which was mismanaged in an era when none of us had any connection with nor influence upon it whatever.

continued ......

The Honourable Herbert E. Gray, P.C., M.P.   August 27, 1980.

If Massey-Ferguson is to be saved from an ignoble and avoidable fate, it will only be by a coalition of effort. Because we know the company well and believe in its prospects and are able to endure the risks involved, risks that deterred virtually every other serious potential investor in the world, we are prepared to play a prominent role in the financial reconstruction of this company. Argus Corporation and its affiliates seek nothing for themselves from any government, and will never under their present management, either ask for preferments from government or attempt to make any government responsible for what is, essentially, a private-sector problem. That Massey-Ferguson has arrived at this embarrassing position is no more the fault or responsibility of government to remedy than it is our's. However, I must advise you in the most unequivocal terms that, unless the federal Government is at least prepared to make "favourable noises" with some possible modest, tangible sequel to them, we should all prepare ourselves for a corporate debacle with no Canadian and few international precedents.

Yours sincerely,

Conrad M. Black.

CMB/jea

P.S. -- Bob Johnstone has just called and told me the Cabinet Committee's
decision. You may wish to have this decision re-considered for
the reasons enumerated above. I have been careful not to beseech
or threaten the federal Government, but you may judge more know-
ledgeably than I the seemliness of the Government's refusal to be
even slightly helpful providing the last straw in the unnecessary
and disastrous collapse of Massey-Ferguson, which will very likely
occur if this decision is not amended.

C.M.B.

Hollinger Argus Limited
10 Toronto Street
Toronto, Canada
M5C 2B7

September 15, 1980.

CONRAD M. BLACK
CHAIRMAN OF THE EXECUTIVE COMMITTEE

The Honourable Herbert E. Gray, P.C., M.P.,
Minister of Industry, Trade and Commerce,
333 West Block,
Parliament Buildings,
OTTAWA, Ontario,
K1A 0A7.

Dear Herb:

At this advanced stage in consideration of the status of
Massey-Ferguson, I hoped it would be useful to you if I debunked, in
writing, some of the myths that have arisen, identified some of the
genuine obstacles that remain, and elaborated the strategy that I recommend for effectively addressing this problem that we have all been
grappling with for some time.

The principal misconceptions that have arisen concern the Argus-
Massey relationship and the nature of the approach that Massey-Ferguson
has made to the federal government. These may be formulated in the
following caricature, most elements of which have been making the rounds
in Ottawa. Black "staked his reputation on Massey;" Argus and Massey
are practically inseparable; the present Argus owners are the continuators
of their forebears who attacked Liberal governments of the past and all
that they stood for. The present managements of both companies are more
or less indistinguishable from Bay Street fat cats of yore who lounged
around the Toronto Club espousing extreme laissez-faire doctrines, and
who are now, by virtue of their own incompetence, "begging" to be "bailed
out" of "another Chrysler" situation.

As you well know, but perhaps not all your colleagues would, the
facts are at drastic variance with this grotesquerie. For 15 years after
the death of W. E. Phillips, as the Argus founders quarrelled, grew old,
moved away, and were otherwise inattentive, Massey-Ferguson was, in good
faith, mismanaged by a coterie of extravagant and unrealistic Americans.
I went into Massey in August 1978, after the most dire warnings from
American lenders about what would happen if drastic measures were not
taken at once. It was obvious to everyone that the company needed a
massive operational wringing-out followed by a comprehensive refinancing.
With no illusions about the gravity of the situation, I embarked upon the
first stage, which Mr. Rice and his new management team have gone a long
way toward completing.

continued ......

The Honourable Herbert E. Gray, P.C., M.P.   September 15, 1980.

However, to anyone who was interested, I made it clear that it was my principal objective to transform the Argus group from a "passive and sclerotic holding" operation (to cite my letter to you of July 4), exercising a tenuous control through token shareholdings in low-yield industries, into an owner-managed, resource-based operating company. Massey-Ferguson, despite its fame and size, was labour and capital intensive, very vulnerable, and technically almost insolvent anyway, and was an uncertain fit. But whatever happens, it has been a great company, was worth the effort, and deserved no less.

As for the heritage of the Argus founders, it is, on the whole, a great one, which we do seek to uphold rather than renounce. However, the founders of Argus Corporation were by-passed by time and events, as surely in political as in commercial matters, and unlike them the present owners are not uncomfortable with the general trajectory of contemporary affairs.

In any case, what Massey-Ferguson is now seeking is an investment in and not a bail-out of a company that has in the last two years been re-made fundamentally sound. What Argus seeks, on Massey's behalf, is even more modest and further removed from mendicancy. All we ever asked for was "favourable noises" or an "expression of support stopping well short of an outright commitment." I have apparently failed, up to now, to convince the federal government that I was not trying to mousetrap it into an open-ended underwriting of Massey, and to convince Massey-Ferguson itself that such noises could, in themselves, possibly be sufficient. I will expand on why I think that they might be sufficient after dealing with some of the other obstacles immediately ahead of us.

The reservations most commonly heard and uttered by my informants in Ottawa are that the federal government is unconvinced that the private sector has been exhausted as a source of support; that if the deal is good enough for us to be in it, why isn't the rest of the private sector crowding forward, money in hand; that any federal support would inevitably give Argus Corporation a risk-free sleigh-ride to undue enrichment; that the federal government can't really afford to extend assistance right now; that such assistance would be a bad and dangerous precedent; that Massey-Ferguson is not really a Canadian company in terms of employment, production, research, and exports; that no amount of money would stabilize a company with such a spendthrift history; and that there is insufficient political support for any aid to Massey.

I submit that most of these reservations would vanish if the federal (and Ontario) governments made only conditional statements of indefinite support. "Favourable noises" will offend no principles of economy or precedent, and not even someone as acquisitive as I am

continued ....

The Honourable Herbert E. Gray, P.C., M.P.   September 15, 1980.

apparently thought by some in Ottawa to be,could line his pockets with air.
As for the venturesomeness of the private sector, you might be the unwitting
victims of some of its rugged individualistic propaganda. Massey-Ferguson
has a terrible track record as an investment and is now in desperate straits.
We know Massey-Ferguson well and would be willing to invest in it under
conditions no less rigorous than those the government itself would impose.
It is asking a lot of the private investor to put much faith in a company
whose history is so strewn with broken promises, disappointments and poor
management decisions.

     The first condition for any participation from us, even more impor-
tant than the size of the ultimate equity package, is a massive reorganization of the worldwide lending arrangements of Massey-Ferguson. We are
violently opposed to any proposal that smacks of raising money in this
country to bail out a bunch of foreign lenders. The international lending
community, which has most at stake in Massey-Ferguson, should take the lead
in solving this problem. Only after this drastic prerequisite has been met
would it be in order for anyone to look to us, let alone you, to produce
tangible support. This procedure would satisfy your well-founded concern
about "the adequacy of private sector support" and would entail a further
drastic retrenchment of the company's manufacturing operations towards or
within Canada, the U.S.A., the U.K. and France, finally making Massey-
Ferguson manageable and comparatively invulnerable to currency fluctuations
and political upheavals. If this were done sensibly, asset and debt-equity
ratios would be greatly alleviated, and might demystify Massey-Ferguson to
the point that the private sector would not be so intimidated at the prospect of investing in it.

     I referred to the fears that have been expressed in Ottawa that
Massey-Ferguson is not really a Canadian company; that it couldn't be made
whole with any amount of money, given its egregious history of cash consumption; and that this is not a politically popular cause. I have repeatedly said that any assistance could be on a project basis to continue the
Canadianization of the company, which is advisable for business as well as
nationalistic reasons. A great deal of work has been done on a diesel project, and I continue to regard this as most promising and uncontroversial,
providing Massey-Ferguson's overall position can be stabilized. The scaling
down of the company and conversion of debt to equity would regularize the
cash flow and improve the yield, otherwise none of us should seriously consider investing in it.

     Massey-Ferguson is certainly regarded throughout the world as
Canadian, and is probably the most familiar Canadian symbol of all in an
absolute majority of countries of the world.

                              continued ....

The Honourable Herbert E. Gray, P.C., M.P.   September 15, 1980.

        You are better qualified than I to judge the political aspects
of this, but I wouldn't underestimate the clangour that would be set up
if this company sank without a ripple in the complete absence of any pro-
fessions of serious government concern. I do re-emphasize that under
no circumstances that are now conceivable to me will Argus Corporation or
I seek to blame Massey-Ferguson's fate on the federal government. As I
wrote to you on August 27, "That Massey-Ferguson has arrived at this
embarrassing position is no more the fault or responsibility of government to remedy than it is our's."

        The strategy I suggest consists of some such comment from the
federal and provincial governments as that they are favourably disposed
to assist in the refinancing of Massey-Ferguson if such assistance proves
necessary, after the fulfilment of various conditions," starting with the
reorganization of the company's international lending relationships and
including whatever is necessary to allay Ottawa's other misgivings. Your
statement need not go much further than a deferral of the decision that
your release of September 8 indicated would come by the end of September.

        With this semblance of some sort of common front of potential
investors including the federal and provincial governments, the principal
lender and shareholder, and a large underwriting group, Massey-Ferguson
could seek a massive reorganization of its lending arrangements from a
position of comparative strength (eliminating once and for all specious
similarities with the Chrysler situation).

        I would envision that Massey-Ferguson could pursue its objectives
in the following sequence:

        First, it would be necessary to make a standfast agreement between
the Canadian, American, and British banks, to which it might be possible to
add some or all of the French banks. Barclay's, who are at the moment the
world's most profitable bank, are Massey's second lender after the C.I.B.C.
I spoke with the Vice-Chairman of Barclay's, Sir Richard Pease, in Toronto
last week, and I think his bank and the other British banks would co-
operate. The American banks would be trickier, as there are more of them,
better secured, but I think it could be managed. The Canadian banks (the
Royal, Montreal, and the Toronto-Dominion between them are now lending
Massey-Ferguson about U.S. $65 million), should not pose too much of a problem.

        Second, these banks would enable Massey-Ferguson to cover its
international loans that are supported by a parent company (Massey-Ferguson
Limited) guaranty, apart from the Canadian, American and British loans so
guaranteed. As the cash requirements of this industry fall off in the
autumn, the back-up facility might not much exceed U.S. $150 million in
November.

        Third, there would then be hard bargaining with the secondary

                                          continued ....

The Honourable Herbert E. Gray, P.C., M.P.   September 15, 1980.

banks in peripheral countries, many of whom would be invited to take some form of Massey-Ferguson paper, or help themselves to some of the company's local assets, which would in some instances, such as Argentina, be redundant to Massey-Ferguson's continuing operations anyway. Some of these institutions would be rather roughly, though honourably treated. This sort of procedure is always distasteful, but in these circumstances there is no alternative, and there is ample precedent for this in the financial industry. What we are envisioning is a reasonably standard, and even comparatively painless, debt reorganization.

Fourth, there would be a partial conversion of debt to equity and liberalization of rates and extension of terms on the part of the continuing lenders. The Canadian Imperial Bank of Commerce could take the lead in this phase.

Fifth, Massey-Ferguson could then return to the equity group who could examine the company's needs more clearly than is the case today. I am in some sympathy with your view that those who have a stake in Massey now should take the lead in refinancing the company, before repairing to us. On this basis, government assistance would be an absolutely last resort, could be minimal, and could, once more, be on the constructive and uncontroversial basis of support for this much-discussed diesel project. The government could justly take some credit for the lenders' concessions, both by having required them as a precondition for assistance, and by having enabled them by its favourable statement of conditional support.

In résumé, the "coalition of efforts" that I wrote about on August 27 would emanate from Massey-Ferguson in concentric circles to include the C.I.B.C., the Argus group, the federal and provincial governments, the Canadian, British and American lenders, until the perimeter is extensive enough that Massey-Ferguson could withdraw within it and rationalize its affairs in an orderly fashion. The company would be revolutionized and partially Canadianized, as we would wish to stipulate in the conditions set for our participation in the new equity issue.

Without the proverbial favourable noises from the federal government, Massey-Ferguson would not be able to seek such rearrangements, except on a basis of unabashed supplication. The withholding of any such comment by the governments at this stage, after all the publicity that has been given to Massey's request, would oblige the other elements, including Argus Corporation, to qualify their support so thoroughly that Massey would have to meet its lenders denuded of any semblance of support or assurance of continuity and would have nothing to show them but a corporate begging bowl. Foreign lenders would be particularly grateful to note federal and Ontario collaboration, after the publicity federal-provincial differences have received abroad.

continued ....

The Honourable Herbert E. Gray, P.C., M.P.   September 15, 1980.

     I would be remiss if I did not mention reports that elements of the Cabinet and senior civil service in Ottawa would be well-disposed to assist Massey-Ferguson only if "Black crawls up the steps of Parliament and begs." In writing to you, I need not dwell again on all the effort Argus Corporation and I personally have made to help Massey-Ferguson through this inherited crisis despite our prodigious lack of enthusiasm and complete blamelessness for it. Under absolutely no circumstances will we inflict further embarrassment upon ourselves than we have already done by maintaining some appearance of solidarity between Massey-Ferguson and ourselves, which is all that has kept Massey afloat for the last two years while its operations have been so impressively streamlined.

     I have been accused both of abandoning Massey-Ferguson and of being inseparable from its anticipated collapse. Both allegations are false. My associates and I took on the task of trying to be helpful to Massey-Ferguson at the most unpromising moment in the entire history of that company out of respect for its past and with a vision of its future that lingers yet, unextinguished. We are loath to relinquish that task. All that now stands between Massey-Ferguson and a gruesome fate are the prospects of favourable gestures from you and of tangible evidences of corporate kinship from us. I have no right or intention to imply either equivalence or intimacy between the Argus group and the federal government, but if you are unable to offer even tentative verbal encouragement to Massey-Ferguson, we cannot honestly maintain any strong prospect of material support for it. With your qualified collaboration, and our support, this great company may yet emerge strengthened from its recent and present ordeal. In the absence of both, an international commercial disaster could be unavoidable. Surely we can do better than that.

Yours sincerely,

Conrad M. Black.

CMB/jea

Appendix D

This list shows how the officers of Argus Corporation succeeded one another from its formation in 1945.

Name	Period	Comment
	Chairman of the Board	
W.E. Phillips	Nov.1945–Dec. 1964	Died Dec. 26, 1964
E.P. Taylor	June 1969–March 1971	Retired March, 1971
John A. McDougald	March 1971–March 1978	Died March 15, 1978
Maxwell C.G. Meighen	April 1978–July 1978	Resigned in July 1978
Nelson M. Davis	July 1978–March 1979	Died March 13, 1979
Conrad M. Black	June 1979–	
	Deputy Chairman of the Board	
A. Bruce Matthews	July 1978–June 1979	Resigned in June 1979
	President	
E.P. Taylor	Nov. 1945–June 1969	Elected Chairman, June 1969
John A. McDougald	June 1969–March 1978	Died March 15, 1978
A. Bruce Matthews	April 1978–July 1978	Resigned in July 1978
Conrad M. Black	July 1978–June 1979	Elected Chairman, June 1979
G. Montegu Black	June 1979–	
	Chairman of the Executive Committee	
E.P. Taylor	Nov. 1945–Jan. 1964	
John A. McDougald	Jan. 1964–June 1969	Elected President, June 1969
Maxwell C.G. Meighen	June 1969–April 1978	Elected Chairman, April 1978
A. Bruce Matthews	April 1978–July 1978	Elected Deputy Chairman, July 1978
Conrad M. Black	July 1978–	
	Vice-President and Managing Director	
M. Wallace McCutcheon	Nov. 1945–Aug. 1962	Resigned to join federal Cabinet

Name	Period	Comment
	Executive Vice-President	
A. Bruce Matthews	June 1969–April 1978	Elected President, April 1978
Alex E. Barron	April 1978–July 1978	Resigned in July 1978
Dixon S. Chant	July 1978–	
	Vice-Presidents	
John A. McDougald	Aug. 1962–June 1969	Elected President, June 1969
A. Bruce Matthews	Sept. 1964–June 1969	Elected Executive Vice-President, June 1969
Maxwell C.G. Meighen	June 1969–April 1978	Elected Chairman, April 1978
George M. Black, Jr.	June 1969–June 1976	Died June 29, 1976
H.N.R. Jackman	July 1978–	
Fredrik S. Eaton	Feb. 1979–	
F. David Radler	June 1979–	
John R. Finlay	Sept. 1980–	

Appendix E

The private dinner given by Hollinger Argus Limited at the Toronto Club after its annual meeting has become the Canadian Establishment's yearly caucus, with not only the list of guests but the tables at which they are placed providing clues to its pecking order. The roster (which includes some local dignitaries) and seating plan are compiled by Conrad Black in the early spring of each year. Here is the list of those invited to the 1981 Hollinger dinner, held on May 7.

Ackroyd, Jack
Chief of Police
Toronto

Aird, Hon. John B.
Lieutenant-Governor of Ontario
Toronto

Albino, George R.
President and CEO
Rio Algom Ltd.
Toronto

Allan, John D.
President
Stelco Inc.
Toronto

Anderson, Robert F.
Chairman
Iron Ore Company of Canada
Cleveland

Archer, Maurice
Chairman
Archer, Seaden & Associates
Brome, Que.

Asper, I.H.
Chairman and CEO
CanWest Capital Corp.
Winnipeg

Ayre, Lewis H.M.
Chairman and President
Ayre & Sons Ltd.
St. John's

Barford, Ralph M.
President
Valleydene Corp. Ltd.
Toronto

Barkwell, Donald D.
Senior Vice-President
Norcen Energy Resources Ltd.
Calgary

Barron, Alex E.
President
Canadian General Investments Ltd.
Toronto

Barry, Hon. Leo
Minister of Mines and Energy
Newfoundland
St. John's

Bassett, Douglas
President and CEO
Baton Broadcasting Inc.
Toronto

Bassett, John W.H.
Chairman
Baton Broadcasting Inc.
Toronto

Bata, Thomas J.
President
Bata Ltd.
Toronto

Battle, Edward G.
President and CEO
Norcen Energy Resources Ltd.
Toronto

Beaubien, Philippe de Gaspé
Chairman and CEO
Télémedia Communications Ltée
Montreal

Bélanger, Michel F.
President and CEO
National Bank of Canada
Montreal

Birks, G. Drummond
President and CEO
Henry Birks & Sons Ltd.
Montreal

Birks, H. Jonathan
President
Henry Birks & Sons (Montreal)
  Ltd.
Montreal

Black, Conrad M.
Vice-Chairman
Hollinger Argus Ltd.
Toronto

Black, G. Montegu, III
President
Hollinger Argus Ltd.
Toronto

Blair, S. Robert
President and CEO
Nova
Calgary

Bolton, Thomas G.
Deputy Chairman and CEO
Dominion Stores Ltd.
Toronto

Bonnycastle, Richard A.N.
Chairman and President
Cavendish Investing Group
Calgary

Bonus, John L.
Managing Director
Mining Association of Canada
Ottawa

Bovey, Edmund C.
Chairman
Norcen Energy Resources Ltd.
Toronto

Brinkos, Joseph S.
Lawyer
Toronto

Bronfman, Charles R.
Chairman of Executive Committee
Seagram Co. Ltd.
Montreal

Burbidge, F.S.
President
Canadian Pacific Ltd.
Montreal

Burns, Latham
Chairman
Burns Fry Ltd.
Toronto

Byrne, J.C.
President and CEO
Discovery Mines Ltd.
Toronto

Campbell, Donald G.
Chairman and CEO
Maclean Hunter Ltd.
Toronto

Carter, G. Emmett
Cardinal
Archbishop of Toronto
Toronto

Chant, Dixon S.
Executive Vice-President
Hollinger Argus Ltd.
Toronto

Coleman, John H.
President
JHC Associates Ltd.
Toronto

Cooper, Marsh A.
Former president
Falconbridge Nickel Mines Ltd.
Toronto

Courtney, James E.
Executive Vice-President
Hanna Mining Co.
Cleveland

Courtois, E. Jacques
Partner
Courtois, Clarkson, Parsons &
  Tetrault
Montreal

Coutts, James A.
Principal Secretary to the
  Prime Minister
Ottawa

322

Cowan, C.G.
Secretary
Hollinger Argus Ltd.
Toronto

Crang, J.H.
Stockbroker
Toronto

Creighton, J. Douglas
Publisher
Toronto Sun
Toronto

Culver, David M.
President and CEO
Alcan Aluminium Ltd.
Montreal

Daniel, C. William
President and CEO
Shell Canada Ltd.
Toronto

Davey, Hon. Keith
The Senate
Ottawa

Davis, Glen W.
President
N.M. Davis Corp. Ltd.
Toronto

Davis, Hon. William G.
Premier of Ontario
Toronto

Desmarais, Paul
Chairman and CEO
Power Corp. of Canada
Montreal

Dewar, John S.
President
Union Carbide Canada Ltd.
Toronto

Dobrin, Melvyn A.
Chairman and CEO
Steinberg Inc.
Montreal

Dunlap, David M.
President
Taper Manufacturing Ltd.
Newmarket, Ont.

Dunlap, J. Moffat
Investor
King, Ont.

Early, Donald C.
Greenshields Inc.
Toronto

Eaton, Fredrik S.
President
Eaton's of Canada Ltd.
Toronto

Eaton, George R.
Executive Vice-President
Eaton's of Canada Ltd.
Toronto

Eaton, John Craig
Chairman
Eaton's of Canada Ltd.
Toronto

Eaton, Thor E.
Vice-President
Eaton's of Canada Ltd.
Toronto

Eby, Peter B.M.
Vice-Chairman
Burns Fry Ltd.
Toronto

Edmison, H.H.
Secretary
Argus Corp. Ltd.
Toronto

Eggleton, Arthur
Mayor
Toronto

Elliott, R. Fraser
Partner
Stikeman, Elliott, Robarts &
  Bowman
Toronto

Eyton, J. Trevor
President and CEO
Brascan Ltd.
Toronto

Fairley, A.L., Jr.
Former president
Hollinger Mines Ltd.
Birmingham, Alabama

Fell, Anthony S.
President and CEO
Dominion Securities Ltd.
Toronto

Finlay, J.R.
Vice-President
Argus Corp. Ltd.
Toronto

Finlay, P.C.
Chairman and CEO
Hollinger Argus Ltd.
Toronto

Fisher, Gordon
President
Southam Inc.
Toronto

Frazee, Rowland C.
Chairman and CEO
Royal Bank of Canada,
Montreal

Fullerton, Donald
Vice-Chairman and President
Canadian Imperial Bank of
  Commerce
Toronto

Gallagher, John E.P.
Chairman and CEO
Dome Petroleum Ltd.
Calgary

Gardiner, George R.
President
Gardiner, Watson Ltd.
Toronto

Geren, Richard
Executive Vice-President
Iron Ore Company of Canada
Sept-Iles, Que.

Gerstein, Irving R.
President
Peoples Jewellers Ltd.
Toronto

Gillespie, Hon. Alastair
Chairman
Carling O'Keefe Ltd.
Toronto

Godfrey, Paul V.
Chairman
Metropolitan Toronto Council
Toronto

de Grandpré, A. Jean
Chairman and CEO
Bell Canada
Montreal

Gray, Hon. Herbert E.
Minister of Industry, Trade and
  Commerce
Ottawa

Hampson, H. Anthony
President and CEO
Canada Development Corp.
Toronto

Harrison, Russell
Chairman and CEO
Canadian Imperial Bank of
  Commerce
Toronto

Heller, Frederick
Senior Vice-President
Hanna Mining Co.
Cleveland

Hewitt, Robert
Chairman and President
Hewitt Equipment Ltd.
Montreal

Honderich, Beland H.
Chairman and CEO
Torstar Corp.
Toronto

Hughes, J.M.
Executive Director
Ontario Mining Association
Toronto

Humphrey, George M., II
Senior Vice-President
Hanna Mining Co.
Cleveland

Jackman, H.N.R.
Chairman
Empire Life Insurance Co.
Toronto

Jackson, Allen C.
President
Dominion Stores Ltd.
Toronto

Juneau, Pierre
Under-Secretary of State
Ottawa

Keenan, P.J.
President and CEO
Patiño NV
Toronto

Kilbourne, William T.
Vice-President and Secretary
Norcen Energy Resources Ltd.
Toronto

Knowles, H.J.
Chairman
Ontario Securities Commission
Toronto

Knudsen, C. Calvert
President and CEO
MacMillan Bloedel Ltd.
Vancouver

Kolber, E. Leo
President
Cemp Investments Ltd.
Montreal

Lalonde, Hon. Marc
Minister of Energy, Mines and
  Resources
Ottawa

Langan, Fred
Commentator
CBC
Toronto

Lebrun, François
Quebec Delegate-General
Toronto

Leitch, John D.
President
Upper Lakes Shipping Ltd.
Toronto

Livingstone, James G.
President
Imperial Oil Ltd.
Toronto

Lodge, Lorne K.
Chairman and President
IBM Canada Ltd.
Don Mills, Ont.

Logan, Frank H.
Chairman
Dominion Securities Ltd.
Toronto

Lutsky, Irvin
Financial writer
Toronto Star
Toronto

MacCulloch, P.C.
President
Selco Inc.
Toronto

Macdonald, Hon. Donald S.
Partner
McCarthy & McCarthy
Toronto

Macdonald, R.D.
Former chief geologist
Labrador Mining & Exploration
  Co. Ltd.
Toronto

MacDougall, Hartland M.
Executive Vice-President
Bank of Montreal
Toronto

McCain, H. Harrison
Chairman
McCain Foods Ltd.
Florenceville, N.B.

McCarthy, Leighton
President and CEO
McCarthy Securities Ltd.
Toronto

McCloskey, Paul H.
President
Madsen Red Lake Gold Mines Ltd.
Toronto

McCurdy, H.T.
President
Standard Broadcasting Corp.
Toronto

McCutcheon, Frederic Y.
President
Arachnae Management Ltd.
Markham, Ont.

McCutcheon, James W.
Partner
Shipley, Righton & McCutcheon
Toronto

McIntosh, D.A.
Partner
Fraser & Beatty
Toronto

McKeough, W. Darcy
President
Union Gas Ltd.
Chatham, Ont.

McKillip, John H.
Deputy Minister of Mines
Newfoundland
St. John's

McMartin, Allen A.
Honorary director,
Hollinger Argus Ltd.
Bermuda

McMartin, Duncan Roy
Hollinger shareholder
Bermuda

McQueen, R.M.
Managing Editor
Maclean's
Toronto

Maloney, Douglas W.
Chairman
Continental Bank of Canada
Toronto

Mara, George E.
Chairman
Jannock Ltd.
Toronto

Matthews, A. Bruce
President
Matthews & Co. Inc.
Toronto

Matthews, Beverley
Partner
McCarthy & McCarthy
Toronto

Medland, C. Edward
President and CEO
Wood Gundy Ltd.
Toronto

Meighen, Michael A.
Vice-President
TV Guide Inc.
Toronto

Meisel, John
Chairman
CRTC
Ottawa

Michener, Rt. Hon. D. Roland
Former Governor General
Toronto

Miller, Hon. Frank S.
Treasurer of Ontario
Toronto

Monast, André
Partner
Létourneau & Stein
Quebec

Mulholland, William D.
President and CEO
Bank of Montreal
Montreal

Mulroney, M. Brian
President
Iron Ore Company of Canada
Montreal

Newman, Peter C.
Editor
Maclean's
Toronto

Nichols, Lawrence M.
President
Bushnell Communications Ltd.
Ottawa

Nickels, Carl E., Jr.
Executive Vice-President
Hanna Mining Co.
Cleveland

Nixon, Peter M.
President
Algoma Steel Corp. Ltd.
Sault Ste Marie, Ont.

Osler, Gordon P.
Chairman
Stanton Pipes Ltd.
Toronto

Ostiguy, Jean P.W.
Chairman
Greenshields Inc.
Montreal

Pearce, R.C.
Chairman
Northern Miner Press Ltd.
Toronto

Peckford, Hon. A. Brian
Premier of Newfoundland
St. John's

Perry, E.A.
Former general manager
Hollinger Mines
Toronto

Phillips, John C.
Chairman
Gulf Canada Ltd.
Toronto

Pitfield, P. Michael
Clerk of the Privy Council
Ottawa

Powis, Alfred
Chairman and President
Noranda Mines Ltd.
Toronto

Radler, F. David
President
Sterling Newspapers Ltd.
Vancouver

Redpath, James B.
Director
Dome Mines Ltd.
Toronto

Reichmann, Albert
President
Olympia & York Developments Ltd.
Toronto

Reichmann, Paul
Executive Vice-President
Olympia & York Developments Ltd.
Toronto

Rice, Victor A.
Chairman, President, and CEO
Massey-Ferguson Ltd.
Toronto

Richardson, George T.
President
James Richardson & Sons Ltd.
Winnipeg

Riley, Conrad S.
Chairman
Dominion Tanners Ltd.
Winnipeg

Riley, C.S., III,
General Manager
Wickett & Craig Ltd.
Toronto

Riley, Ronald T.
Vice-President
Canadian Pacific Ltd.
Montreal

Ritchie, C.E.
Chairman and CEO
Bank of Nova Scotia
Toronto

Robarts, Hon. John P.
Partner
Stikeman, Elliott, Robarts &
    Bowman
Toronto

Roberts, Dr. Kenneth A.
Chairman and CEO
Goldale Investments Ltd.
Toronto

Rogers, Edward S.
Vice-Chairman and CEO
Canadian Cablesystems Ltd.
Toronto

Roman, Stephen B.
Chairman and CEO
Denison Mines Ltd.
Toronto

Rohmer, Richard
Lawyer/author
Toronto

Ross, C. Bruce
Executive Vice-President
Hollinger Argus Ltd.
Toronto

Ryan, Patrick A.
Partner
Thorne Riddell
Toronto

Sarlos, Andrew
President
HCI Holdings Ltd.
Toronto

Schmitt, D.E.G.
President
Pamour Porcupine Mines Ltd.
Toronto

Scott, Fenton
Vice-President
Esso Minerals Canada
Toronto

Sinclair, Ian D.
Chairman and CEO
Canadian Pacific Ltd.
Montreal

Skerrett, G.D.F.
Partner
Aird & Berlis
Toronto

Stock, V.N.
President and CEO
Canada Packers Inc.
Toronto

Stoik, John L.
President and CEO
Gulf Canada Ltd.
Toronto

Stubbins, John B.
Chief Engineer
Labrador Mining & Exploration
    Co. Ltd.
Toronto

Taschereau, Malcolm
President
Dome Mines Ltd.
Toronto

Taylor, E.P.
Lyford Cay Club
Nassau

Taylor, Howard
Partner
Deloitte Haskins & Sells
Toronto

Thomson, Kenneth R.
Chairman and CEO
Thomson Newspapers Ltd.
Toronto

Thomson, Richard M.
Chairman and CEO
Toronto-Dominion Bank
Toronto

Timmins, Gerald L., Jr.
Investor
Toronto

Timmins, Robert N.
Vice-Chairman
Burns Fry & Timmins Inc.
New York

Tomenson, F. Rogers
Director
Tomenson Saunders Whitehead Ltd.
Toronto

Tory, John A.
President
Thomson Corp. Ltd.
Toronto

328

Toyne, William E.
President
Tomenson Saunders Whitehead Ltd.
Toronto

Turner, Hon. John N.
Partner
McMillan, Binch
Toronto

Upham, M.A.
Chairman
Kilborn Engineering Ltd.
Toronto

Van Wielingen, G.A.
Chairman and CEO
Sulpetro Ltd.
Calgary

Wadsworth, J.P.R.
Chairman
Confederation Life Insurance Co.
Toronto

Ward, Douglas H.
Honorary chairman
Dominion Securities Ltd.
Toronto

Ward, Walter G.
Retired chairman
Algoma Steel Corp. Ltd.
Sault Ste Marie, Ont.

Warren, Trumbull
Chairman and President
Rheem Canada Ltd.
Hamilton

Webster, Donald C.
President
Helix Investments Ltd.
Toronto

Webster, Lorne C.
Chairman and CEO
Prenor Group Ltd.
Montreal

Weston, W. Galen
Chairman and President
George Weston Ltd.
Toronto

White, Joseph F.
Exploration Manager
Labrador Mining & Exploration
   Co. Ltd.
Toronto

White, Peter Gerald
President
Peter G. White Management Ltd.
London, Ont.

White, Wendell F.
Vice-President and Treasurer
Laborador Mining & Exploration
   Co. Ltd.
Toronto

Willmot, D.G.
Chairman
Molson Companies Ltd.
Rexdale, Ontario

Wilder, W.P.
President and CEO
Hiram Walker–Consumers Home
   Ltd.
Toronto

Wolfe, Ray D.
Chairman and President
Oshawa Group Ltd.
Toronto

Acknowledgements

Anonymity is all too often the price of candour, and since some of the assessments in this book involved off-the-record comments, I cannot acknowledge all my sources by name. Where no reference to a printed source is indicated in the text, quotations are from my interviews with Conrad Black, who did nothing either to encourage or to suppress this project, having seen the text only after publication day.

A list of all those kind enough to help me with the facts and ideas contained in this book would be too lengthy to reproduce here. But I gratefully acknowledge the assistance of the following:

Robert F. Anderson, chairman, president, and CEO, Hanna Mining Co.; Israel H. Asper, chairman and CEO, CanWest Capital Corp.; Hon. Ronald Atkey, former Minister of Employment and Immigration; Nick Auf der Maur, municipal politician and columnist, Montreal; Alex Barron, president, Canadian General Investments Ltd.; Douglas G. Bassett, president and CEO, Baton Broadcasting Inc.; John W. Bassett, chairman, Baton Broadcasting; Johnny F. Bassett, entrepreneur; Jonathan Birks, president, Henry Birks & Sons (Montreal) Ltd.; Conrad Black; the late George M. Black; G. Montegu Black III; John Bosley, M.P., Don Valley West; Robert Bothwell, professor of history, Trinity College, University of Toronto; Edmund Bovey, former chairman, Norcen Energy Resources Ltd.; Rudolph P. Bratty, partner, Gambin, Bratty; G. Allan Burton, former chairman, Simpsons Ltd.; J.G. Campbell, former president, Canadian Breweries Ltd.; G. Emmett Cardinal Carter, Archbishop of Toronto; Dixon Chant, executive vice-president, Argus Corp.; Michael Cochrane, former vice-president (administration), Massey-Ferguson Ltd.; Peter Cotton, interior decorator; Hon. David Crombie, former Mayor of Toronto; Michael de Pencier, publisher, *Toronto Life*; Ian Dowie, former president, Canadian Breweries; Donald Early, investment counsellor, Greenshields Inc.; Fredrik Eaton, president, Eaton's of Canada Ltd.; John Craig Eaton, chairman, Eaton's of Canada; Harry Edmison, secretary and director, Argus Corp.; Norman Elder, explorer-adventurer; Harry Elton, CBC Radio host, Ottawa; Rev. John Erb, rector, St. Michael and All Angels, Toronto; Albert L. Fairley, Jr., former president, Hollinger Mines Ltd.; Susan Farkas, producer, CBC, New York; Scott Fennell, former parliamentary secretary to the Minister of Communications; John Finlay, vice-president, Argus

Corp.; P.C. Finlay, senior partner, Holden, Murdoch & Finlay; John Fraser, columnist, *Globe and Mail*; Hon. Heward Grafftey, former Minister of State for Science and Technology; Ronald Graham, former senior producer, CBC's "The Canadian Establishment"; Angela Greig, vice-principal, Thornton Hall; Naomi Griffiths, Dean of Arts, Carleton University; the late Charles L. Gundy, chairman, Wood Gundy Ltd.; Peter Harris, former chairman, A.E. Ames & Co. Ltd.; Derek Hayes, former secretary, Massey-Ferguson; George Hayhurst, store owner, Canadian Tire Corp. Ltd., Danforth Avenue, Toronto; Mrs. Cecil E. Hedstrom, real estate agent; Henry N.R. Jackman, chairman, Empire Life Insurance Co.; the late Igor Kaplan; Laurier LaPierre, TV commentator and Quebec historian; Philip B. Lind, senior vice-president, Rogers Cablesystems Inc.; Leighton McCarthy, president, McCarthy Securities Ltd.; Jim McCutcheon, partner, Shibley, Righton & McCutcheon; the late John A. McDougald, chairman, Argus Corp.; Mrs. J.A. McDougald; Donald McIntosh, partner, Fraser & Beatty; Brian McKenna, CBC producer, Montreal; George MacLaren, publisher, *Sherbrooke Daily Record*; Roy MacLaren, parliamentary secretary to the Minister of Energy, Mines and Resources; Maj.-Gen. Bruce Matthews, former president, Argus Corp.; Col. Maxwell Meighen, chairman, Canadian General Investments; Michael Meighen, vice-president, *TV Guide*; Brian Mulroney, president, Iron Ore Co. of Canada; Carl Nickels, executive vice-president, Hanna Mining; Gordon Osler, chairman, Stanton Pipes Ltd.; Steven Otto, former parliamentary secretary to the Minister of Supply and Services; John Parkin, architect; Richard Pogue, partner, Jones, Day, Reavis & Pogue, Cleveland; David Radler, Ravelston partner and president, Sterling Newspapers; Victor Rice, chairman, president, and CEO, Massey-Ferguson; Conrad S. Riley, president, United Canadian Shares Ltd.; Jeremy Riley, educator; Ronald T. Riley, vice-president (corporate), Canadian Pacific Ltd.; T. Stewart Ripley, former president, Metropolitan Trust Co.; Father Jonathan Robinson, pastor, Holy Family Church, Toronto; Edward S. Rogers, vice-chairman and CEO, Rogers Cablesystems Inc.; George Rogerson, Mayor of West Bolton, Quebec; Gerald Schwartz, president, CanWest Capital Corp.; Terence Sheard, counsel, Lash Johnston; Ainslie Shuve, former president, Crown Trust Co.; David Smith, parliamentary assistant to the President of the Privy Council and the Minister of Justice; Brian Stewart, CBC television correspondent, Ottawa; John Strauch, partner, Jones, Day, Reavis & Pogue; Charles Taylor, author; A.A. Thornbrough, former CEO, Massey-Ferguson; Charles W. Tisdall, public relations consultant; Brig. W.C. Wallace, an associate of the late Eric Phillips; Samuel Wakim, Toronto lawyer; Douglas Ward, honorary director, Dominion Securities Ames Ltd.; the Duke of Wellington, corporate director; Peter White, Ravelston partner; Helen West, assistant to Robert Anderson, Hanna Mining; and Donald G. Willmot, chairman, Molson Companies Ltd.

My thanks are also due to Lloyd Hodgkinson, head of the Magazine Division at Maclean Hunter, and to Jim Miller, publisher of *Maclean's*, for allowing me the freedom and opportunity to write this book. I must express my gratitude to Michael Levine, an extraordinary lawyer and literary *agent provocateur* whose wisdom I thoroughly appreciate. I certainly thank Christine Garment for her unflagging help in every phase of the manuscript's preparation, as well as Ann Young and Bev DuBrule for their secretarial assistance.

It is customary for authors to duly note the loving encouragement or benign neglect of spouses. I acknowledge instead, as in two of my previous volumes, the valuable professional contribution of my wife, Camilla, as in-house editor and ever-present prose repair person.

This book owes its existence also to many others not mentioned here; only the responsibility for its imperfections is fully my own.

August 15, 1982   P.C.N.

Index

339

342

348

ABOUT THE AUTHOR

PETER C. NEWMAN is the author whose pioneering studies of power have turned The Canadian Establishment into a household phrase. His seven earlier books have sold a million copies in their various editions and translations.

John Kenneth Galbraith hailed the first volume in the Establishment series as "the best guide anyone will ever encounter to Canada." Social historian William Kilbourn described it as "a Canadian Who's Who as it might exist, if not in the mind of God, then in that of a Canadian Balzac or Scott Fitzgerald."

The recipient of half a dozen of Canada's most coveted journalism awards, Newman has been editor in chief of the country's largest newspaper, the *Toronto Star,* and most influential magazine, *Maclean's,* which he transformed into the country's first national newsweekly. He resigned the magazine's editorship in the summer of 1982 so that he could devote more time to his books and other literary ventures.

He is currently at work on a major popular history of the Hudson's Bay Company as well as continuing his probes of the Canadian Establishment.

SEAL BOOKS

Offers you a list of outstanding fiction, non-fiction and classics of
Canadian literature in paperback by Canadian authors, available at all good bookstores throughout Canada.

The Canadian Establishment	Peter C. Newman
A Jest of God	Margaret Laurence
Lady Oracle	Margaret Atwood
The Snow Walker	Farley Mowat
St. Urbain's Horseman	Mordecai Richler
The Stone Angel	Margaret Laurence
The Back Doctor	Hamilton Hall
Consequences	Margaret Trudeau
Empire Inc.	Clarke Wallace
Lunatic Villas	Marian Engel
Jake and the Kid	W. O. Mitchell
Daddy's Girl	Charlotte Vale Allen
Preparing for Sabbath	Nessa Rapoport
My Country	Pierre Berton
The Diviners	Margaret Laurence
Sunday's Child	Edward Phillips
Ransom Game	Howard Engel
High Crimes	William Deverell
Bronfman Dynasty	Peter C. Newman
Men for the Mountains	Sid Marty
The Canadians (6 volumes)	Robert E. Wall
The Tent Peg	Aritha van Herk
A Woman Called Scylla	David Gurr
Never Cry Wolf	Farley Mowat
Children of My Heart	Gabrielle Roy
Life Before Man	Margaret Atwood
The Wild Frontier	Pierre Berton
Who Has Seen the Wind	W. O. Mitchell
The Acquisitors	Peter C. Newman
Destinies	Charlotte Vale Allen
The Serpent's Coil	Farley Mowat
Bodily Harm	Margaret Atwood
Joshua Then and Now	Mordecai Richler